WINNING
THE
INSURANCE
GAME

Also by Ralph Nader:

Unsafe at Any Speed
The Big Boys: Power and Position in American Business
Taming the Giant Corporation, with Mark Green and Joel Seligman
The Menace of Atomic Energy, with John Abbots

Also by Wesley J. Smith:

The Lawyer Book: A Nuts and Bolts Guide to Client Survival
The Doctor Book: A Nuts and Bolts Guide to Patient Power
The Senior Citizens' Handbook: A Nuts and Bolts Guide to More Comfortable Living

WINNING THE INSURANCE GAME

The Complete Consumer's Guide to Saving Money

RALPH NADER
and WESLEY J. SMITH

FOREWORD BY

J. Robert Hunter
PRESIDENT
NATIONAL INSURANCE CONSUMER ORGANIZATION

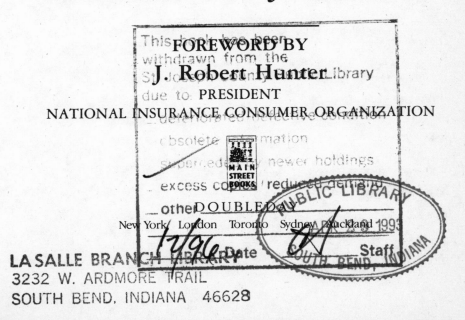

DOUBLEDAY

New York   London   Toronto   Sydney   Auckland   1993

A Main Street Book
PUBLISHED BY DOUBLEDAY
a division of Bantam Doubleday Dell Publishing Group, Inc.
666 Fifth Avenue, New York, New York 10103

Main Street Books, Doubleday, and the portrayal of a building with a tree are trademarks of Doubleday, a division of Bantam Doubleday Dell Publishing Group, Inc.

This book represents the authors' best opinions concerning a financially sound approach to insurance for the average consumer. These guidelines are intended to help you assess your insurance needs and to inform you of various factors that may reduce the cost of insurance coverage. Depending on your particular legal and financial circumstances, the information in this book should be used in conjunction with the advice of your legal, financial, and insurance professionals.

The "Insurance Consumer's Bill of Rights and Responsibilities" reprinted by permission of the National Association of Professional Insurance Agents and the Consumer Insurance Interest Group.

Winning the Insurance Game was originally published in hardcover by the Knightsbridge Publishing Company in 1990.

Design: Mike Yazzolino

Library of Congress Cataloging-in-Publication Data
Nader, Ralph.
    Winning the insurance game : the complete consumer's guide to
    saving money / Ralph Nader and Wesley J. Smith : foreword by
J. Robert Hunter.
        p.   cm.
    "A Main Street book"—T.p. verso.
    Includes bibliographical references and index.
        1. Insurance—United States.   I. Smith, Wesley J.   II. Title.
HG8531.N33   1993
368′.00973—dc20   92-32964
                                                            CIP

ISBN 0-385-46838-5

Printed in the United States of America

10   9   8   7   6   5   4   3   2   1

For Shafeek Nader, who kept the civic vision so fundamental.

—RN

For Julia Micheletti, who lived the American Dream.

—WJS

Contents

Acknowledgments

We would like to acknowledge the following persons and organizations, without whose contributions this book would not have been possible.

Helen Abbott
Mel Budnik
Terrie Frankle-Smith
Ellen Griffin
Katherine Hoffman
J. Robert Hunter
Senator Edward M. Kennedy, United States Senate
Mark Landau, CLU
Barbara Lilly
Carla Mancari
Suzie Matz, R.N.
Ronald Pion
James Quiggle
Jack A. Rameson, III, Esq.
William Rehwald, Esq.

Victoria Roper
Harvey Rosenfield
William Roskam, Ph.D
Leona Smith
Sharon L. Stark
Shirley Strick
Nancy Wexler
Dick and Shirley Willey

Tony Edens
Shelly Usen

Abbott and Associates, Inc.
American Association of Retired Persons
American College
American Express
American Institute for Property and Liability
American Medical Association
American Prepaid Legal Services Institute
American Society of CLU and ChFC
A. M. Best Company
Blue Cross
California State Bar Association
California State Workers Compensation Fund
California State Workers Compensation Institute
California Trial Lawyers Association
Canadian Consulate
Cancervive
Center for the Study of Responsive Law
Coalition for Consumer Justice
Committee of Labor and Human Resources
Consumer Federation of America
Consumer Insurance Interest Group
Consumer Reports Magazine
Consumers Union
Federal Crime Insurance Program
Federal Emergency Management Agency
Group Health Association of America, Inc.

Guaranty Associations
Health Insurance Association of America
Insurance Bureau of Canada
Insurance Information Institute
Insurance Institute of America
Legal Services Plan of America
National Association of Independent Insurers
National Association of Insurance Commissioners
National Association of Life Underwriters
National Association of Professional Insurance
    Agents
National Committee on Property Insurance
National Insurance Consumer Organization
National Organization of Life and Health
    Insurance
New Jersey Department of Insurance
New York State Insurance Department
Public Citizen
SCAN Health Plan
State of California Department of Insurance
20th Century Insurance Company
Underwriters
Underwriters Laboratories Inc.
United States Chamber of Commerce
United States General Accounting Office
USAA Casualty Insurance Company
Vest Insurance Marketing Corporation
Veterans Administration
Voter Revolt
Wausau Insurance Companies
Western Insurance Information Service
Workers Compensation Research Institute

Foreword

Insurance is the number one consumer issue of the early 1990s. Witness California's Proposition 103, the consumer revolt on auto insurance. Witness the mounting pressure for national health insurance. Witness the media alive with insurance stories. Witness the states acting to reform insurance even as I write this.

But reform is really just starting and, where it has begun, the momentum is slow. The key to *reform right now for you* lies in your becoming an informed consumer. *Winning the Insurance Game* brings you to the forefront of insurance reform by teaching you what you need to know about the insurance industry.

Learning about insurance is not as difficult as you may think. This user-friendly book can help you save hundreds, maybe even thousands, of dollars a year. The typical family, in fact, should be able to save at least $500 a year. Even if it takes you 10 hours to read this book, look at it as getting $50 an hour right away and a "dividend" of $50 an hour each year thereafter.

Most of America's consumers of insurance have been illiterate as to what their policies cover and how prices vary. Most receive little or no help from their state or federal legislatures, because insurance regulation is highly limited at the state level and is surprisingly nonexistent at the federal level.

That is why *Winning the Insurance Game* is so welcome. The information in this book is central to helping you make the sort of consumer choices that can discipline this industry. I encourage you to read it carefully, as if you were studying for an exam. The "test" will come soon enough—in the form of your next bill or the next call from an insurance representative.

Ralph Nader and Wesley J. Smith have done all of us a service by writing this important book. Wesley has amassed an incredible amount of information for you to use to save money and to be properly covered and prepared when a loss occurs. Ralph is the man responsible for so much of the progress America has made in treating consumers fairly in all areas of consumer concern. He has been at the forefront of the important consumer issues of our time. He helped me form the National Insurance Consumer Organization in 1980 (quite simply, without Ralph there would be no NICO); he led Proposition 103's movement in California (quite simply, Ralph's support made the difference between success and failure for this initiative).

We are dependent upon one another for becoming informed consumers. But ultimately, *you* are responsible for controlling how your insurance dollars are spent. *The only thing standing between your wallet and your insurance company's hands is your knowledge!*

J. Robert Hunter
President, NICO
September 1990

Introduction

"We regret to inform you . . ."

Your insurance company has just notified you that it will not pay your claim, that it has raised your premium, that it has not accepted your application for coverage.

Now you know the painful truth: you're dealing with the almost inscrutable insurance industry, with its bewildering offerings, fine print, and technical jargon, its soothing symbols of authority, and its promises of reliability. How can you obtain the coverage you need, at a reasonable price and with a fair and responsive claims process? With a good foundation of knowledge, you can make insurance work for you.

In no other sector of our economy can the few hours you will spend reading this book yield such dollar savings, reduce frustrations and eliminate anxieties while, at the same time, inducing insurance companies to become more responsive. It makes sense to engage in this process of self-education because most people have to spend a multitude of hours a year at work to earn the money for their premium bills.

Common sense is so commonly neglected. Obviously, the more you know about what you are being sold, the more you are able to keep dollars in your pocket and obtain a better deal. When millions of consumers are more knowledgeable, the aggregate impact on the insurance industry will be to make it more efficient and more responsive to your needs.

Unfortunately, you can't look to state governments, who are supposed to regulate insurance sellers and educate consumers and who, in the words of the Conference of [state] Insurance Regulators themselves, are "underfunded, understaffed, and underequipped." Nor can you rely on the media, which, with a few notable exceptions, has found the "insurance beat" too mysterious. Even a business editor at the *Washington Post* confessed a few years ago that "nobody around here understands insurance." Well, here is a secret unlocked: *Insurance is purposely made mysterious to exclude you from any role other than to sign the check.*

Succumbing to the soothing but meaningless slogans created by Madison Avenue may be easy, but if we buy our insurance based on name recognition alone, we allow insurance companies to slip off the hook of having to truly compete for our business by offering better prices and better services. We can think of few more beneficial consumer skills you can develop than to become a wise and competent shopper of insurance products. The more you know about what you are being sold, the more you will be able to keep your own dollars in your own pockets while obtaining a better deal for a better product.

And when consumers become filled with the power of knowledge and demand that insurance companies use their political and economic muscle to push for safer cars, safer workplaces, cleaner environments, and fewer fire hazards in an overall drive to prevent damages, injuries, and diseases giving rise to claims, there will be fewer claims, less human suffering, and lower premiums.

Fortunately, as the old song says, the times they are a changing. Consumers are no longer content to spend about *12 percent of their annual income* on insurance (and millions of people spend more for health insurance than they do for food), playing the insurance game on an uneven field. One way change is beginning to occur, as it has in California with Voter Revolt's Proposition 103 and in New Jersey with new statutes concerning auto insurance, is for consumers to insist that laws be passed which force the government to act on behalf of consumers, rather than as a spear carrier doing the bidding of the industry. The Consumers' Agenda sections of this book give suggestions for change citizens can insist upon in their state's laws. Also, included here is an Insurance Consumer's Bill of Rights and Responsibilities, to help you deal with insurance agents and insurance company representatives. This is your legal guide to fair insurance practices, good representation, protection of your insurance dollars, and honest communication.

Consumers have spent so much time fretting about how they are going to collect under their policy that they have developed a *defensive* posture. This book equips you with an *offensive* of knowhow. Familiarize yourself with its format and text. Learn how the insurance marketplace works. Dig in to the policy summaries presented and learn some of the ins and outs of the policies you may already have purchased. Use the tips on shopping around for policies and save literally hundreds of dollars a year and tens of thousands over a lifetime of insurance buying. Find out what to ask your insurance agent or broker. Discover how to ensure that you have as much protection as your premium dollars will buy. Make use of the understanding you will get on how to correctly file a claim. Learn how to push back if your insurance company decides to shove you around. In short, let the insurance companies you deal with know that you are a consuming force to be reckoned with.

This book is also designed to stop insurance inertia. Students of insurance in business curricula, insurance agents, and insurance company staff can become sensitized to the consumer concerns expressed in these pages. And consumers can use the book as a roadmap to the insurance industry for the services they need.

So, down with the fine print, the technical jargon, the tempting symbols of authority, and the slurpy exhortations to trust. Up with putting the insurance companies to the test, forcing them to *earn* your trust, your respect, and your dollars with good products, good prices, and good service. Up with the kind of state regulation that governs insurance industry affordability and responsiveness, thus truly protecting you. And up with an insurance industry that will become health and safety advocates for a more secure society. That, ultimately, is what *Winning the Insurance Game* is all about.

Insurance Consumer's Bill of Rights and Responsibilities

The Insurance Consumer's Bill of Rights and Responsibilities is your guide to fair insurance practices, protection of your insurance dollars, and honest, reliable representation. Take it with you when you interview an insurance agent, and make sure your agent reads and agrees with its principles.

Preamble

We pledge to support these principles as a first step in creating greater understanding of what consumers should expect in buying and using insurance, and to define clearly the responsibilities expected of consumers in return. Using these goals as a yardstick, consumers, agents, and insurers will be able to measure progress as we work together to build the best possible insurance system for the American people.

Bill of Rights

The Right to Protection

The right to purchase insurance that meets your needs, regardless of where you live or work, priced fairly according to your specific risks, without regard to race, color, or creed.

The Right to Be Informed

The right to have your policy printed in clear, easily readable type and written in understandable language; the right to have policy provisions explained to you accurately before purchase; the right to be told in advance, if possible, when the price or terms of your policy are to change, and why.

The Right to Choose

The right to be offered available options for protection; the right to enough time to adequately consider your purchase; and the right to make an informed choice of the coverage that best meets your needs for quality protection, fair value, price, and personal service; the right to a competitive marketplace where several insurance companies compete for your business.

The Right to Be Heard

The right to have a voice in major decisions that affect you, whether made by insurance companies, insurance

Reprinted by permission of National Association of Professional Insurance Agents and Consumer Insurance Interest Group.

agents, or insurance regulators; the right to prompt and constructive replies to suggestions and inquiries; the right to be informed about and participate in consumer organizations that are involved in insurance issues.

The Right to Redress

The right to prompt settlement of just claims; the ability to have access to third parties for mediation and to have access to a responsive state insurance department for further redress.

The Right to Service

The right to be treated with dignity, honesty, and fairness; the right to receive prompt and fair attention to claims, policy changes, and inquiries; the right to be served by an insurance professional who strives to provide you with the best insurance value.

Bill of Responsibilities

The Responsibility to Be Informed

The responsibility to understand the concept of insurance, to read each insurance policy and attempt to understand its terms and, when lacking understanding, the responsibility to seek answers from an insurance professional.

The Responsibility to Help Control Losses

The responsibility to minimize risk through safe driving, loss prevention, vehicle and home maintenance, and caring for your health.

The Responsibility to Report Accurate Information

The responsibility to file insurance applications and report claims accurately and in a timely manner.

The Responsibility to Keep Updated and Accurate Records

The responsibility to maintain in writing the name, address, and telephone number of your insurance agent and your insurance company, and all policy numbers and vehicle make, model, and identification numbers; the responsibility to maintain an updated inventory of household possessions.

The Responsibility to Comply with Policy Provisions

The responsibility to comply with the specific conditions outlined in your policy, including paying premiums on time, cooperating with insurance companies when they defend your claims, and reporting changes that may affect your coverage.

The Responsibility to Report Fraudulent Practices

The responsibility to report to law enforcement and insurance authorities any questionable practices by insurers, agents, consumers, auto body shops, doctors, lawyers, or any other parties seeking to defraud or circumvent the insurance system or consumers.

Part 1

The Nature of the Beast

Life is full of uncertainty, but three things are constant: death, taxes, and insurance. Without insurance, we would not be able to purchase our homes, since no bank would give us the money. Without insurance, many people would not dare to drive a car because of the high financial risk should there be an accident. Without insurance, "The Force" could not be with us, because the film *Star Wars* would never have been made. Without insurance, life and commerce as we know it could not exist.

While we may be unable to prevent death or abolish taxes, we *can* control the cost of insurance and become empowered consumers simply by understanding how insurance works.

1

A Brief History

How did the insurance industry start? Let's step back for a moment and revisit those exciting (and risky) days of yesteryear, before insurance had been invented, before the words "own a piece of the rock" had been coined.

Of course, it could be argued that insurance has been with us since the dawn of civilization. Early Chinese merchants are frequently credited with having been the first to understand the concept of spreading risk. Not that they had a Lloyd's of Peking, mind you, but they reached a clever agreement to protect each individual against the losses and ravages of weather, bandits, and other perils of the time. That agreement allowed each merchant to ship a small part of his cargo in each of several caravans that would be sent out. If a boat sank in the roaring rapids of the Yangtse river, all of the merchants would lose a small portion of their goods instead of one merchant losing everything.

In the West, there have been other such schemes for limiting risk and/or promoting commerce. Seventeen centuries before the time of Christ, at the height of the Babylonian Empire, if a merchant was robbed, the local townspeople had to compensate him for his losses out of their own resources. A thousand years later, during the height of Rhodes, merchants would borrow money to finance shipping. If the ship arrived safe and sound, the lenders would be paid the loan plus a high rate of interest. If the ship was lost at sea, the debt was forgiven. Likewise, during the time of Christ, the Roman legions had burial societies whereby the soldiers each donated a sum to a burial fund that financed their slain brethren's funeral. Since not all of the soldiers would be killed, the many paid for the burial of the few.

Modern insurance practices can be traced back to 17th-century London, where the famous Lloyd's of London had its start. Interestingly, Edward Lloyd's business establishment wasn't an insurance company at all.* It was a dockside coffeehouse where business investors and merchants met to negotiate insurance protection for shipping. Investors, called underwriters, would agree to insure the ship and cargo of a proposed trip. The more dangerous the voyage was thought to be, the higher the price of the insurance. Because travel by ship was, almost by definition, dangerous, few underwriters would agree to be responsible for the entire risk of loss. Instead, several underwriters would typically insure individual voyages, sharing in the benefit and loss proportionate to the percentage of the entire underwriting cost that each individually assumed. Thus, the risk of loss was spread and then spread again.

Fire insurance was first established in London in 1667. Why then? Because in 1666 a major fire devastated the city, destroying 1,400 buildings and leaving 200,000 people homeless. It may have been lucky that the Fire Office, as the company was called by founder Nicholas Barbon, had not been in existence at the time of the fire—no one might have been willing to risk selling fire insurance again.

Benjamin Franklin, that great American genius and institution-builder, formed the first successful American fire insurance

---

*To this day, Lloyd's is not a company as such but a group of independent insurers or syndicates that are in association with one another. For a disturbing look at the practices and power of Lloyd's of London in the United States, see *Goliath: Lloyd's of London in the United States*, by Joanne Doroshow and Adrian J. Wilkes (Washington D.C.: Center for the Study of Responsive Law, 1988).

company in 1752. That company, called Philadelphia Contributorship for the Insurance of Houses from Loss by Fire (try coming up with a catchy advertising slogan for that mouthful!) still exists to this day. (Franklin was many things, but stupid wasn't one of them. His company's charge to insure wooden structures was triple the charge for those made from brick.)

The rest, as they say, is history. As the United States grew, so did insurance companies. Life insurance came onto the scene, and when automobiles were invented, auto insurance quickly followed. Health insurance, workers compensation insurance, and even prepaid legal insurance have all made their appearances on the great underwriting stage of life. In fact, from its humble beginnings, the insurance industry has grown into one of the greatest financial powerhouses in the world.

In the United States alone, there are now over 5,800 different insurance companies. What kind of business does this generate? According to the Insurance Information Institute, total premiums paid to insurance companies for all kinds of insurance in the United States exceed *$600 billion* per year!* Or, to put it into numbers that are easier to comprehend, according to the National Insurance Consumer Organization (NICO), in 1988 the average American family spent

- $2,972 for direct out-of-pocket insurance premiums.

- $4,459 in indirect payments (insurance paid by employers or by businesses with the costs passed through to consumers in the price of goods).

This amounts to 12 percent of the disposable income in the United States. By comparison, people pay more for insurance (direct and indirect) than they do for federal income taxes, not counting Social Security.

But beyond statistics, let's define exactly who and what we are talking about.

*1992 Property/Casualty Insurance Facts, Insurance Information Institute (New York: 1992).

2

The Insurance Umbrella

What is insurance and how does the industry operate? Most of us don't really know. More important, we don't really understand how to make insurance work effectively and efficiently for us. Oh, we complain about the costs of premiums (frequently with justification), but fundamentally, as consumers, too often we just don't know what is going on.

This is a risky state, for while ignorance may be bliss in affairs of the heart, in matters of insurance it's what you don't know that can and often does hurt you. This pain most frequently comes in one of the following forms (and sometimes in all three):

- **The insurance consumer pays more money than necessary for the coverage received.** Many companies charge more than is reasonable for their services. Part of this is the fault of the system, but a great deal of the problem rests with consumers themselves who allow the companies to get away with it because they don't spend the time it takes to find the best deal. Thus, the potential for competition that does still exist is not actualized—to the benefit of the overchargers.

- **The insurance consumer doesn't understand what is being purchased.** As a result, there may be duplication of coverage and a resulting overpayment of premiums.

- **Worst of all, the consumer has no understanding of what is *not* being purchased.** This causes dangerous gaps in coverage, leaving the consumer exposed, unprotected, and ripe for a financial fall or even bankruptcy.

But be of good cheer! None of the above need happen to you. You have what it takes to be an "A #1" consumer of insurance services.

Where should you begin? According to an old Chinese proverb, the longest journey begins with a single step. The first step in becoming a wise insurance consumer is to understand the nuts and bolts of how insurance works.

Risk, Premiums, and Insurance Policies

Basically, insurance is about spreading **risk**. For our purposes let's define risk as the potentiality that on a given day you may incur an incident that causes you to lose something. This may be a fire, in which case you may lose your house; or an auto crash, in which case you risk losing your car, your health, and possibly, after the legal fees, your savings. Then again, the risk could concern your health and the necessity to retain doctors— another expensive proposition. In short, then, every day in virtually every way, we are all at risk of losing something of benefit to ourselves, known in insurance jargon as **loss**.

Losses come in two types: **first-person losses** and **third-party losses**. A first-person loss occurs when the policyholder is personally damaged. For example, if your car is stolen, you have experienced a first-person loss. A third-party loss exists when the damage occurs to someone else but in such a way that the policyholder is responsible. An auto accident is a classic example, where one person often must pay damages to another (the third party) for damages caused by the collision.

Both types of losses can make their unwelcome arrival together. The auto accident is again a good example. If you are in an accident you may incur a third-party loss as we just described. But you may also have a first-person loss in damage to your own car, in your own medical bills, and in legal fees if and when you are sued.

The question then becomes this: Who must bear the burden of loss; that is, who has to pay? Without insurance, if your house burns down, you must pay to rebuild. If you lose a lawsuit, you must pay the verdict (not to mention the lawyers). If your appendix must come out, so must your wallet.

The good news about risk is that the chance of incurring a loss on a given day is usually extremely low. The bad news is that when a loss does occur, its costs can be very high. This dual character of loss is what makes insurance possible and profitable.

When you purchase insurance, you are in essence making a trade. On one hand, you accept a fixed loss, which is the money you pay to the insurance company. It is fixed because you know how much you are going to pay before you write the check. These payments are called **premiums.**

In return for your premiums, the insurance company agrees to accept your risk of loss within the subject matter of the insurance policy (auto, life, health, etc.), in the statistically unlikely event that a loss is incurred. The potential loss to the insurance company from an incident covered by the policy is much higher than the fixed loss of your premium. Thus, you are trading a small but defined loss in order to get the insurance company to absorb an unknown but potentially larger future loss. This agreement is formalized in a written contract.

When this contract, known as an **insurance policy**, has been agreed upon, it is said that the "risk has been spread" from the few (each individually insured party) to the many (all of the policyholders within the insurance company). All policyholders pay for individual losses, because the money to pay claims comes from the earnings of the insurance company. Where does the company earn its money? From premiums and the income earned from investing them. So, the premiums paid by the many fortunate individuals who did not incur a loss have gone, in part, to pay for the losses of the unfortunate few who did. And the insurance company gets to keep the rest as its income to pay for the costs of overhead and to provide it with profits.

The price of the policy you purchase will depend on several factors, which can be boiled down to the natural law of insurance physics: What goes up must go up and what goes down should go down. Among them:

- **The likelihood that a loss will occur.** The higher the probability that an incident will occur that will create a loss your insurance company will have to pay for, the greater the risk to the company and, thus, the higher the premium. (Higher risk equals higher premiums.) For example, if you have three drunk-driving convictions in the last four months, your auto insurer will believe, with justification, that your likelihood of getting into an accident and incurring a loss is very high. As a result of their increased risk of loss, you will incur higher premiums. Conversely, if your driving record is spotless, your premiums should go down with the insurance company's reduced risk.

- **The potential size of the claim.** The higher the potential size of the out-of-pocket loss to the company, the higher the premium. Thus, if you drive a Rolls-Royce Corniche, the potential size of a claim to repair the car is higher than in the case of someone who drives a Toyota Corolla. Thus, the property damage portion of the Toyota driver's policy (see Chapter 11) will be lower than that of the Rolls-Royce owner's.

- **The percentage of the loss the company must pay.** The closer the insurance company comes to having to pay for 100 percent of the loss under the policy, the higher the premium will be. As we will see throughout this book, this aspect of pricing allows consumers great leeway in reducing their premiums by increasing the size of their individual responsibility to pay for a loss. If your health policy, for example, pays 100 percent of your health care costs, your premium will be higher than if you paid the first $500 (known as a **deductible**).

We will deal with the issue of the price of insurance in more detail throughout the book.

Types of Insurance Companies

People tend to view insurance companies as a monolithic whole, with no difference among companies, the policies they offer, or the premiums they charge. The truth is quite the opposite. Insurance companies come in a wide variety of types and sizes and, as we shall see, many approach business in sometimes fundamentally different ways.

Stock Companies

Stock companies are just what the name implies: companies that are owned by stockholders. Like other corporations, stock insurance companies are managed by a board of directors. In theory, the board serves at the discretion of the shareholders. In real life, individual shareholders have a minute impact on the company's management policies or personnel.

Being a for-profit capitalistic concern, a stock company will pay dividends to the stockholders when it is profitable. However, paying stockholders is one thing and benefiting policyholders is quite another. In fact, the profitability of stock companies is usually of little direct consequence to the people who buy insurance from them and who don't specifically benefit from their success. There may, however, be an indirect benefit to policyholders. For example, a company that is doing well may lower premiums (highly unlikely) or, more commonly, raise them more slowly. When their company's profitability is poor, on the other hand, policyholders definitely suffer—in increased premiums. In fact, many industry critics have charged that the horrible premium inflation consumers have suffered through in recent years got its start when insurance company investments turned sour.

A good example of a stock insurance company is Allstate Insurance.

Cooperatives

Mutual insurance companies are formed and operated by consumers of insurance. Unlike a stock company, where the purchase of a policy gives the owner no interest in the insurance company itself, the very act of buying a policy from a mutual company makes the purchaser a proportionate owner of that company. Technically, policyholders own the company but exert little control over management.

Like the owners of stock in a stock company, mutual policy owners benefit with the payment of dividends when the company does well. Dividends are often credited to the benefit of the policy, either reducing premiums or increasing benefits. Mutuals will also accrue surplus funds to protect against a time of heavy claims activities. When a member withdraws from the mutual by canceling coverage, he or she generally receives none of the surplus that may have accrued during his/her tenure as a policyholder. State Farm Insurance is one of the better known mutuals.

Another type of cooperative is the **reciprocal insurance exchange**. Reciprocal exchanges are nonprofit organizations formed and controlled by a large number of people who, in essence, form a group and insure themselves against losses. Participants are both the insured and the insurers. A professional management team is hired to administer the exchange and coordinate collection of premiums and payment of claims. A surplus is usually saved for a rainy day. Some reciprocals pay a withdrawing member's proportionate share of the surplus; others do not.

Another kind of cooperative is a **producer's cooperative**. The most famous producer's cooperative is Blue Cross/Blue Shield, where doctors and hospitals have formed nonprofit insurance companies that sell health insurance to the public. The real power in these organizations lies with the sellers of health care, euphemistically known in the trade as "providers." The organizers control the management of the cooperative. Unlike mutuals or reciprocal exchanges, policyholders obtain no ownership rights.

The Government as an Insurer

Most people don't realize how deeply government is involved with insurance. The federal government has several insurance plans ranging from Social Security and Medicare to the Federal Deposit Insurance Corporation and the Veterans Administration. Some states operate workers compensation insurance companies, and all offer other programs such as unemployment insurance. Government insurance will be covered in detail in Part 6.

The Personal Insurance Marketplace

Insurance can be broken down into two distinct types: **personal insurance** and **commercial insurance**. Personal insurance policies, as the name suggests, are those contracts that protect individuals and families from losses. Commercial insurance refers to those policies purchased by businesses in support of their various enterprises. Since this book is primarily concerned with insurance needs of individuals, commercial insurance will not be discussed, with the exception of workers compensation (see Chapter 37).

Types of Personal Insurance

There are four primary types of personal insurance: **property/casualty insurance, life insurance, health insurance**, and **government benefits**. We will explore each of these in detail later but while we're on the subject, let's test the water.

Property/casualty insurance. Earlier, we touched on first-person and third-party losses. Property/casualty (liability) insurance generally covers both. A good example of this is a homeowner's policy, which protects a dwelling from the hazards of fire and other forms of destruction. But homeowner's policies also provide for protection against liability—for example, if your dog bites the mailman. As you will see, this is not the only case where one insurance policy protects against a wide variety of losses. Property and liability insurance will be discussed in Part 2 and Part 4.

Life insurance. Life insurance, as you undoubtedly know, pays money, sometimes big money, when the person whose life was insured "kicks the bucket," "bites the dust," "meets his Maker," or whatever euphemism you prefer to use to describe the biological process of dying. Some forms of life insurance also act as an investment opportunity by accruing value as premiums are paid, value that can be borrowed against or cashed in during the life of the insured. Because there are so many different types of life insurance (term, whole life, mortgage, etc.), many people consider the subject beyond comprehension. But take heart, Part 5 should wipe those blues away.

Health insurance. Health insurance has become a virtual necessity of life in the United States thanks to the astronomical cost of medical care and the relative paucity of government benefits in the field. Health insurance pays for items such as doctor bills, hospital expenses, and diagnostic tests such as X rays. **Disability insurance**, which is sort of a hybrid between life and health coverages, pays the beneficiary for income lost due to a disabling injury or illness. Part 3 will consider various issues concerning health insurance.

Government benefits. The government is in the insurance game and in it in a big way. Medicare is a health insurance program mostly limited to those age 65 and over. Social Security, among other benefits, provides a form of income insurance (somewhat akin to an annuity) that guarantees a basic level of benefits in return for payments (taxes) paid during working years. Some government entities sell insurance. Others help pay for the cost of insurance that would otherwise be unavailable or cost prohibitive. Parts 6 and 7 will describe many of these government plans and benefits in detail.

How Personal Insurance Is Sold

Virtually everyone is covered by some form of personal insurance, whether from the private sector or as a beneficiary of government benefits. Such coverage is obtained in a variety of ways. Often it is paid for directly by contacting an authorized salesperson and paying the price of the premium. Insurance is also obtained indirectly, often as a benefit of employment or union membership after others have negotiated the coverage and price. At still other times, we receive insurance as a legal right based upon our individual circumstances (e.g., Medicare).

With the exception of group health insurance obtained through work, most people buy their insurance directly. But who sells it and under what circumstances? Let's take a look.

Agents. The image of insurance agents seems to have fallen about as low as the image of lawyers, if that's possible. But is this fair? As in any profession, there are those who are interested only in what you can do for *them*—i.e., buy coverage whether you need it or not. But good insurance agents are primarily interested in what *they can do for you*—i.e., help you find the *right product* at the most *reasonable price* to meet your *individual needs*. In fact, finding a good agent can be one of the best things you can do for yourself as a smart insurance consumer.

Agents are licensed by the state in which they do business. As such, they can be considered professionals. Licensing usually requires a minimum of education and the passing of an examination. *Licensing should not be confused with membership in a national society*, such as being a CLU (Chartered Life Underwriter). (See box on page 19.)

Agents generally come in two types: the **independent agent** and the **exclusive agent**. An independent agent is an entrepreneur who represents many different insurance companies at the same time. He or she is paid through commissions based on a percentage of the price you pay in premiums. The exclusive agent, on the other hand, sells insurance for one company only. Exclusive agents also work on commission.

Which type of agent is better for you? That will depend on the circumstances of each individual transaction. Exclusive agents can often beat the price of independents because of lower selling costs and other factors, such as different underwriting practices (see page 53). Exclusive agents may also have superior product knowledge since they sell only one line of goods. On the downside, the exclusive agent may be more susceptible to the demand of the company for greater productivity (more sales). As in the army, bad news flows downhill, and the result may be high-pressure salesmanship aimed in your direction—with the emphasis not on meeting your insurance needs but on meeting the agent's sales quota.

Independent agents can choose from among several competing companies to find you the policy that will ideally suit your needs and price range. Also, if the independent agent is a high producer, he or she may be able to persuade a company to give you a good deal. Of course, there is a danger that the independent agent may try to put you into the policy that pays him or her the highest commission.

Because agents only earn money when they make a sale, you should always be on guard against agents who are seeking to feather their own nests rather than truly seeking to protect yours (see "How to choose an agent," page 25). That means you should bring a healthy dose of skepticism into your relationship with your agent and that you should act as a powerful and informed consumer.* We'll give you some tips on wise insurance shopping in various places throughout the book (see, for example, page 32, page 101, page 210, chapter 27).

Brokers. People often use the terms "insurance agent" and "insurance broker" as if they were interchangeable. They are not. An agent has a contract with one or more insurance companies and *represents the company*. The broker *represents the buyer*. The broker's job is to search among all insurance companies in the market and find the best policy and price for the client. Brokers are paid by commission from the insurance company. However, the price of the commission is included in the premium you pay (as is true with agents). Brokers are licensed and often will work with company agents to purchase the insurance or will sometimes order it directly. Since brokers represent the buyer, they may be more willing to fight for the client than agents who are tied contractually to the companies they represent.

Direct sales. Many insurance companies do away with agents altogether and market their products and services directly to the buyer. Some do this by mail, others by phone, and still others by salaried sales representatives who are not licensed agents. You can save money by using direct sales insurance companies since there are no commissions to be paid out of the premium. But there is also potential danger in that you will not have the brainpower and experience of a licensed professional to assist you with the selection process. However, according to a 1988 study by *Consumer Reports* magazine, the most satisfied customers are frequently those who purchase directly.

*In fact, J. Robert Hunter, president of the National Insurance Consumer Organization, states, "Be extremely careful when picking an agent and accepting his or her advice. Some agents may put you into higher-priced options rather than the best policy at the most reasonable price."

Agents and brokers can become nationally *credentialed* in addition to being licensed. In order to earn these credentials, special training must be undertaken and additional tests passed. In addition, minimum ethical standards must be adhered to.

Using an agent with one or more of these credentials doesn't guarantee that the agent is competent or honest. But it does show that the agent cared enough about his or her chosen field to take the time and effort to qualify for the credential. Here is a list of some of the more prestigious insurance credentials.

- *CLU (Chartered Life Underwriter)*: The CLU is awarded by the American College at Bryn Mawr in Pennsylvania. It takes the applicant between two and five years of work and study and the passing of 10 tests in order to receive the designation. The CLU is the premier credential for life insurance agents.
- *ChFC (Chartered Financial Consultant)*: This credential is also awarded by the American College but is geared toward financial planners. Like the CLU, the ChFC applicant must take and pass 10 separate courses.
- *CFP (Certified Financial Planner)*: This is a credential given by the College of Financial Planning in Denver and is similar to the ChFC.
- *CPCU (Chartered Property and Casualty Underwriter)*: This credential is the equivalent of a CLU, but applies to the field of property/casualty insurance. In order to earn a CPCU designation, the applicant must pass 10 national examinations, have a minimum of three years experience in the field, and agree to abide by a code of ethics. The program is administered by the American Institute for Property and Liability Insurance Underwriters in Malvern, Pennsylvania.

Group purchases. As we will discuss in detail later (see page 136), a good way to get the best product for the best price is to be a member of a group that has purchased insurance at **group rates**. A group is a collection of people with a common interest (such as a union, corporation, or trade association) who use the concept of "power in numbers" to purchase insurance under the principles of mass merchandising. If the group is big enough, it can usually buy better benefits for a lower price than an individual buyer.

Consumer Alert

If your union, employer, or other group administrators are in the process of negotiating a policy on your behalf, get involved! You will be bound by whatever contract is negotiated, so take a look at the fine print before the deals are signed. If you don't like what you see, speak up. The benefits you save may be important to you later on.

We will deal further with many of these concepts as they become relevant throughout the book. For now, let's get to the heart of the matter: buying insurance. That's the signpost up ahead: you've just crossed over into the insurance zone.

3

How to Buy Insurance

It is safe to say that a great many people in this country are very unhappy about insurance. Some are angry with their individual companies, some with the insurance industry in general, and a great many more with both. True, part of this dissatisfaction is caused by insurance company practices and procedures and by weaknesses in the area of regulation (see Chapter 39). But too many consumers have only themselves to blame because of the poor manner in which they have gone about the task of shopping for insurance coverage.

Too many consumers select their insurance as if they don't care whether they purchase a high- or low-quality product. There are also those who act as if they have money to burn, treating price as a matter of seemingly total indifference. In fact, some insurance shoppers put so little thought into purchasing coverage that they might just as well open the yellow pages to the insurance listings, close their eyes, and point.

But that is definitely not true of you. How do we know? Well, if it were, you wouldn't be reading this book. No, you are a person who cares about buying a quality product. You want to be able to find a company known for good service. And you want any policy you purchase to be at a fair and competitive price.

Happily, this chapter (and of course, the rest of the book) can help your wish become your command. So let's get right to it, with three steps to becoming a wise insurance shopper.

Step 1: Do Your Homework

Before you can be a smart shopper, you should prepare yourself for the task by learning as much as you can about what you are buying. In order to do so, you will need detailed information about the type of policy you are going to purchase, information on the different companies that sell this type of insurance, and, finally, you should get a handle on who you can buy the insurance from.

This isn't as complicated as it might sound! There is a veritable cornucopia of information at your disposal—if you know where to look.

Where to Look

Finding important information about the ins and outs of the type of insurance you want is literally as easy as turning the pages of this book. But you shouldn't stop here. There are 51 different individual markets for insurance in the United States (one for each state and the District of Columbia) and you will want to look for the individual nuances contained in policies where you live. Here are some sources of information you will want to turn to.

Your state insurance department. Most insurance departments provide quite a bit of consumer information about the various policies sold under their jurisdictions. As we shall see, they also can tell you a lot about the specific companies that sell product in your state. The addresses and phone numbers of all of the insurance boards and commissions can be found in Appendix C.

Insurance company representatives. As you compare and contrast the different insurance policies on the market (see below), you will, by definition, discuss what is contained in them with the insurance representatives who are trying to sell them to you. Use these professionals as valuable sources of information who can specifically show you how their policies protect you and your family, based on your individual circumstances. At the same time, always remember that agents earn their living by selling products, so be sure to take what you are told with a grain of salt.

Your local library. There is a great deal of information available to you for free in your local library. The following sources can be especially helpful:

- *Consumer Reports* magazine. This nonprofit periodical (which, by the way, accepts no advertising) is in the business of comparing and contrasting various products and services on the market. From time to time it compares and contrasts the different kinds of personal insurance and the insurance companies that sell them. Ask your librarian how to find back issues on the subject of your choice. Better yet, subscribe. (The address for Consumer Reports is 101 Truman Avenue, Yonkers, NY 10703, (800) 234-1645.

- *Best's Insurance Reports* and other rating publications. There are several business publications that rate the financial condition of insurance companies. The best known is *Best's Insurance Reports,* which comes in two separate volumes: one on property/casual insurance and one on life/health insurance. *Bests's* analyzes the financial strength of insurance companies and rates them from A++ (a new rating recently introduced by *Best's* for the companies they consider to be the most substantial) down through E (under state supervision) and F (in liquidation). *Best's* has also added a rating of NA-11 (rating suspended), which indicates that a previously rated company has experienced a sudden and significant event affecting the company's financial position. The better the rating, the stronger *Best's* believes the immediate financial prospects for a company to be. It is probably not a good idea to do business with a company poorly rated in *Best's* or other publications, such as *Standard and Poor's* and *Moody's*, which publish similar ratings. Remember, *Best's* and the other rating services represent only a snapshot in time. The financial condition of companies can change quickly, as occurred with

Executive Life Insurance in California. Thus, it is a good idea to check more than one service (ask your agent) or to call a particular company to see if there have been any changes since the last published ratings. *Best's* can be reached at (908) 439-2200. *Standard and Poor's* number is (212) 208-1527. (Be sure to ask if the company you are inquiring about is on their Watch List for possible downgrading or upgrading.) *Moody's* (which also has a Watch List) can be reached at (212) 553-0377. If you already have insurance, it is a good idea to monitor your company's rating every year.

Other books. This book is intended to provide all of the information most people need to become wise consumers of insurance (and then some). There are, however, many books on the subject of insurance, usually tackling only one kind of policy. That being so, some have more details about specific coverages than we are able to supply in a general book of this kind. We will recommend some of these from time to time, and we list some in Appendix D, but don't be afraid to call on that hardworking expert who is always there to help: your local librarian.

The National Insurance Consumer Organization (NICO). NICO is a nonprofit national organization whose sole purpose is to be an advocate for, and provide assistance to, insurance consumers. Headed by a former federal insurance administrator and casualty actuary, J. Robert Hunter, NICO can provide you with manuals that give you valuable details about your insurance. NICO also has an excellent book on life insurance, called *Taking the Bite Out of Life Insurance*, by James Hunt. Depending on the type of insurance, NICO may also be able to recommend specific companies that are doing a good job. We urge you to join NICO for a $30 tax-deductible donation. For more information, contact:

NICO
121 N. Payne St.
Alexandria, Virginia 22314

Industry organizations. The insurance industry has established several organizations to promote consumer education (and sometimes, industry propaganda). One organization is the Insurance

Information Institute. A toll-free consumer's hotline will answer questions you may have about property/casualty insurance: (800) 221-4954.

Step 2: Shop Around

The biggest mistake most consumers make when they buy insurance is taking the first good-looking policy that comes along. This is unfortunate, for there are frequently wide variations in the price and quality of the products available on the market. Here are just a few tips to help you find the best buy.

Compare Agents

Choosing the right insurance professional to help you make decisions about your insurance is an essential part of any effective insurance-buying strategy. That professional, whether a broker or agent, should be courteous, knowledgeable, and reliable. He or she should also take additional education classes in the field in order to stay up-to-date on the continuing changes in the insurance industry, and having a special certificate like a CLU doesn't hurt (see page 19). In any event, be sure to speak with several agents and compare them just as you do the products they sell.

Another bonus of shopping among several agents and/or brokers is the increased exposure you will have to the many companies in the market. Remember, when you speak to five independent agents or brokers about insurance, you may be comparing 50 different insurance companies! Finally, don't forget to compare the products of the independents and brokers with those of exclusive agents. By taking a week or so to allow the insurance professionals to do their thing, you will have given yourself a solid grasp of what is available on the market and at what prices.

How to choose an agent. James Quiggle, Director of Public Relations for the National Association of Professional Insurance Agents, offers these helpful hints on how to choose an agent:

- Shop at least three agents. Compare them to see which one offers the insurance package that best meets your needs. This means comparing the poli-

cies, prices, and services to arrive at *your* definition
of the *total value* of the package. Each time you
interview an agent, ask pointed questions about their
policies, prices, and services.

- Check out the agent. Call the Better Business Bureau
  to see if the agent has a history of complaints. Call
  the state insurance department to see if the agent is
  licensed or has disciplinary actions on record. Ask
  friends and neighbors for referrals from agents with
  whom they've personally done business.

- Know the difference among the kinds of agents (see
  page 17).

- Know what insurance you want when deciding which
  agent to do business with. This means understanding
  what insurance *value* means: the price, quality of
  coverage, and the service the agent and company
  offer. Different agents and companies may offer more
  attractive prices but be weaker in services such as
  quick and efficient handling of claims or long-term
  commitment to insurance. If price is most important
  to you, buy primarily on price. But at least be aware
  of *all* options so you can make informed buying
  decisions based on your personal needs.

- Visit the agency before agreeing to do business. Does
  it appear well managed and professional? Do the
  employees appear courteous and helpful?

- Talk with the agent personally, face to face. Does
  the agent appear courteous and informed? Can the
  agent answer your questions about the policy in plain
  English? Does the agent seem to *want* to help you?
  Does the agent ask probing questions about your
  entire insurance needs, or does the agent just want
  to sell a policy and move on? Does the agent gladly
  answer your questions about prices, the company,
  the quality of coverage offered?

All agents are not created equal! The following is a true story and illustrates the importance of utilizing several different agents, even those who represent the same company. One of the authors of this book was shopping for auto insurance. For two cars, he was quoted a price range from $3,000 to $4,200 per year. Undaunted, he checked with an agent who represented a company known for low rates, from whom another agent had previously quoted the $3,000 price. The second agent took extra time looking into the application and discovered that the applicant owned his own home. Based on the agent's superior understanding of the company's underwriting policies, he was able to get a preferred rate for the applicant, *at a savings of more than $900 per year!*

Compare Policies

You should compare what each company is offering you for the premium it is demanding. Frequently, this information is supplied in computer printout comparison sheets. If the agent or company doesn't give you a comparison sheet, create your own by writing down the vital statistics of the proposed coverage—premium price, deductible, maximum benefit, exclusions, etc. This process of comparing and contrasting should allow you to focus on three "finalists" that offer the most coverage for the best prices.

Compare the Intangibles

There are other things you should look at. One is the *ease of making claims*. Some companies make the filing of claims easy by making access to adjusting services readily available in most neighborhoods. Others make processing of claims more difficult, so be sure to ask how each company handles this all-important aspect of the insurance relationship.

Also, see how you *relate to the different agents*. The strength of your relationship with an agent may be important. If you end up in a dispute with the insurance company, a well-connected agent may be able get you a favorable resolution that might not otherwise be available.

You might also look into how the companies *allow you to pay*. For example, some companies accept monthly payments in smaller increments over time while others demand that payment be made in full over two or three months. There are even companies that allow payment by credit card. In short, look at the less obvious things that are important to you and compare them among the policies and companies you are considering.

Compare the Finalists

At some point three or four policies will stand out in your mind as the ones you are interested in. Once you have limited your search to these finalists, review the following for each.

Their respective ratings in *Best's Insurance Reports* and other reporting services. Remember, *Best's* is in your local library, but your agent should have a copy in his or her office as well. If two are A++ or A+ companies and one is a B, chances are you will not want to choose the lower-rated one. Of course, nothing is absolute. Sometimes a lower-rated company will give you a better buy or benefits. In such cases just be sure that the extras you receive are worth the potential risk of choosing an insurance company that is less financially secure.

Their complaint rates. Many insurance departments keep records on the numbers of complaints they receive from consumers against the companies that do business in the state. These records are published. The chart at the top of page 29 is an abridged excerpt of an actual state insurance department complaint report. The names of the insurance companies have been changed to protect the innocent (a company's complaint record in one state

Name	# of Policies Issued	Total Complaints	# of Complaints per 1,000 Policies	Overall Rank
"Stick It to 'Em Insurance"	1,386,404	173	.125	1
"We Never Pay Mutual"	1,215,953	206	.169	2
"Premiums R Us Insurance"	982,186	177	.180	3
"Our Lawyers Are Best"	225,477	54	.239	4

may not be the same as in another). Note: The actual report detailed the complaint record of 25 different companies.

The recommendations of consumer publications. Magazines such as *Consumer Reports* or the opinions published by NICO can reveal a lot about what is going on in the insurance marketplace, and they are a valuable tool to use in your quest for the insurance policy that is perfect for you.

Now that you have come this far, you should know the following about each of the policies you are comparing:

- The scope of coverage
- The price
- The complaint record of the company
- The financial status of the company

Then, by factoring matters such as ease of claims services and the availability of an easy payment plan, you should be able to make an informed and intelligent decision about your insurance.

Step 3: Follow These Helpful Hints

Don't Buy the Company's Advertising

Insurance can be a very impersonal business. It almost has to be, considering the number of people insurance companies deal with and their extreme reliance on statistics when making business decisions.

Yet, insurance executives are smart enough to realize that people long for personal care; they want to be treated as individuals, as "members of the family." That's why insurance companies pay advertising agencies millions of dollars to come up with homey slogans. As a consumer, you must realize that *advertising slogans are just that, no more, no less*. Your decisions about the insurance you ultimately choose must be as cold-eyed and based on rational self-interest as will be the decisions the company makes about you.

Create a "Paper Trail"

Once you realize that insurance is purely a business transaction, treat it as such. One way to do this is by making sure that everything is in writing. Thus, if an agent offers you a certain policy at a certain price, get it in writing. If you decide on a policy and the agent agrees to a binder (an agreement to provide coverage before the formal policy is issued), get it in writing. If the company wants some information from you, give it to them by letter and keep a copy for your records. Also, be sure to keep any correspondence or other communications you receive from the company. In this way, if there is ever a dispute (and there are an abundance of disputes between insurance companies and their customers every day) you will have the ammunition you need to be able to effectively present your side of the matter (see Chapter 40).

Make Sure the Insurance You Buy Meets Your Needs

Determining the appropriate amount and types of insurance to buy will depend on several factors that are unique to each individual. Discuss these matters at length with the insurance company representative *before* you buy.

What is the need? One person may have a great deal to insure, another much less. For example, if your monthly budget is $2,800 and you are looking for life insurance to protect your family for 10 years after your death, chances are you can buy less coverage (and therefore spend less money) than someone whose monthly budget is $6,500.

What perils exist that can create a loss, and does the insurance cover them? A **peril** is something that causes loss, such as earthquake in a homeowner's policy or theft in an automobile policy. Perils differ from place to place and from coverage to coverage. This being so, you probably don't want to buy coverage for something that presents you with little or no risk of loss.

How much money can you afford to spend? If money is a big consideration regarding insurance, you need to make sure that you get the most insurance bang for your premium buck. You may also need to set your insurance priorities, making sure that those things of most importance are protected first before you consider less substantial matters. J. Robert Hunter of NICO recommends that you think "comprehensive" and "catastrophic." By *comprehensive*, he means to achieve as broad an umbrella of protection as possible. By *catastrophic*, he means that you should strive to cover yourself for the worst-case scenario. Thus, being covered by a broad-based health insurance policy is probably more important than a disability policy. In turn, the disability policy is more important than prepaid legal insurance.

In later chapters we will refer to these three issues in detail as they relate to different types of insurance.

Save Money On What You Buy

Part of what we hope to help you do with this book is save money. You will see that each kind of insurance involves different strategies for economy, but in the meantime here are some thoughts that should serve you well regardless of the kind of insurance you are buying.

Increase your deductibles. A **deductible** is the money that must come out of your pocket after a loss *before* any money comes out of the insurance company's. Health insurance typically will have a $200 deductible, which means you pay for the first $200 of health expenses per year before you receive any benefits. Since a great number of claims deal with relatively small amounts of money, the higher the deductible, the less risk the insurance company is exposed to, and thus the lower your premium will be.

Avoid unneeded coverage. Many policies can be tailored to fit individual needs. For example, if you own an older car, you may not want to insure it against property damage because the amount you can collect probably isn't worth the premium. (The insurance company has the option to pay you the value of your car rather than repair it, and an old car may be "worth" only a few hundred dollars.) Likewise, many homeowner's policies allow for an economy version of protection that does not include theft losses. If you have few possessions of significant value, you may want to look into this source of significant savings.

Look for ways to earn special savings. Many policies will reward you with lower premiums if you meet certain criteria. For example, there may be a nonsmoker's discount for auto, life, and property insurance. Most auto insurers also give a two-car discount. Others allow for a lower premium for senior citizens who take special driver awareness classes.

Conduct your life like a preferred risk. One way to pay less for insurance is to live your life in such a way that the insurance company believes you are less of a risk than others of your class. Some things, such as age, cannot be changed, but others can with a little forethought and discipline. For example, if you maintain a good driving record you will pay less for auto insurance. If you keep yourself in good shape by eating right and getting enough sleep and exercise and by refraining from smoking, you should pay less for life insurance. In short, live life in the slow lane. Not only will you live longer but you'll also pay less for insurance.

Join a group. The old saying that there is power in numbers is especially pertinent in the area of insurance. Thus, whenever possible, obtain your insurance through a group rather than on an individual basis. Not only will you save money but you will have the power of the group to keep you from being penalized (by increased premiums or refusal to renew) if you make what the company thinks are excessive claims.

Get Involved

A lot of us treat insurance like the weather; we gripe and complain but don't do anything about it. Luckily, insurance is *not* like the weather. We *can* do something about prices that are too high and insurance departments that are biased in favor of the companies. But to do so we must get involved and we must have an *agenda*. And that is what the Consumers' Agendas are about.

4

The Insurance Contract

Now that you are familiar with the basic principles of purchasing insurance, you are ready to tackle the insurance policy itself. As we stated in Chapter 2, a policy of insurance is a written **contract**. Without getting too deeply into legalese, let's define a contract as an *exchange of promises* among two or more people (or companies) that is *enforceable by law*.

In order for the law to recognize and enforce mutual promises as a contract, each promisor must agree to do something that he, she, or it *would not otherwise have done*. Usually this involves both sides giving the other something of value, or one side giving something of value and the other assuming an obligation. The assumption of these burdens is called **consideration**.

For example, if your friend promised you that he would buy you a steak dinner based on your promise to mow his lawn, you'd have a contract. Your friend had no duty to buy you the steak and only agreed to do so because you agreed to do something you didn't have to do; i.e., mow the lawn. If, however, your friend promised to pay his own income taxes if you mowed his lawn, there would not be a contract because his promise involved doing something he already was under an obligation to do.

Keeping this in mind, let's look at the insurance contract. When you buy an insurance policy, you promise to pay the insurance company a specific amount of money within a specific period of time. In return, your insurance company agrees to pay **benefits** upon the occurrence of a specified event or events. Benefits are the payments by the insurance company (to you or others) as required under the insurance policy. In life insurance, the "event" is the death of the named insured. In an auto insurance policy, the event might be an auto accident in which the insured is injured. In health insurance, it is receiving medical care covered by the policy. As long as you pay your premiums, the court will enforce the insurance company's obligation to pay you benefits.

General Principles of Insurance Contracts

Here are some general principles you should know about insurance contracts:

- **There must be an *insurable interest* in order for the insurance contract to be legal.** An insurable interest is usually defined as an exposure to direct financial loss. Thus, if Uncle Pete rents an apartment, he cannot take out insurance on the apartment complex itself because he has no personal financial interest to protect in it. He can, however, insure the contents of his apartment through renter's insurance.

- **Insurance contracts are almost always *contracts of adhesion*.** A contract of adhesion is where one party controls the writing of its terms, thereby making the contract a "take it or leave it" proposition. The bad news about this is that the terms are written to be as favorable to the insurance company as is legally possible. The good news is that any vague terms or ambiguities will be construed by the courts against the insurance company that wrote the policy.

- **Both parties owe the other the utmost good faith in insurance contracts.** This means that both parties must deal with each other in complete honesty and candor and must not act out of malice or ill toward the other.

    If the insurance company acts with ill will or dishonesty, some states (but not nearly enough) allow injured insureds to sue for damages above and beyond the losses incurred that are covered by the policy. These are called **bad-faith cases**; they are discussed in detail in Chapter 42.

Your Obligations Under the Contract

As a policyholder, you also have obligations under the contract (in addition to paying premiums). If you act improperly, the insurance company may be able to get out of paying benefits. There are usually three ways in which a policyholder may be subject to the loss of benefits.

Breach of Warranty

A warranty is a fancy name for a promise that is part of the insurance contract. In many insurance contracts, the policyholder will promise that something is true at the start of the policy or will continue to be true during the duration of the policy. Based on these warranties, certain underwriting decisions (see page 53) will have been made. For example, a homeowner who owns a dog known for biting may have a homeowner's policy issued where the owner warrants that a muzzle will be kept on the dog when the animal is out in the yard. Failure to muzzle the pet could lead to the release of the insurance company from liability should the dog bite the mailman.

Misrepresentation

When you fill out an insurance application, you make **representations** to the company concerning facts about yourself. Many of these facts are vital to the underwriting process—for example, whether you smoke, in the case of a life insurance policy. If you lie about any of these facts and the company catches you, and if a court concludes that the lie was material (important) to the underwriting decisions of the company, you could lose some benefits or the company may be allowed to cancel the policy.

Concealment

Sometimes people are dishonest by keeping quiet. Since an insurance contract is a contract of utmost good faith, failure to reveal a matter material to the underwriting decision of the insurance company may again be grounds for loss of benefits. For example, if you know that a forest fire is heading toward your house, you can't call a property insurance agent, get an agreement for immediate coverage (see "Where Does Coverage Begin?" below), and expect to collect benefits when your house burns down. That just wouldn't be cricket.

Usually, but not always (many states hold that a warranty violation is actionable by the very fact that it occurred), an insurance company seeking to escape liability based on improper conduct must prove the bad intent of the policyholder. They must also show that the false information was of great significance. Thus, to use a ridiculous example, if you lied about the color of your eyes and the insurance company found out, they would be unlikely to get out of the contract. On the other hand, if you lived in a very rural area and you warranted in a homeowner's policy that you had a phone with which to call the fire department, when in fact you did not, that could be a different story.

When Does Coverage Begin?

We now know what an insurance contract is and what parts it is made of. But when does the insurance contract actually begin? In other words, when is the company on the hook if a loss occurs—until you've paid a premium, or as soon as you sign on the dotted line? The answer to this question can be very important if a loss covered by the policy occurs after you have requested to be covered but before the policy has been formally issued. Let's call this time period the *gray area*.

The gray area is entered as soon as you fill out and sign an application for insurance and the agent accepts it. In the application, you will supply basic facts to the insurance company, such as your name, address, age, and gender. Information pertinent to the kind of insurance you desire and the extent of the risk you present to the insurance company will also be solicited in the application. For example, you will have to disclose your medical history in an application for health or life insurance. The value of your car and the existence of extras, such as a car phone, will be pertinent to an automobile policy. When an insurance application is taken over the phone, the same principles apply.

Consumer Alert

Material misrepresentations in the application may be grounds for the insurance company to be relieved from its obligations under the insurance contract. So be honest, even if the agent suggests you fudge on the truth, which some commission-hungry agents sometimes do. The benefits you save may be your own.

After you have filled out the application, the agent will decide whether to accept it. If he or she does not believe you will be an acceptable risk under the guidelines of the insurance company, your application may be rejected then and there. In such case, there is obviously no contract. If the application is acceptable to the agent, you and the agent will discuss important matters such as the terms of the contract (see below) and the price.

At that point, if you wish to be obligated (bound), a contract may or may not occur, depending on which of the following two scenarios occurs.

Scenario 1: Binder

If he or she has authority from the company, the agent may fill out a document obligating the company to provide immediate coverage. This may occur even before you have actually paid any part of the premium. This document is called a **binder**, and it will remain in effect until the actual policy is issued. Once a binder has been issued and accepted, a *contract exists* between you and the insurance company the agent represents. Property and casualty agents often have the power to bind the company. Life and health insurance agents usually do not. If your agent agrees to give you a binder, *make sure it is in writing*. In that way, an unscrupulous agent won't be able to say, "Binder, what binder?" in the event you have a claim. (If you are given an oral binder, be sure to write down what was said, the time it was said, and who said it. Then, make sure you get a written copy of the binder as fast as possible. You might even write a confirming letter yourself, just to be sure—see Chapter 40.)

Scenario 2: No Binder

If the agent does not have the power to bind the company or chooses not to do so, the agent will merely accept the application and send it to the insurance company for underwriting. During this period, a *contract does not exist* because the insurance company, through its agent, has not promised to do anything of value; all it has agreed to do is review the application. During this time period, you may be requested to do some things to help the insurance company make a decision about whether to insure you and/or how much to charge. For example, in a homeowner's policy, you may be asked to get a formal appraisal of your valuables. In a life insurance policy, you may be asked to have a physical examination. In any event, *if no binder was issued, you are not covered until you have been notified that the company has accepted your application*. This is true even if you send a premium check along with your insurance application. In such cases, without a binder, the company can reject the application or offer to issue a policy for a different price than what was quoted you.

Consumer Alert

If you are in a hurry to find coverage—or even if you are not—always ask the agent if he or she has been given authority by the insurance company or companies to issue binders. If the answer is yes and you sign up for insurance, be sure you get the binder in writing.

5

How to Read an Insurance Policy

All right, it's time for a little "i" dotting and "t" crossing. Have you ever read your insurance policies? Not just glanced at, but truly read them? Do you really know what each of your insurance policies contains—what each covers and, equally important, what each does not cover? If you are like most people, the answer is an unqualified no.

Most policyholders don't bother to read their policies, relying instead on what the agent tells them or a brief summary that may be supplied by the insurance company. And let's face it: the text of an insurance policy isn't exactly *Gone With the Wind* (although it may seem just as long).

Exciting or not, however, it really behooves you to know your insurance policy inside-out. Otherwise, how will you know what is covered? How will you know the circumstances under which you can collect? How, indeed, can you know how much you are entitled to collect?

As we have stated before, an insurance policy is, in reality, a written contract. The contract itself is broken down into several parts.

Consumer Alert

Frequently you will not receive the actual policy until after you have decided to buy. You will also often have the right to inspect the policy and cancel. When you receive your policy, *read it* to make sure the promises about the terms of the policy made to get you to buy were actually kept in the contract itself. Few of us do this, but we should.

The Declarations Page

The **declarations page** is the part of the insurance policy with which you are probably most familiar. It is the one- or two-page form that lists the basic information of the coverages and terms that have been purchased. In most cases, this is the only part of the policy that is personalized to you. Here is a basic list of what can be found in a typical declarations page:

The name of the company issuing the policy. This is very basic, yet very necessary information. After all, you need to know who to turn to in time of need.

The type of policy. Each type of policy will have a different form as each policy has different terms and conditions.

The name and address of the insured. This identifies you as the person to whom the insurance has been issued.

The exact time the policy will be in effect. Policy declarations are very precise about this, generally starting at 12:01 A.M. on the date the policy commences and ending at 12:00 noon or 12:00 midnight the day it ends. There is no such thing as a grace period, so if you suffer a loss outside of these time periods, you are on your own.

The extent of coverage. The amount of coverage will be typed in at the appropriate place. Many insurance policies cover several different types of risk. For example, an automobile policy may cover liability, property damage, medical pay, etc. (see Part 2). When there is more than one kind of coverage provided, the differing terms will be broken down into different sections. Each section will in turn be listed separately on the declarations page.

Important information. The declarations page will contain other important matters. In an auto insurance policy it will identify the specific car(s) covered by the insurance. In a property insurance policy, the address of the insured property will be set forth. If there is a deductible, the amount will be listed, as will the amount of the premium. One thing the declarations page will *not* list is **exclusions**. Exclusions are matters specifically not included in coverage. This is one reason why you need to look beyond the declarations page if you are to truly understand your policy.

Endorsements or riders. As we will discuss in greater detail, many policies provide basic but not all-inclusive coverage over the subject matter of the policy. If additional protection is requested, it can often be obtained for extra money. The additional items of coverage are called **endorsements** in property/casualty insurance and **riders** in life and health insurance. If they have been purchased, they will be listed in the declarations page.

Signature of the company representative. Written contracts must be signed to be valid. The declarations page will contain the authorized signature of an officer of the insurance company. (Your signature is usually on the application.)

In short, the declarations page gives you a brief *but not all-inclusive* overview of your insurance policy—its face, if you will, but not its heart and soul.

Definitions

Before the terms of the contract are set forth, they must be defined. The section of the policy that does this is called the **definitions** section. For example, the word "you" will be used quite a bit in most policies. Therefore, the term "you" must be defined. That definition might read something like this:

> Throughout this policy "you" and "your" refer to: 1. The "named insured" shown in the Declarations; and 2. The spouse if a resident of the same household.

The language of the agreement usually starts out very simply. Here is a typical example: "In return for payment of the premium and subject to all the terms of this policy, we agree with you as follows:" Clear and to the point . . . so far.

Of course, life is rarely that simple. The terms of the agreement itself must be set forth. The purpose of the definitions section is to limit the parameters of the coverage by specifying exactly what various terms, which might otherwise be subject to more than one interpretation, really mean in the context of the policy. Here is an example of how this works:

Assume that injuries to a "residence employee" are covered under the terms of a particular insurance policy. Assume further that you work out of your home and employ a secretary, who is injured while at work. The question would arise as to whether or not the secretary was a "residence employee." After all, the secretary is employed by you and works in your home. If that isn't a residence employee, what is?

The answer should be in your policy's definitions section. Here is some typical language used by the insurance industry to define a residence employee:

> Residence employee means: an employee of an insured whose duties are related to the maintenance or use of the residence premises, including household or domestic services.

Thus, under this definition the secretary would *not* be a "residence employee," since the work he or she performed was not "related to the maintenance of the residence premises." Therefore, at least in the case of this particular hypothetical policy, the secretary's injuries would not be covered.

Thus, it is easy to see how important definitions are to the insurance agreement and why you need to understand them if you are to be an effective insurance consumer.

Agreement

If the declarations page can be thought of as the face of the policy, then the **agreement** portion is its heart, for here will be found the exact terms of the contract itself.

Having defined the vital terms of the contract, the contract will set forth the exact terms of the agreement. Most policies are written in outline form and organized around **sections**. Each section of the policy covers one specific topic of the agreement. For example, Section I of a homeowner's insurance policy deals with property coverages, and Section II with liability. Thus, each area of the contract that deals with property coverage in the policy will be labeled as "Section I" material and each part that sets forth the terms of liability coverage will be labeled as "Section II." Most policies have several sections within each insurance agreement.

Subjects within each section may be further broken down into different **parts**, each part designated by a letter. Again using the homeowner's policy as an illustration, the parts will be labeled Part A, "Dwelling," Part B, "Other Structures," and Part C, "Personal Property" (see Part 4). Regardless of the type of insurance, there will be a different part for each subject covered within each individual section of the policy.

Here are brief excerpts from a typical homeowner's policy to help you visualize the point.

SECTION I: PROPERTY COVERAGES

COVERAGE A: *Dwelling*

We cover:

1. the dwelling on the residence premises shown in the declarations, including structures attached to the dwelling; and

2. materials and supplies located . . . etc.

[Body of Text re Part A coverages omitted]

COVERAGE B: *Other Structures*

We cover other structures on the residence premises set apart from the dwelling by clear space. This includes structures connected to the dwelling by only a fence, utility line or similar connection.

[Body of text re Part B coverages omitted]

COVERAGE C: *Personal Property*

We cover personal property owned or used by an insured while it is anywhere in the world. At your request . . .

[Body of text re Part C coverages omitted]

Note that there are three different *parts* (dwelling, other structures, and personal property) covered within the individual *section* on property damage. For organizational purposes, those subjects were broken down individually and labeled with the letters A, B, and C.

The agreement portion of the policy will refer to each section number and part letter when outlining coverage pertinent to each. As an illustration, the homeowner's insurance policy quoted on page 47 deals with the **perils** (see Glossary) insured against, using the same format just described. Notice that the different section numbers and part letters are consistent throughout the insurance policy.

And so it will go, section by section, part by part. The policy will specify the terms of the insurance agreement, the exact level

SECTION I PERILS INSURED AGAINST

COVERAGE A: DWELLINGS and
COVERAGE B: OTHER STRUCTURES

We insure against risks of direct loss to property described in Coverages A and B only if that loss is a physical loss to property; however we do not insure loss:

1) involving collapse, other than as provided in . . . etc.
   [Body of text re Part A and B perils omitted]

COVERAGE C: PERSONAL PROPERTY

We insure for direct physical loss to the property described in Coverage C caused by a peril listed below unless the loss is excluded in Section I—Exclusions . . . etc.
   [Body of text re Part C perils omitted]

of coverage (by reference to the declarations page), and the exclusions and conditions of coverage, which shall be described below.

Exclusions

Exclusions tell you exactly what areas are specifically *not covered* by the insurance contract. In other words, where an exclusion exists, there is *no protection* afforded by the policy (unless purchased separately as a rider or endorsement—see "Endorsements and Riders" below).

Many people resent exclusions because they claim insurance companies give with one hand in the agreement and take away with another in the exclusions portion of the contract—sort of an act of prestidigitation that really sticks it to consumers. However, exclusions are often designed to prevent coverage that is more appropriate to other types of insurance. Exclusions also eliminate exposures that the industry would refuse to insure without charging a premium that would break Fort Knox, such as protecting property against acts of war.

Here is some typical exclusionary language, using the same homeowner's policy quoted above. Note that the exclusions portion of the policy also utilizes the sections and parts breakdown of the policy. Thus these terms are concerned with the property portion of the insurance policy and not the liability portion.

SECTION I EXCLUSIONS

1. We do not insure for loss caused directly or indirectly by any of the following. Such loss is excluded regardless of any other cause or event contributing concurrently or in any sequence to the loss.

   a. *Ordinance or Law*, meaning enforcement of any ordinance or law regulating the construction, repair or demolition of a building or other structure, unless specifically provided under this policy.

   b. *Earth Movement*, meaning earthquake including land shock waves or tremors before, during or after a volcanic eruption; landslide; mud flow; earth sinking, rising or shifting: unless direct loss by:

   (1) fire;

   (2) explosion; or

   (3) breakage of glass or . . . etc.

   [Body of exclusions text omitted]

Not being covered is bad enough, but it's even worse when you could have made an end run around the exclusion by purchasing additional protection. For example, assume that the exclusion quoted above concerning earthquakes was in effect in your homeowner's policy when nature cut loose with an 8.2 temblor, reducing your house to so much kindling wood. Under the terms of the homeowner's policy we have quoted, the damage caused by the earthquake would not be covered and you would

Consumer Alert

It is *absolutely essential* that you understand what is excluded under your insurance policies. Otherwise, you may end up with a loss for which you mistakenly thought there was a remedy within the policy.

have to personally absorb the consequences of the destructive event. If you didn't know going in that earthquake damage was excluded from coverage, you would never know that you had an opportunity to get around the exclusion by purchasing extra coverage by way of an earthquake endorsement.

Conditions

For the most part, the **conditions** portion of the policy describes your obligations under the policy—for example, your duties after a loss. These may include giving prompt notice to the company and protecting against further loss.

The terms under which a loss will be settled also appear in the conditions portion. For example, our old friend, the homeowner's policy, has the following language under Section I:

SECTION I: CONDITIONS

[Previous text omitted]

3. Loss Settlement. Covered property losses are settled as follows:

a) Personal property;

b) Awnings, carpeting, household appliances, outdoor antennas and outdoor equipment, whether or not attached to buildings;

c) Structures that are not buildings;

at actual cash value at the time of loss but not more than the amount required to repair or replace.

Understanding the conditions section can be very important, especially with regard to preserving your rights under the policy should you incur a loss. This portion of the contract will also tell you how your losses will be measured pursuant to the policy. Most policies require you to comply with specific procedures when filing claims and disputing insurance company decisions with regard to those claims. These requirements and procedures will be found in the conditions portion of your policy. Your failure to comply could result in loss of money you would otherwise have obtained, or at least may delay payment, and can prevent you from having the right to take the insurance company to court.

Consumer Alert

If you have a question about the terms of your contract, contact your agent and have your questions answered in writing (see Chapter 40).

Endorsements and Riders

If you read your policy carefully and discuss it thoroughly with the agent or other insurance company representative before you buy (or after, for that matter), you will soon learn the areas in which you are not protected. Often, for an extra premium, you can fill in the exclusionary gaps that disturb you. Note, however, that *no affordable policy will ever protect you against every single possible loss*. We will discuss the different riders and endorsements you can purchase for each type of policy covered in this book as they become relevant.

Many consumers are completely baffled as to how insurance companies decide to price their products. Do they close their eyes and throw a dart at a big board marked "High," "Higher," and "Highest"? No, there is a method to their madness. Let's look next at the mysterious world of insurance pricing.

6

What Price Security?

Insurance companies put a lot of time and effort into pricing their wares. We will now take a peek behind the scenes at this area of vital concern to you.

The Importance of Statistics

The key word to remember about insurance is *statistics*. The industry breathes, eats, and bleeds statistics. Minutiae that would cure the worst case of insomnia for us, such as the number of people who have had a home fire in a given town over the last 50 years due to smoking in bed, is the stuff of which dreams are made to the dedicated insurance executive in charge of figuring out what to charge for insurance.

Each of you reading this book is an individual. But to an insurance company looking at you as a potential policyholder, what you really are is a statistic. Your age, gender, life history, residence locale, occupation, and more are all of considerable interest to an insurance company when you apply for insurance.

To the insurance company, these statistics make you a member of a **class**—a group of people sharing common characteristics relevant to the issue of pricing. For example, men under the age of 25 might be a preferred class for the purposes of buying life insurance but would probably be less desirable when it comes to auto insurance.

Once your relevant class is determined, the company looks even more deeply into the statistics. Based on the class involved and the type of insurance being sought, the insurance company will determine what the average **expectancy of loss** will be within the class. For example, in a given community, five houses may be expected to burn per year. This information is important in setting prices, as we shall soon see.

Once your class has been determined, then, the insurance company will determine whether you have a *greater risk of loss*, an *average risk of loss*, or a *lower risk of loss* compared to an average member of the class. To state the obvious, insurance companies love to land those with statistically low risks as policyholders, since the likelihood that they will have to shell out insurance benefits is then greatly reduced.

Underwriting

This brings us to **underwriting**. Before the price of a product can be set, an applicant for an insurance policy must first be accepted by the company as an eligible policyholder. How is that done? By reviewing the relevant statistics. Who does it? A faceless (in the sense that they don't deal directly with the customers) but very powerful person known as an underwriter.

As an extreme example, assume that a 95-year-old man who smokes three packs of cigarettes a day, and who is going into the hospital in two weeks for a triple bypass, comes to the "Easy Pay Insurance Company" looking for $1 million in life insurance. Assume again that you are the underwriter who is responsible for deciding whether to take this million-dollar gamble (and who, not irrelevantly, has a family to support). What would you do? Of course, you'd say, "No way, Jose." Why? The statistical chance of the applicant living very long and helping to fill the insurance company's coffers with premium payments would be very small indeed. Moreover, the chance that the company would shortly have to shell out big bucks in benefits would be very, very high. Thus, the chance that this poor fellow would be issued a life insurance policy would be virtually nonexistent.

Obviously, in real life few underwriting decisions are that easy or clear-cut. When you apply for insurance you come to the underwriting table with a mix of characteristics that will be considered as either *positive* (presenting a low risk to the company) or *negative* (presenting a high risk to the company). The underwriters will then consider your entire statistical profile and decide whether, overall, you present an average risk to the company (**standard**), a high risk (**substandard**), or a low risk (**preferred**). Preferred risks will be quickly accepted and offered the best price. Standard risks will be accepted and offered the standard price. Substandard risks will either be rejected, or accepted on the condition that they pay a higher price or, sometimes, that they accept lower benefits.

Rates

We now come to the subject of rates. We have already learned that a premium is the amount we pay for insurance. That is a good general definition. But how is the premium determined? By magic? No. By the number of **units** of insurance purchased multiplied by the **rate** per unit.

Units of Coverage

A unit of insurance is the building block of pricing. It varies from one type of insurance to another. For now, think of a unit of coverage as a pound of meat. Visualize the rate as the price you pay per pound.

When you buy insurance, you buy units of coverage. For

Consumer Alert

The statistics used by insurance companies in determining the level of risk you present to them will vary from company to company. What one may consider important, another may not. Thus, if you are branded substandard by one company, don't hang your head in shame! Keep looking for a company that will give you a better deal. You may just find a company that thinks better of you.

example, assume that a unit of life insurance is $1,000 for one year's coverage and that you want $10,000 worth of life insurance. Let's further assume that the rate per unit is $20 per year. You would have to pay $200 for one year's worth of life insurance with a benefit of $10,000 (10 units × $20 rate = $200).

The next question is, how is the rate per unit determined? Statistics, of course! The insurance company (or an independent rate bureau to which the company subscribes) will establish rates based on what its statistics tell it to expect the cost of the anticipated claims and losses to be. From that figure, the premiums will be set so as to be sufficient (and profitable), equitable (and profitable), nongouging (and profitable), competitive (and profitable), and safety conscious (and above all, profitable).

Let's look at these criteria a little more closely.

Sufficient. The rates must be sufficient to pay the company's anticipated losses from claims and the overhead expenses. No state insurance department will permit any insurance company to set its basic rates so low as to result in its insolvency (see Chapter 39).

Profitable. The rate will be established so that the insurance company can expect to make a profit. But what kind of profit?

The insurance industry believes it should always be able to have rates high enough to make an **underwriting profit**. An underwriting profit is where the premiums received pay for (1) all losses and (2) all overhead expenses, with some money left over, which is the overhead profit. Insurance companies also make tons of money investing your premiums. The companies believe this area to be their exclusive business and use arcane bookkeeping methods that keep the exact amount of investment profits they earn a well-guarded secret. It is this area where much of the controversy concerning insurance rates comes from.

Equitable. The methods of establishing classes and setting rates should be fair. There is also tremendous controversy here, especially regarding auto insurance and the fairness of establishing rates based on residence, called **territorial rating**. Those who support territorial rating contend it is the fairest way to set rates because most accidents happen within a few miles of a driver's home. Opponents contend that territorial rating discriminates against minorities and those who live in cities. (For more information on this ongoing dispute and California's Proposition 103, see Chapter 13.)

Nongouging. In theory, at least, rates are set to provide a fair **rate of return** (profit) but not an excessive rate of return (exploitation).

Competitive. Insurance rates should be competitive vis-à-vis other insurance companies selling similar lines of insurance. Otherwise, no customers will come knocking on the company's door.

Safety conscious. Some insurance companies determine rates by how willing you are to take steps to reduce your risk. This helps both of you, since reduced risk leads to fewer claims and fewer claims means that your life has been less "eventful." For example, companies offering homeowner's insurance often reward nonsmokers with a small savings in the premium since statistics prove that nonsmokers have less likelihood of suffering a fire than smokers do. Fewer claims should also mean lower premiums.

Rating Systems

Once a rate has been set for each unit of coverage using the above criteria, adjustments can be made for individual cases and/or classes. As we saw in Chapter 1, Ben Franklin's old fire insurance company set lower rates for brick houses than wooden houses. This is an example of a **blanket rating**, where different classes of applicants for the same kind of insurance receive different rates per unit of insurance. **Gender rating** in life insurance, where women receive better rates than men because they live longer, is a current example of blanket rating. (Gender rating is now prohibited by law in some states.)

Merit rating is another way that basic rates are often modified. The type of merit rating you are most likely to run into is **experience rating**. In experience rating, factors that make a person a preferred, substandard, or standard risk (e.g., a person's driving record in auto insurance) are looked into and the premium is adjusted up, down, or not at all, as the underwriter deems appropriate.

We'll be discussing issues of pricing for many different types of insurance in more detail as we get to them. We'll also teach you how to use the various systems of pricing to your advantage in order to save money.

7

Consumers' Agenda

As things stand right now, regulators allow insurance companies to charge too much for many of their products. One way to combat this outrage is to demand that your state legislature create the political office of a **Public Advocate**.

A Public Advocate acts as a representative for the consumer before the state insurance commissioner when insurance companies request the right to raise their rates. This is an important concept since most insurance commissioners view themselves as impartial decision makers regarding matters of insurance rather than as advocates for the consumer. Commissioners are barraged by insurance company lawyers and representatives in support of rate increases, but there are usually few advocates for the consumer. The office of Public Advocate changes that inequity.

Currently, several states have advocates working on behalf of the consumer. These states include Maine, Massachusetts (through the office of the state attorney general), New Jersey, Ohio, Florida, and Texas.

The office of the Public Advocate should be financed by the insurance industry or, if necessary, by the taxpayers. Without such a public office, the insurance industry gets to do most of the talking when it comes to raising rates. And that simply isn't fair.

If you agree that a Public Advocate is an idea that could help keep insurance rates down, become an activist and write your legislators and governor demanding that the office be established in your state. You never know, your letter could be the first step in the long journey toward the mythical destination of pricing fairness. Here is a sample letter you may send to your state representative.

> John (Judy) Goodrepresentative (or Industrystooge, if ap-
>   plicable)
> State Representative
> Capitol Office Building
> Your Capital City, Your State
> Proper Zip Code

Dear Mr. (Ms.) Goodrepresentative:

I am very displeased with the regulation of the insurance industry in our state. It seems to me that the money and power of the insurance industry gives them disproportionate power in the halls of legislature and before the state insurance department.

One solution to this problem would be to create a new state office: Public Advocate. The job of Public Advocate would be to take the side of the average insurance consumer when matters of premium rate increases, insurance policy wording, insurance legislation, or other issues of vital import to consumers are being debated in the legislature or decided by the insurance commissioner. A Public Advocate would have the time, money, information, and ability to effectively represent the consumer's point of view. This is extremely important from my perspective because I do not believe that the consumer is adequately represented in government. This new office would balance the equation.

This matter is very important to me and will affect my voting in the next election.

Sincerely,

Mary P. Involvedconsumer

Part 2

Automobile Insurance

We now take up the volatile issue of auto insurance. At one time, auto insurance was not a subject that was likely to raise the hackles or pump up the adrenaline of anyone. Now, because of the tremendous increases in the price of auto insurance in many parts of the country, the topic is one that generates anger, controversy, and resentment—even before the envelope containing the bill is opened. Once people actually see what they are being asked to pay, their reaction can be much more pronounced. For one thing, auto insurance is mandatory in many states. That means consumers can't "Just Say No," thereby reducing the incentives of the companies to keep prices low.

The reasons for this superinflation vary, depending on whose opinion is being expressed. Ask the insurance industry and it will carry on about greedy lawyers bringing frivolous lawsuits that the insurance companies have to spend millions to defend. It will rail against unethical body shops that charge unconscionable fees to repair damaged cars and about the outrageous costs of medical care.

Ask the lawyers and they will yell about recalcitrant insurance companies that force injured parties into attorneys' waiting arms due to unfair practices. Lawyers will also point to the power of insurance companies to water down legislation intended to keep the cost of insurance in line and to their power to influence the regulators to speak softly and carry a small stick.

For this reason, our discussion of auto insurance will deal with topics that would have seemed almost irrelevant only a few years ago. Issues such as limiting the legal rights of injured people to have their day in court, no-fault versus fault insurance systems, and the concept of territorial rating will be addressed. In addition, we will introduce you to the ins and outs of your auto insurance policy, a less dramatic but still necessary step toward helping you achieve a state of "consumer power." We will take you into the world of the personal injury lawsuit and contingency fee lawyers ("Toto, I've a feeling we're not in Kansas anymore"). Finally, we will recommend ways both today and in the future to keep the price of your auto insurance from forcing you out of car and garage. So, to paraphrase a famous Bette Davis line, fasten your seat belts, it's going to be a bumpy ride.

The Question of Fault

8

When we were kids and something went wrong, our first response was usually, "It's not my fault!" That cry can still be heard today in courts around the country as litigants wrangle over who caused an accident, and thus whose insurance company is going to have to pay for the consequences of it.

The **fault system** of redressing civil grievances is as old as the country itself. From the beginning of our history, people have taken each other to court when they felt they had been wronged at the hands of another.

When the automobile came into being and, by definition, auto accidents followed, the legal system didn't skip a beat as people sued each other for damages and injuries caused when great-grandpa's Model A ran into his neighbor's Model T.

How the Fault System Works

In order to be a fully informed consumer, you need to understand how the fault system works. This isn't as easy as it sounds, since each state has different laws concerning negligence and auto accidents. However, there are some general principles that can be discussed.

Negligence Is a Tort

When we discuss the issue of negligence or fault, we are talking about something called a **tort**. In legal terms, a tort can be defined as a civil wrong committed by one person against another that causes damages. If someone commits a tort, be it negligence, libel, fraud, or whatever, he or she can be held responsible in a court of law for the damages caused.

The Damages That Can Be Collected

In an auto accident, different types of damages can be incurred. Lawyers call these **special damages, general damages**, and **punitive damages**.

Special damages. **Special damages** are out-of-pocket losses incurred by the injured party. They usually include items such as medical bills, lost wages, property damage, and funeral expenses. When someone is seriously injured, special damages can be exceedingly high. For example, imagine the expenses and losses of an injury that takes six months to heal. We could easily be talking six figures. Even relatively minor injuries can cost thousands of dollars in medical bills, lost wages, and property repair costs.

General damages. It is in the area of **general damages** that most of the controversy over the fault system can be found. General damages refer to real losses, but losses that cannot be objectively measured in that there is no bill or receipt or loss of money in a bank account to prove the loss. The concepts of **pain and suffering** and **loss of use** come under general damages.

It is often said that if you have your health you have everything. A person who is in chronic pain might tell you to add exclamation points to that sentence! Even if the pain ultimately disappears, the discomfort, as the doctors euphemistically call it, can be a searing experience while it lasts.

So, how do you compensate someone for putting them through the experience of pain? In our system, we don't extract an eye for an eye or a tooth for a tooth. Rather, we try to put a price tag on that which cannot really be valued. General damages, then, try to compensate the accident victim for the pain and discomfort he or she experienced or will continue to experience due to an accident. Loss of use, likewise, attempts to compensate a person for the loss of a body part or function.

What is an arm or a leg worth? What is the price of chronic back pain? These are questions that lawyers, insurance adjusters, and juries have grappled with every working day for years in states that have fault laws.

Punitive damages. Punitive damages are designed to punish wrongdoers who intentionally engage in despicable misconduct. Sometimes punitive damages are also awarded for **gross negligence**, which can be defined as negligence so horrible that it deserves punishment. Punitive damages are rarely an issue in auto accident cases, and car insurance policies usually will not pay for awards of punitive damages. Thus, we will not discuss them further here, although they will be covered in Chapter 42.

Computing a Fault Award

Putting all of this together, here is how a fault award might be computed.

Assume that Harry Leadfoot rear-ends Maggie Neckbrace. Maggie is taken to the hospital. She spends three days in the hospital and then one week at home recuperating. Thereafter, she returns to work but continues to suffer chronic headaches as a result of the accident. She is treated for headaches for one year, and her doctors believe she will experience severe headaches from time to time for the rest of her life. They also predict that, because of the accident, she will probably develop an arthritic condition in her neck as she ages.

The following are Maggie's special damages:

> $4,250 hospital bill
> $3,125 doctors' bills
> $1,800 lost wages
> $1,250 physical therapy
> $425 medications
> Property damage paid by
>   Harry's insurance
> _____
> **$10,850 Total Special Damages**

What is Maggie's case worth? That may not be as easy to determine as it looks. Computing her special damages seems simple, and it often is. However, sometimes things aren't always as they appear at first. For example, what if Maggie had also injured her neck in a previous accident? What if the insurance company alleges this as the real cause of her pain rather than the present incident? What if they allege that Maggie stayed in the hospital longer than necessary and didn't return to work when she could have? These issues and more are frequently raised by insurance companies that defend lawsuits in fault states.

Then there is the issue of general damages. What is the value of the discomfort and pain that Maggie experienced? How much should she receive for her future headaches and potential pain from arthritis? This is where many lawsuits get down and dirty, with the injured party's lawyer arguing for a high figure of compensation and the defense lawyer urging a low recovery.

Assuming that the accident is the sole cause of Maggie's injuries and damages, her case would probably be worth anywhere from $20,000 to $50,000, depending on state law and the mood of the jury that hears the case. There's simply no way to calculate the amount for sure, due to the subjectivity of general damages (although lawyers will tell you that a case is generally worth between three and five times the "specials").

The Meaning of "Fault"

The meaning of fault can be very important in determining whether someone is entitled to damages, and if so, in what amount. Exactly what "fault" is will vary from state to state. Here is an overview of the differing ways this concept is looked at.

Contributory negligence. Under the old rules of negligence (which are still followed in some states), if the injured party was even partially at fault, he or she could receive nothing since the policy of the law was not to reward people for their own negligence. Thus, a defense to the tort of negligence was **contributory negligence**; i.e., the person bringing the suit (the plaintiff) was partially at fault and thus entitled to nothing from the person sued (the defendant). This resulted in some cases of injustice where a person only slightly at fault received nothing from a clearly negligent defendant.

Comparative negligence. This potential for injustice has, for the most part, been corrected in most states by changing the law from contributory negligence to a system of **comparative negligence**. Under comparative negligence, the injured party is entitled to recover that percentage of damages that he or she did not cause, as determined by a jury. Thus, if you are in an accident and found to be 20 percent at fault and you were damaged to the tune of $100,000, you would receive $80,000.

There are various kinds of comparative negligence among the states that follow this type of law. Some permit both sides to sue each other for the percentage they are not at fault. Others require that a plaintiff be less than 50 percent at fault in order to recover damages. In any event, the percentage that each party is at fault in an accident can be a big issue in settling or bringing auto accident disputes to court.

The Need for Lawyers

We have only scratched the surface of the potential disputes that can arise between an insurance company and the injured party.

Under such circumstances, is it any wonder that people often feel the need to call in a lawyer to assist them?

Lawyers are an integral component in the fault system of many states. Some claim that this is because of lawyers' alleged greed and/or "ambulance chasing" propensities. Others blame insurance company adjusters who are so penny-pinching that they literally force people into the courts to recover their losses. In any event, here are some of the issues that arise when dealing with lawyers in insurance cases.

Plaintiff's expenses. Plaintiffs usually hire a lawyer on a contingency basis. That means that they will pay the attorney a percentage of the amount of money the attorney actually collects on their behalf.

Lawyers who advertise on daytime television like to say that means that if there's no recovery of damages, there's no fee. That's true as far as it goes. But attorneys' fees are not the only expense to the client. There are other costs, such as paying a court reporter to record a deposition, and court filing fees. Costs can run from hundreds of dollars in small cases, to thousands in average cases, to tens or even hundreds of thousands in very large cases. *Clients are responsible for costs regardless of who wins the lawsuit.* Sometimes lawyers "advance" costs for their clients because the client can't afford to pay them. This is perfectly proper, but remember, "advance" is just another name lawyers use for "loan." The client will have to pay it back out of the recovery proceeds if the suit is successful, or out of his or her own pocket if no money is collected.

Another expense that is often incurred is for medical treatment and doctors' testimony. Often the client does not have the money to pay for these doctors. The doctors will often respond by "taking a lien" on the case. This means that the doctor gets paid out of the proceeds before the client receives a dime.

Often, clients grumble that they receive less money out of a personal injury award than do the lawyer, doctor, and others. Here's how that situation can come about:

- Assume a trial recovery of $100,000.
- Assume further that the retainer agreement with the lawyer gives him or her 33 percent of the recovery.

- Assume the costs of the case were $6,500.

- Assume that two doctors had liens on the case totaling $8,000.

In such a case the client would receive "only" $52,500 ($100,000 minus $47,500, which is the total of the attorney's fees, court costs, and doctors' liens). But hey, *it's tax free*.

▶ **NOTE:** The insurance industry and other business groups attack the contingency fee as being unfair to the client. What they don't tell you is that without a contingency fee, you would have to pay an attorney an hourly fee, which can range upward from *$150 per hour*. Were that the case, *the insurance companies could bankrupt you* by having their lawyers drag their feet to force you to incur excessive fees. Rather than being a problem for clients, contingency fees allow the consumer to have a fighting chance against powerful and rich insurance companies. No wonder the insurance industry is trying to eliminate contingency fees in the litigation marketplace.

Defendants' expenses. Luckily, those who are sued, called **defendants**, have less to worry about—other than an increase in their rates, of course—since their lawyers' fees and court costs are paid by the insurance company. Defense lawyers charge the insurance company an hourly rate, usually at a premium because of the volume of cases a defense firm will handle.

Despite the fact that a defendant does not have to pay for the lawyer, if you are sued you should be actively involved in the case. An adverse judgment or settlement can be the cause of your insurance being canceled or your premiums raised.

The Stages of a Typical Case

A typical case will go through several stages before it is resolved. Here, in chronological order, is an outline of what you can expect if you get into a controversy surrounding an auto accident.

1. **The accident.** Car meets truck, car meets car, car meets pedestrian, whatever. Sometimes bad things happen to good people.

2. **The investigation.** After the accident occurs, both parties take action that starts matters in motion. There may be a police report. The accident will be reported to the insurance companies of the parties involved.

3. **Medical treatment.** If there is an injury, medical care is given. Often medical care will continue for some time. In some cases, especially in soft-tissue injuries such as whiplash, the effects of the injury may not be felt immediately.

4. **Settlement negotiations.** Once there is a clear picture of what happened and the consequences of the accident, an insurance adjuster will attempt to resolve the case. If the person not at fault has hired a lawyer, the discussions will be with the attorney; otherwise, they will be with the injured party.

5. **Filing a lawsuit.** If the matter is not settled at the adjuster stage, a lawsuit is often filed. This brings in defense lawyers, and both parties usually go to their corners in preparation for the combat ahead. At this point, other people who may have helped cause the accident can also be sued, either by the plaintiff or the defendant.

6. **Discovery.** After the initial stages of a lawsuit, both parties will attempt to find out as much as they can about the case. This process is known as **discovery**. During discovery, a plaintiff's medical history will be thoroughly reviewed, witnesses will be interviewed or deposed, experts may be hired to give their opinion. Discovery can be a long, grueling, and time-consuming process.

Consumer Alert

In any civil case, there is a time limit within which a case must be filed in court or it is barred forever. This is called the *Statute of Limitations*. Generally, you have one year from the date of the accident to bring an action, although the time varies from state to state. If you are injured in an auto accident, make a point of finding out what the statute of limitations is and make sure your case is filed on time if you don't otherwise settle the matter.

7. **Settlement negotiations.** As discovery proceeds and the lawyers for both sides learn more about the case, they will form conclusions as to who will win and who will lose. They also arrive at a general idea as to how much the case is worth. At any time they can (and often do) discuss settlement.

8. **Settlement conference.** As the matter approaches trial or arbitration, the court will often call all parties into court for a settlement conference. At the conference both lawyers informally present their case to the judge, who will give a nonbinding opinion as to its value. Often the parties settle their cases at such conferences.

9. **Trial.** If push comes to shove and the parties cannot reach agreement, the matter will go to trial or arbitration, where a jury, judge, or arbitrator will decide who wins and how much, if any, the insurance company will have to pay in damages.

10. **Appeal.** If the loser is unhappy with the result and believes that the decision can be overturned on ap-

peal, an appeal will be filed. If the appeal is successful, there will usually be a new trial. If not, the decision stands and must be carried out by the parties.

Criticism of the Fault System

This fault system of redressing grievances arising out of automobile accidents has increasingly come under attack in recent years. The criticism has been broad-ranged and has come from both the insurance industry and from some consumer advocates, most particularly Consumers Union. It can be summarized as follows:

- **The fault system causes high auto insurance rates.** The fault system is time-consuming and expensive. Thus, critics charge that it is a major cause of high auto insurance premiums.

- **It only protects those "not at fault."** When an accident occurs, only the person adjudged not at fault or less at fault (depending on the laws of each state) is able to collect damages for items such as lost wages and pain and suffering from the person who caused the accident. Yet, just because a person may have caused an accident doesn't mean that he or she does not also have significant injuries and expenses arising from it. Under the fault concept, the only benefits that persons at fault can collect will be from their own insurance policies, be it auto, health, or disability insurance. Unfortunately, many have little or no insurance protection and thus end up in severe financial straits.

- **It is a primary cause of court congestion.** Auto accident cases make up a significant part of the civil case court load in states that have a fault system. Some states have such an overload of civil cases that it can literally take years to get to court.

- **It can take years to receive benefits.** When an injured person seeks damages under the fault system, he or she must often go through years of waiting to receive damages due to the time-consuming exercise of bringing a lawsuit and waiting for a court date (assuming a quick settlement can't be reached with the insurance company of the person at fault). Unfortunately, bill collectors, like the tides, wait for no man. Thus, many have been financially ruined while waiting to collect their money.

- **Only the lawyers benefit.** As we have noted, lawyers in automobile accidents usually work on a contingency fee, meaning they collect a percentage of the recovery rather than an hourly fee. If there is no recovery, there is no fee. The percentage charged can be significant, running from 25 to 40 percent.

With all this criticism and with so much fussing and fighting, it is no wonder that there is an effort under way to change the way we settle differences arising out of auto accidents. This new approach is called no-fault. How no-fault works and its pros and cons are the subjects of our next chapter.

9

The No-Fault Alternative

With the cost of auto insurance premiums rising at truly alarming rates, there has been a movement in many states in the last decade to alter the fault system. This movement supports a concept generically referred to as **no-fault** insurance.

Basically, no-fault insurance is designed so that the victims of an automobile accident receive compensation from their *own* insurance company for damages that result from the collision. It is called no-fault because the respective insurance companies are responsible for the damages to their own clients without regard to whose driving errors caused the accident.

How No-Fault Is Supposed to Work

In theory, no-fault insurance is designed to do away with many of the annoying and time-consuming delays that are found in the fault system.

- **The issue of fault does not have to be proved.** Injured parties no longer have to wait months and years to receive benefits when they are not the primary cause of the accident.

- **The party primarily at fault can also have his or her damages paid.** In addition to medical bills, items such as lost wages, which would not normally be paid by a fault system insurance policy, would be compensated for.

- **Lawyers are supposed to be unnecessary in the system.** Insurance companies pay claims in most cases upon appropriate proof of loss, through objective records easily obtained by the injured parties and/or insurance companies.

- **Benefits cover a broad range of losses to the victims of accidents.** These include:

  medical expenses to a limit as defined in the policy.

  rehabilitation expenses, if necessary.

  a proportion of lost earnings.

  indemnity-type payments as reimbursement for money paid to others for "essential services" that cannot be performed due to injuries. Essential services include housework and home maintenance.

  funeral expenses.

  payments to survivors of those killed in the accident to compensate for the loss of a family member.

New York's No-Fault System

Let's see how these general principles have been applied in real life. One of the more successful no-fault systems in the United States is that of New York. The state adopted "the no-fault solution" in 1974. Currently, if a New York resident is injured in an accident, his or her insurance company must provide coverage up to $50,000 per person, consisting of the following basic benefits:

- **All necessary medical and hospital bills and other health-service expenses.** These are payable in accordance with fee schedules established by the state. Doctors and hospitals are restricted from charging more than the fees allowed in the schedule except under unusual circumstances.

- **Eighty percent of lost earnings up to a maximum of $2,000 per month for up to three years following the date of the accident.**

- **Up to $25 per day for a year for other reasonable and necessary expenses resulting from the accident.** For example, this could include the cost of hiring a housekeeper or necessary transportation expenses to and from a health care provider.

- **A $2,000 death benefit payable to the estate of a covered person.** This is in addition to the $50,000 coverage for medical losses.

All benefits must be paid within 30 days of providing the insurance company appropriate proof of loss.

In addition to the above, consumers can buy additional coverage to increase the amount of medical bills that will be paid and the amount of lost earnings that will be compensated. However, there will be a reduction in payments if the injured party also receives benefits from Social Security disability and/or workers compensation.

If all of this sounds so good that you are wondering "What's the catch?" then you are asking a very intelligent and relevant question. There are indeed several catches. You must give up some things to the insurance companies in return for their agreeing to compensate you immediately for covered losses. Here are the tradeoffs:

Collection for pain and suffering. Under New York's and other no-fault systems, you lose the right to be compensated for your pain and suffering in most circumstances. (For the exceptions, see "The Concept of Thresholds," below.) Thus, if you suffered agonizing headaches, there is no recovery. If you will suffer chronic pain for the rest of your life, chances are there is no recovery.

Undercompensation for lost wages. Note that the basic coverage in New York is 80 percent of the basic lost wage to a maximum of $2,000 per month. Minnesota, another no-fault state, has an even lower maximum payment: only $250 per week. Such capped payments may be inadequate to meet the needs of the injured party.

Undercompensation for other out-of-pocket expenses. The New York law provides for $25 per day for items such as house-keeping and transportation. How many housekeepers do you know who will work for $25 per day? How much is taxi fare across town to your doctor's office?

You lose the right to sue. If you are not at fault in an accident and you live in a no-fault state, you cannot sue for redress of grievances unless your injuries are very severe. This means, almost by definition, that you are not going to receive full compensation for your losses.

Compensation for property damage remains under the fault concept in most states with no-fault. This may seem like small potatoes, but it isn't. Assume that your car is damaged to the tune of $5,000. Assume further that you don't have collision coverage. You will have to sue the driver at fault for your damages—only there's a catch. Most people don't have the time or ability to bring a suit without using a lawyer. And no lawyer will take a $5,000 case on a contingency basis. Therefore, you will have to pay the lawyer an hourly fee, probably about $150 an hour. At that rate, you could end up spending as much to bring the suit as you will receive in damages *if* you win.

The Concept of Thresholds

People who are very seriously injured need more in compensation than no-fault laws typically allow for. This fact has not escaped the lawmakers who have installed no-fault in their states. Thus, each state permits those who are *badly hurt* to bring suit under the fault concept. The line that divides cases where no-fault applies from circumstances where lawsuits are permitted is called the **threshold**. The threshold varies from state to state, but it is always based on one of the following plans.

Verbal threshold. A **verbal threshold** is one where the right to sue depends on the nature of the injuries. In order to sue in a verbal threshold state, the victim must suffer serious impairment of body function, permanent serious disfigurement, or death. Exactly what this means is defined in the law as the courts interpret it. The insurance industry favors this type of threshold because it is easier to keep a case within the no-fault dividing line.

Monetary threshold. A **monetary threshold** is easier to understand because it is based on a more objective criterion: whether the cost of medical treatment exceeds a base amount established in the no-fault law. If it does, the victim is free to sue based on fault. The insurance industry disapproves of this type of threshold, asserting that thresholds are often too low (for example, $400 in Connecticut), resulting in too few cases coming under the no-fault category. In addition, the insurance industry believes that a monetary threshold only encourages accident victims to run up unnecessary medical bills in order to be able to sue and go for the big bucks in a fault-type lawsuit.

Add-on states. Some states mandate first-party no-fault-type payments while still permitting third-party suits based on fault. In these states you can receive compensation from your own insurance company for damages you sustain while at the same time being sued by a third party if your driving contributed to their injuries. These are known as **add-on laws**.

Currently, 14 states and Puerto Rico have some form of no-fault law. So does the province of Quebec in Canada. At least two states, Pennsylvania and Nevada, have repealed no-fault laws. In addition, several states are toying with the idea of allowing insurance consumers to choose which system to be under.

How the no-fault controversy will ultimately play itself out is still up in the air. The insurance industry favors it. So does Consumers Union. Both point to a reduction in lawsuits in strong no-fault states and a reduced need to hire lawyers. The authors of this book are not in favor of no-fault in its present forms. We believe that the compensation is often inadequate and that the victims of accidents are asked to pay for the wrongdoing of those who cause the accidents. In other words, safe drivers are penalized while unsafe drivers benefit through no-fault. And why should people give up compensation for pain and suffering in order to expand insurance company profits, anyway?

The No-Fault Insurance Policy

Most of the terms in a no-fault insurance policy remain the same as in a fault policy. The major difference is the personal injury protection coverage, known as PIP. The PIP portion of the insurance policy pays for the no-fault benefits that are mandated by state laws.

Your no-fault insurance policy must also provide benefits for fault auto accidents. Fault auto accidents are those that occur in

Consumer Alert

A good way to save money on your no-fault premium is to agree to coordinate no-fault benefits with those of your own health insurance policy, with health insurance being first in line to pay. If such coordination is available to you, think seriously about signing up. And while you are at it, apply the saved premiums toward giving yourself better wage protection in the event an accident makes it impossible for you to work.

a fault state or those in which the injuries exceed the threshold limits of state no-fault law. Liability policies work in a way similar to traditional fault policies.

Whether your state adopts or rejects the no-fault concept is up to you, *if you get involved*. Otherwise, special interests will make the decision for you, and that decision could be based on who contributes the most to campaign funds of state politicians. So become an active consumer. Your financial well-being may depend on it if you are ever involved in an auto accident.

▶ **NOTE:** If you live in Canada, this doesn't matter as much to you because of the extensive health services safety net you enjoy. We in the United States can learn from you.

Now that we're past the controversy, let's get into the nuts and bolts of auto insurance.

10

The Typical Auto Insurance Policy

Americans are in love with their cars, but they sure don't love their auto insurance. Unfortunately, the joys of owning a car are often diminished by the realities of auto insurance. Or, to put it more graphically, auto insurance is to cars what buffalo chips are to bison.

As unpleasant as it may be to purchase auto insurance, it will be even more distasteful if you don't fully understand the who's, why's, what's, and how's of your coverage. And since ignorance is never bliss when it comes to insurance, it pays to know your policy, from the declarations page to the fine print.

Who Is Covered?

When you purchase auto insurance, *you are insuring a specifically identified automobile*. But you are also insuring people, who are known in "insurancespeak" as the **insureds**. Without turning this into a discussion of how many insureds can dance on the head of a pin, there are generally three different categories of parties who can qualify as an insured under your policy.

The Named Insured

If you buy insurance for your car, you are a **named insured**. So is your spouse if you are married, as well as any other family members who reside with you.

"Permissive Users"

If you allow your brother-in-law to borrow your car, he also becomes an insured, since insurance coverage usually follows the car wherever it goes, as long as it goes with your permission. This is important because liability also follows the vehicle wherever it goes—again, as long as it is driven with your permission or by someone who could reasonably believe you had given permission. (Many states limit the liability of the insured for damages caused to others by a permissive driver. For example, California limits such damages to $15,000. Of course, this limit does not protect the *driver* from further liability.)

Other Legally Responsible Parties

Another category of insured includes persons or organizations legally responsible for the acts of a covered person while using an automobile. Sometimes we use our cars for other than personal purposes. For example, if your boss asks you to drive to the airport to pick up an important customer, you are using *your car* for your employer's purposes. If you had an accident under such conditions, your employer could be sued as well as you, because you were conducting company business while driving the car. Should such an unfortunate incident take place, your employer would be considered an insured for purposes of auto insurance protection. (This would not apply if you were driving a company car rather than your own. In such circumstances, the company insurance policy would be primarily responsible.)

Types of Coverage

An auto insurance policy, whether in a fault or no-fault state, is really a combination of several different coverages tied up in one package. Some of these coverages protect third parties and some protect the insured directly. Some of the coverages are mandatory and some optional. The differing coverages are priced separately and added together to come up with the total premium cost.

Liability Coverage

The issue of **liability insurance** is the most controversial aspect of auto insurance and the most expensive to purchase. Liability insurance is designed to protect you against the costs of being sued should your or another insured's negligent driving cause injury.

Without sounding too much like the lawyers we are, negligent driving can be defined as *driving outside the standard of care* required of the operators of an automobile. What constitutes driving beyond the standard of care will depend on each state's individual laws. A good universal example would be running a red light.

Negligence requires more than the "mere" act of driving badly. In order for liability to arise there must also be some form of actual harm, called *damages*, which directly result from the bad driving. In other words, under the "no harm, no foul" principle, if you run a red light and get away with it without incident, you will not be subject to liability to anyone. However, if you run a red light and hit someone, you can be held liable for all of the monetary damages allowed by law that result from your negligence.

An auto insurance policy addresses three separate aspects of this liability: bodily injury, property damage, and the cost of defending a lawsuit.

Bodily injury. If your driving negligence causes the injury or death of another, you must pay the monetary damages that result from the accident. This includes medical bills, lost wages, and money to compensate the victim for pain and suffering (in fault states) that result from the injury. In some cases, you can also be held responsible for damages that the injury to one person causes to others. For example, if the injured person is killed, you can be held responsible to the deceased's spouse and children for loss of the support they would have received had the person lived. You can also be sued for something called *loss of consortium* if the injuries prevent a spouse from enjoying the "comforts of the marital bed."

When you purchase liability insurance as part of an auto insurance policy, you have the power to choose how much protection from liability you want to buy. This liability coverage will be expressed in terms of a **single-limit amount** or a **split-limit amount**.

Split-limit liability packages are the kind the majority of people purchase. The risk accepted by the insurance company is expressed in terms of the maximum amount that will be paid under the policy *per injured person* and *per accident for all injured persons*. A typical example is $100,000 per person and $300,000 per accident.

A single-limit policy will not limit the amount payable to an individual but only per accident—for example, $300,000 per accident.

The distinction can be important. Assume that you rear-end a car full of people. Five people are injured. However, only one person is seriously hurt while the other four suffer minor injuries. Assume that the seriously injured person incurs $80,000 in medical bills and loses $50,000 in wages because of the injuries. The total damages, without pain and suffering, are already $130,000. Add pain and suffering and the potential loss of future health and earning capacity, and you could be facing $500,000 or more in liability.

Under a split-limit type of coverage, the *most* the severely injured person could be paid under your liability insurance would be what is called the **policy limits**—$100,000 in our example.

You could be forced to pay the difference out of your own pocket if the injured person (or his or her lawyer) decides to pursue you in court. Under a single-limit policy, however, you would have less to worry about because your insurance would be more productive. Most of your liability coverage could be applied to the seriously injured party, $300,000 in our example, which the victim might be willing to accept as payment in full. At the very least, the amount you could be forced to take out of your own wallet would be significantly less than under the split-limit format.

Liability policies are sold in states that have a fault system of redressing damages caused by auto accidents as well as in no-fault states, which modify this aspect of the auto insurance policy (see Chapters 8 and 9).

Consumer Alert

Many states require by law that a minimum level of liability insurance be carried by each person insuring a vehicle, in the absence of other proof of financial responsibility. The amounts required vary from state to state (see chart on page 115). However, if you have property of any significance or you earn wages that could be subject to attachment, you should carry more than the minimum to be sure you are adequately protected against liability. In such matters, to underinsure is being penny-wise and pound-foolish.

Property damage. The property damage aspect of the liability portion of an auto insurance policy pays for damages to another's property caused by negligent driving. Usually the damage is to another vehicle, but it doesn't have to be. For example, if you lose control of your car and crash into a fence, you would probably be responsible for the cost of repairing the fence—a legal burden you would transfer to your auto insurance company under the contract of insurance.

Like coverage for personal injury, the policy will provide for maximum benefits that the insurance company has to pay. Many states require a minimum amount of coverage, usually $10,000 or so. However, with the expense of vehicle repair today, the minimum usually isn't enough. Thus, you should probably add to the minimum coverage so that you are protected for at least $25,000.

Coverage for property damage, like personal injury in a fault state, is based on negligence. However, the extent of risk for property damage is far less than for personal injury, so the cost of the coverage is also far less.

It is interesting to note that over 50 percent of all insurance payouts are made for property damage and not for personal injuries. It is worth pointing out that insurance industry schemes to limit your rights to recover for personal injuries you have suffered in an auto accident leave untouched this important area of insurance company overhead. Could it be that the personal injury lawsuit crisis the insurance industry complains so bitterly about is really a mirage? We think so.

The cost of defense. To rewrite that great old rock 'n' roll standard, "there's a whole lot of suin' goin' on!" Sometimes people get sued when they didn't do anything wrong. Sometimes people who did make a mistake get sued for far more than the damage their negligence truly caused. And sometimes no one really knows who was at fault, so they sue each other.

This being so, a very important part of your auto liability policy is the company's obligation to pay for your defense should you get sued because of an accident or other incident covered by the policy. This **cost of defense** coverage can literally save you thousands of dollars since it includes high-priced items such as the cost of lawyers, specialists in accident reconstruction (if necessary), doctors who work for the defense, and other similar expenditures that are often needed to adequately defend an auto accident case. (Imagine the despair you would feel if you had to pay directly for all these. And imagine the corner-cutting you might do to save money if you had to pay for your own defense—corner-cutting that could cost you the lawsuit. The word *bankruptcy* could take on a new personal meaning.)

Medical Pay

As the name implies, the medical payments coverage in an auto insurance policy is designed to pay for some of the medical consequences that can result from an accident. Unlike the liability portion of the insurance policy, "med pay" has no relationship to fault but will pay benefits to eligible beneficiaries for the cost of medical care and funeral expenses up to the policy limits.

Who gets benefits under med pay. Two classes of persons are entitled to receive benefits under med pay:

The insured and family members who live in the same household. Thus, if you run a red light and cause an accident, your insurance will protect you against the financial consequences of your negligence, while at the same time the med pay portion of the policy will pay for the treatment of your injuries, up to the extent of coverage.

An insured and covered family are also protected under med pay if they are hit as pedestrians by a vehicle intended to be driven on public roads, regardless of who caused the accident. This "no-fault" aspect of med pay coverage can be important, since you don't have to wait until the matter is resolved in court to receive benefits—which in some states can take years.

Any passenger injured while in the "covered vehicle". Regardless of who is at fault in the accident, your passengers are entitled to receive payment for medical expenses caused by the accident —again, up to the maximum amount provided in the policy. The key phrase here is "covered vehicle," or the car listed in your policy. Thus, if you are driving *someone else's car*, your med pay would not cover the accident injuries of a passenger. That would be up to the med pay portion of the car owner's policy.

Most people elect not to take out large amounts of med pay since they are usually covered by some form of health insurance and there could be duplicate coverage. However, med pay will cover one thing that health insurance will not: funeral expenses. Since the price of med pay is relatively small, it is a good idea to have at least a few thousand dollars in coverage.

Now, take a look at the typical auto insurance declarations page shown opposite. If you do purchase med pay, the declarations page will tell you how much you are selecting. Did you know that the limit of coverage is not necessarily the maximum your company could have to pay? That's because, unlike liability coverage, the med pay policy limits do not refer to the total coverage available, but rather to the total that can be collected by *each covered injured individual*. Thus, if three people are seriously injured in an accident where the owner/driver of the car had $2,000 in med pay coverage, the insurance company could be on the hook for $6,000 under the med pay clause.

It is noteworthy that your auto insurance company will try to restrict you—and properly so—from receiving a double benefit from them. Thus, if your company pays for covered injuries out of the med pay portion of the policy, it will not pay the same bills under the liability section and will be permitted to deduct those payments from the final award.

Consumer Alert

If you don't have health insurance, be sure to buy large amounts of med pay. It's relatively inexpensive, and if you are injured in an auto accident it may mean the difference between adequate care and a trip to your county hospital, where treatment could be catch-as-catch-can.

TYPICAL AUTO INSURANCE DECLARATIONS PAGE

AGENT

Sunspot Insurance Co.   3752   29
26 Underwrite Drive.
Marino, CA

SUNSPOT INSURANCE CO.
AUTOMOBILE POLICY

IMPORTANT COVERAGE EXCLUSION

POLICY NUMBER	FROM 12:01 A M	POLICY PERIOD	TO 12:01 A M
00000000000	01/15/90		07/15/90
	PERSONS INSURED		

NAMED INSURED

1 Joe S. Citizen

OTHER DRIVERS

2 Sarah P. Consumer

APPLICABLE. TO ALL COVERAGES. INCLUDING BUT NOT LIMITED TO, LIABILITY AND UNINSURED MOTORISTS. PROVIDED NOW OR LATER.
It is agreed that the insurance afforded by this policy shall not apply nor accrue to the benefit of any insured or any third party claimant when any motor vehicle is being used or operated by a "designated person" listed below regardless of where the person resides or whether the person is licensed to drive.

1 Allan Consumer

MAILING ADDRESS

CAR	YEAR	VEHICLE DESCRIPTION	SERIAL NUMBER	COST OR VALUE	NEW USED	PURCH DATE	H P C/D
1	87	BMW 325I 4DR SED		25000	N	11/87	
2	89	BMW 735I 4DR.		55000	N	08/89	

CAR	LP-AI RO	NAMES AND ADDRESSES OF LIEN HOLDERS, ADDITIONAL INTERESTS AND REGISTERED OWNERS OTHER THAN THOSE LISTED ABOVE.			
1	LP	GEN. ELEC. AUTO LEASE	P.O. BOX 490	SPRINGFIELD	OH 45501
1	AI	GEN. ELEC. CR. AUTO LEASE	P.O. BOX 310	BARRINGTON	IL 60011
2	LP	GEN. ELEC. AUTO LEASE	P.O. BOX 490	SPRINGFIELD	OH 45501
2	AI	GEN. ELEC. CR. AUTO LEASE	P.O. BOX 310	BARRINGTON	IL 60011

THE INSURANCE AFFORDED IS ONLY WITH RESPECT TO SUCH OF THE FOLLOWING COVERAGES AS ARE INDICATED BY A SPECIFIC PREMIUM CHARGE OR CHARGES. THE LIMIT OF THE COMPANY'S LIABILITY FOR EACH SUCH COVERAGE IS STATED BELOW SUBJECT TO ALL THE TERMS OF THE POLICY. THE LIMIT OF LIABILITY FOR COMPREHENSIVE AND COLLISION COVERAGE SHALL NOT EXCEED THE 'COST' SHOWN ABOVE

COVERAGES	LIMITS OF LIABILITY			PREMIUMS		
BODILY INJURY LIABILITY	$ 100,000 EACH PERSON	$ 300,000 EACH ACCIDENT		CAR 1	CAR 2	CAR
PROPERTY DAMAGE LIABILITY	$ 100,000 EACH ACCIDENT			287	355	
UNINSURED MOTORIST Bodily Injury	$ 30,000 EACH PERSON	$ 60,000 EACH ACCIDENT		38	38	
UNINSURED MOTORIST Property Damage	$3500 MAXIMUM					
COLLISION DEDUCTIBLE WAIVER				3	3	
MEDICAL EXPENSE	$ 5000 EACH PERSON ☒ EXCESS WITH REIMBURSEMENT TO COMPANY	☐ NO EXCESS NO REIMBURSEMENT		19	19	
COMPREHENSIVE	DEDUCTIBLES CAR $ 500 CAR $ 500 CAR $			71	123	
COLLISION	DEDUCTIBLES CAR $ 500 CAR $ 500 CAR $			118	202	
TOWING AND LABOR	$ 35 EACH DISABLEMENT			4	4	
RENTAL CAR BENEFIT	$ 15 PER DAY - 15 DAYS COLLISION ONLY			5	5	

SPECIAL EQUIPMENT:	CAR. NO.	ITEM INSURED	LIMIT	CAR. NO.	ITEM INSURED	LIMIT	PREMIUMS PER CAR	
ITEMS INSURED AND AMOUNTS OF INSURANCE FOR EACH ITEM ARE STATED HEREIN.							543	749

POLICY FEE	
CA SURCHARGE	13
TOTAL PREMIUM	1307

ENDORSEMENTS ATTACHED TO THE POLICY   U-10   10/89   U-45

Collision and Comprehensive

Another important aspect of an auto insurance policy is the part that protects the value of your vehicle. This part of the contract is called **collision coverage** and its cost is about one-third of the total cost of the policy.

Types of collision coverage

Collision. Collision is usually defined as "the upset of 'your covered auto' or its impact with another vehicle or object." That means there has to be a physical contact between your vehicle and another car, truck, or object, which causes physical damage to your auto. (Any damages to the other vehicle would be paid by the liability portion of your coverage, *if*, that is, you were at fault.)

Comprehensive. Loss caused by flying objects, fire, theft, windstorm, hail, malicious mischief, riot, hitting an animal, etc., is considered "other than collision" coverage, more commonly called **comprehensive coverage**.

▶ **NOTE:** It is important to note that collision and comprehensive are separately provided for and charged. In order for the company

Consumer Alert

There is an important exclusion to collision coverage that you should know about. It is "loss to equipment for the reproduction of sound," known in the vernacular as a stereo. If the stereo is permanently installed in the car, it is covered. But if you purchase the kind of stereo that you can take out of the car to thwart thieves, the stereo is no longer considered "permanently installed," and there will be no coverage if it is ever stolen.

Other exclusions of note include: CB equipment, car telephones, wear and tear and mechanical breakdown, camper body or trailer (unless specifically paid for and shown in the declarations), and customized equipment.

to consider you to be covered by either or both, the declarations page must show that you have selected that protection.

Deductibles and payment options. Unlike some other aspects of auto insurance, the collision protection of the policy is subject to a deductible (the amount you pay before any insurance benefits kick in). Most deductibles are around $200 but you can elect to have a higher or lower amount. The higher the deductible, the lower the premium.

If your vehicle is damaged or stolen, the company has the right to choose one of two ways in which to pay you benefits:

The amount necessary to repair the vehicle or replace property that was lost. This method is simple. If the repair bill comes to $1,500, the insurance company pays $1,500 (less the deductible). If a radio is stolen and it costs $500 to replace it and $150 to repair a window broken in the theft, the insurance company pays $650 (less the deductible).

The cash value of the stolen or damaged property. Here's where a lot of people feel they get burned. Under the terms of the policy, the insurance company may elect to "cash you out" for the loss rather than repair the vehicle, if this method will cost them less money. In addition, they can deduct for depreciation and adjust for a deteriorated physical condition of your vehicle.

When the insurance company elects not to repair your car but to pay you its value, it is sometimes called "totaling" the vehicle. When the company totals your car, you receive what the vehicle is "worth" on the open market—even if (as is often the case) this amount is less than it will cost you to actually replace the car.

Other aspects of collision coverage

Collision is not a mandatory coverage. You don't have to take out collision coverage, and many people with older vehicles don't. It is simply not worth the money if the company is likely to "total" the vehicle rather than pay for its repair. Or, you can elect to take either collision or comprehensive and not the other.

Consumer Alert

If your insurance company tells you they want to total your damaged car, don't just roll over when they tell you how little they think your car is worth. Look in the Kelly Blue Book, which should be at your local library, and in your local paper at the classified ads to see what cars like yours are selling for. It will often be more than the company wanted to pay. This proof of value may carry the day if you present it to the company. Also, if your car includes extra equipment, such as a valuable stereo system, air conditioning, special tires, etc., be sure to let them know. It can add to the value of your car when the company "totals" it. Some companies will sell you an endorsement that will add a benefit requiring the company to pay for a new car if the covered car must be totaled.

Collision coverage is not dependent on fault. Like medical pay, if you have a claim for collision damage, you are entitled to benefits even if you caused the accident.

Your collision policy will pay benefits for vehicles you don't own. If you are driving a car you do not own and are in an accident or the car is stolen while in your possession, your collision coverage will pay benefits for the loss. However, this protection will not apply if you drive the car on a regular basis.

If you are covered for auto theft, there is a transportation benefit. If your car is stolen, and if you are covered under the collision aspect of your policy for other than collision loss, you will be entitled to reimbursement for some of the transportation costs you incur until benefits are paid under the policy. Benefits are payable daily, typically $10 or so, and there will be a maximum total benefit defined in the policy.

Uninsured Motorist

Imagine the horror of being involved in a serious auto accident and having the other driver run away from the scene. Or think about how you would feel if you were seriously injured by a negligent driver who had no liability insurance. To put it mildly, you would not be a happy motorist.

With the rapidly climbing cost of auto insurance, uninsured drivers are becoming an increasing menace on the highways. That is why the **uninsured** and/or **underinsured motorist coverage** on your auto insurance is so important. It protects you if you are injured by someone who has no car insurance or is uninsured.

What you need to know about uninsured motorist protection. Uninsured motorist coverage is optional. But if you can afford it we urge you to purchase it. If you don't, the only protection you have if you are hit by an uninsured driver will be your med pay, which is rarely enough to pay for all of the bills of a serious accident. The additional expenses of your injury—such as medical bills beyond that covered by med pay, lost wages, and pain and suffering—will simply not be covered if you don't have the protection of uninsured motorist coverage.

Uninsured motorist protection has nothing to do with property damage. It is specifically designed to pay your losses for *bodily injury*. Thus, the more you have, the safer you will be. It is better to err on the side of paying a little extra premium than to have inadequate coverage. Here are some of the important points that you should know about the protection.

It is based on fault. If you caused the accident and the other car was not insured, you will not receive benefits. Uninsured motorist protection pays you what you *would have been entitled to* had the other driver had insurance. In other words, the uninsured driver must have been liable to you for damages in order for you to collect.

You can collect for pain and suffering. The measure of damages is the same in uninsured motorist proceedings as in a fault lawsuit. Thus, that chronic pain in the neck caused by the accident can be translated into money in your bank account. Such things as medical bills, lost wages, and pain and suffering are all included in determining the amount of compensation you will receive.

Three groups are covered under the uninsured motorist provision. The insured, members of his or her household, and any other person legally entitled to recover damages are protected under the uninsured motorist provision of an auto policy. The coverage also applies to injuries sustained by the insured or householders who are injured as pedestrians by an uninsured motorist.

You do not go to court if you have a dispute with your company. If you and the company cannot agree on a fair compensation for damages caused by an uninsured motorist, you do not go to court. Instead, you engage in an arbitration. In the arbitration, there may be one arbitrator, for whom you and the company pay mutually; or three arbitrators—one selected (and paid for) by you, one by the company, and one by both of the previously selected arbitrators, for whom both parties pay equally. (We think this method is unjust because it forces you to pay for the privilege of having a dispute with your company. For more on this topic, see Chapter 42.) The arbitrator(s) must determine whether you are entitled to damages and, if so, in what amount.

The limit of liability will be shown on the declarations page. The limit of insurance company liability for uninsured motorist coverage is shown on the declarations page just as it is in the liability portion of the policy. Thus, "$15,000/$30,000" on the declarations page means $15,000 maximum coverage per individual and a maximum of $30,000 total per covered accident.

Some companies offer underinsured motorist protection. What if you are in an accident where the person at fault is insured but woefully underinsured to pay for the total damages sustained? For example, many motorists only have $15,000/$30,000 in liability coverage. These days $15,000 doesn't go very far. Many companies recognize this problem and allow you to purchase underinsured protection, which will pay the amount not covered by the other driver's insurance to the maximum of your own policy. This is excellent coverage to purchase since many drivers are forced to underinsure themselves due to the high cost of premiums.

Miscellaneous Coverages

There are other smaller coverages you can purchase at a nominal cost when you buy auto insurance, including:

Rental car reimbursement.   If you have to rent a car while yours is being repaired after an accident, you can be partially protected by indemnity-type payments (fixed amounts) per day in an amount set forth in the policy.

Towing.   If you are not a member of an automobile club you may want this benefit, which will pay up to $50 for the cost of towing your car from the scene of an accident. If you are a member of an auto club, you already have paid for this benefit and you don't need to purchase duplicate coverage.

You now know much, but not all, of the contents of a basic auto insurance policy. We will discuss this more later, but now let's get to the fun part—how you can save money today on your auto insurance policy.

11

Saving Money on Auto Insurance

When it comes to auto insurance, the word *frustration* comes quickly to mind. So do the words *anxiety* and *insomnia*. It's not that people feel badly about auto insurance itself. They recognize it as a necessary expenditure. It's the *high cost* of auto insurance that they are disgusted with, and the fear that the price will continue to go through the roof in years to come no matter what they try to do to stop it.

We will discuss reform and consumer activism in Chapter 13. But first, let's take a look at how auto insurance is priced. Then we'll deal with what you can do to keep your auto insurance premiums as reasonable as possible.

How Auto Insurance Is Priced

Several factors determine the pricing of auto insurance. Some are absolutely legitimate. Some, we believe, are not. Saving that discussion for later (see page 123), the following considerations are the factors insurance companies look at when they determine the premium you will pay.

Where You Live

The single largest factor in 49 of the 50 states (excluding California, thanks to Proposition 103 [see page 127]), and throughout Canada, is the neighborhood where you reside. This concept of pricing is called **territorial rating**. Here's how it works.

Insurance companies break down the various localities in each state into what are known as territories. Some companies may establish territories by using zip codes, others by neighborhood, town, or county.

However the territories are determined, companies use their statistical-gathering abilities to compute the rates of auto insurance claims within each established region. The insurance industry's reasoning for this pricing mechanism is the fact that most accidents occur within a few miles of where the vehicle is garaged. Thus, the companies believe that territories provide an accurate basis for determining their risk. And, as we saw in Chapter 2, the price of insurance is based on the risk of loss to the company.

From these statistics, the underwriters then determine the risk of loss for cars garaged in each territory. Once this has been done, they determine a **base rate** for each territory. The base rate is the starting point from which each person's actual premium will be established.

Your Personal Statistics

The statistics of the insurance industry indicate that certain members of the driving public are more likely to be involved in accidents than others. Thus, the following are looked into as important factors in determining insurability as well as the price of the premium:

- **Age.** Younger drivers tend to be accident prone. For this reason, drivers under the age of 25 pay more in premiums than those aged 25 to 64. Similarly, drivers over the age of 65 tend to have more accidents than younger ones and thus may find their premiums going up.

- **Gender.** Statistics show that there is a gender difference in the rate of automobile accidents. For example, young unmarried men are statistically the worst drivers in the country. Thus, they will pay more in premiums than women of the same age, all other things being equal.

- **Marital status.** Married drivers are statistically less likely to have accidents than single drivers—proving, if nothing else, that two can live more cheaply than one, at least when it comes to auto insurance premiums.

What You Use the Car For

Another important factor in fixing rates is what you primarily use your car for. For example, if the car is mainly used for pleasure as opposed to business, you will probably have a lower premium. The mileage driven as part of that usage is also reviewed. Thus, if you use your car to drive to work each day, you will pay more if you drive 15 miles each way than if you drive less than 5 miles each way.

The Kind of Car You Drive

The kind of car you drive is also used to determine the premium. For example, the cost of repairing a Mercedes-Benz is likely to be much higher than that of a Ford sedan. Thus, the collision premium for a Mercedes will be higher than for a Ford. Likewise, some cars are safer to the driver and passenger than others. The safer the car, the more reasonable the premium should be. Other factors are also important, such as the car's age, original cost, and ease of repair.

Your Personal Driving Record

If you have a bad driving record, the statistical chances of your being in an accident are higher than if you have a good driving record. Thus, the good driver should pay less for insurance. But what distinguishes a good from a bad driver, especially if you have had no accidents in the last few years? The answer is convictions—convictions for moving violations, to be specific. Your driving record is reviewed continually to see whether you have been convicted of crimes such as drunk driving or of violations such as speeding or running a red light.

The Extent of Your Insurance

The extent of your coverage also plays a large part in determining the premium you will pay. If you have low deductibles you can expect to pay higher premiums than if you have high deductibles. Likewise, if you have high limits of liability, you will have to pay for the added protection. If you choose to select comprehensive coverage, you will pay for it in the total cost of your premium.

How You Can Save Money Now

We have seen that many different factors go into the cost of your premium. The good news about most of the auto insurance pricing mechanisms is that they are based on matters purely *within your control*. This being so, there are steps you can take to help keep your premiums down.

Step 1: Shop Around

There can be a tremendous variety in the level of rates charged among the various companies that sell auto insurance within a given state market. For example, according to the California

Passenger Auto Insurance Premium Survey of 1988, conducted by the California Department of Insurance, the following annual prices were charged by the following companies to a hypothetical 45-year-old couple with no accidents or tickets in the city of Alhambra, a suburb of greater Los Angeles:

Aetna	$1,145
Allstate	$1,091
Auto Club	$1,404
Colonial Penn	$1,011
Farmers	$1,007
Mercury	$810
Ohio Casualty	$1,073
Progressive	$1,511
Safeco	$965
State Farm	$898
Transamerica	$1,186
20th Century	$814
Wawanesa	$692

The difference between the most expensive rate and the most reasonable was $819! So, how come anybody purchases the expensive coverages? For the most part, *they simply do not take the time to find out that better prices are available.*

If you are comparison shopping, it is important that each agent or sales representative you consult uses the same information to work with. Thus, before you make your first call or attend your first appointment, be prepared by writing down the following information to share with the sales rep:

• The types of coverage you want.

• The levels of liability coverage you want.

Consumer Alert

This comparison chart is not intended to be a valid comparison of the companies that sell auto insurance in *your* area. It is an illustration only. *Do not use it to determine which company you should give your business to.* Beyond that, it is important to note that the comparative rating levels of the companies vis-à-vis one another will vary from locale to locale. The company that is the lowest in one area may not have the lowest rate in a different area, since companies determine their territories and other underwriting factors differently. As an illustration, Wawanesa, which had the lowest hypothetical rate in this example in Alhambra, had the third-lowest rate based on the same hypothetical situation in Berkeley, California.

- The size of the deductibles you want.

- Details of your driving record, including any convictions for moving violations and any accidents you may have had within the last three to five years.

- Your daily and annual mileage.

- Basic information on all drivers within your household, including their age, gender, marital status, driving record, and driver's license numbers.

- Vital information about your car, such as its age, mileage, the purchase price, and any equipment that might qualify you for discounts (see below).

Step 2: Be a Good Driver

Your driving record is the key to keeping down your insurance rates. Without a good record there is virtually nothing you can do to keep from paying dearly for coverage. Here is an example of the increases you can expect if you are an unsafe driver. Remember our hypothetical example of the 45-year-old couple living in Alhambra, California? Well, here are the rates the same couple would be charged if one of them had one drunk driving conviction within the last three years, according to the same California Department of Insurance survey:

> Mercury: $1,790, an increase of $980 *over the same hypothetical couple with a safe driving record!*

> Ohio Casualty Group: $3,751, an increase of $2,678 *over the same hypothetical couple with a safe driving record!*

> Progressive: $1,625, an increase of $114. But note that Progressive was already the highest-priced company in Alhambra for the good driver.

None of the other 10 companies listed will sell the hypothetical couple insurance *at all*.

Clearly, then, the most important thing you can do to keep your rates low is to drive like a preferred risk. We cannot over-emphasize this point. Otherwise, you are likely to hear those fateful words, "Get thee to the assigned risk pool, do not pass GO, do pay an extra $1,000!"

Step 3: Purchase Cars Subject to Lower Rates

As far as insurance premiums go, some cars are more costly to own than others. Those that are expensive to repair, subject to a higher risk of theft, or that have a higher statistical rate of bodily injury claims are going to cost more to insure. Also, if you are presently with a "discount" insurance company, check to make sure they cover that new car you may be thinking of purchasing. Some companies keep their prices lower by refusing to insure expensive or exotic vehicles.

Consumer Alert

If you are going to buy a new car, it is a good idea to contact your insurance company to see which cars have the lowest rates. You can also obtain the loss data on almost 200 makes and models of cars as compiled by the Insurance Institute for Public Safety. If you are interested, write to their publication department at Watergate, 600, Suite 300, Washington, DC 20037.

Step 4: Modify Your Coverage

As with most kinds of insurance, you can lower your premiums by increasing the risk of loss that you will absorb yourself. In other words, you can save more now, but if you have a claim, you will have to pay more out of your own pocket later. This tradeoff can be done in several ways.

Raise the deductibles. Many of the benefits paid by auto insurance companies deal with relatively low payments for covered incidents. If you agree to absorb more of this potential loss by raising the money you have to pay before benefits kick in, you can lower your premiums.

Lower the maximums. By agreeing to accept less overall protection, you reduce the total out-of-pocket risk the company accepts by insuring you. This, in turn, allows them to lower your overall premium.

Refuse optional coverage. The mandatory insurance or financial responsibility laws of the various states do not compel you to purchase every aspect of coverage. You can reduce your rates by rejecting some forms of protection—which in some cases are not a good investment in any event. Thus, if you have a car with little value, you may wish to omit collision or comprehensive coverage from your insurance package. You can use your premium savings to pay for the rising cost of your health insurance policy. A word of advice, though: Don't omit uninsured motorist protection unless you otherwise have excellent health and disability benefits.

Step 5: Take Advantage of Offered Discounts

Many insurance companies offer discounts for a wide variety of reasons. If yours does, find out which discounts are available and act to place yourself within their parameters. Here is a list of many discounts available from most major companies.

Multi-car discount. It makes no sense to insure different vehicles with different companies, since that will increase the expenses of your policies. You will lose the discount you would receive for insuring more than one car with the same company.

Multiple-policy discount. If you purchase more than one kind of policy, usually homeowner's and auto, from the same company, you may be eligible for a discount, sometimes as high as 10 percent. Thus, when you compare the price of policies before you buy, be sure to cross-check with the companies to see whether you can strike a deal by giving them your business in more than one area of coverage.

Driver's education discount. Several states require, and many companies offer, discounts for drivers who have successfully completed driver's education courses. There may also be discounts for classes specifically geared to defensive driving skills. So, take some time and go back to school. You might lower your insurance premiums. More important, you might save someone's life, maybe even your own.

Nonsmoker's discount. Any way you look at it, it costs to smoke, and not only in terms of your health. It can cost you applicable discounts in your auto insurance premium.

Anti-theft devices. Companies in a few states will give you a discount on your comprehensive premium if you install anti-theft devices in your car to discourage would-be thieves.

Passive restraints discount. Some companies will give you a break on your no-fault coverage or med pay if your car has seat belts and/or air bags installed.

Good driver discount. Many companies give discounts if you have not been convicted of a moving violation or been in an accident over the term of the policy. If you have had a good record, check with your agent to see whether you qualify for such a discount.

Good student discount. Young people pay the highest premiums for insurance. This burden can be reduced for good students. If you have a high school or college student in the family who gets good grades, let your insurance company know about it. It can save you money.

Mature driver discount. If you are over 50, don't be quiet about it. Your age can save you up to 10 percent on your auto insurance premiums.

Low mileage discount. Some companies offer discounts to motorists who drive fewer than a predetermined number of miles a year.

Step 6: Coordinate PIP Coverage with Health Insurance

Those of you who reside in no-fault states can save premium dollars by agreeing with your company that the first benefits to be paid will come from health insurance rather than your auto insurance. According to Consumers Union, savings of up to 40 percent may be possible from your personal injury protection premium by utilizing this strategy.

12

Avoiding Insurance Roadblocks

We have covered much in the preceding pages. But wait! There's more! By minimizing your problems, you minimize your costs. And we still have to discuss issues such as your obligation after an accident, the issues surrounding cancellation of your policy, and what to do if you can't get a regular auto insurance policy.

If You Have an Accident

Your automobile insurance policy specifically spells out your duties to the company if you have an accident, as the following sections outline.

Notification

You must promptly notify your insurance company of any accident you are involved in, regardless of who you think is at fault. The reason for this is so that the company can conduct an investigation of the incident before the trail gets cold. When reporting the accident, be ready to advise the company of the following.

How the accident happened. Write down what happened while it is fresh in your mind. Then, send a copy of your recollections to the company, keeping a copy for your own records. In fact, you should set up your own file about the accident in case you find yourself in a lawsuit with the other party or a dispute with your own company.

Other parties involved in the accident. Your company will need the name, address, home and work phone numbers of the other party or parties to the mishap. You should also obtain the name of the other driver's insurance company and his or her policy number, if you can. In addition, include the make, model, and license number of the other automobile(s) involved in the collision.

The name and address of any witnesses. It is common for the participants in an accident to have differing versions, often self-serving ones at that, of how the collision occurred. This often leads to a situation where it is one driver's word against the other's. For this reason, it is vital that you obtain the names and addresses of witnesses to the mishap who can assist in determining what happened. This is important even if your company will pay benefits, since they have the right to sue the party at fault or his or her insurance company for reimbursement for the benefits paid. This kind of lawsuit is called **subrogation**.

Notify the police. Each state has its own laws regarding when the police must be notified after an accident. In addition to that, your policy will require you to report an incident to the police if you seek to present a claim for an uninsured motorist based on a hit-and-run driver leaving the scene of an accident.

Cooperation

You must cooperate with your company if you seek the benefits of coverage. If you want to receive the benefits of coverage you must be prepared to do the following.

Cooperate with the company in its investigation. This can mean meeting with investigators, lawyers for the company, or adjusters concerning the facts of the accident and other relevant areas of concern.

Promptly send the company copies of any notices or legal papers you receive. If a lawyer contacts you regarding the accident or you are sued, you must immediately turn the matter over to your insurance company so it can put its people to work on the case. Failure to comply can be grounds for your company to attempt to deny coverage or to refuse to defend you.

Submit to examinations. If you are injured, you have the obligation to allow your insurance company to have you examined by a physician of its choosing. You may also be required to submit to an oral examination under oath regarding the facts of the case, called a **deposition**.

Allow the company access to relevant personal records. When an insurance company investigates a case, it sometimes really *investigates*. Often, this includes reviewing your past medical records and other relevant material. You may be asked to sign authorizations for the company to obtain such documentation, which you must do unless you have valid grounds for denying the request (such as being asked to divulge personal information that has nothing to do with your claim).

Protection

If you seek benefits under the collision portion of your policy, you must do all that you reasonably can to protect the vehicle from further damage, including towing it if necessary to a place of safe storage.

Inspection

Before repairing the damage to the car, you must allow the company to inspect the vehicle if you intend to seek reimbursement for the repairs.

Cancellation Rights

A major source of anger and frustration to insurance consumers is the seeming unfairness with which companies choose to raise rates or cancel policies if a policyholder makes a claim. You know the scenario: Someone has been with a company for 10 years without a claim and then, BANG, they are in an accident. The company pays the benefits and then, POW, it cuts the policyholder loose as a poor risk.

How can the companies get away with this? Simple. The language of the insurance contract permits them to do it, and inadequate enforcement by most state insurance departments doesn't stop the companies from wielding the ax in an unfair and capricious manner.

Cancellation of an Existing Policy

There are two issues of concern to this discussion: cancellation of an existing policy, and refusal to renew a policy once its term has expired. First, let's look at a typical insurance policy regarding the issue of cancellation.

You can cancel at any time. If you become unhappy with your company or wish to cancel, you can do so by giving the company written notice of when the cancellation is to take effect or by returning the policy. If this is done, the company must return to you any unearned premiums.

The company can cancel for several reasons. It is rare for a company to cancel a policy *while it is in effect*. However, it may do so under certain conditions. These include:

- **Nonpayment of premiums.** If you don't pay in a timely fashion, the company can cancel you on 10 days' (or so) written notice.

- **During the first 60 days.** During the first 60 days the policy is in effect, it is subject to cancellation upon reasonable notice (often 10 days) for any reason. Since agents often bind their company to a policy, the laws of the states permit companies to cancel. If this is done, it is usually because the insured has somehow misrepresented the facts and circumstances surrounding the issuance of the policy.

- **If your driver's license or that of a covered householder is cancelled.** The insurance industry keeps a constant watch on the driving records of its insureds. If you or a covered member of your household has their license suspended or revoked, your company may follow suit with your insurance coverage.

- **If you or a covered member of your household is convicted of drunk driving.** Clearly it is not in the interests of an insurance company to insure the automobiles of those foolish enough to endanger themselves and others by driving while intoxicated. And it doesn't take much to be legally drunk. *Often a couple of drinks or several beers over an hour or so will make you a prime candidate for an accident, jail, or both, if you then are irresponsible enough to try to drive a car.*

- **If you misrepresent information to the company or submit a fraudulent claim.** As the old saying goes, honesty is the best policy. Lying to your insurance company can lead to cancellation. You could also get sued if the company paid you benefits to which you were not entitled.

Refusal to Renew

Cancellation of an existing policy is not usually a problem after the first 60 days of coverage have elapsed. After that, the company can only cancel for cause; i.e., nonpayment of premiums. The real problem most consumers fear is their company's refusal to renew a policy at the end of the coverage period. *Unfortunately, unlike health insurance, auto insurance companies don't issue policies that are guaranteed to be renewable.* Thus, a company can usually refuse to renew your policy or raise your rates upon the following terms and conditions.

Prior notification. You have to be told of the company's intended action at least 30 days (the time may vary) prior to the end of the policy period. The purpose of the notification is to allow you to make other arrangements. The only problem is that a new company will rarely take the "rejects" of another company, which may force you into the assigned risk pool (see below).

Written notification. In order for the refusal-to-renew notice to be valid, it must be in writing. With word processors being what they are, this requirement is not much of a burden on the companies.

Compliance with state law. Most states allow insurance companies to refuse to renew for just about any reason. Some, however, prevent nonrenewal based on age, sex, race, or occupation.

That's about it. Oh, some states require that you be told the reason you are not being renewed, but that isn't usually tough to figure out. It may be a ticket or two, an accident, or any activity the company believes increases your risk. Far too often, it means merely applying for insurance benefits to which you are legally entitled.

If You Can't Get Insurance

When it comes to auto insurance, some consumers find themselves between the proverbial rock and a hard place. On the one hand, they cannot get an insurance company to sell them a policy (due to high risk factors); and on the other, their state laws compel them to buy insurance or otherwise prove financial responsibility.

The chart on page 115 lists the minimum auto insurance requirements of the 50 states, the District of Columbia, and the provinces of Canada, according to the 1990 *Property/Casualty Fact Book*.

Shared Markets

If you cannot convince an auto insurance company to sell you a policy, you will be forced into the netherworld of what the industry calls the **shared market**. Every state provides some mechanism of guaranteeing access to the purchase of auto insurance through these shared markets. There's one other thing that is also almost guaranteed in these shared markets: the cost will be much higher than for a regularly issued policy.

There are four different types of shared markets.

Assigned-risk plans. In an assigned-risk-type plan, each auto insurance company doing business in a state must write insurance for those who cannot otherwise obtain insurance, in a percentage equal to its share of the state's auto insurance market. Thus, if a company issues 12 percent of the auto insurance in the state, that company will have to provide insurance for 12 percent of those drivers who can't otherwise get insurance. In assigned-risk plans, the company that issues the policy services it as it would any of its other customers.

Joint underwriting associations (JUAs). A JUA is a form of pooling association that sells insurance to the otherwise uninsurable. All companies writing insurance in a state share in the profits and losses of the insurance business written by the JUA.

Reinsurance facility. A reinsurance facility is an organization that issues insurance to insurance companies. The reinsurance

AUTOMOBILE FINANCIAL RESPONSIBILITY/COMPULSORY LIMITS

United States

State	Liability Limits[1]	State	Liability Limits[1]
Alabama	20/40/10	Montana	25/50/5
Alaska	50/100/25	Nebraska	25/50/25
Arizona	15/30/10	Nevada	15/30/10
Arkansas	25/50/15	New Hampshire	25/50/25
California	15/30/5	New Jersey	15/30/5
Colorado	25/50/15	New Mexico	25/50/10
Connecticut	20/40/10	New York	10/20/5[2]
Delaware	15/30/10	North Carolina	25/50/10
District of Columbia	25/50/10	North Dakota	25/50/25
Florida	10/20/10	Ohio	12.5/25/7.5
Georgia	15/30/10	Oklahoma	10/20/10
Hawaii	15/35/10	Oregon	25/50/15
Idaho	25/50/15	Pennsylvania	15/30/5
Illinois	20/40/15	Rhode Island	25/50/25
Indiana	25/50/10	South Carolina	15/30/5
Iowa	20/40/15	South Dakota	25/50/25
Kansas	25/50/10	Tennessee	20/50/10
Kentucky	25/50/10	Texas	20/40/15
Louisiana	10/20/10	Utah	20/40/10
Maine	20/40/10	Vermont	20/40/10
Maryland	20/40/10	Virginia	25/50/20
Massachusetts	10/20/5	Washington	25/50/10
Michigan	20/40/15	West Virginia	20/40/10
Minnesota	30/60/10	Wisconsin	25/50/10
Mississippi	10/20/5	Wyoming	25/50/20
Missouri	25/50/10		

[1]The first two figures refer to bodily injury liability limits and the third figure to property damage liability. For example, 10/20/5 means coverage up to $20,000 for all persons injured in an accident, subject to a limit of $10,000 for one individual, and $5,000 coverage for property damage.
[2]50/100 if injury results in death.

CANADA[3]

Province	Liability Limit	Province	Liability Limit
Alberta	$200,000	Nova Scotia	$200,000
British Columbia	200,000	Ontario	200,000
Manitoba	200,000	Prince Edward Island	200,000
New Brunswick	200,000	Quebec	50,000
Newfoundland	200,000	Saskatchewan	200,000
Northwest Territories	200,000	Yukon	200,000

[3]In all Canadian provinces except Quebec, the amount of liability insurance shown is available to settle either bodily injury or property damage—or both. When a claim involving both bodily injury and property damage reaches this "inclusive" limit, payment for property damage is limited to $20,000 in British Columbia, Manitoba, New Brunswick, and Newfoundland, and to $10,000 in the other provinces and territories having "inclusive" limits. Quebec laws provide that people injured in accidents in Quebec be compensated by a government fund. Benefits paid to nonresidents are scaled down in proportion to their degree of fault. The $50,000 limit relates to liability for damage to property in Quebec and to liability for bodily injury and property damage outside Quebec.
Sources: American Insurance Association; Insurance Bureau of Canada. Reprinted courtesy of Insurance Information Institute.

facility format allows companies to transfer a percentage of their policies to the reinsurance facility. The profits and losses are shared by all insurers writing business in the state. In states with reinsurance facilities, no one can be refused a policy.

The Maryland State Fund. The state of Maryland has a state-funded insurance company for those who cannot otherwise obtain insurance. The policy is administered by the state but private insurers are required to subsidize losses from the fund, for which they can be recouped by their own policyholders.

Any of these shared-market policies invariably cost more to purchase than regular policies. The way most people get into the shared market is by having poor driving records or, sometimes, automobiles so customized that insurance companies are loathe to issue a policy. The good news is that the door to the shared marketplace swings both ways. Improve your driving record and you can probably get a regular and less expensive policy within a few years.

Endorsements

You can purchase extra protection for your auto for an extra premium. These extras in the field of auto insurance are called **endorsements**.

There are several types of endorsements that you may wish to consider purchasing.

Miscellaneous vehicle. This endorsement allows coverage of vehicles normally excluded from coverage in the typical auto insurance policy, such as motor homes, motorcycles, and recreational vehicles. If you own vehicles such as these, *make sure you're covered* by asking your agent whether you need to purchase this endorsement.

Nonowner coverage. If someone who is not an owner of the car and not a covered family member is going to be driving your car, seriously consider adding that person's name as a covered driver. This is done through the **nonowner coverage** endorsement.

Underinsured motorist. As we discussed earlier, having a healthy uninsured motorist coverage is almost a necessity. Adding to that an endorsement for underinsured motorists is also important.

Sound receiving and transmitting equipment. As we stated earlier, items such as car phones and CBs are generally not covered in a basic automobile policy. Unfortunately, these items attract thieves like honey attracts flies. If you want to be protected against the loss of these items, look into purchasing an endorsement.

Stated amount. If you have a unique or classic vehicle, you can agree ahead of time with your insurance company as to just how much the car will be worth should a claim be made. This is done with a **stated amount** endorsement. However, if you choose to state the values of the vehicles you are insuring, you may not actually get that figure if your car is totaled, since the insurance company can pay you less if the actual cash value of the vehicle has slipped beneath the amount stated in the endorsement.

Customized equipment. If you have customized a van or pickup truck, you can be covered for items such as refrigerators, special carpeting, and cooking or sleeping facilities. All it takes is to pay a little extra by adding the endorsement.

Tapes coverage. Your auto policy will not reimburse you for the loss of audio tapes or discs. If you carry an extended or valuable collection of such items in your vehicle, consider insuring them by endorsement.

There are other endorsements in addition to these, such as those that will cover you if you drive a short distance into Mexico, and those that cover snowmobiles. Ask your agent or company for a complete list of endorsements available.

Consumer Alert

Endorsements are usually identified by letters and numbers. For example, the snowmobile endorsement is "PP 03 20." Numbers and letters—not the name of the endorsement—will appear on your declarations page if you purchase the added coverage. If you do purchase extra coverage, get copies of the endorsement contract language, *read it*, and *ask questions*. This is the only way you can be sure you understand the details of what the added coverage protects and what it does not.

We'll finish our discussion of auto insurance in the next chapter, where we cover the reforms we believe are necessary in the auto insurance industry itself and within each state's regulatory process if rates are to be permanently stabilized.

13

Consumers' Agenda

The price of auto insurance is too high. Consumers know it. Politicians know it. The insurance industry knows it, too. In fact, since approximately 1986, auto insurance rates have increased at more than four times the rate of inflation, with even higher levels of increase in some states.

What can you do about it? At this point the consensus breaks down. The primary response of the auto insurance companies has been to push for no-fault insurance and otherwise limit the liability of perpetrators of harm. They have been joined by some consumer organizations, most notably Consumers Union. The principal arguments that support the no-fault concept are that premiums can be reduced under a no-fault system because smaller lawsuits are taken out of the picture and the claims can be processed with less investigation and greater speed, both of which act to reduce insurance company costs.

We believe "the no-fault solution" is not the answer, for several reasons. For one thing, it does not adequately compensate the victims of auto accidents. For another, we don't believe that the potential reductions in premiums are worth the elimination of victims' rights. In fact, there is significant disagreement as to whether there has been any premium relief in the states that have tried no-fault—one of the reasons why three states have repealed no-fault laws in the past several years.

However, the main reason for our opposition to no-fault goes deeper than quibbling over whether premiums are moderately reduced in states that adopt the concept. According to J. Robert Hunter, president of NICO, good no-fault laws, like Michigan's, that pay unlimited medical and rehabilitation expenses, do not lower rates. Such laws might even raise them modestly. But Hunter believes it is a good trade-off, as does Consumers Union, which believes that *good* no-fault laws deliver more benefits for the same cost more promptly. Our opposition comes from our strongly held beliefs that no-fault simply does not address the central reasons why auto insurance premiums have gotten so out of hand. In fact, the political efforts on the part of the insurance industry are really a smoke screen designed to mask the deep and abiding need for fundamental change in the automobile insurance industry and other aspects of state law. In our opinion, then, only fundamental reform is the true key to permanent control of auto insurance premiums.

A Proposal for Reform

Public Citizen, the famous consumer-protection organization, and the National Insurance Consumer Organization (NICO) have joined to formulate the following proposals, which we believe will go a long way toward ending the inequitable and outrageous condition of the current auto insurance marketplace.

Step 1: Make Insurance Companies Cost-Effective

Regulators must demand that auto insurance companies reduce their costs of doing business. Many of the largest national auto insurance companies simply do not run their businesses in a cost-effective manner, resulting in higher premiums for the consumer. It does not have to be that way. Much can be done by the companies to reduce their operating expenses, as shown by a minority of firms that do a significantly better job than most at running their businesses. These efficient companies offer their customers lower premiums. According to NICO, if the industry as a whole were able to compete at this level, premiums could be reduced by more than 16 percent.

Step 2: Repeal the State and Federal Insurance Industry Antitrust Exemption

Currently, the Insurance Services Office (ISO) sets "advisory rates," which most insurers use as a reference point in pricing their wares. ISO rates reflect what the least efficient companies need to charge in order to make a profit. Therefore, rates based on ISO advice tend to push the rates of all companies upward, regardless of each company's individual profit-and-loss picture. Repealing the antitrust exemption would prohibit ISO from issuing such advisory rates. This, in turn, would force companies to base their prices on their own economic projections and productivity levels. True competition would be introduced into the picture, strengthening the forces of the marketplace that reward efficiency and productivity. The result: lower premiums overall.

Step 3: Repeal Anti-Group Laws

Unlike health and life insurance, most states currently prohibit auto insurance "group" plans. Such laws were enacted years ago and were backed strongly by the insurance industry lobby. These laws are anti-consumer. Since the individual does not have the bargaining power of a large group, anti-group laws act to keep prices high. By allowing groups to form for the purpose of purchasing auto insurance, the power of the marketplace will be freed to do its thing. The result will be to allow groups to negotiate policies with higher benefits for a lower premium.

Step 4: Repeal Anti-Rebate Laws

In a free marketplace, agents who sell insurance would be able to reduce the cost of premiums to their customers by voluntarily reducing their commissions, if the agents believe doing so is necessary to get the sale. Unfortunately, insurance industry interests oppose this freedom, and as a result many states have laws prohibiting such "rebates" to the consumer. In these states, efficient agents cannot lower commissions to compete better for a higher market share. Such laws are purely and simply anti-consumer, and they should be repealed.

Step 5: Strengthen Rate Regulation by the States

Since people are compelled to purchase insurance by state financial responsibility laws and cannot simply walk away from the sale or do without the product, it is necessary for insurance companies to be regulated. There are several ways for state insurance departments to increase price regulation.

Make the office of insurance commissioner an elected post. Traditionally, the office of insurance commissioner has been an appointed position. Those selected to this important post have usually been people who have made their careers in the insurance industry and who intend to return to it after public service. Their attitudes often reflect insurance industry attitudes and prejudices. By making the post elective rather than appointive, the point of view of the consumers, if they are organized and alert, will have to be taken into account. This will reduce the power of the industry to control those who are in the position to regulate them and will make life much easier for the consumer.

Require regulatory approval of rate increases. In order for insurance premiums to be kept down, the companies should be required to justify their proposed rate increases *before* they go into effect. The regulatory process should include public hearings. The point of all of this is to force insurance companies to prove the business necessity for a rate hike. Rate increases should not be granted unless the company shows it has been operating in an efficient manner.

Step 6: Reduce the Weight of Territorial Rating in Setting Prices

Territorial rating has the effect of punishing people because of where they live. It also has the frequent effect of making insurance unaffordable to some of the poorest people in the country, those who live and work in inner cities. To eliminate these inequities, laws should be passed mandating rate-setting based more on the individual policyholder's driving record, mileage driven, and years of driving experience and less upon residence. "Good driver" discounts of up to 20 percent should also be mandated by law. This would act as an incentive to drivers to obey traffic laws, which would have the beneficial side effect of reducing accidents and saving lives.

Step 7: Establish Computerized Consumer Information Services

Each state should establish consumer information bureaus to help consumers comparison shop for auto insurance (and, eventually, other types of insurance as well). In addition to price information, the state should make available data on how long it takes to settle claims, the percentage of claims that go to court, the costs of providing insurance in the state, assessments of reserve accuracy, and similar information. Applicants would be able to either call an 800 phone number or access computers to obtain the information. Such a service would increase competition within the industry—and, as any good capitalist will tell you, increased competition should decrease prices and improve service.

Step 8: Establish Consumer Advocacy Organizations

One of the major problems facing consumers of insurance is their voicelessness in the corridors of power. Lacking an organized and informed organization to represent them in front of state legislative committees and administrative agencies, consumers' rights often take a backseat to the moneyed interests who use their wealth and power to influence state legislatures and the executive administration of state law. The playing field could become more level if citizen insurance boards were established to represent consumer concerns in rate proceedings and in front of legislatures considering insurance legislation. The boards would be financed through individual membership fees inserted in motor vehicle registration envelopes, along with some state subsidies.

What Else Can Be Done?

In addition to these proposals, there is another source of reform: passage of state laws that compel companies to issue guaranteed-renewable policies.

Much of the fear and loathing people feel toward auto insurance companies comes from their knowledge that if they use their insurance, their company will make them pay dearly for the privilege or cancel them altogether, even if they are not at fault. This inequity can be substantially reduced if companies are compelled by law to offer policies in which the consumer is guaranteed renewal, without a rate increase above that charged all other policyholders as approved by the state insurance commissioner. The only grounds for an individual increase in premiums (other than changes in the risk of coverage, such as the purchase of a new car) would be a poor driving record based on the concept of fault. In other words, if you made claims against the company for benefits as the result of an accident that was not primarily your fault, your rates could not be raised.

Auto insurance costs can also be greatly reduced if the federal government were to push much harder than it does now for safer, more crashworthy automobiles and laws that would reduce injuries and save lives. We should all insist upon the following items.

Better Consumer Information

The government should require ratings of crashworthiness placed on new-car window stickers to assist buyers in selecting safer cars. If this were done, safety would become a larger factor in consumer purchasing decisions. In a competitive marketplace, the auto manufacturers that best respond to the public's safety concerns will garner the largest shares of the market. This, in turn, will serve as an incentive to the auto companies to increase the safety of their vehicles.

Increased Auto Safety

Much can be done to increase the crashworthiness of the cars we drive. Safety improvement items must be addressed. *Side-impact protection standards* should be upgraded to reduce thoracic/abdominal injuries and head injuries from contact with the A-pillar and from side-door ejection, particularly in car-to-car side-impact crashes. *Increased rollover protection* is needed, with a requirement that anti-lock brakes be installed in every car to reduce rollovers. *Automatic passive restraint safety requirements*, currently established for passenger cars, should be broadened to include light trucks and vans, which are becoming more and more popular with the driving public. Safer cars equal fewer injuries. Fewer injuries change insurance companies' statistics regarding their risk of loss. A lower risk of loss allows the companies to reduce premiums.

Reduced Property Damage

More insurance money could be saved if cars were manufactured so as to decrease property damage incurred in minor mishaps. Among the matters that should be required are the following.

0–10 MPH bumper standards. Technologically, the auto industry has the ability to manufacture bumpers that can withstand low-speed collisions. The 5 MPH standard set in 1980 has been reduced to 2.5 MPH, resulting in *hundreds of millions of dollars* more each year in repair costs. These costs, which would have been unnecessary under the higher standard, are part of the total price of your insurance premiums.

Small accidents can be quite expensive, depending on the manufacturer and model of the car involved. The Insurance Institute for Highway Safety recently published a survey that compared the repair costs of low-speed (5 MPH) crashes of small four-door 1990 cars. The costs varied widely: a Honda Civic DX, when backed into a pole, incurred $225 worth of damage; a Daihatsu Charade SE backed into the same pole would cost $1,372 to repair. Clearly, higher-quality bumpers on all cars could bring down the cost of repairs—costs that are now paid with insurance benefits. With better bumper standards in place, "fender benders" would be eliminated, resulting—*in theory*—in lower premiums.

Increase competition to lower the price of parts. One major expense item in repairing any damaged car is the price of parts. A major reason for this is the monopolistic control original equipment manufacturers (OEMs) have over the parts market. Competition in this lucrative market must be encouraged. Any state laws that prevent use of competitive replacement parts should be repealed.

Increase the prevention of theft and fraud. Existing steering-wheel lock and other such anti-theft requirements should be reevaluated and upgraded. In addition, insurers should push auto companies to design more theft-resistant locks. Laws that punish insurance fraud by fake accident specialists should be toughened and enforcement increased so that this drain on auto insurance funds can be reduced.

The above proposals, if adopted, would go a long way toward getting the runaway costs of auto insurance under control. In addition, other approaches are possible, such as establishing state-run nonprofit auto insurance companies similar to the workers compensation funds that have been created in many states (see page 130).

The war to bring reason and fairness to the pricing and administration of auto insurance will be hard-fought. No one expects the entrenched and powerful forces of the insurance establishment to surrender their immense power easily. In fact, it will take years of energetic consumer activism to stop the pricing abuses of the auto insurance industry.

Let's take a look at one of the early conflicts in the war to reduce auto insurance premiums: California's Proposition 103.

The Saga of Proposition 103

The first blow for auto insurance consumer rights was struck in November 1988, in California, with the passage of Proposition 103. California has had a bona fide auto insurance crisis that has been accelerated in recent years. As a result, consumer advocate Harvey Rosenfield formed an organization called Voter Revolt and wrote an auto insurance reform initiative that qualified for the ballot. The measure became known as Proposition 103.

Proposition 103 was one of five ballot initiatives on the state's 1988 general election ballot that dealt with insurance. Others included an attempt by the auto insurance industry to institute no-fault insurance and restrict the ability of consumers to hire lawyers on a contingency fee. Of the five initiatives, only 103 passed.

Proposition 103 provided for the following:

1. **A 20 percent rollback and rebate on auto policy premiums and homeowner's premiums from November 1987.** Language in the initiative provided relief from the rebate for insurance companies that could prove that the rebate would create a substantial threat of insolvency.

2. **A mandated 20 percent discount for good drivers.** This was to begin in November 1989.

3. **Changing the post of insurance commissioner from appointive to elective.**

4. **A freeze on rate increases for one year.**

5. **Removal of the precedence of territorial rating.** Instead, the rating system will look at individual driving records and patterns.

6. **Increasing the potential for competition by allowing banks to sell insurance.** Economists will tell you that true competition is the consumer's best friend because it forces prices down and quality up. By allowing banks to enter the field of insurance, competitive pressures will be increased in the insurance industry, and this will be of great benefit to the consumer.

7. **Groups may now form in California to negotiate the purchase of auto insurance.** The power of a group to negotiate substantial benefits at a good price is far greater than that of an individual. There is no rational basis for preventing the sale of group auto insurance, as the voters demonstrated by passing Proposition 103.

8. **Agents may rebate portions of their commissions to the consumer.** As discussed above, in a truly competitive market, agents can rebate portions of their commissions to the consumer in order to get the sale. Proposition 103 did away with the previous legal ban on such practices.

9. **A 900 phone number allowing consumers to get consumer price information from the state insurance department.**

As you would expect, the insurance industry has howled in rage and pain at the prospect that its reign of unfettered power may be coming to an end. Insurance companies have challenged the law in court. So far, the pro-business California Supreme Court has upheld the law but also engaged in some "judicial amending"; they removed the language exempting companies in danger of insolvency from the law and replaced it with a different standard. Under the law as rewritten by the court, insurance companies have to be guaranteed a "fair and reasonable profit" before they can be forced to roll back prices or partake in the rate freeze. (Isn't it ironic that conservatives, who usually rail against "judicial legislation," were so quiet when the California Supreme Court engaged in one of the most outrageous cases of such practices in the postwar period?)

The effect of the court's rewriting of Proposition 103 was to gut much of its short-term rollback impact. The law was thrown into confusion: What is a fair and reasonable profit? How is it to be determined? Roxani Gillespie, the California state insurance commissioner, vacillated between being soft on the companies and surrendering to them. Hearings were promised and some were even held. The bottom line is that most of the promised rebates and rollbacks were stalled as the companies collectively spent over $100 million to thwart the people's will. (Source: Office of the California Insurance Commissioner.)

Then, in 1991, John Garamendi was inaugurated as California's first elected insurance commissioner. Unlike his appointed predecessor, Mr. Garamendi has worked to enforce Proposition 103. As of this writing, three of the top ten insurance companies in Caifornia—The Automobile Club of Southern California, Mercury Insurance, and Progressive Insurance—have agreed to pay rebates averaging between $172 and $204 per policyholder. Three other, small medical malpractice insurance carriers have also given rebates, as have a few homeowner insurance carriers. The 900-phone-number rate comparison hotline is set to go on-line in the winter of 1992–93, adding needed competition to the automobile insurance market, which should increase pressure to bring prices down. More needs to be done, but by any measure, Proposition 103 must be judged an unfolding success.

Should All Auto Insurance Be State Operated?

With the auto insurance mess being what it is in many states, some people have begun to suggest that the simplest and fairest approach to the problem is to incorporate insurance premiums into the price drivers pay at the pump for gasoline. Thus, those who drive the most will pay the most, which is fair since the more you drive, the greater the likelihood is that you will have an accident. This concept would also eliminate issues such as territorial rating, insurance cancellations, and the other areas of controversy that currently rage in the field of auto insurance. While we are not ready to endorse this proposal, we believe it is certainly worth investigating.

Part 3

Health Insurance

We've all heard the old adage, "If you've got your health, you've got everything." And that's true, as far as it goes, but it does not go far enough. Unfortunately, in today's medical marketplace you need something more, something that may hold the key to your continued good health or the solution to curing whatever might be ailing you. That something is a good health insurance policy.

Without health insurance, it is unlikely that you will be able to find a doctor to call your own or to obtain treatment for illness or injury. Without health insurance, you could even be turned away from hospital emergency rooms unless it is a life-or-death situation. Even then, patients have died because treatment was refused. In short, health insurance is vital to the health and welfare of each and every one of us.

In the chapters that follow, we will cover traditional health insurance and hospitalization policies. We will also discuss the newer models of health insurance, such as health maintenance organizations (HMOs) and preferred provider organizations (PPOs), which have been developed to reduce costs. Your rights to continue your group health insurance coverage or to convert it to an individual policy, should you become ineligible for group coverage due to loss of a job or divorce from an insured spouse, will also be detailed. We will look into disability insurance. Finally, we will investigate some proposed solutions to our health care delivery mess.

Why do we call it a mess? Those unlucky Americans who do not obtain health insurance as a benefit through their places of employment or unions must purchase it in the open market, where the prices alone are enough to reduce life expectancy. And there are many uninsured—over 37 *million people* do not have any health insurance at all and therefore, almost by definition, receive inadequate health care. Many of these uninsured are children. Even those with group coverage can lose their insurance if they become ineligible for group membership, a particular problem for divorcing spouses.

To address these issues, we will take a quick look at the famous Canadian system of health insurance as well as some of the solutions that have been proposed for us here in the United States.

So take a deep breath. Hold it, that's right. Now, exhale. Once again, please. That's fine. Now, cough. Good. You seem fit as a fiddle. You can turn the page now. This won't hurt a bit . . . well, maybe just a little.

14

To Your Health . . . Insurance

Ask any patient (except the president of the United States and members of Congress, who are insulated from such things), and they will uniformly agree that health care costs money, lots and lots of money. In fact, unless you are a Donald Trump, a major illness requiring a couple of weeks in the hospital is enough to flush your life savings right down the drain and into the hands of doctors, hospitals, drug companies, and medical laboratories.

This being so, there are only two things keeping most of us from bankruptcy court: the good fortune of not becoming ill or injured, and health insurance. Thus, health insurance may be the most important insurance need most of us face, since sooner or later we or a loved one are bound to need the services of a physician and/or a stay in the hospital.

How Health Insurance Is Obtained

You can acquire health insurance in several different ways: through individual policies, group coverage, and government benefits.

Individual Policies

If you are not in a group, you can usually purchase insurance either directly from an insurance provider or through agents and brokers (see page 16). The unfortunate part of purchasing individual or family policies is that they are extremely expensive. Worse, an applicant with any significant health problem may not be able to obtain coverage, or may find so many exclusions in the policy that it resembles Swiss cheese.

Group Insurance

A group insurance policy is sold to an organization of people who share a common interest. This organization may be a corporation, union, trade association, club, religious society, or any other identifiable collection of people an insurance company is willing to recognize as a "group."

Benefits. Because the group has power in numbers, it can usually get insurance coverage for less cost per individual and/or family than would be obtainable if the insurance shoppers were buying on their own.

In addition to reduced premiums, there are other health insurance benefits to joining a group. These include the following.

Preexisting conditions are likely to be covered. As we will discuss in more detail, many health insurance policies will exclude identified medical conditions that existed prior to the health insurance going into effect. These are called **preexisting conditions**. Many people who have had the misfortune to experience serious illness find that exclusions for preexisting conditions often keep them from reaching the promised land of health insurance coverage.

Often, the only way around this difficulty is to somehow join a group that is large enough to have negotiated a concession from the insurance carrier whereby the company gives up the right to exclude such preexisting conditions. This concession is often the difference between obtaining coverage or risking health and prosperity as a member of the unfortunate uninsured.

Medical exams are often not required. Health insurance companies, like life insurance companies, usually require a close look into the health of the individual applicant during the underwriting of the application. This can include a physical examination. Group members often are able to obtain insurance without this investigation into their health.

Benefits are frequently higher. The negotiating power of a group, especially a large group, often allows members to receive better total benefits at a lower out-of-pocket price, not only in terms of premiums but also with regard to expenses that individuals must pay themselves.

Deductibles are lower. People can afford lower deductibles because the group pays a lower rate overall, and a lower deductible means less money out of your pocket should you need to file a claim.

▶ **NOTE:** Small groups frequently have difficulties similar to individual insurance shoppers. Letters received by the Center for the Study of Responsive Law attest to this fact. Here's an excerpt from one such letter sent by Richard Darby, of Holmdel, New Jersey:

> My wife and a friend currently have a small manufacturing business and applied for group medical insurance. . . . The only medical item reported to them on the application was a small cancerous mole that was removed from my wife's partner's back five years ago. Exams each year have proved negative and still they (insurance companies) will not consider *anyone* in the group [emphasis added].

Moreover, NICO president J. Robert Hunter has testified that insurance companies are now using age as a criterion of pricing, thereby doing away with universal premium pricing within the group. This could, in turn, lead to increased age discrimination in employment. Hunter also reports that members of small groups are increasingly having all preexisting conditions excluded from coverage.

This is a shameful state of affairs. People need access to health care, and too often our system of private insurance doesn't give it to them.

Consumer Alert

One of the most important benefits of employment is often group health insurance. Thus, if you are thinking of changing jobs, be sure to check out what your health insurance situation will be if you do so. For example, will there be a waiting period for preexisting conditions? Will the level of protection be better or worse than your old plan? Don't hesitate to question your prospective employer on health insurance matters.

Government Benefits

The federal and state governments provide health benefits to various people in different ways. These include **Medicare**, which partially pays the medical bills for those 65 and over as well as the blind and disabled; **Medicaid**, a state and federally funded health insurance for the poor; and the health benefits of the **Veterans Administration**. We will discuss these in detail in Part 6.

Different Kinds of Health Insurance

Whether you buy group or individual insurance, the options you have regarding the different types of insurance are generally the same. In some groups you can even choose from a menu of available plans. These different types are **traditional health insurance, health maintenance organizations (HMOs), and preferred provider organizations (PPOs)**.

Traditional Health Insurance

The traditional health care delivery system is based on a fee-for-service type of arrangement. In a fee-for-service system, you pay for each itemized medical service you receive. In the days of the frontier, "Doc" often received a chicken as payment. Today, physicians are paid with money, lots and lots of it. Fee-for-service health insurance recognizes this practice and is designed to reduce or even eliminate your duty to pay directly for your medical care.

Traditional health insurance comes in three parts:

Hospitalization. Hospitalization covers defined expenses incurred while in the hospital. Generally, the insurance will pay for all of the covered services rendered by the hospital staff. However, if the insurance benefit is an **indemnity payment** plan (see Glossary), the payment will be for a fixed sum regardless of the actual expenses incurred. This fixed sum will usually be far below the daily charge actually made by the hospital.

Medical/surgical. This part of a traditional health plan covers the expensive costs of medical care other than the bill from the hospital. Services such as doctor visits, treatment charges, etc., are covered here. Medical/surgical usually has a deductible (see page 12) and requires **copayments** by the insured (payments you make for charges not covered by the insurance), typically 20 percent of the doctor's fee.

Catastrophic or major medical. There are usually lifetime maximum payments that hospitalization and medical/surgical plans will pay, after which the well runs dry. Unfortunately, these maximums may not be sufficient to pay for all of the care required if a major illness or injury should strike, since such afflictions can eat up hundreds of thousands or even millions of dollars worth of health services. Thus, catastrophic coverage adds to your umbrella of protection in an amount sufficient to protect you from the horrendous expenses of such serious and prolonged illnesses. These policies also fill in some of the gaps not covered by hospitalization or medical/surgical.

Health Maintenance Organizations

The health maintenance organization (HMO) is a relatively new player in the health insurance game, although it has been around in a limited fashion since the 1930s. The idea behind an HMO is to pay one premium and receive all of your health care at no or a nominal additional cost. The point is to save money compared to traditional health plans that cost more to purchase and require more out-of-pocket payments from the insured. What you, the insured, give in exchange for reduced cost is a substantial loss of your freedom to choose who will take care of your health needs. HMOs will be considered in Chapter 16.

Preferred Provider Organizations

Preferred provider organizations (PPOs) seek to give both the benefits of traditional health plans and the money savings of HMOs. They do this by paying higher benefits as a reward for your using the doctors or hospitals they preselect for that purpose. PPOs will also be discussed in Chapter 16.

Disability Insurance

Disability insurance does not pay for health care; rather it pays for lost wages caused by a disabling injury or illness. Disability insurance will be detailed in Chapter 18.

How Health Insurance Is Priced

Ask anyone how health insurance is priced and you will get a simple answer: expensively! Beyond that, there are underwriting criteria used by health insurance providers, whether they are for-profit or, like Blue Shield/Blue Cross, nonprofit.

Underwriting Criteria

Age. The older you are, the more likely you are to get sick; ergo, the higher your health insurance premiums.

Number of people covered. Many people buy family coverage rather than individual policies. This means that there will be adults as well as minor children protected by the same plan. Some companies will charge based on the size of the family. Others charge a basic family rate without regard to the number of members.

Gender. Unlike life insurance, where women get the better end of the bargain than men, in health insurance women often pay higher premiums. This is based on health insurance industry statistics which indicate that the female of the species tends to need medical care more often than the male.

Health history. Insurance operates on statistical probabilities. If you have had a poor health history, statistically you are more likely to have a more expensive health care future. This, in turn, means that you will pay higher premiums—if you can get health insurance at all. For example, Susan A. Nessim, the founder of Cancervive, an organization dedicated to assisting those who have fought cancer, states that many former cancer victims are considered uninsurable by insurance companies, even years after they defeated the disease (as was the case with Richard Darby's letter quoted earlier). Hence the importance of becoming a member of a large group for health insurance purposes. (Why is it that insurance companies are a lot like banks—if you need them they don't want you, but if it looks like you don't need them, you can have their services on a silver platter?)

Occupation. The more likely you are to suffer injury or illness because of the work you do, the more likely the health insurance industry will be to charge excessively for benefits.

This may be well and good for professional deep-sea divers. But the industry has begun to stretch the concept into areas that have nothing to do with the inherent danger of the work. The *New York Times* recently published an exposé on the increasing number of professions to which health insurance companies will not issue policies. According to the *Times*, coverage is not denied because the professions are inherently dangerous, but because high numbers of homosexuals are thought to be among their members. In essence, what the health insurance carriers are trying to avoid is the likelihood of paying for the treatment of AIDS.

Lifestyle. In your application for health insurance you will be asked questions about your personal habits. Your answers will have a lot to do with the cost of your premiums. If you smoke, you will probably pay more for health insurance. If you drink to excess, you will probably pay more for health insurance. If you are known to be under a great deal of stress, you may pay more for health insurance. Remember, insurance companies try to avoid having to pay benefits; thus, the greater the likelihood that your lifestyle will make you sick, the greater the likelihood that you will need medical care, and thus the more expensive your health insurance will be.

What You Don't Know
Can Hurt You

Regardless of the kind of insurance you select, there are certain important contract provisions to watch out for.

Exclusions

As you will recall from some of our earlier discussions, **exclusions** in an insurance policy remove areas from coverage that would otherwise come under the protection of the insurance umbrella. Understanding the exclusions in your policy is vital if you are to truly understand your rights under the policy.

Here are some typical exclusions found in health insurance policies.

Preexisting conditions. Preexisting condition exclusions are the bane of the health insurance consumer. They can be so broad that they make a joke of health insurance "coverage."

A **preexisting condition** is often defined as "the existence of symptoms that would cause an ordinary prudent person to seek diagnosis, care, or treatment within a five-year period, or a condition for which a physician either recommended or rendered care." That leaves a pretty wide latitude, as an angry health insurance consumer living in Florida discovered when she searched for health insurance. She writes:

> My search for health insurance was due to the fact my employer decided to discontinue the group plan under which I had been covered. The insurance premium had been increased drastically at regular intervals until the premium for three adults and two teenagers had reached nearly $50,000 per year.

She went on to relate how she applied for insurance. After several months she was told that a policy would be issued but that there would be three areas of exclusion, one for her left hip, one for her back, and one for her female organs. She continues:

> I was stunned, to say the least and asked [the underwriter] why. He told me that since I had been in an auto accident in 1983 and had received treatment for a back sprain, they could not cover my back; that since I had inflammation in my left hip, even though I had not seen a doctor about the condition

for over a year, they could not cover my hip. And since they could not locate the gynecologist who had treated me for what I listed as minor female irregularities, they would not cover my female organs. I was told that these exclusions would apply for two years and then they would review my case and a decision would be made as to whether to remove the exclusions.

Thus, under today's privatized system of health insurance, you don't even have to have a chronic illness such as diabetes or have had a heart attack or a major injury to be left out in the cold by a preexisting condition exclusion. So, be sure to check very carefully the preexisting clause of any new health insurance you are thinking of purchasing. You may find that you are paying full premiums for only a shell of a policy.

Substance abuse. Many policies exclude coverage for illnesses or injuries that arise out of the abuse of narcotics or other controlled substances not prescribed by a physician.

Attempted suicide. If things are so bad that you are contemplating ending it all, be aware that any treatment you receive because of the effort will probably be on your own dime.

Mental illness. Some policies exclude benefits for mental or emotional illness that does not have an organic (bodily) cause. Others provide specifically defined and limited benefits for such things as psychotherapy. Be sure you understand your rights under your policy if you feel the need to consult a psychiatrist, psychologist, or other mental-health professional.

Workers compensation claims. If the injury or illness is subject to workers compensation medical benefits, the private or group policy will generally exclude itself from paying the medical bills.

Cosmetic surgery. If you don't like your looks and you seek plastic surgery to fix what you find offensive about your body, don't expect your health insurance to pay the bill. However, if the cosmetic surgery is required due to injury (or birth defect in a child born under the protection of the health policy), the cost will be covered.

Pregnancy. Many insurance policies do not cover normal pregnancy. Often they will also not pay for an elective cesarean section. Some even exclude miscarriages from coverage, and very few will pay for an abortion. Thus, if you are pregnant or planning to be, be sure to check your policy to see what prenatal and obstetric delivery services are covered by your health insurance plan.

Eyeglasses and dental work. These services are not covered. However, dental insurance can usually be purchased as an add-on to the policy.

Treatment paid for by the government. If a government benefit will pay the bill, your health insurance company will try not to.

Prescription drugs. Unfortunately, many policies don't pay for the cost of medication. And with the cost of drugs these days, that lapse can prove expensive and potentially dangerous to your health if you can't afford to pay for necessary medicine.

Preventive care. Many traditional health insurance policies will not pay for things such as routine physicals or medical tests where no symptoms are present. Apparently these companies have never heard that an ounce of prevention is worth a pound of cure.

Renewability

Another very important area of your health insurance policy is your all-important right to renew the policy at the end of its term. After all, if you get sick and the terms of the policy allow the company not to renew your coverage, you can kiss good-bye any hope of purchasing other health insurance. Thus, check the policy carefully to see what your renewal rights are and whether the company has the right to raise your rates. (Renewal provisions also control your company's right to raise your rates.)

Following are the different types of renewal provisions usually found in health insurance contracts.

Cancelable. If your policy is **cancelable**, it can be canceled at any time at the discretion of the insurance company, even during the term of the policy itself. The only limitation is your right to receive advance notice in writing, typically a week or so before coverage lapses. Avoid cancelable policies if you possibly can, since they provide a very low margin of security.

Nonrenewable. In **nonrenewable** policies, the company can't cancel you but you can't force them to renew you. This can work well in the short term—say, if you are between jobs. But these policies offer little security since your company can terminate the policy at the end of its term, even if (some would say, especially if) you are in the middle of treatment for an illness or serious injury.

Conditionally renewable. Some policies guarantee renewability unless certain conditions arise, such as their canceling of all policies of the type you have purchased. In such cases, there is no restriction on the insurance company's ability to raise the rates upon renewal.

Guaranteed renewable. A truly renewable policy guarantees your right to renew at the end of the term without regard to the state of your health. There is, however, often a time when the renewability guarantee will cease, usually at age 65. Renewable policies can be raised in price as long as the company raises rates for all policies of the same class. Clearly, if you can get guaranteed renewable health insurance, do so. The only way you can be cut off is if the rates rise above your ability to pay the premiums (which can happen) or if the company goes bankrupt (which can also happen).

Noncancelable. A **noncancelable** policy is one that cannot be canceled as long as you pay your premiums. Moreover, your rates cannot be raised. Not bad, not bad at all—if you can get a company to issue such a policy and if you can afford to pay for it.

Time Requirements

Your health insurance will require that certain time conditions be met, including the time within which you must make a claim. There will also be a grace period during which nonpayment of premiums will not be grounds for cancellation. There may also be a *waiting period* before benefits begin. Most policies also have a **free look** provision that allows you 10 days or so to review the policy to see if you really want it.

Waiver of Premium

Many policies allow premium payment to be suspended during periods of disability. Look to see what the waiting period is for the waiver of premium clause to go into effect and the way the policy defines the term "disability."

Coordination of Benefits

If you are covered under more than one policy—if you and your spouse have group coverage from your respective jobs, for example—you should learn how the companies will coordinate their obligation to pay benefits.

Having multiple protection should work to your advantage. You should be able to have the benefits not paid by one company paid by the other. Unfortunately, the industry has found a way around this equitable approach to coordination of benefits. What they often do is insert a "birthday rule" into the group insurance contract. The effect is to deny many insureds the total coverage that two insurance policies should give them. We'll let Charles and Joann Roth of Louisville, Kentucky, describe how the birthday clauses deprive them of health insurance benefits. They write:

> Most insurance companies are now practicing a rule which they have named the "birthday rule." This rule states that if you and your spouse are covered under a medical or dental policy, the person whose birthday falls first in the year is the primary carrier. The rule goes on to state that if the spouse who is the primary carrier has coverage which pays 1¢ more than the other spouse's coverage, then the other carrier doesn't pay anything, no matter how much the primary carrier doesn't pay for. . . .

My daughter needs braces which will cost $2,700. My carrier would pay $1,500 and my husband's would pay $1,000, leaving us with a burden of $200. But because my birthday falls earlier in the year than his, his insurance will not pay anything. As a result, my daughter is not going to be able to get braces.

Unfortunately, people like the Roths have little individual power to force their benefit negotiators to resist unfair policy clauses like the birthday rule. But regulators do. The fact that they don't try to stop practices such as this illustrates the power insurance companies have over the regulatory process.

The Roths also did something that saved them from deep debt. They took the time to learn how their benefits would be coordinated (or in their case, would not be) before they incurred a health care debt they could not afford. You should do likewise.

Now that you have a running start on some of the general provisions of a health insurance contract and some of the items that are excluded from benefits, let's get into the flesh and blood of the various health insurance policies. We will start with traditional health insurance.

If You Think a Mistake Has Been Made

If the insurance company believes you have a past health problem, they may not sell you insurance. If the insurance company is correct, your only recourse may be to try another insurance company or attempt to get into a group with a policy that does not take preexisting conditions or past illnesses into account. On the other hand, if you believe the insurance company has made an error about your health, here are a few things you can do:

Ask for additional tests. Screening health tests can be performed in a perfunctory manner. If you believe the test results are wrong, you can ask for additional tests. Unfortunately, if you choose to go this route, you will probably have to pay for the tests yourself.

Ask the insurance company to send the tests to your doctor. Your doctor can review the insurance company tests against your medical records. If a mistake has been made, your doctor may be able to locate the error and inform the company, which may get them to change their minds.

Get copies of your medical information bureau records. You may not know it, but your medical history may be on file in the Medical Information Bureau (MIB), in much the same way as your credit record is on file with TRW. When you apply for insurance, your company may have contacted the MIB and received an erroneous report. In such cases, you will want to receive a copy of the report, and under the Fair Credit Reporting Act, you have a right to if the report is the cause of the denial. MIB can be contacted at (617) 426-3660.

Consumer Alert

The health insurance crisis has gotten beyond the point where individual consumers can do much to protect themselves against increasing premiums. Oh, you can increase your deductible and copayments, but that is only a holding action at best. And you can switch companies—*if* you can get past the preexisting condition exclusions and waiting periods. But, even then, your next premium notice will undoubtedly put you back into the same fix you were in when your former company raised its rates.

No, the only way the entire system can be stopped from imploding will be for national action to be taken to control the costs of medical care and guarantee universal health insurance coverage, either through the private or public sectors or a combination of both.

With so much money at stake, with the power of the health insurance industry, and with the medical community resisting change, it will take vigorous and concerted grass-roots activism to bring about needed reforms. That means you—Uncle Sam wants you to demand reform and not take no for an answer!

15

Traditional Health Insurance

Health insurance has traditionally come in two parts, with an optional third sometimes thrown in for good measure. These are **hospitalization, surgical/medical**, and **major medical** (also known as **catastrophic coverage**). We will cover all three in this chapter.

Hospitalization

Any hospital stay is going to cost a great deal of money. The more care you need, the higher the bill. For example, some intensive care units cost up to $1,000 a day, and that doesn't include the cost of the doctors. Regular care isn't cheap either. In fact, you could live one day at the nicest hotels in the world (meals included) for just the cost of one day's uneventful stay in an ordinary hospital. This being so, it is very important to have hospitalization insurance.

Types of Policies

Hospitalization policies generally come in two varieties.

Indemnity plan. This kind of policy is the easiest to understand. Basically, if you are hospitalized for covered services, the insurance company must pay a flat fee directly to you. You, of course, must pay the hospital. Unfortunately, the difference between what you receive in payments and what the hospital wants to collect may be enough to put you right back in the hospital.

Fee for service. Most hospitalization policies pay for part or all of the following hospital services.

Room and board. Whether you are in intensive care or an ordinary semiprivate room, your room and board expenses will be paid for by the insurance company. Frequently, there is a maximum number of days covered per stay, after which coverage ceases unless you are protected by catastrophic care insurance. Happily, this time period is usually quite long. Private rooms will be paid for only when there is a medical necessity for you to be placed in one.

Routine nursing care. If you have ever stayed in a hospital, you know how important the nurses and medical staff are to your care and comfort. Your hospital bill includes these basic services (the cost of bringing you food, the cost of a nurse administering medication, etc.). These basics are paid for by your hospitalization coverage.

Miscellaneous medical services and supplies provided by hospital personnel. As you know, the aspirin you can buy for a dollar a bottle in a drugstore can cost you a dollar a pill in a hospital. Expenses such as these are paid by the hospitalization coverage to the maximum allowed under the terms of the policy.

Food. Hospital food is paid for by insurance. Oh boy! Now, if only there were a policy clause guaranteeing good nutrition and taste . . .

Use of the surgical suite. If you are in the hospital for surgery, your hospitalization policy will pay for the cost you will be charged by the hospital for the use of the operating room.

Hospitalization for treatment of substance abuse. If you listen to the advertisements for treatment programs on daytime television, you know that this country has a terrible drug and alcohol abuse problem. Listen further to these ads, and you will know that many hospitalization policies will pay benefits for inpatient (hospitalized) treatment of such afflictions. Usually, such treatment is restricted to one hospitalization in a year's time and a maximum of 45 days, although the terms in your policy may vary.

Hospital outpatient services. More and more, insurance companies are insisting that surgery be done on an outpatient basis. As an outpatient, you check in before breakfast, have surgery before lunch, and return home before dinner. Such brief non-overnight stays will usually be paid for by the hospitalization portion of your health insurance. Likewise, emergency outpatient care is also usually covered under your hospitalization coverage.

Doctor bills. Some fees charged by doctors may be paid under the hospitalization portion of your health policy, especially for services, such as surgery, rendered in the hospital.

Policy Restrictions

Almost as important as knowing what is covered under your plan is knowing the policy limitations. The following are some of the things to look out for in a hospitalization plan that can leap out of the tall weeds and bite you on the ankle if you don't know they are there.

Waiting periods before coverage begins. If your hospitalization plan requires a waiting period before coverage begins, you could end up in big financial trouble. Most hospital stays are relatively short and they have become even shorter in recent years thanks to insurance company pressure to keep costs down. Thus if your policy contains a three-day waiting period and you are in the hospital for four days, you will receive only one day's worth of benefits. You will have to pay the remaining three days' worth of care yourself, which in all likelihood will be in the thousands of dollars.

Short periods of coverage. At the other end of the hospitalization spectrum are policies that cover only brief periods of hospitalization. These can be even more dangerous to your economic health since the amount of time they would not cover can be very long if you are seriously injured or ill. Moreover, if your policy restricts the length of your stay unreasonably, you could find yourself forced into a public facility that you would not choose for yourself.

Maximum payments that are too low. Some policies are deceptive in their appearance. On one hand they will set a seemingly high maximum number of days permitted to be paid under the policy. Then, on the other, they limit their maximum financial exposure to $10,000 or $25,000. Such financial maximums make a mockery of the "days in hospital maximums," and unless supplemented by a catastrophic care policy, they are much too small to protect you against serious illness or injury.

Restricted payments for specialty care. Sometimes patients need the special attention provided by intensive care units or other specialty care wards. In these settings the patient receives a lot of attention—attention that can mean the difference between life and death. However, this extra-special treatment comes at a very high cost, often double the hospital's normal daily charge. If your hospitalization policy puts a cap on payments for this type of care, you may find your pocketbook in need of intensive care.

Limitations on hospitals. Many hospitalization policies now require you to be hospitalized at specifically identified hospitals that have contracted with the health insurance company to provide care at reduced rates. These hospitals are called **contract**

hospitals. If you are admitted to a noncontract hospital (in other than a life-threatening emergency), your benefits are subject to being significantly reduced. Thus, if your doctor and you conclude you need care in a hospital, ask the doctor to admit you into a hospital where you will receive full benefits. If you don't know which hospitals qualify, be sure to contact your plan administrator.

Obviously, there's far more to receiving complete health insurance protection than is covered under a hospitalization policy. There is a second part of most traditional health insurance, called a surgical/medical policy. Hospitalization and surgical/medical coverage make up what is called a **basic policy**.

Surgical/Medical

The surgical/medical (S&M) policy is meant to complete your basic health protection package. Typically S&M policies pay for physician's services; the nonhospital costs of surgery, including the anesthesiologist; the cost of diagnostic testing; in-home health care, if provided; skilled nursing, if provided; medically necessary ambulance services; the use of wheelchairs, etc.; and services such as physical therapy.

The plans usually work something like this.

Deductibles

Most policies do not pay from dollar one but require you to pay a certain amount before benefits kick in. This payment is called the **deductible**. Deductibles usually are set at approximately $200 per person, although they can be much higher. (For example, some people with preexisting conditions can only obtain policies with deductibles in the thousands of dollars.) Most policy deductibles are for a calendar year but some policies have deductibles per malady. If you have a choice and can afford a deductible per calendar year, go for it since having to pay a deductible every time you have a health problem could get very expensive.

Copayments

Most S&M policies require you to pay a portion of the total bill, typically 20 percent after the deductible has been met. There will often be a **stop-loss provision** that limits your yearly total copayment to a defined figure, such as $3,500 or $5,000. Thus, if you incurred a $2,000 medical bill on a policy where you had to pay 20 percent, you would be responsible for $400 (assuming you had paid your deductible). However, if you had previously paid all of your yearly copayment obligation, your bill would be paid in full by your insurance company.

Limitations on Covered Charges

Unfortunately, insurance companies don't usually make it as easy as the equation set forth above. In an effort to hold down costs, they often try to put a **cap** (highest limit) on the amount of the doctor's charges that they will pay. This cost containment can come in the form of paying only those fees the insurance company considers to be proper—what are called "usual, customary, and reasonable charges." Thus, in the scenario of the $2,000 medical charge, if the insurance company only allowed $1,600 as a usual, customary, and reasonable fee, the company would pay 80 percent of $1,600, or $1,280 (assuming a previously paid deductible). Their arbitrary determination would increase your copayment accordingly from $400 (20 percent of $2,000) to $720.

Another practice of some insurance companies is to publish a schedule of benefits that will be paid per diagnosis. These payment schedules are invariably far less than the actual fees charged by doctors. When that happens, the patient must pay the difference.

Consumer Alert

By limiting payments to "usual, customary, and reasonable" charges, insurance companies make it difficult for you to control your out-of-pocket expenses for medical care since you won't know what a "reasonable" charge is until you receive your benefit statement from the company.

However, you might be able to get around this problem by asking your doctor to accept what the insurance company pays as payment in full or, at least, to accept the insurance company's determination of a fair fee. It's worth a try. The worst thing that can happen is the doctor will say no.

Also, if you owe the doctor a significant amount of money for services not fully paid for by insurance, ask him or her to accept monthly payments. Most will be glad to accommodate you if they receive the bulk of their fees from insurance benefits and if the monthly payment you offer to make is a fair one.

Other Cost-Containment Provisions

There are other things that many traditional insurance policies require of their insureds in order for full benefits to be paid. Some of these policies involve the use of **medical review committees** that work for the insurance company. These medical review committees will look over your doctor's shoulder to make sure that unnecessary treatment is not rendered. *It is vital that you understand your company's rules regarding cost containment* if you are to avoid having to pay for treatment yourself or getting into a major conflict with your carrier.

Most company cost-containment provisions include the following.

Same-day admission for surgery. It used to be that patients were admitted to the hospital the night before surgery. Today, many companies won't pay for this and require the patient to go into the hospital the *morning of surgery*. They claim that this is just as safe for the patient, but we note that when Mrs. Reagan had her mastectomy, she was admitted the night before surgery. So was Mrs. Ford. So was Ronald Reagan before his colon surgery. Maybe that tells us something.

Pre-admission testing. It is less expensive for the insurance company if the tests that must be taken before admission to a hospital are made on an outpatient basis. As a result, most policies require you to undergo pre-admission testing in non-emergency situations.

Outpatient surgery. There is a growing trend for insurance companies to insist that minor surgeries be performed on an outpatient basis. This means that all recovery is done at home.

Second-opinion requirements. In nonemergency situations, many insurance companies require you to get a second opinion before submitting to surgery in order for you to receive full benefits. Since studies have found that many surgeries are unnecessary (particularly hysterectomies and cesarean sections), this requirement may do you a very big favor.

Prior consent for hospitalization. Some policies will not pay full benefits for hospitalization unless the company agrees ahead of time that it is required (in nonemergency situations).

Managed care. Increasingly, insurers are insisting on "managing" your health care as a way to reduce their costs. Usually this means getting prior approval for hospitalization and some forms of medical treatment. For example, under many managed care programs, the insurer will not only require pre-approval of hospitalization, but their review staff will determine whether your hospitalization is "medically necessary." If they conclude it is not, you will receive no benefits to pay for the hospitalization. Also, the managed care staff may approve treatment, but in a different, less expensive manner than that suggested by your doctor. Fail to follow the staff's decision and there will be a reduction or an elimination of benefits. If hospitalization is approved, the managed care staff will specify the number of days you will be permitted to stay in the hospital and receive insurance benefits. Managed care can also apply to long-term illness or recovery from injuries where a case manager determines the parameters of care that will be allowed under the insurance policy. Managed care is being touted as an effective method of reducing insurance company costs. But it can also be used as a mechanism for rationing needed health care.

It is vital that you understand your responsibilities under the managed care provisions of your health insurance policy. If you have any questions about your policy's managed care provisions, be sure to contact your plan administrator and get educated.

The appropriateness of care given. Some insurance companies have become so involved in cost containment that they sometimes second-guess the total scope of your doctor's treatment. In such cases, the company may even *refuse payment* if they disagree with the manner in which your doctor proceeded with your care.

Hospice Care

Many policies will pay for hospice services for the treatment of terminally ill patients. The focus of hospice care is not to save the patient's life but to make it more comfortable, thereby allowing the patient to die with dignity. Less expensive than fighting the terminal illness to the bitter end in the hospital (using respirators and other wonders of medical science to keep the patient alive), hospice care can take place in the home or in a hospital unit set aside for the terminally ill.

The above coverages usually have a lifetime cap on benefits, which might not be high enough to pay for a catastrophic illness that requires long-term care and hundreds of thousands of dollars to treat. That is why everyone who can afford it should also purchase major medical protection (also called a catastrophic care policy).

Major Medical

Major medical policies are designed to supplement your basic policy protection provided through hospitalization and S&M coverages and to pay for just about everything you need while recovering from a catastrophic condition. These include:

A High Total Benefit Package

One of the important provisions of these policies is a high maximum level of benefits, typically $1 million. You should not elect to be protected for less than $1 million unless you can't afford full coverage.

Extended Hospital Stays

Any basic hospitalization policy will limit the number of days you can receive benefits per hospital stay. Major medical will pay for hospitalization that goes beyond the basic plan maximums.

Extended Home Care

Often, catastrophic care involves extended periods of recuperation at home using private nurses and other health professionals to assist with care. Usually, the basic coverages do not pay for most of these services, or if they do it will be only for a brief period of time. A major medical plan will often cover these important health services for an extended period. The same applies for extended periods of physical therapy, speech therapy, or respiratory therapy.

Durable Medical Equipment

Some illnesses or injuries require the continuing use of durable medical equipment such as respirators, special toilets, wheelchairs, and the like. Often the basic policies do not pay for these items, or do so only for a limited time. Major medical policies, on the other hand, pay for these life-saving or quality-of-life-enhancing tools over the long haul. (Durable medical equipment is especially vital for those who become handicapped by their medical catastrophe. Wheelchairs and catheters can make the difference between a wasted life and one that can still be pursued productively and enjoyably.)

Skilled Nursing Home Care

If a patient needs to be placed into a skilled nursing home, major medical will cover the tab. It will not, as a general rule, pay for unskilled nursing, also known as custodial care. (There are insurance policies on the market that do cover convalescent home care. For discussion of these policies, please refer to Chapter 36.)

Prescription Costs

The basic plans generally don't pay for prescription expenses, although some, especially large group plans, do. Major medical policies usually do cover most prescription expenses.

Processing the Forms

Last but not least, let's take a brief look at how health insurance benefits are processed. This is no small subject. A recent study indicates that $50 billion per year is spent on billing and collecting fees for Medicare and insurance companies.

In order to obtain benefits, you have to file a claim form. (For more information on claims, see Chapter 41). This bit of bureaucracy is a necessary evil. Luckily, many doctors will process the claim forms for you, either as a goodwill gesture or at extra charge. If your doctor will do this, by all means let his or her trained staff assist with this vital piece of work.

There are two ways in which your health insurance benefits will be paid.

1. You pay the doctor and the company repays you. Or,

2. The company pays the doctor directly and you pay him or her the difference that has not been paid by insurance benefits.

If the doctor will process the claim and submit it for you in order to receive direct payment from the company (option 2 above), he or she **accepts the assignment** of benefits that would normally be due to you. This approach is easier on you and on your pocketbook and should be your preferred method of handling your health insurance business with your doctor. Thus, always ask if your doctor will accept assignment.

Whether or not the doctor accepts assignment, the insurance company will issue you statements explaining why and how benefits were paid or denied. Be sure you understand these statements and keep copies for your records. And if you disagree with your company's actions, don't hesitate to let them know. (See Part 8.)

Incomplete Coverage for Preventive Care

One of the most important things you can do as a health care consumer is to engage in preventive care. Not only will you be able to spot serious diseases at an early stage, thereby increasing your chances of effective treatment and cure, but you should be able to save money as well, since it is usually far less expensive to treat a disease when it's a molehill rather than a mountain.

Unfortunately, most traditional health insurance policies *do not* pay benefits for the most important preventive medical procedures. Although policies differ (be sure to read yours), the chart on pages 162–163 is a good summary of which types of insurance cover the various preventive care procedures.

WHO COVERS PREVENTIVE PROCEDURES?

Procedure	Purpose/Cost*	Recommended Frequency	Insurance Coverage
Mammogram	Early detection of breast cancer. $50 to $150.	Every two years for women over 50; recommendations for women in 30's and 40's vary.	Medicare: none. Private: 30 states require some coverage.
Sigmoidoscopy	Early detection of colon cancer. About $200.	Often recommended every three to five years after 50, sometimes for high-risk individuals only.	Medicare: none. Private: none.
Cholesterol screening	Detection of high cholesterol, which can lead to coronary artery disease. $7 to $20.	Every five years for those over 20; applicability to women and the elderly unclear.	Medicare: none. Private: none.
Blood pressure measurement	Detection of hypertension, which raises risk of stroke, heart disease, etc. May be part of office visit.	Most recommend test every two to five years for those over 20, with increasing frequency for the elderly.	Medicare: none. Private: none.
Pap smear	Early detection of cervical and uterine cancer. $20 to $48.	Annually for women over 18; after three negative smears, doctor may cut frequency to every three years.	Medicare: covered as of July 1, 1990. Private: generally none.
Professional breast examination	Early detection of breast cancer. May be part of office visit.	Every year.	None.

Procedure	Purpose/Cost*	Recommended Frequency	Insurance Coverage
Influenza vaccine	Gives some immunity to influenza A and B. $10 to $30.	Annually for people over 65.	Medicare: none. Private: none.
Tetanus immunization	Protection against tetanus. May be part of office visit.	Every 10 years.	Medicare: none. Private: none.
Pneumococcal vaccine	Protection against infections from common pneumonia-causing bacteria, pneumococcus. $15 to $20.	At least once; length of immunity uncertain.	Medicare: covered. Private: Usually not covered.
Counseling	May be part of office visit.	As needed.	Not covered.
Tonometry	Early detection of glaucoma. $20 to $30.	Data unclear, but some screening considered prudent after 65.	Medicare: none. Private: none.

*Does not include office visit fee.
Copyright © 1990 by The New York Times Company. Reprinted by permission.

As the costs of medical care, and thus insurance, have skyrocketed in recent years, there has been a revolution in health insurance. New forms of coverage have come onto the market that vary from the fee-for-service health insurance described above. These policies, designed to be cost-effective, are the subject of our next chapter.

16

HMOs and PPOs

In recent years, a financial crisis has descended on the field of medicine as the cost of medical care has skyrocketed, almost without regard for what is true, proper, and just. Doctors have been accused of ordering unnecessary tests and of keeping patients in hospitals for too long, while the fees charged by specialist consultants have soared. There seems to be no limit on how high the price of good health care can go.

This out-of-control inflation has triggered increases in health insurance premiums that could turn your hair white. The industry is well aware that they are pricing health insurance to the point where people can no longer afford it. Thus, they are working to keep the increase in premiums to a minimum (or so they claim). The rallying cry of the industry in this battle has become "cost containment," as insurance plan after insurance plan seeks to adjust its way of doing business to keep accounts payable in line, and thus premium increases from going through the roof.

Out of this quest for cost containment have come two new major types of insurance plans whose purpose it is to control the cost of medical care, with the savings supposedly passed on to you by way of lower premiums. These two new players are the **health maintenance organization (HMO)** and the **preferred provider organization (PPO)**.

Health Maintenance Organizations

In a sense, HMOs are a form of socialized medicine, capitalism style. In socialized medicine, taxes help pay for the cost of all citizens' health care. Beyond the money you pay to the government (which can be considerable), there are few health care costs you have to pay out of your own pocket. And, in theory, your basic medical needs are guaranteed to be taken care of—everything from the prescribing of antibiotics to heart bypass surgery.

This is similar to the way an HMO works. Instead of the government paying the tab, you do through premiums paid to the health maintenance organization plan. These premiums are sometimes paid by individuals and sometimes by a group for its members.

When you join an HMO, you are called a **plan member**. As a member you are entitled to receive all of the health care you need, including preventive health services, with very little money coming out of your pocket by way of copayments or deductibles. Thus, the primary benefit of an HMO is almost complete *control over out-of-pocket health care expenses*. Once your premiums have been paid, you're home free.

What's the catch, you ask? Good question. Well, it's this: If you join an HMO, in all but *life-threatening* emergency situations *you must use the doctors and facilities authorized by the HMO*. In other words, in return for lower premiums and little or no copayments, you *give up your freedom of choice*. You can only use doctors approved by the HMO.

This lack of freedom of choice can cause problems. While most HMOs have a wide selection of primary care physicians, they usually have far fewer subspecialists (such as cardiologists, gastroenterologists, rheumatologists, etc.) who are authorized to handle specialty care. And if you should need a subspecialist, your doctor may be reluctant to refer you since pressure is brought to bear on HMO physicians to keep costs down. Moreover, when a referral is made, it may not be to the best subspecialist your doctor knows since he or she can only refer you to doctors who work with the HMO. Your choice of hospitals is also limited to those owned or authorized by the plan.

HMOs put heavy emphasis on cost-cutting because their profits come from doing *less* rather than doing more. Some HMO members complain that this emphasis on saving money makes it difficult for them to receive all the care they require, especially in the area of diagnostic testing.

Types of HMOs

There are three different types of HMOs, each of which puts a slightly different twist on the way health benefits are delivered to plan members.

The group model. Although the first group model was established in 1929 at a cooperatively owned hospital in Elk City, Oklahoma, by Michael Shadid, the most famous group model HMO is probably Kaiser Permanente, located in California and several other states. Group models are essentially partnerships among the medical plan, usually a large number of doctors who work within the HMO (called the group) and sometimes hospitals (as with Kaiser). The plan will only refer you to doctors in the group. In return, doctors will not work for anyone who is not a member of the plan. The doctors work in clinics and hospitals that are either partners in the HMO or contract with it to provide services. At the Puget Sound Health Cooperative in Seattle, decisions about patient care are made with the patient, the plan, and the doctors, with a lot of peer oversight to make sure costs are kept down and the quality of care is kept high.

The staff model. In staff type HMOs, the doctors are not equal partners with the plan but, rather, are employees of the plan. This means the plan has a lot of power (the power of an employer) over how patients are treated, since the doctors are hired as individuals and do not have the clout of a group behind them. Most treatment is done at plan-owned hospitals and clinics, and only plan doctors can treat plan members. Doctors in staff type HMOs, like group systems, can only work for the HMO and do not have individual practices.

The IPA Model. IPA stands for **independent physician association**. An IPA is a group of doctors who, for the limited purpose of working with an HMO, form a legal entity that contracts with the health plan. In other words, doctors who are in private practice, and who cooperate with traditional health insurance companies, can at the same time be members of an IPA model HMO. However, unlike the referrals that might be made in a traditional health insurance situation, if the case comes to the doctor from the HMO, he or she can only use plan-authorized physicians for referrals and can only hospitalize patients in plan contract hospitals.

Criticisms of HMOs

The recent expansion of HMOs into a significant force in the health care marketplace has created a controversy over the quality of care given by them. This is because the profit margin in an HMO is increased when the extent of medical care is decreased. Most complaints about HMOs concern the following.

Insufficient testing. Some plan members complain that it is hard to get the HMO to adequately test them regarding their health complaints. Of course, traditional health insurance administrators complain that *too much* testing goes on.

Time delays. Some HMOs are well known for the waits required both to get in to see a doctor and to obtain medical tests.

Difficulty in getting nonplan emergency room treatment. When we suddenly become ill or are injured, our first instinct is to get to the nearest emergency room, pronto. However, if you are an HMO plan member, you may not be able to get authorization for treatment unless the situation is a matter of life and death. When nonplan testing and treatment is allowed, it is often given piecemeal, requiring far more time in the emergency room than would otherwise be the case. Should you decide to go ahead with treatment without authorization, you may have to pay the bill yourself.

Difficulty in getting treatment outside the plan area. If you are outside the geographic area covered by the HMO and require medical treatment, you may find it difficult to obtain quick approval in non-life-threatening situations.

Difficulty in getting specialists. HMOs may be less likely to allow their primary care physicians to refer a difficult case to a specialist or to several specialists. This can create a conflict between patient and doctor or member and plan administration. The following is a true story of such a difficulty (the names have been changed to protect the privacy of the family).

Todd is six years old. During the fall, he suddenly began to experience an abrupt increase in his rate of urination. At one point, he was urinating over 50 times per day. This situation forced the boy out of school.

The family's HMO pediatrician did his best to treat Todd but to no avail. The desperate parents asked the doctor to refer the case to a pediatric urologist. The plan refused until certain tests were run, which would take several months to schedule. Besides, they said, they suspected a psychological cause. Meanwhile, the boy was out of school and semisuicidal over his predicament.

The parents refused to take the HMO attitude lying down. Todd's mother hit the local medical library and did some research. She discovered that there are highly trained specialists who handle cases such as her son's. She begged the plan to allow her to consult one of the specialists. The plan refused. Putting their son's health before the family pocketbook, the parents nevertheless consulted the specialist, who came up with a diagnosis and surgical treatment.

Happily, the treatment worked and the boy returned to nearly normal urination patterns. Thinking the plan would be happy the problem had been solved, the parents requested reimbursement for the more than $3,500 they had spent to help their son. The plan refused and forced the parents to choose between doing nothing and an arbitration that would have cost them as much as the bill itself (see Part 8). Luckily, the group insurance that provided the health insurance for the family allowed them to choose how they wished to be covered: either an HMO or traditional health insurance. After this incident the family left the HMO and entered into a fee-for-service arrangement, which would pay for the subspecialist should the boy need his services again.

Postscript: After a year or so with the traditional health insurance plan, Todd's folks are back with the HMO, "with caution," as the mother says. The reason? Money. The traditional health insurance plan, although available through the group, cost the family $2,000 a year more than the HMO in premiums. At such rates, freedom of choice was more than the family could afford, despite their unhappiness with the HMO concept.

If you join an HMO, you may have to change doctors. If you have had traditional health insurance and join an HMO, you may have to give up a doctor who has treated you for a long time and whom you trust, unless that doctor practices in an IPA that has a contract with your HMO. Good doctors are hard to find, and changing doctors is something most of us don't relish.

The Sunny Side of the HMO Street

Notwithstanding the above criticism, a lot of people actually prefer HMOs. These contented souls generally point to the following in support of their preference.

Lower premiums. As stated, HMOs generally charge less for their coverage than do traditional health insurance companies.

No copayments or deductibles. We've said it before but it bears repeating: With HMOs there are little or no deductibles or copayments. This can save you thousands of dollars a year.

Prescriptions are paid. In most if not all HMOs the cost of prescriptions is borne by the plan with little or no copayment by the member. The same cannot be said of many traditional health insurance plans.

You can choose your own primary care physician. While HMOs require members to select their doctor from a list, the number of available primary care physicians is usually quite high. Thus, most people can find a doctor they like. Moreover, if you are dissatisfied with a doctor, it is usually easy to get a change approved.

Preventive health care is covered. Most traditional health plans pay little or no benefits for preventive care such as regular, nonsymptomatic physical examinations. Not so with HMOs. Of all of the benefits of an HMO, preventive care is one of the most important. As a nation we put too little stress on preventing illness. *Good* HMOs do just the opposite. They put great emphasis on catching illness or disease early, thereby saving the plan money and increasing the chances of a successful course of treatment. Most traditional health plans pay little or no benefits for preventive care such as general physicals.

In group and staff model HMOs, your records are always available. Because doctors at group and staff HMOs take care of their patients from the HMO facility, the patient records will always be available at a moment's notice, even when the doctor is not available.

To HMO or not to HMO, That Is the Question

Should you go with a traditional fee-for-service method of health insurance or choose an HMO? As with most issues such as this, there just isn't one right answer. Choosing the way to go will depend on your personal needs and preferences. Studies seem to indicate a high level of satisfaction on the part of HMO members. In fact, over 32 million Americans are serviced by over 600 different HMOs in the United States. On the other hand, there is an increasing number of bankruptcies in the HMO industry, and unfortunate stories abound like that of Todd's family described above.

There is one thing we can say for sure: If you decide the HMO concept is right for you and your family, be sure to be an *assertive* plan member. Be prepared to fight, if necessary, to make sure that you receive the care and treatment you are entitled to. Don't be afraid to urge doctors to give you good service. Complain to plan administration whenever the plan falls short. In short, be the squeaky wheel. You will be much more likely to get the grease.

Consumer Alert

If you are a Medicare recipient, you can trade your government benefits for membership in an HMO. This issue will be discussed in Chapter 33.

Preferred Provider Organizations

Many of the traditional health insurance carriers have responded to the out-of-control inflation in the medical industry and the economic challenge of HMOs by devising a hybrid type of insurance plan called a preferred provider organization, or PPO for short.

The PPO works as follows. Your health insurance company, employer, union, or other deliverer of group health protection signs contracts with doctors, hospitals, and other health service providers to supply health care at a discount price.

In return, the service providers receive monthly payments called **capitation** for each person serviced by the PPO. If the cost of care exceeds the capitation fee, the doctor or other service provider will be paid by the plan for the extra care, usually at a discount price.

If you utilize PPO contract physicians and hospitals, it will cost you less than if you use physicians who are not in the plan. Frequently, the health care provider will accept your insurance benefits as payment in full. In other words, the copayments required of traditional health insurance consumers may be done away with altogether if the "preferred provider" is utilized.

Deductibles generally work in the same way as they do in traditional fee-for-service insurance.

Costs for PPOs are kept down as they are in HMOs by rewarding cost efficiency and penalizing overutilization of services. It is also important to remember that unauthorized treatment from nonpreferred service providers (in other than life-or-death situations) can leave you exposed to an obligation to pay a substantial copayment.

If you are interested in the PPO concept, be sure to find out whether you need to add a major medical provision to the basic policy, since many limits on care exist similar to those of traditional insurance. A major medical policy should not be required in an HMO, since your monthly premiums entitle you to receive all of the care you need.

How to Choose a Good HMO/PPO Plan

Make sure the HMO or PPO provides, at minimum, the following services (which are required in order to meet federal approval standards):

- Physician services, including referrals to specialists.

- Inpatient and outpatient hospital services.

- Short-term mental health services sufficient to provide crisis intervention and evaluation capabilities.

- Medical services for chemical dependency or substance abuse.

- Preventive health, including immunizations, well child care, regular adult health evaluations, family planning, and children's eye and ear examinations.

Other Questions to Ask

Here are some other questions to ask the sales or group health insurance representative if you are thinking of joining an HMO or PPO.

What are the credentials of the authorized plan physicians? Any plan that restricts your freedom to choose doctors is only as good as the doctors who are on staff. Thus, you want to find out about the quality of doctors you can choose from. For example, are all primary care specialists board certified in either internal medicine or family care (for adults) or pediatrics or family care (for children)? Board certification does not guarantee quality of care but does show that the doctor in question had the intelligence and commitment to take extra training and education and to pass a national test.

Which hospitals are available? All hospitals are not created equal. Some simply provide better patient care. Ask the hospital what its rating by the Joint Committee on the Accreditation of Hospitals (JCAH) is. (Three years accreditation is best; probation or no accreditation, worse.) Call your state department of health to see if there are any serious complaints on file against the hospital. Check to see if there is a high level of incidental infections.

What is the policy toward emergency services? It is important to know your rights and responsibilities toward emergency situations when you might not be able to get to an authorized service provider.

Where are the authorized facilities located? If you have trouble getting around, the locale of authorized service providers will be especially important. If you can't use the facilities because of their location, what good is the money you have saved by joining an HMO or PPO?

Can you see the same doctor every time? Having your own doctor is an important part of an effective health care strategy. This may be particularly important if you are in an HMO or PPO where great emphasis is put on saving costs and where a good relationship with your doctor may make the difference in the energy he or she puts into getting you the extra services you may need.

What is the grievance procedure? If you end up in a squabble over your health care, you want grievance procedures that give you a fair chance to have your side of the controversy heard and acted upon. If the grievance procedure will cost you more money than the amount in dispute, you may be at the mercy of the consciences of the plan administrators.

What about issues of concern in traditional health insurance? Just because you are in a cost-reducing plan doesn't mean you should ignore important health insurance questions such as issues of renewability, preexisting conditions, and so on (see page 143).

One of the worst things that can happen to you in our defective health care delivery system is to lose the right to maintain group health insurance. At one time, losing coverage by the group meant you were immediately locked out of the benefits you had enjoyed. That may no longer be the case. We'll talk about this and steps you can take to protect your health coverage in our next chapter.

17

Filling the Gap
When You Lose
Group Coverage

Everyone reading these pages knows how important group health insurance is to maintaining quality coverage at a "reasonable" price. In fact, without groups, there would be a lot more people without health insurance than the 37 million Americans who don't have protection now.

But what happens if you lose your status as a group member? Unfortunately, such nightmares happen every day. For example, you lose your job and with it your "fringe benefits," which include health insurance. Or you get a divorce from a spouse who remains covered by group health insurance. Alas, once the marital knot is untied so is your connection with the group.

At one time, people who lost their group coverages had only two choices: buy coverage themselves or go without. And with the price of individual policies ranging between outrageous and exorbitant, too often the loss of group benefits left the formerly insured person as vulnerable as Eliza crossing the ice in *Uncle Tom's Cabin*.

Group Health Insurance Continuation Rights

Happily, things have changed for the better. Now, by federal law—i.e., the Congressional Omnibus Budget Reconciliation Act (COBRA) and a subsequent omnibus bill (OBRA)—you have the right to continue your group health insurance for a period of time after you lose your membership, if the group coverage was provided through employment or union membership. This additional protection can be crucial, especially if you have a preexisting condition or lack the funds to purchase a high-priced individual plan.

How COBRA Works

Not everyone who is a member of a group comes under the protection of the COBRA law. For those who do, here's how it works.

Widow/widower and children of a deceased covered employee. If you are the spouse of a group member who dies, you and your dependent children must be allowed to continue the group coverage for *three years* at the same price the insurance would have cost the employer (had the employee not died), plus a small administrative fee. There's only one catch: you have to pay for the coverage, but at least it's at group rather than individual rates.

Covered employee becomes eligible for Medicare. Companies usually stop providing group health insurance to employees at age 65 when they become eligible for Medicare. But what about the employee's spouse if he or she is not also eligible for Medicare? And what if the employee has kids who are otherwise eligible for group coverage? Well, the same rules apply as when an employee dies: three years of group coverage at group rates (on your dime).

Covered employee and spouse divorce. If you get a divorce and lose coverage under your former spouse's group insurance, you can continue coverage at your expense for three years. Some good news—the dependent children of the employee can still be protected by the employee's coverage. For example, if you are divorced and you are the noncovered spouse, you will lose group health insurance, but the dependent children of your former spouse will not. Thus, you'll only have to pay for your own coverage and you'll get group rates to boot.

Covered employee becomes unemployed. If you (or your spouse) lose your job or have your work hours reduced with a subsequent loss of group health insurance privileges, you can extend group coverage for *18 months*. (If the loss of the job was "for cause," this right may not apply.) If, during the 18 months, an event occurs (such as a death or divorce) that would have qualified the nonemployee to extend coverage, you can purchase additional coverage for up to 18 months.

Children who grow out of eligibility. When a child reaches majority, he or she usually loses the insurance protection that had been provided by a working parent's group health insurance. If that happens, COBRA allows the children to extend group coverage for three years at group rates.

Activating COBRA Benefits

Should you have to avail yourself of the protection of extending group health benefits, you must remember that the continuation of the coverage is *not automatic*. You must take affirmative action to make sure you obtain the extended coverage, and you *must do it in a timely manner*. Here's how matters are generally handled:

- **If your group eligibility is lost, the insurance company is notified by your former employer.**

- **The insurance company then sends out a notice within two weeks giving you information on con-**

tinued coverage. If you don't receive it, call the company and ask why.

- **The formerly eligible group member then has 60 days within which to accept the extension of group health insurance.** This time limit is *strictly enforced*, so be sure to communicate your acceptance *in writing*, sending the correspondence by registered mail, return receipt requested. Always keep copies of your correspondence and your receipt from the post office proving your letter was delivered.

- **If minor children come into adulthood, the employee must remember to inform the health carrier of the children's age.** The company then has two weeks to give the employee notification of the children's right to extend coverage. The acceptance of the children must also come within 60 days.

Importance of Continued Group Coverage

The importance of the right to extend group coverage cannot be overstated. By continuing coverage, the former group member receives the following important benefits:

- The right to continue to receive health insurance with no break in coverage.

- The right to buy health insurance for a price not otherwise obtainable.

- Relief from worrying about things such as preexisting conditions for the term of the continued coverage.

- Some breathing room within which to find new work or take other action to become eligible for another group's insurance.

If you continue group coverage, here are some other things you need to know:

- **If you don't pay your premiums you will lose your coverage.** You will not be able to get it back, either, at least not at group rates.

- **If you are eligible for continued coverage as the former spouse of a covered employee, you lose your rights to maintain the extended group insurance if you remarry.** This is true regardless of whether your new spouse is covered by group health insurance.

- **Once you become eligible for other group health insurance because of employment, your rights to continue on the old group plan end.**

- **If the former employer drops group coverage for current employees, yours ends too.**

Consumer Alert

COBRA-type benefits also apply if you are changing jobs. This is important if you have a preexisting-condition waiting period or other exclusions under your new employer's group plan. The maximum extension of group coverage in such cases is 18 months, and as with other COBRA rights, you will have to pick up the premium tab yourself.

Other Options If You Lose Group Coverage

If you are a member of a group insurance plan but are not in one governed by the federal law that permits you to extend your benefits, there may still be some things you can do if you lose your group benefits.

Convert Your Group Policy into an Individual Policy

Most group plans allow departing members to convert their insurance into an individual plan. And *you don't have to qualify for the converted policy, nor are there waiting periods or preexisting health exclusions* since your right to convert is usually built in to the group insurance contract itself. This can be very important to your future health insurance well-being, especially if your health history is such that you will find it difficult or impossible to obtain another insurance policy.

Before you decide to convert your group benefits into an individual health plan, you should check into the coverage and the price.

Coverage. Converted policies generally give you *fewer benefits* than you would have had under the group plan. That's because as an individual you lack the clout of the group.

Price. Even though your benefits in a converted policy will probably be lower, the *price will be higher*. Again, this is caused by the loss of the clout of the group and by the fact that you don't have to qualify as a standard or preferred risk when you convert to an individual health plan.

Thus, when deciding whether to convert your group benefits into an individual policy, be sure to compare the "converted plan" with the other plans on the market, including individual health carriers, HMOs, and PPOs. After all, it's better to pay a little more for your coverage if the benefits you thereby receive can save you money in case of health problems.

Purchase a Short-Term Policy

If you are between jobs or otherwise lose your group health insurance, you may wish to think about buying an interim policy to tide you over until your health insurance situation becomes more stabilized.

Short-term policies generally protect you for a period of two to six months. They often work similarly to traditional health insurance, covering basic hospitalization, surgical fees, laboratory tests, and doctor's services. There will be deductibles, usually around $500, and a copayment responsibility. Maximum benefits will be limited to less than you would receive from traditional renewable health insurance. But that is to be expected since the insurance is only intended as a stopgap measure until more permanent arrangements can be made. Most short-term policies are not renewable.

Sign Up on Your Spouse's Group Insurance Plan

Many of today's families have two wage earners. Often, the family has not taken advantage of a health plan available from one spouse's employment or trade association because the other spouse's group plan provided better benefits or a more reasonable price. However, the once-shunned group plan may begin to look awfully sweet when compared to the price and coverage of an individual policy—or, worse, no health protection at all.

Qualify for Group Rates Any Way You Can

Employment and union membership are not the only ways to be eligible for group health insurance. If you find yourself looking for health insurance and you don't qualify for a group plan through your work, find out if there is another possibility. You'll be surprised how easy it can be. For example, if you work in a trade, there are trade associations you can join that usually offer group insurance in addition to other support services. Large organizations, such as the American Association of Retired Persons, often offer insurance priced at group rates as a benefit of membership. Even credit card companies sometimes offer group health benefits to cardholders, although usually on a limited basis. The key is to review your circumstances and use your imagination. That group plan may be just around the corner.

Purchase an Individual or Family Policy

If push comes to shove and you can't find a good group rate, purchase an individual plan with the best benefits you can afford. Do this even if it means a leaner Christmas, putting off buying a new car, or wearing last year's fashions. Remember, living without health insurance is like playing financial Russian roulette; it is not a matter of whether disaster will strike, just a matter of when.

Consumer Alert

There may come a time when you should consider purchasing two health policies at the same time. Such drastic action might become necessary if you lose your group coverage and decide to purchase an individual policy. If the new policy has a waiting period before taking effect or does not cover preexisting conditions for a period of time, you may have to seriously consider converting or continuing group coverage *while at the same time* purchasing the individual policy. This would allow you to have uninterrupted health insurance protection while you are waiting for the new policy to go into full effect. Of course, once it does, you can drop the converted or continued group plan. We realize this means paying twice the premiums, but that is cheaper in the long run than facing a health crisis with no health insurance.

Look into State Health Insurance
Risk Pools

Some states have begun to create risk pools for persons whose health precludes them from obtaining an individual policy. If you are such a person, contact your local state legislator to see if such a pool exists in your state. Be warned, though, risk pools are expensive, so don't expect to get a good price. However, as the old saying goes, "any port in a storm."

So far, our discussion of health insurance, whether traditional fee-for-service, HMO, or PPO, has dealt with policies designed to pay for the costs of medical care. But there is another type of health insurance, one that protects your income if you become disabled. This insurance is called **disability insurance**, and it is our next topic.

18

Disability Insurance

Disability insurance can be as important to a good personal insurance backup system as health and life insurance are. It's fine to have the bulk of health expenses paid should a serious illness or incapacity strike, but that alone may not be enough to stave off family disaster brought on by the inability of a breadwinner to work.

Disability insurance is designed to pay monetary benefits during times when an illness or injury prevents the insured from earning an income. It is, in essence, an *income replacement policy*, which pays money when a disability arises from some cause recognized in the policy to qualify the insured for benefits.

What Is Disability?

When you are looking to purchase disability insurance, you need to know what the term *disability* means within the context of the policy. Be very careful here, because the manner in which the policy defines the term will determine what benefits you will receive if you can't work because of illness or injury.

Disability will usually be defined in one of the following ways:

- **The inability of the insured to work and perform the duties of his or her usual occupation, when the insured is not otherwise working.** The key phrase here is *usual occupation*. This does not mean the disability prevents you from doing anything, but from working in the job or occupation you are used to (which will often be listed in the application for insurance). Thus, a nurse who cannot give injections or render other medical care because of muscle weakness would be disabled. However, there is also the requirement that the disabled person is *not working* because of injury or disease. Thus, the nurse who cannot work with patients but who is given a job supervising other nurses would not be considered disabled.

- **The inability of the insured to perform duties in *any* occupation for which he or she should be able to work due to education, training, and experience.** This is a far more stringent definition. Under this concept of disability, not only would your usual occupation have to be out of the question, but any equivalent occupations. Thus, the nurse with the muscle problem who could work as a consultant, a teacher, or in some other nonnursing job, would probably not be considered disabled under this definition.

- **The inability of the insured to work at all.** Few injuries or illnesses are so bad that they fall under this strict standard. After all, most humans have the capacity to be productive unless they are comatose. This definition is rarely used in private disability policies.

Since the definition of disability has such a direct bearing on whether benefits will be paid, always look for the definition *in relation to the time periods during which the definition is in effect*, when you are looking for a policy to buy. For example, some policies utilize a version of the first definition (usual occupation) for the first two years and then require the disability to be so bad that it qualifies under the second definition (equivalent occupation) for benefits to continue.

Consumer Alert

Most policies require a *total* disability of the insured before benefits are payable. Thus, if you have only lost the capacity to perform some of the duties but not all of your occupation, the insurance company may call it a partial disability and refuse benefits. You may then find yourself involved in a lawsuit.

Causes of Disability

You will also want to see if the policy places any restrictions on the cause of disability. Some policies limit benefits to disabilities that have a specific cause, such as an accident, and exclude those that fall outside those listed in the policy, such as an illness. The better policies cover disability *whatever the cause*, and those are the kinds of policies you will want.

Some policies may also exclude disabilities created by accidents or hazards at work. These are called **nonoccupational policies**. The theory behind them is that workers compensation will pay for disabilities arising from employment activities or accidents (although such coverage can be woefully inadequate, as you shall see in our discussion of workers compensation in Chapter 37). On the other hand, **occupational policies** allow benefits regardless of the cause of disability, although they will usually reduce their benefits by any amount the insured receives from workers compensation. Thus, if the policy calls for $1,000 a month in benefits and the insured receives workers compensation of $450 a month, the policy may then pay only $550.

Exclusions

As you would expect, there are exclusions in disability policies that preclude the payment of any benefits. Typical exclusions include the following.

Suicide attempts. If you become disabled in the process of a suicide attempt, don't expect to receive benefits.

Drug abuse. If you become disabled through the use of illegal drugs, no benefits will be paid.

Plane crashes. If the disability arises from injuries in the crash of a *noncommercial* plane, the company will often deny benefits, unless the insured was not in the plane but injured on the ground.

Military service or acts of war. If a soldier is shot in war and becomes disabled, a private disability policy will not pay benefits.

Normal pregnancy. If a woman becomes pregnant and cannot work at her usual occupation, the policy will not pay. However, if complications in the pregnancy cause the work stoppage, benefits may be payable.

Benefits

The purpose of disability insurance is to replace lost employment income. However, that does not mean that the insurance company will sell you a policy that will replace *all* of the income you would lose should you become disabled. In fact, insurance companies will only sell you a policy that will pay about two-thirds of your normal income. The reasons for this are severalfold.

- **They want you to have an incentive to go back to work.** The way insurance companies look at it, if you were to receive as an insurance benefit 100 percent of the income you used to make, your desire to jump back into the old salt mine might be less than zealous. By limiting your benefits, they hope to increase your desire to get off of their dime and back onto your own.

- **You usually receive the benefits tax free.** If you become disabled and rely on your disability insurance for your livelihood, you usually don't have to pay income tax on the insurance money received. Thus, since most of us pay the government at least 33 percent of our earnings, we end up in about the same place.

- **It is anticipated that your expenses will be reduced.** If you are disabled, the company anticipates that your out-of-pocket living expenses will be less than when you were in good health. Of course, this doesn't include medical expenses, but you should have a good medical policy to take care of those costs. *If you don't, finding one should probably take priority over purchasing disability insurance.*

The amount you receive may also be reduced if you are the beneficiary of other disability funds such as Social Security, workers compensation, or state disability. This is especially true in group policies.

It is also important to know *when and for how long* you are entitled to receive benefits. Disability policies have designated waiting periods before they will pay benefits. These waiting periods are often called **elimination periods**. In essence they act as a form of deductible, only expressed in *time* rather than dollars.

If you regain your ability to work during the waiting period, the company will owe you no benefits.

The elimination period will vary from policy to policy. Generally, the wait is rather long, ranging from a few months to even years. However, some policies allow for immediate benefits if the disability was caused by an accident.

Most disability policies also have a *time limit* during which benefits are payable, often called the **benefits period**. The policy may run for a period of years or until a certain age is reached, often 65. Short-term disability policies generally run to a maximum of two years, while long-term policies obviously run much longer.

Some policies provide benefits for a continuing **partial disability**. Others allow riders such as a **cost-of-living rider**, which increases the benefit as the cost of living rises. Most disability policies also include a waiver of premiums benefit, similar to those found in life insurance policies (see page 330).

Benefits are usually paid in weekly or monthly increments. However, sometimes the company will pay the insured a lump sum for the disability as a buy-out of the insurance company's obligation. In addition, some policies provide for lump-sum payments, especially if the disability was caused by an accidental dismemberment.

Some policies agree to pay to help a disabled person receive training in a new line of work after a disability strikes. Usually, such action is at the discretion of the insurance company.

How Much Disability Insurance Should You Buy?

To determine how much disability insurance you need, fill out the income and expense work sheet in the life insurance section of this book (see page 281). This will tell you how much you earn and spend per month. Then, do a little research. Find out how much you would receive from Social Security, state disability, any group disability you may be entitled to, and any other source. Subtract the benefits you would receive from the expenses you will incur each month, and you should have a pretty good idea of how much disability insurance to buy. This will also help save you money since you will probably not be overinsured.

Consumer Alert

If you want to save money when you purchase a disability policy:

- **Increase the length of the waiting period.**

- **Reduce the percentage of income that you will receive upon disability. (This may not be a sacrifice once you determine the extent of other disability benefits to which you may be entitled.) And/or:**

- **Shorten the length of time the insurance company will have to pay benefits.**

Final Comments

If you are thinking of purchasing a disability policy, remember the following:

- **Make sure you have the right to renew.** Guaranteed renewability is just as important in disability insurance as it is in traditional health insurance.

- **Make sure you pay your premiums in a timely fashion.** Most policies have a grace period (typically

30 days), but failure to pay premiums on time can result in cancellation of your policy. And with the ironic way life sometimes works, disability would probably strike when you no longer had insurance protection. *Don't let such a double tragedy ever happen to you!*

- **Make sure you understand the time limits for filing a claim.** You must report the disability to the insurance company and keep them apprised of your condition in a timely manner. Understanding *your* obligations in this regard will keep the company from having an excuse with which to wiggle out of its obligations.

- **Make sure you have enough savings to see you through the elimination period.** Disability insurance is designed to keep the wolf from your family door. However, if you are already broke by the time your benefits kick in, the money you receive may not be enough to keep hearth and home together. Thus, try to have a nest egg set aside to pay your expenses until you qualify for benefits.

- **Purchase disability insurance through a group if you can.** Just as with health insurance, the power of a group usually means you can obtain higher benefits for a lower price. However, many group policies only offer partial protection. If that is the situation you find yourself in, see about *purchasing a supplemental individual policy with a rider that allows you to increase your benefits* should you need them in the future.

19

Consumers' Agenda

If there is one thing that can be said for the health care delivery system in the United States, it is this: To put it bluntly, it is falling apart piece by piece. The cost of medicine is way too high; those people most in need of medical insurance often can't get it; and those who can get insurance, whether a company in private enterprise or a family of four, are paying through the nose for diminishing levels of protection. Clearly, something must be done.

The United States is the only industrialized nation other than South Africa that does not provide some form of universal health care for its citizens. Instead, we've bought the line of the health insurance companies that *they* are the answer to ensuring health care access to Americans.

Yet, a look at the record proves their answer rates a grade of "incomplete." What health insurance companies are really about is earning profits—or, at the very least, not losing money if they are nonprofit organizations. In and of itself, that is certainly a worthy thing, but it comes at a terrible cost to millions of people who can't get health insurance.

Currently over 37 million people in the United States have no health insurance. For some, the cost is just too high. When it comes to choosing between health insurance and feeding the kids, food has to win every time. Of course, they can always go on welfare, but that option is not available to working folk. Besides, Americans simply should not have to become indigent to receive a decent standard of medical treatment.

Beyond the cost, others can't buy health insurance at all, not because they can't afford it but because they need it, *now*—and if there is one thing health insurance companies don't want to do, it is to insure people who are ill or have a demonstrated need for coverage. Bad business, don't you know.

There are a myriad of proposals for change. We will look at some of these and offer our suggestions to the question, Where do we go from here?

The Canadian System of Universal Health Insurance

Many of us in the United States look longingly at Canada's system of universal health insurance. Canada, like the United States, has a federal system with a national government and 12 provincial governments, similar to our states. The Canadian system, called **Medicare**, is funded jointly by the federal government and each province, not unlike our Medicaid system of medical insurance for the poor (see Chapter 34).

In essence, the Canadian health care system is really 12 different systems, since each province has a different benefit package. However, there are minimum standards of coverage that each province must provide. The system guarantees the following coverages:

- **Medically necessary hospital care.** This includes inpatient and outpatient treatment of acute illnesses (such as a heart attack or pneumonia), rehabilitative conditions, or chronic conditions (such as diabetes or arthritis).

- **Medically necessary physician care.**

- **Surgical-dental services where a hospital is required for the proper delivery of services.**

In essence, the items covered are equivalent to a good fee-for-service health insurance plan. Beyond these basics, provinces may at their discretion cover some of the costs of "extended health care," which includes nursing home intermediate care, adult residential care, home care, and ambulatory health care. Grants from the national government help the provinces pay for these services.

The only criterion for eligibility in the health care system is residency. The waiting period for residency cannot exceed three months. If a resident of one province is temporarily in another province, they are entitled to full services at no extra charge.

The Canadian Health Act penalizes physicians and dentists for billing extra for covered services. This means that the doctor or dentist is only entitled to receive what the health system agrees to pay. Hospitals are likewise penalized for charging fees beyond what the system pays for acute, rehabilitative, or chronic health care. However, chronic care charges for meals and accommodations are permitted.

Let's get down to brass tacks and show how user-friendly this health care system really can be. Most services, as stated above, are free ("paid for by the taxpayers" might be more accurate). However, some extra charges are permitted. For example, the province of British Columbia charges a nominal fee per day for emergency services or a hospital bed. Alberta is much tougher, charging more than $20 per day for a hospital bed. Imagine the nerve—$20! Some provinces charge nothing at all.

▶ **NOTE:** It is interesting to note that the United States spends 12 percent of its gross national product for grossly incompetent health care, while Canada spends only 9 percent for broader coverage.

The Canadian plan does have some problems. Sometimes there is a waiting list for life-sustaining surgery. Emergency rooms are often overcrowded and the costs to the taxpayers are rising. There is also a shortage of funds available for capital improvement for hospitals, most of which are nonprofit institutions.

Yet, person for person, dollar for dollar, the average Canadian has access to quality care without the out-of-pocket burdens that Americans have to face.

The Oil, Chemical and Atomic Workers International Union, AFL-CIO (OCAW) endorses the National Health Program (NHP) advanced by the Physicians for a National Health Program and modeled after the 20-year-old Canadian health care system. According to the OCAW:

> Every Canadian is fully covered by the government insurance program and can go for care to any hospital or doctor in the country. Since the public program covers the costs for everyone, private insurance has been phased out. Hospitals and doctors get all their payments from the National Health Program, and have been able to eliminate most of the expensive billing bureaucracy. A typical Canadian hospital has three people in its billing office who use a single personal computer. A comparable American hospital employs 50 billing clerks and a $2 million billing computer.
>
> Canada also saves money because since the public insurance pays all the bills, it is able to closely regulate doctors' fees and hold down exorbitant hospital spending. With a single payor, cost containment is possible—as you can see, all health care dollars flow from a single spigot as opposed to the U.S. where the health care dollars flow from thousands of spigots. You can see the advantage when attempting to control costs.
>
> As a result, every Canadian gets free, comprehensive, high-quality care, and costs are 30 percent lower than in the U.S. In summary, an NHP would improve access; minimize bureaucracy; cover all Americans; provide free choice of physicians, clinics, hospitals; and abolish discriminatory private insurance.*

*OCAW National Health Care Information Manual. Published by the Oil, Chemical and Atomic Workers International Union, AFL-CIO. For further information, contact "Cradle to Grave" OCAW National Health Program, PO Box 2812, Denver, Colorado 80201, (303) 987-2229.

We should consider the benefits of such a plan. Sure, the tax costs would rise, but at a concurrent savings from insurance premiums. We have a lot we can learn from our Canadian cousins, and it's high time we began the process of doing so.

The American Medical Association (AMA) Plan

Physicians are not oblivious to the inequities of our health care delivery system. They realize that the uninsured are mostly unable to obtain quality health care. They also know that bringing those unfortunate folks under some form of health insurance umbrella will help these potential patients without hurting the doctors' financial statements.

The medical establishment, which finds its loudest voice in the AMA, strongly believes in the traditional fee-for-service approach to medical care. Their current proposals are geared toward maintaining this approach. The AMA position has two principal parts, one arising out of the private sector and the other from government benefits.

The AMA Plan for Uninsured Workers

The first part of the AMA plan covers employed uninsured workers, who, according to AMA studies, constitute 75 to 80 percent of the populace not protected by insurance. The AMA proposes the following.

Employers should be required to provide adequate health insurance for their employees. The AMA believes that employers should be required by law to provide health insurance for their full-time employees. This requirement would be phased in over a period of years starting with larger companies. In order to soften the financial blow, tax credits would offset some of the additional costs companies would incur. Part-time employees would evidently not be covered by this proposal, depending on how the term *full-time* is defined. This loophole would probably be recognized by many employers, leading them to hire fewer full-time workers. (One large retail chain already embodies this policy to avoid having to pay employee benefits.)

State pools would be created to assist small businesses in obtaining reasonably priced coverage. The AMA recognizes that small businesses would not have the clout to purchase quality group coverage at a reasonable price. Therefore, they recommend the expansion of **multiple employer trusts (METs)**, where many small businesses pool their health insurance purchasing powers to be able to negotiate a favorable group policy.

AMA's Plan for Uninsurable Citizens and Those in Need

The AMA estimates that the majority of the currently uninsured would find protection in the above proposed laws. However, they recognize that a significant number of people would remain unprotected. These include, according to AMA estimates, about 11 million who live below the poverty level and 1 million who are uninsurable or unable to afford individual policies. For these people in need, the AMA proposes an increase in state and federal government involvement, including the following.

The standardization of Medicaid eligibility requirements for all states. Currently, Medicaid, the medical program to assist the poor with their medical care (see Chapter 34), has widely diverse eligibility requirements among the states that administer the programs. The AMA believes this can be resolved by federal regulation standardizing eligibility while allowing each state to adjust for its own economic circumstances. The point would be to catch those individuals who fall between the cracks of the current system of Medicaid.

The creation of basic national minimum benefit standards. Each state's program would have to meet minimum national standards in terms of benefits provided. This would eliminate the inequities in the current system, which finds Medicaid recipients receiving superior benefits in some states and inferior benefits in others.

Sufficient physician and hospital reimbursement to assure broad access to health care for the poor. The way the AMA figures it, payments to doctors and hospitals must be high enough to make sure that providing care to the poor will be worth the while of the health care providers.

The AMA also recommends that **risk pools** be established in each state that will provide health insurance coverage for the uninsurable and for medically standard risks who cannot afford rates for individual coverage. The coverage would be sufficient to ensure care and the premiums priced at a slightly higher level than a comparable group policy. For those who are close to the poverty level, the AMA proposes publicly funded vouchers to help pay for the pool coverage.

The Kennedy Proposal

Senator Edward M. Kennedy (Democrat, Massachusetts) has proposed a new law entitled "The Basic Health Benefits for All Americans Act." According to Senator Kennedy, not only are 37 million Americans uninsured, but 60 million more have insurance that is inadequate to pay the expenses of serious illness. Annually, 2.5 million people are crushed by the costs of catastrophic illness, and over 15 million Americans each year are turned away from health coverage or do not seek it because of the cost.

The purpose of the Kennedy plan is to erase this disgraceful situation. The proposal consists, in part, of a law requiring employers to provide basic health coverage in the same way they must pay a minimum wage. This provision is similar to the AMA proposal, with the following specifics:

- **A full-time worker would be defined as a worker who normally works more than 17½ hours per**

Consumer Alert

The idea of risk pools is gaining acceptance among the various states. Currently, 15 states have enacted legislation authorizing risk pools: Connecticut, Florida, Illinois, Indiana, Iowa, Minnesota, Montana, Nebraska, New Mexico, North Dakota, Oregon, Rhode Island, Tennessee, Washington, and Wisconsin.

Contact the authorities in your state for information on how the risk pools operate, or to review plans to create risk pools in your state if they do not already exist.

week. This would eliminate any loophole whereby employers would hire mostly part-time workers, since few employers would hire workers for less than 17½ hours per week.

- **The health package paid for by the employer would have to include the following**:

    1. Medically necessary hospital care, physician care, diagnostic tests, prenatal care, well baby care, and a limited mental health care benefit.

    2. Catastrophic coverage that limits out-of-pocket costs per family to $3,000.

- **There could be no exclusions for preexisting conditions.** (Hip, hip, hooray!)

- **Deductibles could not exceed $250 per individual and $500 per family.** There would be an exception for well baby care and prenatal care, which would have no deductibles.

- **Copayments could not exceed 20 percent.**

- **Employers would be required to pay 80 percent of the premium.** For low-wage workers (those working at or near the minimum wage), the employer would be required to pay the entire premium.

The Kennedy bill also contains special provisions for small-business employers. These include:

- **A system of private regional insurers would be established in each geographical region.** Small-business employers would be pooled into larger insurance units to give them the purchasing power of a large group. Each certified regional insurer must offer a standard set of insurance options and offer PPOs and HMOs if it does so as part of its regular business activities.

- **A federal subsidy would be available to small-business employers who could demonstrate need.** If a small-business employer can demonstrate financial hardship, the government would lend a helping financial hand.

- **A companion bill would increase the business deduction for health insurance.** Currently, 25 percent of a company's health insurance premium is deductible on federal income tax returns. Senator Kennedy proposes that this amount be increased to 100 percent of the insurance costs for small businesses or the self-employed.

For those not covered by the above, the law would mandate a federal/state program that would take effect by the year 2000. This plan would be phased in as follows:

- **All uninsured children below the poverty line and pregnant women who fall between 100 percent and 185 percent of the poverty line.** This would be phased in at the same time as the employer requirements.

- **Uninsured adults below 185 percent of the poverty line.** This second phase would begin in 1996.

- **Thereafter, the remaining uninsured would be covered by the year 2000.**

The benefits of the public health insurance plan would be identical to those required of the employer-based plans. For individuals under the poverty level, the public, through taxes, would pay all premiums, deductibles, and copayments. Copayments, premiums, and deductibles for those under 185 percent of the poverty line could be imposed at state option. Premiums would be limited to a maximum of 3 percent of the person's gross salary. Deductibles would be limited to $125 per individual and $250 per family. The maximum copayment cap would be one-third of that required in a private plan. Those above 185 percent of the poverty line would have payments similar to those in a private plan.

The Bush Proposal

In February 1992, with an election pending and his popularity slipping, President Bush entered the debate over national health insurance with the Bush "Comprehensive Health Reform Program." The Bush plan rejects any form of national health insurance and instead would rely on some window-dressing reforms consisting of tax credits and deductions to assist low- and moderate-income families pay for health insurance. The proposal also would permit self-employed individuals to deduct completely the cost of their health insurance. The best portion of the proposal would compel insurers to offer groups guaranteed renewable policies and remove preexisting exclusion clauses from the policies issued under the plan. Health Insurance Networks (HINs) would be created, allowing small firms to pool themselves into a larger group—thereby reducing premiums. There would also be an attempt to standardize claims procedures to reduce inefficiency in the system. Finally, some ill-advised restrictions on the rights of medical malpractice victims would be enacted in the name of cost containment.

At best, the Bush proposal is inadequate in that it does little to assist those who cannot afford health insurance and avoids true cost containment in return for the little that would be accomplished. It would also make the highly profitable medical marketplace less safe to consumers by gutting malpractice laws that compensate injured patients and deter future negligent medical practice.

Get Involved—Without You It Won't Happen!

The issue of national health insurance looks to be one of the political hot spots in the 1990s. And with so much at stake, it should be. However, nothing is going to be accomplished that will benefit average, everyday people unless most of us get involved in this issue.

We suggest that you take some of the following steps.

Write a letter to your representative in Congress, both of your senators, and the president of the United States. Tell them in no uncertain terms that you want some form of universal health coverage *now*. Let them know your future vote for or against them depends on their involvement in this issue.

Don't let it go at that. Keep at them. If the issue makes the news, fire off another letter. When your representative or senator comes into the district for political gatherings, attend them and raise the issue again and again. In short, let "the powers that be" know that business as usual simply will not cut it.

You might also write letters to the editors of your local newspapers urging the papers and your fellow citizens to get on the national health care bandwagon. When the issue comes up on your local radio talk shows, call and get on the air supporting a national health insurance plan.

Get involved with national health organizations that promote the concept of national health insurance. One such organization is the Committee for National Health Insurance. They promote a national health insurance plan that would be a combination of individual state, federal, and private involvement. If you are interested in their program, they can be reached at:

Committee for National Health Insurance
1757 N Street N.W.
Washington, DC 20036

Get involved at the local level with organizations that support national health insurance and/or work to keep the delivery of health care at an optimum level.

One such group is the Champaign County Health Care Consumers Organization (CCHCC) of Champaign, Illinois. The CCHCC is a nonprofit community-based citizens organization with over 4,000 dues-paying members. It was founded in 1977 by people just like you who became convinced that health care reform was necessary and that it was *up to consumers to get active* and make these reforms happen. Among the programs operated by the CCHCC are the following:

- **Consumer advocacy.** CCHCC established a consumer hotline to assist local residents in the resolution of complaints regarding health care services and fees and in explaining government health benefits to those entitled to receive them.

- **Community education.** The CCHCC works hard to educate the members of its communities on matters concerning their care, their insurance, and their rights.

- **Collective action.** The CCHCC believes in promoting collective action by citizens everywhere. Thus, they encourage each of you to contact them and receive their assistance in establishing organizations like the CCHCC. If you are interested in the concept and would be interested in getting involved at the local level, contact:

Champaign County Health Care Consumers Organization
44 Main Street, Suite 208
Champaign, Illinois 61820
(217) 352-6533

Part 4

Residential Insurance

Earthquake, flood and fire;
Lightning, windstorm, hail.
The earth can be a perilous place
Through which our lives do sail.

Burglary, theft, and vandalism;
People can be hazardous too.
That's the way it has always been;
And will be till we're through.

All right, all right, so we're not Robert Frost. But that poor excuse of a poem does illustrate one point: Our lives, which often seem so secure, orderly, and protected, are really lived on the edge of the precipice. Catastrophe can strike at any moment. Each of us can lose all we have in a few minutes or even seconds, to the ravages of man or the power of nature.

The insurance industry has long recognized this fact of life and over the years has developed insurance products that offer protection for hearth, home, and property from many of these perils. Generically, such policies are known as property insurance. Property insurance comes in several types, but we'll deal almost exclusively with the most common: homeowner's insurance.

Homeowner's insurance is usually thought of in connection with the ownership of single-family residences. However, homes come in other shapes and sizes too. Condominium owners have policies of their own to cover their somewhat different sets of needs. People who rent need protection too, and so the industry also sells renter's insurance. These and other types of coverage will be discussed in the following pages.

Another important part of our discussion will focus on the exclusions contained in homeowner's policies. Why? Because far too many people feel that homeowner's insurance covers their property come what may. Unfortunately, it does not. Knowing what is not covered under the basic policy is vital if you are to reach a complete understanding of your policy.

Far too many consumers find out about these areas of exposure after a loss occurs. Then, insult is added to injury when they discover that they could have purchased coverage to fill in these gaps. It is for this reason that we will also spend some time focusing on the extras that are available to you as a homeowner or renter.

First, we will discuss ways to effectively shop for homeowner's insurance, including ways in which you can save money on your premiums.

20

How to Buy Homeowner's Insurance

Nearly everyone reading this book, whether a renter or property owner, either has a residential policy or should have one. That being so, it pays to know how to plan your purchase or renewal so that you have the correct level of coverage at the best obtainable price.

How Homeowner's Insurance Is Priced

The premiums charged for homeowner's policies have remained relatively stable over the years, especially when compared to the volatility of auto insurance. There are several reasons for this.

The major factor in homeowner's insurance is the protection of property. Liability coverages, while important, are not utilized by consumers nearly as often as in auto insurance, where there are more accidents. Thus liability rates, which can be so high in auto insurance, are a much smaller slice of the premium pie in homeowner's coverage.

In addition, while it is certainly not a universal truth, most people tend to be very careful about protecting their residential property. Thus, the chance that you will have to make a claim against your homeowner's policy is less than it is against your automobile insurance.

Finally, property doesn't move. By their very nature, homeowner's and auto policies cover very different human activities. In auto insurance, the car is being driven from place to place, often at high speeds. This being so, the chances of even a good driver being in an accident are significant over a period of, say, 10 years. In contrast, the risk factors that govern the price of insurance for a home are relatively fixed, knowable, and unchanging. Thus, the price of premiums is less likely to jump.

As with auto insurance, territorial rating is a major part of the price-setting formula. Once a company sets the perimeters of a territory, it is relatively easy to get a statistical fix on the risks. For example, how many fires occurred in the area over a given period of time? How many claims for burglary? How good is the fire department in the area? (ISO, the Insurance Services Office [see Appendix E] investigates and grades fire departments for rating purposes.) How likely is wind damage in the area? These factors and more go into the territorial statistical review, which is an ongoing insurance company activity.

In addition to territory, the insurance company will look at other factors—for example, quality of construction. If your house is fire-resistant, you will probably pay less in premiums than if it is not. How close is the home to the nearest fire station and fire hydrant? These matters will affect your insurance rates.

Saving Money on Your Premiums

Many of the underwriting factors that go into setting prices are out of your direct control. But not all of them. As with auto insurance and other lines of coverage, there are some direct steps you can take to reduce the premiums you have to pay for protection.

Step 1: Shop Around

The homeowner's insurance field is an extremely profitable one for the insurance industry. In fact, it is one of the most profitable types of insurance the industry sells. In 1988, over $17 billion worth of premiums were collected in the United States alone. This provided very large profit for the insurance companies. One of your jobs as a consumer is to do all you can to keep to a minimum the amount of that profit that comes out of your own wallet.

Your best bet in this regard is to put the competitive marketplace to work for you. And the best way to do this is to simply let your fingers do the walking and use your phone to shop around for the best price provided by a company that is financially secure according to *Best's Reports* (see page 23).

Here is an illustration of the wide range of prices, as published by the California Department of Insurance. These prices were reported for Bakersfield, a rural city about an hour's drive north of Los Angeles. The coverage quoted is for a hypothetical single-family residence, built in 1982, which suffered no losses for the last five years. The applicable deductible is $500. The dwelling is valued at $200,000 with protection of contents at $100,000. The liability protection is valued at $300,000.

AAA	$747
Aetna	$621
Allstate	$712
Blue Ridge	$569
Cal Mutual	$538
Chubb Group	$698
Continental	$701
Farmers	$646
Firemans Fund	$575
Industrial Indemnity	$713

The difference between the highest-priced company and the lowest-priced is over $200 a year! In 10 years, that amounts to more than $2,000, enough to make a dent in the cost of your kid's college education! So don't let laziness cost you money. Check around. Find the best price. Reward companies that are operated in a competitive and productive manner.

Step 2: Don't Overinsure

A large part of what you pay in premiums is determined by the amount of coverage you select. Thus, some significant dollars can be saved by taking a close look at the following.

The size of the deductibles. The basic homeowner's insurance deductible is usually $250. If you think you can afford to pay a higher deductible amount in the event you have a claim tomorrow, you can save big money by increasing that amount today.

The size of the liability protection. If the basic liability protection is sufficient to suit your needs, don't pay more for higher levels of protection.

The amount of money to replace your dwelling. You want to be insured for an amount sufficient to rebuild your dwelling should it be destroyed. However, many people make the mistake of insuring in an amount equal to the entire value of the property, *including the land*. Thus they are paying more than they have to for protection.

Step 3: Investigate Discounts

There are several discounts available to consumers of homeowner's insurance. Ask the agent you are discussing the matter with to see if the companies he or she represents offer any of the following discounts.

Multiple-policy discount. If you use the same company to write your homeowner's, auto, and umbrella policies (see page 254), you should be able to save as much as 15 percent on your premiums.

Safety device discount. If your house is fitted with smoke detectors, tell your insurance company, since you can save money on your premiums. Ditto if you have a burglar alarm.

Nonsmoker's discount. Smokers have a higher likelihood of seeing their homes go up in smoke than do nonsmokers. Some companies recognize this fact by reducing your premiums if you don't smoke.

Fire-resistant material discount. A house constructed of fire-resistant materials can significantly reduce the chance of fire. This may result in reduced premiums.

Mature homeowner discount. Some companies reward longevity by reducing the premiums on homeowner's insurance.

Loyal customer discount. Usually the insurance industry is impersonal when it comes to setting rates. However, some companies reward long-time customers with discounts.

Exclude coverage for wind and hail. In some areas of the country, the danger from wind and hail is substantial. In these locales, a significant amount of homeowner's premiums go to cover these perils. If you want to take your chances, you can save on your premiums by agreeing to exclude these coverages.

The Question of Endorsements

Another important job you have as a consumer is making sure you are adequately protected based on your individual needs. As we have seen, the basic policy covers a wide range of insurance protection. However, it is not complete. You may wish to add the following protections through endorsements to your coverage.

Earthquake coverage. For details, please refer to our discussion of earthquake insurance in Chapter 23.

Home office coverage. The basic homeowner's policy will cover $2,500 worth of business equipment. If you work out of your home and have business equipment in excess of that amount, you may wish to increase your protection.

Personal articles floater. The basic coverage for personal property loss is sometimes inadequate to fully protect valuables such as jewels, fur coats, or antique furniture. If you have valuables such as these, you may wish to specifically identify them with the company and establish their value. This is done by appraisal or using purchase receipts. Be sure to keep the receipts, photographs, schedules, or other proof of value of your personal property in a safe and secure place. A bank safety deposit box is ideal; however, if you would rather keep that material at home, be sure to store it in a fireproof safe or container.

Increased blanket coverage. If the total of your personal property is worth more than the policy's basic coverage will apply to a loss, you can increase the blanket coverage. To determine the value of your property, have your agent supply you with a *personal property inventory form*.

Buy replacement cost insurance. Unless you make other arrangements, if you suffer a loss to personal property, you will be paid what it is worth as of the date of the loss. This is often less than the replacement cost, since depreciation is deducted from your payment. If you choose, you can pay for coverage that will replace the lost items regardless of their actual worth on the date of loss.

Building code coverage. Many older homes no longer meet current building and safety codes. In such cases, if the home is substantially damaged, local law may require that the entire building be demolished and rebuilt. The only problem is that the policy coverage will not be enough for this demolition and rebuilding process, leaving you with a coverage gap. If such a situation may apply to you, you should investigate purchasing an endorsement that will pay for the costs of rebuilding as dictated by local building and safety codes.

21

Protecting Hearth and Home

There is probably no country on earth that places greater importance on the right to own property than the United States. For most of us, this national yearning to own property translates into the "American dream" of owning our own homes.

Since World War II, there has been a veritable explosion in the number of people who own and live in their own residential property. In recent years, despite inflated prices and high interest rates, many of us have still been fortunate enough to fulfill this desire. But with the fulfillment comes risk—the potential of losing our home due to physical destruction of the property or due to its being taken from us by law to pay our debts. Homeowner's insurance is designed to mitigate the consequences of such potential losses.

Types of Policies

More than any other line of coverage, homeowner's insurance is substantially standardized throughout the United States. There are four basic types of policies sold to homeowners. These are labeled **"HO"** for "homeowner's," with a number that designates different policy packages: **HO 1** provides basic coverage; **HO 2** provides broad coverage; **HO 8** protects older homes; and **HO 3** provides special coverage. Of the group, HO 3 offers the widest protection and will be the subject of most of our discussion (see chart on pages 218–219). In Appendix F, we have excerpted sections from a sample HO 3 policy.

A homeowner's policy is divided into two basic parts: **property protection** and **coverage for liability**. We'll take up the property issues first.

Protection of Your Property

Five basic areas are protected in the property section of a homeowner's policy:

> The dwelling itself
>
> Other structures on the property
>
> Personal property
>
> Loss of use
>
> Miscellaneous coverages

We'll discuss each of these areas and their coverages and illustrate why the distinctions among them can be important.

The Dwelling and Other Structures

The dwelling. The dwelling consists of the living structure itself (house) along with attached structures such as a garage. This coverage is identified in the policy as **Section I, Coverage A**. (See sample policy in Appendix F.)

There was a time when a person whose house was damaged or destroyed was rescued from his plight by neighbors who rolled

BASIC HOMEOWNER INSURANCE POLICIES

Kinds of Losses (Perils) Covered	Type of Policy				
	HO1	HO2	HO3	Renters	Condo
1. Fire or lightning	X*	X*	X*	*	*
2. Windstorm or hail	X*	X*	X*	*	*
3. Explosion	X*	X*	X*	*	*
4. Riot or civil commotion	X*	X*	X*	*	*
5. Aircraft	X*	X*	X*	*	*
6. Vehicles	X*	X*	X*	*	*
7. Smoke	X*	X*	X*	*	*
8. Vandalism and malicious mischief	X*	X*	X*	*	*
9. Theft	X*	X*	X*	*	*
10. Breakage of glass constituting a part of the building	X*	X*	X*	*	*
11. Falling objects		X*	X*	*	*
12. Weight of ice, snow, sleet		X*	X*	*	*
13. Accidental discharge, leakage, or overflow of water or steam from within a plumbing, heating, or air-conditioning system, or household appliance		X*	X*	*	*
14. Sudden and accidental tearing apart, cracking, burning, or bulging of a steam or hot water heating system or of appliances for heating water		X*	X*	*	*
15. Freezing of plumbing, heating, and air-conditioning systems, and household appliances		X*	X*	*	*
16. Sudden and accidental injury from artificially generated currents (loss to a tube, transistor, or similar electronic component not included)		X*	X*	*	*
17. Volcanic eruption		X*	X*	*	*

BASIC HOMEOWNER INSURANCE POLICIES

Kinds of Losses (Perils) Covered	Type of Policy				
	HO1	HO2	HO3	Renters	Condo
— Other perils except flood, earthquake, war, nuclear accident, and those specified in your policy. Check your policy for a complete listing of excluded perils.		X			

X—Dwelling coverage   *—Contents coverage
READ YOUR POLICY FOR EXACT EXCLUSIONS
AND COVERAGES PROVIDED

up their sleeves and pitched in to rebuild what was lost. No more. Now insurance has to do the job.

In the homeowner's policy, a major part of your coverage is designed to pay for the cost of rebuilding. Many believe this means that they should insure their property in an amount equal to its worth on the open market. Not so. Remember, the *land* the house is built on also has value, and its worth does not need to be included in the amount of coverage you select—only the cost of rebuilding.

A key question, then, is determining how much coverage you should take out. The best way to do that is to work with your agent. Consumers Union also suggests that you contact your local builders association to determine how much it costs to build a home per square foot in your locality. After that, multiply that figure by the square footage of your home. The answer is the approximate cost to rebuild your home should it be destroyed. If you insure above that price, you are probably paying more in premiums than you need to.

However, a bigger potential problem than overinsuring is underinsuring. In order for protection to be complete, the coverage you take out *must be at least equal to 80 percent of the actual replacement cost* to rebuild your home. Many consumers forget to review and update their coverage as the cost of building increases. Thus they may be left underinsured.

The consequences of underinsuring can be profound. For one thing, if you suffer a total loss and you are underinsured, your policy will not fully pay you for your damages. This might force you to dig into your own pockets or to go into debt in order to fully rebuild. Or worse, you might have to sell the property at a loss.

Beyond that, there is the issue of partial losses. Let's say you decide to roast marshmallows in the fireplace one cold winter's eve and end up setting fire to the living room. If you are not fully insured, your company is only obliged to pay an amount equivalent to the percentage of the total value you were insured for. For example, assume the great marshmallow fire caused damage in the amount of $5,000. If the company determined that your policy insured you for only 75 percent of the full replacement value of the home itself, the company would only have to pay for 75 percent of the $5,000 in damage. In other words, you would have to pay $1,250 out of your own pocket to rebuild your living room.

Consumer Alert

The best way to avoid this potential problem is to purchase a *guaranteed-replacement-cost policy* (see page 214). Under this type of policy, the company guarantees to pay whatever it takes to fully replace your home, even if the face amount on the policy is inadequate to the task at hand. If you choose to purchase this option, the company may raise the face amount of the policy to reflect changing costs of construction.

Other structures.   Other structures are those on the same parcel of land but not directly attached to the residential premises itself. For example, if you grow orchids and erect a greenhouse in your yard, this would be defined as a **nonattached covered structure**. This comes under **Section I, Coverage B**. (See sample policy in Appendix F.)

Coverage for the Dwelling and Other Structures

The following are some of the important terms and conditions you should be aware of in regard to Coverages A and B.

How losses are paid.   As we have discussed, covered property losses to the dwelling and other structures are paid so as to replace the structures themselves. However, in all but the smaller cases, you must actually repair or replace the property. Otherwise, only the actual cash value will be paid to you, which is often a lesser figure than the amount of money it would take to replace damaged dwellings or other structures. Remember, however, that if you are underinsured, you could be paid substantially less than the actual replacement value.

▶ **NOTE:** Few of us own our homes outright. Most carry mortgages or deeds of trust against the property. In such cases, the mortgage contract compels you to name the mortgagor or holder of the trust deed as a named insured. If a loss occurs, the insurance company will usually make out settlement checks in both names.

Perils covered against.   The homeowner's policy does not protect your home against *all* forms of damage or destruction. Therefore, knowing what is and is not covered is one of the primary responsibilities of the consumer.

All of the differing forms of coverage protect against the following perils to hearth and home:

Fire or lightning

Windstorms or hail

Explosion

Riot

Aircraft crashes

Damage caused by vehicles

Smoke damage

Damage caused by malicious mischief or vandalism

Volcanic eruptions

The HO 1 and HO 8 policies stop there. (This restricted breadth of coverage is one reason why HO 1 policies are being phased out in many states.) HO 2 and HO 3 add some significant other protections against the following potential causes of property damage, at a cost of about a 15 percent additional premium:

- **Falling objects.** (This protection is not as weird as it may sound. Have you noticed that jets are beginning to lose pieces of their structure in flight?)

- **The weight of snow, sleet, or ice.**

- **Water damage caused by household appliances.** This includes appliances such as a water heater or air conditioner and items such as a broken sprinkler system.

- **Other forms of damage resulting from defects in heating systems, air conditioning, or other such items.**

- **Freezing of water systems, air conditioners, plumbing, or other such items.**

- **Damage caused by electrical malfunctions.**

HO 3 adds an important general protection coverage of insuring against all perils *except those specifically excluded* (see "Exclusions," below). The important thing to remember is that *no policy covers all sources of damage*; and some, such as HO 1 and HO 8 policies, are rather restricted in what they cover.

Exclusions. When it comes to your homeowner's policy, understanding the exclusions is vital if you are to accurately assess the risks you choose to insure against and those you will take on yourself. The following are excluded from protection under all policies unless you purchase an endorsement (if available):

- **Loss caused by collapse of the structure.** If a sinkhole opens under your house or it collapses under its own weight due to faulty construction, your company will not pay for the damages.

- **Freezing, when the dwelling is vacant.** If the property is vacant, damage caused by freezing will not be protected. The purpose of this exclusion is to ensure that property owners heat and otherwise properly care for any vacant dwellings they own.

Consumer Alert

For insurance purposes, it is important that you know the difference between "vacant property" and "unoccupied property." A dwelling is vacant if it is empty and unfurnished. A property is unoccupied if it is furnished but the owners are not living there at the time of the loss. The distinction can be very important, as many of these exclusions demonstrate.

- **Vandalism or malicious mischief caused after a dwelling has been vacant for more than 30 days.** Thus, if you intend to vacate your dwelling, be sure to hire a caretaker or otherwise take measures to provide security since you will not be able to count on your insurance policy to pay for any damage vandals may cause to your property.

- **Constant or repeated seepage.** If an appliance bursts and causes damage, you are covered. But if the damage is caused by a slow leak or by seepage that recurs over and over again, your insurance company is probably off the hook.

- **Water damage.** Water damage includes flood, surface water, waves, tidal water, overflow of a body of water, or spray from any of these whether or not driven by wind. The definition also includes backed-up sewers, underground streams, and seepage from swimming pools.

- **Power failure.** Damage resulting from a general power failure will not be paid for. However, if the power failure occurred on your residential premises only, you are protected.

- **Neglect.** If you do not properly maintain your property, your insurance company won't pay for your errors.

- **Intentional loss.** If you intentionally cause damage to your own property or direct others to do so, your company will not bail you out for the losses your conduct causes.

- **Earth movement.** Earthquakes, landslides, and mudslides can destroy property. If they do, your basic property policy will not cover the loss. However, you can buy some protection through endorsements (see Chapter 23).

- **War.** As usual, insurance policy protection excludes damages occasioned by acts of war. (After the recent American incursion into Panama, it was reported that many insurers of Panamanian property denied coverage based on this exclusion.)

- **Nuclear hazard.** If your home is destroyed by a radiation accident you'd better not look to your policy to protect you, since your insurance will not pay for the loss. This is very interesting, considering all of the propaganda put out about the safety of nuclear power. Apparently the insurance industry just doesn't buy it. Otherwise, why exclude nuclear hazards from coverage *at any price?*

- **Acts or decisions of governmental bodies.** If a loss is caused by enforcement of an ordinance or law, or the failure to enforce such laws, insurance will not pay you for the losses incurred. In such a case you may need a good lawyer if you are to avoid eating the entire loss yourself.

Personal Property

An important part of the coverage of any homeowner's policy is the portion that protects **personal property**—items such as furniture, stereos, appliances, and the like. In the policy itself, personal property is called **Section 1, Coverage C**. (See sample policy in Appendix F.)

Personal property is covered as long as it is owned or used by the insured, *anywhere in the world*. In other words, the loss to the property need not occur at the covered dwelling. The personal property of others can also be included in the policy protection, if it is located at the residence *occupied by the insured*. Thus, personal property owned by the tenant in a rented house would not be covered by the homeowner's policy, but personal property brought by a guest visiting the policyowner would be.

Coverage for personal property is not unlimited. In fact, unless endorsements are purchased (see Chapter 20), the protection can be rather limited.

You are entitled to receive the actual value of your personal property at the time of loss. Note that this is *not the replacement value*, which is usually a far higher amount. Also note that there is a limit of coverage in which benefits for the loss of personal property do not exceed 50 percent of the total amount taken out to protect the dwelling (Coverage A). (If you have property located at a secondary residence, the coverage may be less.) Thus, if you had your primary home insured for $100,000, you would be protected for no more than $50,000 for loss of personal property.

Limits of liability.   There are also special limits of liability that apply to the insurance company's liability for the following items:

- **$200 on money, bank notes, bullion, gold other than goldware, silver other than silverware, platinum, coins, and medals.** In such cases 200 bucks isn't very much, so if you have such items of value and you want adequate protection, you are going to have to pay extra for it.

- **$1,000 on securities, accounts, deeds, evidences of debt, letters of credit, notes other than bank notes, manuscripts, passports, tickets, and stamps.** Again, items such as this often have a higher extrinsic value and you may need to purchase extra coverage.

- **$1,000 on watercraft, including their trailers, furnishings, equipment, and outboard motors.** Since coverage is so low, consider purchasing boat insurance if you own one.

- **$1,000 on trailers not used with watercraft.** Again, if you have an expensive trailer, you will have to insure it separately since the basic homeowner's coverage provides only nominal benefits.

- **$1,000 on grave markers.** This will not come up too often, but you need to know just in case.

- **$1,000 for losses due to theft of jewelry, watches, furs, precious and semiprecious stones.** Again, the low coverage means you should probably purchase extra protection. A thousand bucks might not even pay the tax on some of these luxury items.

- **$2,000 for loss of firearms by theft.** (It's curious that the insurance industry will pay more for firearm losses than for theft of jewelry.)

- **$2,500 for loss by theft of silverware, silver-plated ware, goldware, gold-plated ware, and pewterware.** This includes flatware, hollowware, tea sets, trays, and trophies made of these metals.

- **$2,500 for property, on the residence premises, used for business purposes.** Thus, if you work from your home and have expensive computers, desks, or other equipment, you should think seriously of purchasing additional protection.

- **$250 on personal property, away from the residential premises, used for business purposes.** The key to the lower limit is the business purpose.

Exclusions. Personal property protection generally has the following exclusions:

- **Articles separately described and specifically insured in the homeowner's policy or other policy.** The protection of the homeowner's policy for personal property is intended to provide blanket coverage within its limits for unscheduled property. If you decide to specifically insure items of value by way of endorsement, that coverage will be determined by the language of the endorsement or other policy and will not be protected by Coverage C.

- **Animals, birds, or fish.** You may think Rover is worth a million dollars, but your insurance company won't pay one dime if Rover meets an untimely end.

- **Motor vehicles and all other motorized land conveyances.** That's why they invented auto insurance. There are two exceptions to this exclusion: if the motor vehicle is not subject to motor vehicle registration and is used to service an insured's residence or designed for assisting the handicapped.

- **Aircraft and parts.** That's why they invented aircraft insurance.

- **Property of roomers, boarders, and other tenants, except property of roomers related to the insured.** That's why they invented renter's insurance (see Chapter 22).

- **Property in an apartment regularly rented or held for rental to others by an insured.** Ditto.

- **Property rented or held for rental to others off the residence premises.** Ditto, again.

- **Books of account and drawings.** This includes bookkeeping records on paper, electronic data, computer software, and so on containing business data.

- **Credit cards.** If you lose your credit cards or are the victim of credit fraud, your basic homeowner's policy will not protect you. However, you may be covered in another part of the policy; see "Additional Coverages" below.

Perils protected against. As we have stated, your policy is not all-inclusive and does not protect you against everything that can cause damage to your property. The good news is that personal property is covered against the same perils as dwellings are, except for the general protection against all nonexcluded perils provided by HO 3.

In addition to the perils already discussed, losses due to theft become a large issue regarding personal property losses. Not all thefts are protected by the coverage. *The following are excluded under Coverage C:*

- Thefts by the insured.

- Thefts from part of the residence rented to another.

- Theft in or to a building under construction.

- Theft from a secondary residence unless the insured is living there when the theft occurs.

- Theft of watercraft, outboard motors, trailers, or campers that occurs away from the residence premises.

Loss of Use

An important part of the homeowner's policy provides funds to compensate you for the loss of the use of your property, should it be damaged by peril covered under the policy. This aspect of the policy is known as **Section I, Coverage D**. (See sample policy in Appendix F.)

There are two ways in which you can elect to be compensated under the Loss of Use portion of the policy: payment for additional living expenses or payment for the fair rental value of the uninhabitable property.

Additional living expenses. If your house becomes uninhabitable, your monthly outlay for living expenses is bound to rise. For example, if your house is destroyed by fire, you will have to rent another residence while it is rebuilt.

One of the benefit options you can choose if your house becomes uninhabitable is to have these added living expenses paid for. The additional living expenses allowed are those incurred so that your household *"can maintain its normal standard of living."* In other words, if your house is in Beverly Hills, you don't have to rent an apartment in Hobo Alley.

Fair rental value. Your other option is to receive according to policy language the "fair rental value of that part of the premises where you reside, less any expenses that do not continue while the premises is not fit to live in."

Whichever way you choose to go, it must be for the shortest time required to replace or repair the damages to the property, or if you permanently relocate, the shortest time within which you can do so.

If the property that has become uninhabitable was not your principal place of residence, you will not have a choice of benefits. In that case, the only compensation for loss of use will be for additional living expenses. If the property that was destroyed was rented to others, however, then payments will be on the basis of fair rental value.

Additional Coverages

The HO 3 homeowner's policy, which most people now purchase, also includes some benefits you may not be aware you have.

Debris removal. If a covered loss creates the necessity of removing debris, the homeowner's policy will pick up the tab. It will also pay for the removal of ash caused by a volcanic eruption to the extent that the ash damages the property or buildings thereon. The amount available for debris removal is included in the total limit of liability under the policy. However, if the debris removal expenses exceed that amount, an additional 5 percent is available to complete the job. Fallen trees often come under this portion of the policy, but there is a dollar limit of $500 in the aggregate for any one claim.

Reasonable repairs. The homeowner's policy covers the reasonable cost incurred by you for necessary repairs made solely to protect covered property from further damages if a peril insured against causes the loss.

Trees, shrubs, and other plants. This section of the homeowner's policy will compensate you for the loss of trees, shrubs, and other plants caused by most covered losses (not including windstorm). The most you can receive for this coverage is 5 percent of the limit of liability that applies to the dwelling, with no more than $500 allowable for any one tree, shrub, or plant. If you grow the plants for commercial purposes, however, no benefits will be paid.

Fire department service charges. HO 3 coverage will pay up to $500 for your liability assumed by contract or agreement for any fire department charges incurred when the fire department is called upon to save or protect covered property from a peril insured against (i.e., fire, volcanic eruption, etc.). If a city provides the services without charge, your insurance company owes no benefits.

Property removed. If you have property that must be removed due to a covered peril (e.g., a windstorm destroys your wall), the additional coverages portion of the policy will pay for the costs. There is a time limit of 30 days for this coverage to apply.

Credit card, fund transfer card, forgery, and counterfeit money. Interestingly, an HO 3 policy will pay up to $500 for:

- Your legal obligation to pay because of theft or un-authorized use of credit cards issued to or registered in your name.

- Loss resulting from theft or unauthorized use of a fund transfer card used for deposit, withdrawal, or transfer of funds. These cards are also known as ATM cards.

- Loss due to the forgery or alteration of any check or negotiable instrument.

- Loss to an insured through acceptance in good faith of counterfeit United States or Canadian paper currency. In all such cases, the insurance company reserves the right to investigate the circumstances of the loss and is under no obligation to pay for losses arising out of the insured's dishonesty.

Loss assessment. The policy pays up to $1,000 for your share of any loss assessment charged to you by a corporation or association of property owners. This only applies if the assessment against you was caused by a loss covered under the terms of the policy. If the assessment is made by a governmental body, no payments will be made by the insurance company.

Collapse. The HO 3 policy insures you against direct physical loss to covered property involving collapse of a building or any part of a building caused by one or more of the following:

- The perils insured against regarding personal property losses in Coverage C.

- Hidden decay.

- Hidden insect or vermin damage.

- Weight of contents, equipment, animals, or people.

- Weight of rain that collects on the roof.

- Use of defective material or methods in construction, remodeling, or renovation if the collapse occurs during the course of such work. *Note that collapse does not include damage caused by settling, cracking, shrinking, bulging, or expansion.*

Protection Against Liability

Your standard homeowner's policy also includes a very important protection against personal liability. This is known as **Section II** (see sample policy in Appendix F). **Coverage E, Personal Liability**, states that "if a claim is made or a suit is brought against an insured for damages because of bodily injury or property damage caused by an occurrence" to which the coverage applies, your insurance company will:

- Pay up to the limit of liability as appears on the declarations page if the insured is legally liable.

- Provide a defense at company expense by counsel of

their choice, even if the suit is groundless, false, or fraudulent.

In addition, under **Section II, Coverage F**, the company will pay for *medical expenses* to others who are injured while *on the insured location* with the permission of the insured. They will also pay medical expenses of others injured *off of the insured location*, if the bodily injury:

- **Arises out of a condition on the insured location or the ways immediately adjoining.** If your tree hangs over into your neighbor's yard and a branch falls and hits your neighbor in the head, you can expect your insurance company to pay for the medical costs.

- **Is caused by the activities of the insured.** If you play golf and slice the ball into the opposite fairway, hitting another golfer, your homeowner's policy will pay that poor soul's medical bills. (It won't, however, compensate you for the increase to your golf handicap.)

- **Is caused by a residence employee in the course of the employee's work.**

- **Is caused by an animal owned or in the care of the insured.** If Rover bites the mailman, your insurance pays for the stitches.

Liability Exclusions

We all may need the benefits of good liability insurance protection. However, before you believe that your homeowner's policy protects you against the world, you'd better have a look at the exclusions. For as we all know, what the policy gives with one hand, it can specifically limit with the other.

The following are the exclusions that are not covered by the liability portion (Section II) of your homeowner's policy.

Intentional acts of the insured. If you intend to cause someone harm, don't expect your insurance company to pay for your malice.

Bodily injury to the insured. If you are injured on your own property or due to your own negligence, your homeowner's insurance policy is not the place to turn for payment of the damages.

Damage arising out of business activities. If the damage that gives cause for liability arises out of business pursuits of an insured, the protection of the homeowner's policy does not apply. In such a case, you would need a business liability policy for protection.

Damage caused by the rendering or failure to rend professional services. Thus, if you are an engineer and your work is defective, your homeowner's policy will not pay anyone for the damages your faulty work causes. In such cases, you would need a professional errors and omissions policy.

Noninsured locations. If injuries are caused on property owned by you but not listed in your policy, you're on your own.

Damages caused by motor vehicles. That's what you buy auto insurance for.

Damages caused by watercraft. If you own certain watercraft as described in the policy, damages resulting from the usage of the craft will not be paid by your homeowner's policy. In such cases, seek shelter in a good watercraft insurance policy.

Damages caused by the operation of aircraft. However, this does not apply to injuries caused by model hobby planes, which would be paid by the homeowner's policy.

War. If the damage is caused directly or indirectly by war, whether declared or not, it is excluded. Some more good news: If a nuclear device is detonated, it will be deemed an act of war even if the explosion was an accident. (Who thinks of these things?)

Communicable diseases. If you give someone a disease and get sued for it, your homeowner's policy probably does not protect you. This can be a very important exclusion in these days of AIDS and other sexually transmitted diseases.

Injuries covered by workers compensation. If a worker at your home is injured and the injury is one covered under workers compensation insurance, the homeowner's policy is off the hook.

Now that we have covered the most important parts of the typical homeowner's policy, let's see how other types of residential policies differ.

22

Insurance for Condominiums, Rentals, and Mobile Homes

As we approach the end of the 20th century, we are experiencing a change in the patterns of American housing. In many parts of the country, the proverbial Cape Cod house with the white picket fence is no longer affordable to a husband and wife with 2.5 children to feed. If it's hard for a traditional family to afford a house, imagine the difficulty a single-parent household faces in finding quality housing. And of the younger generation, how many can afford to buy a house? Unfortunately, not very many.

Over the last 10 to 20 years, as the prices of homes inflated, the types of property ownership available expanded. Condominiums and townhouses came into vogue. Mobile homes were not simple trailers anymore. With these new forms of home ownership came new forms of property insurance.

Then there are the renters. Millions upon millions of people in this country, either by force of circumstances or by preference, rent their residence rather than own it. Many of these people think they don't need insurance. Unfortunately, some find out they were wrong when they return home one fine day to find that someone helped themselves to the furniture.

Condominium Insurance

Condominiums are an interesting variation on the theme of home ownership. When you purchase a condo you are, in essence, buying two things at the same time:

- **You are buying sole ownership of your "home space."** Because this area of the property is yours and yours alone, much of the risk of loss is yours alone too. Thus, if you have a fire in your condominium kitchen, the cost of repair comes out of your wallet.

- **You are buying a small piece of the entire complex, known as the "common areas."** Areas such as lawns, swimming pools, and walkways are owned by everyone in the condominium complex. Thus, if you own one of 20 individual condos in the entire complex, you own a 1/20 interest in the entire common area.

This ownership interest comes with a price tag. You are obliged to pay for your proportionate share of upkeep and improvements for the commonly held areas. The money for this comes from your monthly condominium association dues. However, you may also be required to put out *extra* money if work on the common areas of property is required beyond normal maintenance. This extra charge is known as **loss assessment**. If the assessment is required because of damage caused by a peril covered by insurance (such as fire), benefits from insurance taken out by the association for the entire complex will be available to pay for part or all of the amount to be assessed.

Keeping these aspects of condominium life in mind, what are the insurance issues you need to think about if you own a condominium or cooperative? Again, there are two:

- The insurance you need to purchase for your own residence.

- The coordination of your policy with the insurance that the condominium association has purchased to protect the common areas and the complex itself.

Your Individual Policy

The insurance you purchase as an individual condominium owner to protect your unit is very similar to the homeowner's insurance discussed in the last chapter.

It protects the property you own individually. Usually, the insurance the condominium association purchases covers damage to the physical space you live in. However, if the policy is not enough to completely protect you, your individual coverage should fill in the difference.

It protects certain portions of the common area. If you have a legal duty under the condominium association agreement to keep and maintain portions of the common area, your individual policy will pay benefits for the destruction or loss of that area.

It covers destruction or theft of your personal property. For the most part, this is the same as the homeowner's agreement.

It protects you against liability. In our society, where lawsuits can become a reality in your life, liability insurance is a must if you have a reasonable amount of assets to protect. (See the discussion on "Protection Against Liability" in the last chapter, page 232.)

The Insurance Policy
for the Entire Complex

Your condominium association purchases the policy that covers the complex as a whole with funds collected from all of the individual unit owners. However, just as with individual policies, the terms of the overall coverage may not be adequate to completely pay for covered losses. Thus, it is vital that you have a copy of the association policy so that you can take it to your insurance agent and coordinate its terms with those of your individual policy. In that regard, there are at least three things you need to ask you agent.

Do I have adequate protection for my home space? The policy for the entire complex will pay for reconstruction of your space if it is damaged or destroyed by an event covered by insurance. This reduces your out-of-pocket costs and the price of your individual policy. However, many association policies only provide enough insurance protection to rebuild the space itself. But there's more to a home than the four walls surrounding it. What about the built-in appliances, fixtures, stairs? Is the association policy really enough to completely restore your home? If not—if your association has purchased a stripped-down model of insurance— you had better make sure your individual policy will fill in the gaps.

Are improvements I have made to my unit covered under the association policy? When you buy a condominium, you give up some of the rights to do with your property as you please. For example, you probably can't paint the exterior walls of your unit hot pink when the rest of the complex is brown. However, when it comes to the interior of the premises, your home remains your castle. Do you want to install a special tile floor? Just write the check. Do you want to install special bathroom fixtures? Most bathroom fixture showrooms take credit cards (but it is OK to pay cash and save money on interest, too!).

The only problem in improving your home in this way is that you may find that your all-new-and-improved condo is only protected for loss by the association policy as if it were still the old, unexciting unit. Thus, you will want to make sure your individual policy picks up the slack between the actual cost of the loss and the amount that will be paid for by the association policy.

Am I covered for loss assessments? If the policy taken out by the association is not sufficient to pay for the entire cost of repair or rebuilding of the common areas, you could be asked to pay your proportionate share of the amount not paid for by insurance (loss assessment). In a serious catastrophe, the loss assessment could run into big bucks.

Consumer Alert

When you buy an endorsement to cover loss assessments, you must *name the specific portions of common area for which you want the extra coverage*. So, when you discuss the matter with your agent, be sure to bring a list of the areas you believe may be expensive to repair.

The basic individual condominium policy protects you for up to $1,000 in coverage if the loss assessment is required due to damage covered by insurance. That may not be enough. Sometimes loss assessments can be staggering. For example, assume a clubhouse is destroyed along with exercise and weight-lifting equipment and a sauna. If the association policy only pays to restore the premises but not the equipment, you could be hit for a loss assessment far in excess of $1,000. In such cases, you can increase the protection your individual policy provides by paying a little extra in premiums.

Consumer Alert

As an informed consumer, you should be active in your condominium association. As this discussion illustrates, the decisions made by the association directly affect you. This includes matters of insurance coverage. The better the commercial policy the association buys, the less you will have to pay for adequate individual protection.

Renter's Insurance

Tenants need residential insurance, too. Oh, not that they need to cover the building they live in—that's the responsibility of the landlord. But there are areas of protection that a good renter's policy covers that can help the renter sleep well at night.

Insurance on Personal Property

Renters need to protect their personal property against perils such as fire and theft, just as homeowners do. The renter's policy provides this coverage in a manner similar to the homeowner's policy discussed in the last chapter.

The amount of insurance you should purchase in this regard should be sufficient to pay for the value of your property at the time of loss. In order to be fully protected, be sure to take a complete inventory or have the property professionally appraised.

Liability Protection

Many renters believe they are not responsible for people who are injured while visiting their home, believing that such injuries

Consumer Alert

Many landlords will not rent to tenants who have waterbeds unless the tenant is insured against damage caused should the bed spring a leak. Many insurance companies offer a waterbed endorsement to renters and condominium owners to protect against such an occurrence.

are the responsibility of the landlord. Unfortunately, as the old song says, "It ain't necessarily so." It all depends on where the injury happens.

For example, assume your friend comes to visit you. He climbs the stairs toward your second-floor apartment. While he's on the stairs, the bannister breaks and he falls, breaking his leg. In such a case, the owner of the apartment and his or her insurance policy would indeed be on the hook, not you.

On the other hand, assume your friend gets up the stairs safely and rings your doorbell. You let him in. Immediately, your attack-trained toddler pushes his favorite toy fire engine into the path of your friend, who trips on it and breaks his leg. Is the landlord on the hook for your friend's shattered tibia? No, you are. And without renter's insurance, you may not only lose a friend but you could have several fewer zeros to print at the end of your bank account.

Beyond such "internal injuries," renters can also get into trouble in the world outside their apartment door. The liability portion of the renter's policy protects the insured from these potential perils in the same manner as does the homeowner's policy described in the last chapter.

Tenant Improvements

Sometimes tenants improve their landlord's property in order to make the living space more enjoyable. If the improvements are considered "fixtures"—for example, if the tenant installs new kitchen cabinets—the property becomes the landlord's when the tenant moves out.

Many tenants realize that the improvements they make to their homes will ultimately become the property of the landlord. However, they may not realize that these new and valuable improvements may not be covered under the landlord's insurance policy and would thus not be replaced should they be damaged or destroyed by a loss covered by the landlord's policy. In this case, the tenant's renter's insurance will cover these improvements *if*:

- The improvement was paid for by the insured tenant, and

- It was used exclusively by that tenant.

Consumer Alert

While improvements and additions can be covered in a renter's policy, the extent of coverage is very thin— 10 percent of the amount taken out to protect personal property. Thus, if the improvements that you have made as a tenant are substantial, think seriously about purchasing extra protection with a building additions and alterations endorsement to the basic policy.

Additional Living Expenses

Your renter's coverage will also pay for any increase in living expenses made necessary when your residence cannot be occupied because of damage caused by the usual listed perils. (Read your policy for the specifics.)

Mobile Home Insurance

People who live in mobile homes are kind of a cross between the traditional homeowner and the renter. Like a tenant, the mobile home owner usually doesn't own the land upon which his or her mobile home sits. However, like the owner of a house, the owner of a mobile home does own his or her physical abode.

Needless to say, the insurance industry sells mobile home insurance. They do so either by creating a mobile home policy or by selling a traditional homeowner's policy modified by endorsement to fit the unique needs of the mobile home owner. Whichever way it goes, the following areas of coverage must be met.

The Mobile Home Itself

Like a house, a mobile home has value. Your mobile home insurance should have liability amounts sufficient to fully replace or repair the home should it be damaged or destroyed. The cost of this coverage may be greater than the traditional homeowner's policy since mobile homes are more easily damaged by the elements than a house is. (Remember the tale of the three little pigs? Well, there were actually four. One owned a mobile home.)

Other Standard Coverages

Your basic protections regarding personal property, loss of use, liability, and such are the same for mobile home owners as for the owners of single-family residences (see pages 225–235).

Unique Problems

Mobile homes have one characteristic that separates them from other residences: they can be readily moved. This provides some unique insurance problems that can be resolved by endorsements.

Damages caused during a move. When you move your mobile home, there are dangers that you should insure against. For example, what if the home is in an accident? It happens. Thus, if you are going to move your mobile home, purchase an endorsement that will cover you against such mishaps.

The costs of avoiding an insured peril. If you own a mobile home and see that a large forest fire is heading your way, you can move your home to a safe locale until the peril passes. The basic policy provides for $500 for this kind of expense. However, it usually costs far more than that to move a mobile home. If you wish, you can add to the $500 coverage by purchasing an endorsement in an amount more likely to cover the cost of moving out of harm's way and returning once the danger has passed.

Protection of the lienholder. Mobile homes don't cost as much as houses, but they are not cheap. Few purchasers pay cash. For those who buy on credit, the mobile home will be the security for the loan in the same way that a mortgage is for the purchase of a house.

This creates a problem for the lender: you can move the mobile home and thus the piece of property that "secures" the loan. For this reason, many lenders require mobile home purchasers to buy insurance that protects the lender should the purchaser default on the loan and abscond with the mobile home. This lienholder protection policy is offered by way of an endorsement that also insures the lender from risk of loss during delivery.

We've now told you more than you probably wanted to know about the basic coverages you can purchase to protect your home. Now, let's turn to the extras that are available to add to the scope of your insurance umbrella.

23

"Add-on" Protection

So far we've described in detail the glories of the basic homeowner's coverages. However, for many people, these basic plans, as extensive as they might be, do not provide adequate insurance protection. For these needy souls, the insurance industry offers more: more protection of valuables, higher limits of liability—and, of course, added premiums to pay for them.

Earthquake Insurance

Perhaps no natural disaster can cause more damage to life and property than an earthquake. That's probably why earthquake damage is specifically excluded from coverage in all homeowner's policies. Many people don't believe this exclusion affects them. After all, outside of California, where does the ground shake, rattle, and roll? Unfortunately, in a lot of places.

California's Not the Only Danger Zone

Recent news stories have indicated that there is a significant earthquake danger in some areas of the country that don't usually leap to mind when you hear the words "The Big One."

The Pacific Northwest. New evidence indicates that the coasts of Oregon and Washington have been raised above sea level and lowered beneath it by strong earthquake activity over the millennia. There's no reason to believe that history will not repeat itself. Alaska is also a very active earthquake area, as the citizens of Anchorage will tell you.

The Middle Mississippi. One of the greatest earthquakes in American history occurred near the Mississippi River in the early 19th century. It was so strong that it literally changed the course of the Mississippi River. Few people were hurt at the time because the region was relatively unpopulated. But times have changed. Large population centers such as Memphis, Tennessee, or Saint Louis, Missouri, may lie directly in harm's way. The potential for a major disaster is very real indeed.

The East Coast. Not even the East Coast is immune to earthquake threat. New England is in danger, and there is talk among scientists who know about such things that New York City could be hit.

The South. Parts of the South are also endangered by the threat of earthquake. For example, on August 31, 1886, the city of Charleston, South Carolina, was hit hard by a temblor that killed 60 people.

A big problem for many of these vulnerable areas is that they do not have earthquake building and safety codes like those that exist in California. This means that an earthquake that would do little or moderate damage in California could do tremendous harm in other parts of the nation. This being so, property owners should seriously consider purchasing earthquake coverage as an endorsement to their homeowner's policy.

Earthquake Coverage Can Be Expensive

Depending on where you live, it can cost quite a bit to protect against earthquake damage. In California, the coverage for earthquake is almost as expensive as the basic homeowner's policy itself.

There is a deductible. Earthquake coverage comes with a deductible. The amount is not usually stated in dollars but in percentages of the limits of liability for property damage. For example, in California the deductible is usually 10 percent. Thus, if the dwelling is insured for $125,000, the deductible is $12,500.

The sale of earthquake insurance can be suspended. Many people don't think of purchasing earthquake insurance until a small quake hits nearby. Then they rush to purchase coverage, only to find that their insurance company has suspended the sale of earthquake protection on the theory that some smaller quakes are warnings of bigger things to follow. So, if you believe that it is better to be safe than sorry, purchase your coverage when things are calm and quiet. It only takes an instant to turn the world upside down.

Earthquake insurance can be purchased independently of your homeowner's insurance. Some companies sell earthquake insurance directly rather than through endorsement on a traditional homeowner's policy. If you decide to go this route, make sure the company has a high rating in *Best's* (see page 23) and is not a company that will be here today and gone the day after the earthquake.

Flood Insurance

Another form of natural disaster that causes significant levels of destruction is flood. (See page 251 for what constitutes a flood for insurance purposes.) It is not surprising, then, to note that flood damage is excluded from coverage in your homeowner's policy.

National Flood Insurance Program

Up until 1968, people whose property was damaged by a flood were usually out of luck unless some government disaster assistance was made available. Then, the federal government created the National Flood Insurance Program (NFIP), which made flood insurance available to everyone—everyone, that is, whose community agreed to participate in the NFIP program.

The flood insurance program works as follows.

A community agrees to participate in the program. Communities throughout the country face varying degrees of flood risk. If a community believes that the danger of flood in the area justifies joining the NFIP program, it does so. When a community agrees to participate, individual members of the community will have flood insurance made available to them. In return, the community must take steps to manage and reduce the local dangers of flood.

Consumer Alert

If your community does not join the National Flood Insurance Program, you as an individual are ineligible to buy flood insurance protection. You may also be unable to obtain certain forms of disaster relief should a flood hit your community if it has been identified as having a flood risk but has refused to participate in NFIP.

**Individuals purchase insurance through community property/
casualty agents.** The insurance is sold by local agents or brokers.
The program used to be administered by the Federal Insurance
Administration. However, that changed in the early 1980s when
the Reagan administration put great emphasis on bringing private insurance carriers into the field. Currently, the program has
brought over 200 private companies into selling and administering flood insurance in their own names. In return, the insurance companies are guaranteed that any losses they incur above
the premiums received (and income earned thereon) will be reimbursed by the government. In other words, the insurance companies can't lose.

A flood insurance rate map (FIRM) is prepared. The rate map
will determine the rates you will pay if you elect to purchase
flood insurance. Naturally, the higher the risk of flood, the higher
the premiums.

There is a waiting period. Once your community is in the NFIP
program and you elect to cover your property, there is a five-day
wait for the insurance to take effect.

**Most walled and roofed structures that are above ground may
be insured.** As long as the property you wish to insure is a
roofed structure with walls and is not below ground or wholly
over water, it can be insured. So can the personal property contained therein. However, if the building to be insured is below
the government's flood-control building standards, insurance can
be refused.

The amount of insurance is limited. There are limits to the
amount of flood insurance you can buy. If a community decides
to join the system, it is initially part of the "emergency program."
At this time the community is required to adapt initial measures
to control flooding. Once this has been done and the FIRM has
been prepared, the community joins the "regular program."

Building Coverage	Emergency Program	Regular Program
Single-family dwelling	$35,000 (higher in Alaska, Hawaii, U.S. Virgin Islands, and Guam)	$185,000
Other residential	$100,000	$250,000
Nonresidential	$100,000	$200,000
Small business	$100,000	$250,000
Contents Coverage		
Residential	$10,000	$60,000
Nonresidential	$100,000	$200,000
Small business	$100,000	$300,000

▶ **NOTE:** These figures are subject to change. Ask your local home-owner's insurance agent for current figures. Also ask about the minimum levels below which the program will not sell policies.

Limits of coverage. Following are the limits of coverage available under the emergency and regular programs.

Definition of "flood". Several hazards come under the term. A "flood" is defined as a "temporary condition of partial or complete inundation of normally dry land areas" caused by:

- The overflow of inland or tidal waters.

- The unusual and rapid accumulation of runoff of surface waters from any source.

- Mudslides that are proximately caused by flooding as defined above if they are akin to a river of liquid and if they occur on what is normally dry land.

- The collapse of land along a shore as a result of erosion or undermining caused by waves or currents of water.

Flood insurance has deductibles. Varying levels of deductibles are available. Ask your agent for details.

The flood insurance program shows what can be done by a concerned federal government working with local communities. Thanks to the program, communities are making themselves less vulnerable to flood damage and individuals can insure themselves against losses. As the old saying goes, "Such a deal!"

For more information on flood insurance, contact your local property insurance agent or:

> The Federal Emergency Management Agency
> Federal Insurance Administration
> 500 C Street S.W.
> Washington, DC 20472

Or you can call toll free at (800) 638-6620. In Maryland, the number is (800) 492-6605. In Alaska, Puerto Rico, Guam, Hawaii, or the Virgin Islands, call (800) 638-6831.

Crime Insurance

There are limits to what the government can do about crime. But there is something you can do, and that is to purchase Federal Crime Insurance to protect your valuables.

The Federal Crime Insurance Program is a federally funded project in which robbery and burglary coverage is sold directly by the federal government. The purpose of the program is to make crime insurance available in areas where it is not otherwise easily obtained. Such insurance can come in handy, too. According to the FBI, in 1988, $343 million was lost to robbery. And burglary? Hold on to your hat—$3.4 *billion* worth of money and property was taken by burglars.

Coverage is *guaranteed* to applicants in eligible states who meet minimum protective device requirements, regardless of where in the state they live. The eligible states and territories are:

Alabama, California, Connecticut, Delaware, the District of Columbia, Florida, Georgia, Illinois, Kansas, Maryland, New Jersey, New York, Pennsylvania, Puerto Rico, Rhode Island, Tennessee, and the Virgin Islands.

Crime insurance is sold in both commercial policies and residential coverages. The maximum coverage on residences is $10,000; for commercial protection, $15,000.

Losses from both burglary and robbery are protected against. **Burglary** is the crime of stealing property by means of feloniously entering the premises in order to commit the crime. **Robbery** is theft using the means of violence or threat of violence.

If you need to buy crime insurance from the government, you can at least take heart in the fact that it is relatively affordable. A thousand dollars of coverage costs $32 per year. If you take advantage of a 5 percent discount for burglar alarms, the cost is $30. Ten thousand dollars' worth of coverage costs $126 without the burglar alarm discount and $120 with it.

If you would like more information on Federal Crime Insurance, telephone the following toll-free number: (800) 638-8780.

The FAIR Plan

Just as some automobile owners must rely on assigned-risk programs in order to find auto insurance, some property owners must turn to the FAIR plan in order to find insurance protection.

FAIR stands for Fair Access to Insurance Requirements. Its purpose is to make sure that high-risk properties have access to insurance. If you live near the ocean, subject to damage by wind or tide, or if you live in an inner city where crimes such as arson are a big problem, the only protection you may be able to obtain may be through this program.

Twenty-seven states participate in the program, as well as the District of Columbia and Puerto Rico. A similar program to protect coastal properties is available in seven states along the Eastern and Gulf coasts.

The policies are sold by local agents, so if you are having

difficulty obtaining property insurance, ask yours if he or she can investigate obtaining property coverage for you under the FAIR plan.

Consumer Alert

FAIR plan policies are limited in scope and do not provide the breadth of protection that a standard homeowner's policy does. Thus, if you must make use of the program for your insurance, think about coordinating it with other types of insurance, such as crime insurance, in order to broaden the scope of your insurance safety net.

Umbrella Liability Policies

Some of us have more to lose than others and thus require more insurance protection than the standard homeowner's policy supplies. If you are one of these lucky people, extended policies are available to protect you against liability should you mess up and find yourself liable to someone for big bucks.

The **excess liability policy**, also known as an **umbrella policy**, is designed to provide wide-ranging protection against huge liability exposure. It is designed to supplement other forms of liability protection, whether in auto insurance, homeowner's insurance, or other types such as watercraft insurance. The policy pays only after these other liability coverage benefits have been exhausted. Umbrella policies generally start at providing $1 million in protection and go up from there.

What Is Covered

As with most liability policies, the consequences of personal injury liability, property damage liability, and the costs of defense are provided by umbrella coverage. However, some umbrella coverages apply the cost of defense to the total amount of protection instead of its being an additional protection. In such cases, the benefit of the umbrella is reduced since the cost of litigation, which can be considerable, is taken off of the limits of liability, potentially exposing the insured to an **excess judgment** (a judgment above the limit of insurance coverage). Should that happen, the insured would be obliged to pay the difference between the total cost of liability and defense and the limits of coverage.

Exclusions

The usual exclusions regarding war and nuclear accident apply to umbrella coverages. In addition, umbrella coverage does not pay for damage to property owned or controlled by the insured, nor does it pay if the matter in dispute is a workers compensation case. In addition, business activities that give rise to liability are not included in the umbrella, nor are professional liability cases. Insurance specific to those needs is available.

24

Consumers' Agenda

Many people don't realize it, but California's Proposition 103 applied to homeowner's insurance as well as auto insurance. And in the brouhaha that followed, it was discovered that the profit margins in these lines were very high. (For a review of Proposition 103, see Chapter 13.) There may be grounds for rate relief in your state, too.

Another area of very real concern to homeowner's insurance consumers is earthquake coverage. The power of an earthquake is awesome. Billions of dollars' worth of property can literally be destroyed in less than 60 seconds. The October 1989 earthquake in the San Francisco Bay area was not "THE BIG ONE," yet it caused approximately *$4 billion* in economic damage! Of course, a major part of this damage was to public facilities like the Oakland Bay Bridge, but we're still talking real money!

A very real question exists as to whether insurance companies have sufficient reserves to pay for property damage caused by a large earthquake. If you live in an area prone to earthquake damage, encourage your state insurance regulators to seriously address this potential problem and make sure that some of the enormous profit made by insurance companies that sell policies in the field is placed in reserve, "just in case." After all, what good is earthquake coverage that you pay hundreds of dollars a year for if your company goes broke because it doesn't have enough to pay claims?

Homeowners should begin to emulate in the field of property insurance what many on the East Coast are doing in regard to heating and oil. These self-help activists are forming buying groups, which allow them to negotiate substantial discounts with oil distributors, thereby keeping their heating bills lower than is generally available to the public at large. There is no reason why the same consumer activism cannot be applied to property insurance, as long as any legal impediments that may exist are removed from state law.

Part 5

Life Insurance

Life insurance. The very mention of the subject drains the color from one's face. Many view life insurance as a "lose-lose" situation. Under this theory, if you die you lose, because—well, you're dead. If you live, you lose again since you spent so much money on premiums that turned out to be unnecessary. Of course, less cynical types argue that life insurance is actually a "win-win" endeavor. If you die, you win because your family or other beneficiaries are protected from the consequences of your death. If you live, you win again since, by definition, you are not dead. We'll leave this argument to the world's great philosophers to tackle.

The morbidity of the subject matter isn't the only reason many of us find the topic distasteful. We worry about the potential hassle of purchasing life insurance. Will we have to take a physical? Are we too old to qualify? Do we have to take an AIDS test? Then there's the cost. Not that life insurance is necessarily expensive. It's not—not if you're a 25-year-old Olympic qualifier for the decathlon. But if you're a 45-year-old man with a history of angina, the words "sock it to me" take on a whole new meaning. And we mustn't forget the complexity of the subject, either. What do those murky projection charts mean, anyway? How much should we buy? Is $100,000 too much or too little? What about the tax benefits, and what the heck is an annuity?

Finally, there is the one person in life most people attempt to avoid even more than lawyers—the life insurance agent. Oh, you know the type . . . *"If (God forbid) something (God forbid) should happen to you (God forbid), then what kind of a person would you be [guilt, guilt, guilt!] if you didn't provide for little Jamie's college education?"*

The worst part of all this is that our semifictional life insurance agent has a point. It is a cold, cruel world and we must work for the best as we prepare for the worst. It is, indeed, important that our loved ones be protected should we, as Shakespeare so artfully put it, "shuffle off this mortal coil."

So wish as we might, for most of us there is no escaping the need for life insurance. Therefore, it must be dealt with, not by throwing up our hands and signing on the dotted line, but from a position of empowerment—empowerment that comes from making the right decisions based on the knowledge of what is best for us and our families.

So get comfortable, take a deep breath, and stretch your arms. You can even crack your knuckles if you must. You are about to enter the mysterious world of life insurance, where you will learn about such things as cash surrender value and mortality charges; the difference between participating policies and non-participating policies; and the benefits and pitfalls of term insurance versus a cash value policy. And when you're done, you'll see that it really isn't so mysterious after all.

25

You Bet Your Life

At its core, the concept of life insurance is very simple. A person called the **owner** buys a policy wherein he or she "bets" that a specifically named individual, called the **insured**, will die at some point during the existence of the policy. The owner may or may not be the insured. The life insurance company, in turn, "bets" that the insured will not die during the life of the policy.

If the insurance company loses the bet, it pays the amount set forth in the insurance agreement, called the **face amount** of the policy. This money is paid to those named in the policy called **beneficiaries**. If the insured does not die while the policy is in effect, the company keep the premiums that have been paid and pays no benefits—unless, that is, the policy is the kind that accrues cash value (see "Cash Value Policies," below, and Chapters 29 and 30).

The Purposes of Life Insurance

Depending on the kind of policy you select, life insurance can have several purposes.

Protection of Beneficiaries

The most obvious reason for life insurance is to provide financial support (the face amount of the policy) for the beneficiaries named in the policy. People name beneficiaries for many reasons, including the following:

Income protection. The most common reason people buy life insurance is to protect their immediate family from the financial consequences of the death of the breadwinner(s) and to give the survivors time to adjust to the loss without having to reduce their standard of living.

Payment of debts. Some people take out life insurance to make sure that certain debts they have accrued will be paid if they die. **Mortgage insurance**, which pays off the balance due on a mortgage or deed of trust, is typical of life insurance taken out for this purpose.

To resolve potential business disputes. People who go into business together usually want to avoid the legal hassles that can result when one of the principals dies. For this reason, they enter into "buy/sell" agreements. These important business contracts fix the price ahead of time that will be paid to the deceased owner's family for the deceased's share of the business. This arrangement allows everyone involved to avoid expensive and time-consuming endeavors such as determining the value of the deceased person's share of the business or deciding whether the family of the deceased should be given an ownership stake in the business. Such buy/sell agreements are often funded by life insurance policies taken out by the business on the lives of the principals.

As an Investment

Some forms of insurance accrue cash values and are thus deemed investments. Over a period of time, portions of the premiums paid to the life insurance company are invested by the company to earn money, some of which accrues over the years to the life insurance policy itself. This accumulating worth is known as the **cash value** of the policy. Cash value policies are discussed in detail in Chapters 29 and 30. Some forms of life insurance, called **annuities**, are used to guarantee a specific level of income in later years. Annuities are also discussed in Chapter 30.

As a Tax Shelter

Unlike some investments, the income earned during the existence of a cash value life insurance policy is *tax deferred*. That is, while dividends payments and interest earned in a bank savings account will be taxed in the year the income accrues, earnings that accumulate as cash value in life insurance policies are not taxed until withdrawn. This can be a significant advantage, especially since the money can be used as collateral for a loan (which is also nontaxable) from the insurance company.

In addition, life insurance proceeds paid upon the death of the insured *are not income taxable*. Thus, if you protect your family by buying life insurance equal to five years of your earnings, the actual protection given is much higher since the income taxes you would have paid had you earned that amount of income will not be paid when that same amount of money comes to your survivors from life insurance.

As a Tool of Estate Planning

Some wealthier persons use life insurance to avoid estate taxes or to pay probate expenses. However, the federal estate tax doesn't tax the first $600,000 of an estate, and some states don't even have inheritance taxes. Thus, for the average family, life insurance as a form of estate planning is not a major issue. It will not be discussed here in detail. If you have any questions, contact a lawyer who specializes in probate law or is a qualified estate planner.

How Charges Are Determined

The price of your life insurance premium is based on several factors.

The Mortality Charges

Each company uses established mortality rating tables as a base for determining the cost of premiums. These base rates, called **mortality charges**, originate from the statistics each company has kept or upon the rate tables published by such companies as the National Association of Insurance Commissioners, concerning the rate of death of various segments of society. The mortality charge can be thought of as the *wholesale cost of the life insurance policy*. Generally, here's how mortality charges are established.

A basic rate number is derived for each age level. Statistics are used to determine how much $1,000 of life insurance should cost based on the likelihood that an insured will die. This is done for each age group rated; e.g., 30–34, 35–40, etc. Once established, this number is the foundation amount from which the mortality charge is based. Since, statistically speaking, an older person has a higher probability of dying than a younger person, the *mortality rate increases with age*.

Other factors are added. As with any wholesale cost, the amount includes the anticipated costs of doing business such as payment of benefits, maintenance of buildings, clerical costs, salaries of employees, and executive bonuses. Of course, profit is also included.

The rate based on age and the cost of the other factors are added together. This determines the actual mortality charge. This total represents the base rate to be charged per each $1,000 of coverage. Thus, if at age 40 a nonsmoking male in average health for his age has a rating of 4.20, he will be charged $4.20 per year for each $1,000 of coverage. Under this example, the base yearly premium for $100,000 of coverage would be $420.

Underwriting

As we saw in Chapter 5, underwriting is the process that determines the insurability of a person and the amount to be charged in premiums. In life insurance, the information supplied in the application will be used to determine whether the applicant is a standard, preferred, or substandard risk. This classification will be based on factors that either *increase, decrease*, or *don't change* the chances that the person seeking insurance will die, as already factored into the mortality charge.

The company will look at the following factors when underwriting your application for life insurance.

Your health. Your actual health condition will increase or decrease the likelihood that you will die during the life of the policy, thereby costing the company benefits that they would rather not pay. For example, if you are a 25-year-old who has diabetes, you have a statistically higher risk of dying sooner than someone your age who has had no significant health difficulties.

Life insurance companies try to be careful about who they accept as insureds. Thus, they reserve the right to have you take a physical and/or medical tests before issuing a policy. You will not be charged for this exam, but if you refuse their request you will not be issued a policy. (Of course, the expense of such physicals is part of the cost of doing business that has been factored into the mortality charge.) Many states also permit the company to engage in AIDS testing. If this is a concern to you, check with your state insurance commission.

Your occupation. High-risk occupations will usually trigger an increased cost in the premium. This makes sense since a professional helicopter pilot probably has a greater risk of dying than a shoe clerk the same age, all other things being equal.

Your personal habits. If you have an unhealthy lifestyle, the underwriting department may penalize you with higher premiums. *This is especially true for smokers*, who can expect to pay far more for insurance than nonsmokers.

Consumer Alert

Companies usually publish guidelines that will tell you whether they will require you to take medical tests. The determining factors are generally your *age* and the *amount* of insurance you want to purchase. The older you are and/or the higher the amount of insurance you are seeking, the greater the likelihood that you will have to take an insurance physical. These guidelines will vary from company to company, so you should look around before you apply if you don't want to have to take medical tests before getting your insurance.

The results of a "special investigation". If the application doesn't "smell right" to the underwriter or if the amount of insurance requested is unusually high, a special investigation may be ordered that will dig deeply into your background. Not only will you be interviewed, but so may friends, relatives, and colleagues. If the result reveals a special risk, it will be factored into the underwriting decision, which could increase your premiums or result in denial of coverage.

Once the underwriting process is completed, you will be labeled a standard risk (average risk of dying while the policy is in effect), a substandard risk (higher than average risk), or preferred risk (lower than average risk), and your premium will be set accordingly.

The Type of Policy Issued

Other charges may be added depending on the type of policy being purchased. For example, if you are looking for a policy that will accrue cash value, the old saying "It takes money to make money" definitely applies. The reason is simple: In order for the insurance company to make money for you, your premium payments must be higher than the basic cost of the insurance itself. Thus, an amount is added to the premium from which you can accrue value. A charge is also factored in for the company's management of your money. In other words, you make money off of the increased premiums, but so does your insurance company.

Policy Costs

Your premium also pays the costs directly associated with your purchase. This is called **loading**. An example of a cost built into your premium is the commission your sales agent will be paid for "lassoing" you and bringing you into the life insurance company's "corral."

When all of the above have been factored in, a premium will be established and if agreeable to you, a deal will be struck. Once the policy is in effect, you are insured against your death according to the terms contained within the policy.

Types of Policies

Life insurance comes in several styles and models from which to choose. Each type will be discussed in detail in later chapters, but here is a brief overview.

Term Insurance

Term insurance is the equivalent of the basic stripped-down model you might find in an automobile sales showroom. It's basic transportation—no frills and nothing fancy. In a term policy, you are covered for a specific time period (the *term*), as established in the contract of insurance. The only obligation of the insurance company is to pay benefits should the insured die within that time. No cash value accrues in a term insurance policy, and once it lapses, you have no rights to a refund of any of your premiums. Term life insurance will be discussed in Chapter 28.

Cash Value Policies

As discussed earlier, some life insurance policies accrue a **cash value** over the years. This is accomplished in a variety of ways by different kinds of policies. Some, called **mutual policies**, are issued by mutual companies and accrue dividends. Others accrue interest or earnings from investments. Once a death occurs, the company does not have to pay any of the cash value, only the face amount of the policy. However, if you decide to cancel your policy, you are entitled to receive the cash value you have accrued so far. You can also borrow against the cash value while keeping your life insurance in full force and effect. Cash value policies are discussed in Chapters 29 and 30.

Annuities

Some policies are primarily designed to pay benefits during the life of the insured rather than waiting for him or her to die. These policies are called **annuities**. Sometimes annuity payments terminate upon the death of the insured and sometimes they do not. Annuities are discussed in Chapter 30.

Now, armed with a general working knowledge of the world of life insurance and familiarity with some of the industry's jargon, we're ready to dig a little deeper.

26

Understanding the Life Insurance Contract

As we discussed in Chapter 4, an insurance policy is a contract that is legally binding on all parties to its execution. Life insurance is no exception. In fact, you could say that your rights and those of the beneficiaries live or die (figuratively speaking, of course) by the terms of the agreement you sign.

For this reason it is always very important to understand the terms of the contract. This chapter will make you aware of some of the important terms that you agree to when you purchase a life insurance policy.

The Ownership Clause

Life insurance contracts are owned as pieces of property. The owner is usually, but not always, the person paying the premiums.

Rights of Ownership

As you would expect, the owner has the *right to exercise control over the policy* and the right to direct the life insurance company that sold the policy to take or refrain from action with regard to the policy itself. The owner can usually exercise his or her prerogatives with regard to the policy without the consent of beneficiaries or anyone else.

Among the rights of the owner are the following:

The right to name beneficiaries. As we know, the beneficiaries of a life insurance contract are the ones who usually get the money when the insured dies. It is the owner of the policy who has the right to name the beneficiaries. The owner also has the right to change beneficiaries as he or she sees fit. However, owners can sometimes be prevented by law from changing beneficiaries. For example, many divorce decrees compel that a former spouse or children be named as beneficiaries of existing life insurance policies. Under such circumstances the owner's right to name beneficiaries would be suspended as long as the court order remained in effect. At other times, the life insurance contract itself might prevent the changing of beneficiaries. These are known as **irrevocable beneficiaries.**

The ability to make decisions regarding the cash value. The owner is the one who has the right to:

> borrow against the cash proceeds
>
> cash in the policy; and/or
>
> determine how dividends will be dealt with once they are declared by the company.

This is true regardless of who the beneficiary is unless, as was stated above, some legal impediment prevents this exercise of control.

Consumer Alert

It is very important to be precise when you name beneficiaries in order to avoid unnecessary complications and to avoid lawsuits among those you want to protect. You should also list *contingent beneficiaries*, those whom you want to receive the benefits in the event the beneficiaries predecease you. (These contingent beneficiaries can be related to the beneficiaries or not, as you see fit.)

If you choose, you can name your estate as beneficiary. In this case, the proceeds will be paid to your legal heirs or according to the provisions of your will. Be warned, however, that if you do name your estate as beneficiary, there may be significant estate or inheritance tax consequences.

Also, *if the insured under the life insurance contract is also the owner*, the proceeds of the life insurance may be subject to estate tax. Thus, many wealthier individuals choose to create irrevocable *life insurance trusts* to avoid this potential estate tax problem. (It's not as bad as it sounds. There is a marital deduction that will protect your spouse if he or she is named as beneficiary.)

The right to choose to exercise policy options. The owner has the right to make decisions with regard to policy options. We'll discuss these options next.

Settlement Option Clauses

In "insurancespeak," the payment of benefits upon the death of the insured is called the **settlement** of the policy. *The owner of* *the policy is the one who chooses how the benefits will be settled* should the insured pass away.

The following options are among those available.

Lump Sum Settlement

This is the kind of payment option most people think about when they think of life insurance benefits. As the name states, when you elect to have benefits paid in a lump sum, a one-time-only payment is made of all money due under the policy.

Interest Payments Only

This settlement sets up an account for the beneficiaries out of the death benefit and pays them the interest earned thereon. The principal acts as a form of savings account available to the beneficiaries. The beneficiaries usually have the right to withdraw principal if they choose.

Installment Payments

The owner of the policy can elect to have the beneficiaries receive their benefits in periodic payments over time. The benefits that remain on account at the insurance company earn interest for the beneficiaries as long as there are proceeds left to be paid. Usually, the beneficiary has the right to withdraw principal. Should the beneficiary die prior to the full payment of benefits, the remaining amount will be paid to his or her heirs or as directed under the policy. Installment payments can be designed to provide a specific amount of money per payment or to have the payments last for a specific period of time.

Life Income

Some policies provide for equal periodic payments for the life of the beneficiary. The amount of the payment will depend on the size of the benefits, the age of the beneficiary, and whether the payments are guaranteed to last a minimum amount of time. Unlike the other options we have mentioned, *the beneficiary usually does not have the right to withdraw principal.*

Customized Arrangements

If you want to tailor the settlement to meet specific needs not mentioned above, most companies will try to accommodate your special requests. So, if you feel like being creative, go for it! The worst thing that can happen is that the insurance company will say no.

Other Important Policy Terms

Life insurance policies have several other potentially important clauses you need to be aware of. Here are a few things to look for.

Exclusions

You can never escape from exclusions when you buy insurance. However, there are fewer exclusions in life insurance policies than in most other types of insurance. Sometimes there is only one: the suicide clause.

Suicide exclusion. Most people believe that suicide invalidates a life insurance policy. This isn't true. What the suicide exclusion usually says is, "If the insured commits suicide within two years from the Date of Issue, we will limit our payment to a refund of premiums paid, less any indebtedness."

Aviation exclusion. Some life insurance companies exclude deaths caused by air crash unless the insured was a fee-paying passenger on a commercial airline. This seems like a rip-off to us, but if you fly in a private plane, you'd be wise to buy an insurance policy that will not leave your beneficiaries out in the cold merely because you meet the grim reaper in a private airplane crash. (See also Chapter 31.)

Inherently dangerous activity exclusion. Some but certainly not all insurance companies will exclude benefits if the insured dies while performing dangerous activities such as hang gliding or skydiving. (Many companies don't exclude dangerous activities but charge a higher premium for those policyholders who engage in them.)

War exclusion. Some policies exclude death caused by acts of war.

Incontestability Clause

Here's a provision of the contract that works to your advantage. The **incontestability clause** protects the policyholder from having benefits contested by the company due to misstatements or misrepresentation made about the insurability of the insured (for example, if the insured had a heart attack that had not been disclosed to the company). Under this clause, if the error is not discovered within a period of time defined in the contract, the insurance company is out of luck. This is why companies put such a strong emphasis on screening applicants before issuing policies. However, *misstatements of age and/or gender are usually not excused by incontestability clauses*. In such cases the amount of the benefit will be reduced by an amount equal to the higher premiums that would have been charged had the application been truthful.

Unpaid Premium Provisions

Life insurance policies generally cannot lapse as long as the premium is paid in a timely manner. Once lapsed, there are provisions that govern what happens next.

Grace periods. Sometimes a payment gets lost in the mail or is made a little late because of financial or other difficulties. In such cases, life insurance contracts provide a grace period, typically 31 days, within which the insurance remains in effect and the premium can still be paid. If death occurs during the grace period, the benefit will be paid minus the unpaid premium.

Reinstatement rights. If the premium remains unpaid after the passing of the grace period, the company will notify the owner that the policy has lapsed. In such cases all is not necessarily lost, for the policy can often be reinstated under certain conditions specified in the terms of the insurance contract. Before they will reinstate the policy, companies typically demand renewed proof of insurability requirements, payment of all unpaid premiums in full, and the repayment of policy loans.

The policy will also detail the amount of premiums and how they are to be paid, the face value of the insurance and details regarding renewal, borrowing from cash values, and other matters. Any questions about policy terms should be directed to the agent or company and the answers confirmed in writing.

27

Shopping Tips

For most people, shopping for life insurance is about as pleasant as having a root canal without anesthesia. First, there's the topic: death, especially your own, is never pleasant to contemplate. Second, there are all those darned charts (where are they when you are suffering from insomnia?). Third, there's the lack of knowledge. Is $100,000 too little, $500,000 too much? Fourth, there's the doubt about whether you are truly getting the best policy at the best price.

But be of good cheer. Help is on the way. And while we can't make the process a pleasant experience, we can point you in the right direction toward effective purchasing decisions. (The authors strongly suggest that you review Chapter 3, "How to Buy Insurance," before proceeding.)

How Much to Buy

The first task you will face is to answer the somewhat elusive question of how much life insurance to buy. In many ways, this is the most important issue if your primary purpose in buying life insurance is the protection of those you love. The decision concerning the size of the face amount is uniquely individual and will be based on several factors.

Your Income

Life insurance benefits are intended to enable survivors to maintain their lifestyle should a breadwinner die and the family's income be lost. The amount of income also determines how much can be set aside from the needs of the moment to pay for life insurance.

The Cost of Family Living

Of perhaps greater importance than income is the expense side of family life. After all, you want your insurance benefits to be high enough to pay for the family expenses that will remain after your death. The level of your expenses as compared to your income will also give you an idea of how much you have to spend on life insurance premiums. Use the work sheet on page 281 to determine your monthly income and expenses. Don't be surprised if you find you spend more than you make. A lot of people do, thanks to the modern magic of credit cards.

The completed worksheet will tell you information about your finances that is important for two reasons:

- In determining the amount of insurance to purchase, you will want to protect your family both in the present and in the future. Usually, life insurance is about maintaining a lifestyle for the family that loses a breadwinner.

- In looking at your expenses, you have a better idea about how much insurance you need to protect your family and how much you can afford to buy. It makes no sense to miss meals in order to buy excessive amounts of life insurance.

Future expenses you will want to make sure will be paid. The expense side of the ledger will not remain static but will change over the years. In this regard, consider the following:

- **Monthly expenses will grow or shrink depending on life circumstances.** For example, a family with two young children can be guaranteed to have their monthly expense acorn turn into a formidable oak tree when the kids hit the dreaded teenage years. On the other hand, a couple whose chicks have left the nest may have lower expenses now that they aren't buying the kid's clothes or feeding the voracious appetites of growing children.

- **Debts may have to be paid.** There may be lump-sum debts that will have to be paid in the future. Many people take out second and even third mortgages to finance home improvement or educational expenses. Typically, these debts become due in a lump sum. Many people count on refinancing these bills when they come due, but the death of a breadwinner may make refinancing impossible to obtain.

- **Future obligations will have to be provided for.** Some future obligations, such as college tuition, estate taxes (if any), and funeral expenses, can be generally predicted. Others, such as the aftermath of a natural disaster, cannot. Sufficient funds will have to be provided to meet both.

Figuring It All Out

Now, let's pull all of this together. There are a lot of different methods out there as to how to come up with the right amount of life insurance. We believe there is no magic formula, although many agents may tell you there is. Some will talk in terms of

INCOME AND EXPENSE WORK SHEET

A. First, determine your monthly spendable income. If there is more than one breadwinner, include all sources of income.

Gross Income

1. Add the total gross income received during the last year, including wages, commissions, bonuses, and overtime. _____

2. Add the gross money received during the last year from _____
all other sources, interest, dividends, etc.   Total: _____

3. Divide by 12 for total monthly gross income.
                       Monthly Gross: _____

Deductions

4. Add total of federal income tax withheld for last 12 months. _____

5. Add total of state income tax withheld for last 12 months. _____

6. Add total of Social Security withheld for last 12 months. _____

7. Add total of state disability and unemployment insurance withheld for last 12 months. _____

8. Add total of other withholding, e.g., health insurance, union dues, pension fund, etc. _____

9. Add any taxes due caused by inadequate withholding. _____

10. Subtract any income tax refunds. _____

                       Total: _____

11. Divide by 12 for total monthly deductions. _____

12. Subtract the monthly deductions (#11) from the monthly gross (#3) to determine monthly spendable income. _____

B. Second, determine your monthly expenses.

1. Residence expenses
   A. Rent or mortgage _____
   B. Taxes and insurance _____
   C. Maintenance _____
2. Food and supplies _____
3. Eating out _____
4. Utilities _____
5. Telephone _____
6. Laundry and cleaning _____
7. Clothing _____
8. Medical and dental _____

9. Insurance (auto, life, etc.) _____
10. Child care _____
11. Education _____
12. Entertainment _____
13. Transportation and auto (gas, oil, repair, etc.) _____
14. Installment payments _____
15. Incidentals (charity, maid, etc.) _____

                  Total monthly expenses: _____

"real money" values and what money will be worth in 10 years, and other such gobbledygook. We believe, however, that for the average life insurance consumer, things should be kept rather simple.

Use the following to determine the face amount of insurance you should buy.

Yearly income. You will want to have enough life insurance to at least replace your yearly family income for an extended period of time. The exact time will depend on your desires and, of course, on how much you can afford. *Many in the insurance industry recommend that you have 10 years' worth of income protection* as your face value. Thus, if your spendable income is $40,000 a year, that would require *$400,000* worth of insurance, which can get pretty expensive. *NICO, on the other hand, recommends that a multiple of 5 be chosen, believing that level to be a good balance between protection and cost.* Under the NICO formula, the family with $40,000 annual spendable income would choose $200,000 worth of life insurance.

Yearly expenses. Expenses are as important as income. *If your expenses exceed your income* (which is true for many Americans), *use your yearly expense total* as the multiple rather than your income.

Special expenses. If you wish to provide for special expenses such as college tuition, add that amount to the total. In such a case, you may wish to direct that the benefits be set aside in trust for the stated purpose.

Emergency fund. Some people like to add an emergency fund of $10,000 or so to their face amount to provide that little extra cushion between loved ones and the harsh realities of living.

Debt payoff. If you can afford the extra premiums, you may wish to add an amount to the face value of the life insurance to pay off the family's debts. By doing this, you also reduce the family's monthly living expenses.

Funeral expenses. Funerals can cost a lot of money. If your good-bye celebration is likely to be on the lavish side, you may wish to pay for it ahead of time with a little extra face value of life insurance.

A sample calculation. Under the above formula, using a multiple of 5 as recommended by NICO, a family earning $40,000 per year, having two children who wish to attend college (at $10,000 per year apiece) and a $25,000 second trust deed due in four years, would want the following total life insurance protection:

$200,000 (5 times income)
+   80,000 (college tuition for two)
+   25,000 (trust deed payoff)
+   10,000 (emergency fund)
= **$315,000 in death benefits**

If you want to pay for funeral expenses, add $5,000 to $10,000 for that purpose.

Many authorities contend that you should also deduct liquid assets (such as savings accounts) from the face value total. Thus, in the example above, if the family had $15,000 in a certificate of deposit, that amount could be deducted from the total face value needed.

If the family income is made up of two breadwinners, both should have life insurance at face value at least 5 times their respective take-home salary. Thus, if the $40,000 is made up of one salary of $25,000 and one of $15,000, the two policies purchased would not be of the same value. However, each policy alone should carry enough face value to pay for the college tuition, emergency fund, etc.

What Kind of Insurance to Purchase

Once you have figured out the correct amount of face value to purchase, your next step is to decide whether you should buy term insurance or cash value. Most consumer organizations recommend annual renewable term insurance, while the insurance industry recommends cash value.

Whichever way you go, be sure that you have a sufficient face value to protect your loved ones in case you die. Thus, if it comes to a decision about whether to buy a larger face value term policy or a lower face value cash policy, *CHOOSE THE TERM POLICY*. Make it convertible to cash value if you believe you'd prefer a cash value policy when you can afford higher premiums.

If you have enough money to pay for a sufficient death benefit, you can:

- Take out a cash value policy and turn your family protection into an investment.

- Increase the face amount of your term policy to provide your loved ones greater protection. Or

- Take the money you save in premiums by buying term, and invest it yourself.

Then again, you might want to take a trip to Hawaii. After all, you only live once.

Tips on Saving Money

Life insurance may be one of life's less pleasant necessities but that doesn't mean it should be one of its more expensive ones. Happily, there are ways to save yourself significant money on your life insurance. Here are some do's and don'ts.

Do Shop Around

As we stated at the outset of this book, there are a multitude of companies to choose from to fill your insurance needs. In fact, there are *over 2,000 insurance companies that sell life insurance in the United States alone*. And each of these companies has its own philosophy about how to make profits. Some place greater emphasis on investments. These companies often charge lower premiums in order to obtain more sales so that they will have more money to invest. Others choose to make a higher profit off of the premiums themselves. So take the time to find the company that's right for you. The money you save will be your own.

Consumer Alert

There is a very valuable *term* life insurance shopping service available that can do the comparison shopping for you. It is called *Insurance Information Inc*. Within 24 hours of receiving an inquiry from you, they will be able to send you a report on five of the lowest-cost insurance companies to fill your needs. The report will include *Best's* rating of each company mentioned. The price charged for the service is modest, and the company does not sell insurance itself, so there will be no sales pressure whatsoever. If you are interested in term insurance, call them toll-free at (800) 472-5800.

Don't Smoke

If there is one thing that will send the cost of your premiums through the roof, it is smoking within 12 months of applying for life insurance. So don't smoke. Not only will you be saving money, you may be saving your life.

Do Consider a Mail-Order Policy

If you order your life insurance by mail, you can save significantly because you will not be paying for the agent's commission. Of course, you should investigate a mail-order company as thoroughly as a company that uses commissioned sales personnel. NICO keeps tabs on some of the better mail-order companies and can recommend the ones they believe are offering the best coverage at the best price.

Don't Buy the Company Propaganda

Certified Life Underwriter Mark Landau, who owns Insurance by Design in Sherman Oaks, California, states that life insurance companies have a double-edged sword when it comes to marketing. One side is aimed directly at the consumer, in ads that do not specifically mention benefits or costs but attempt to stimulate name recognition. For example, one company uses a beloved cartoon dog to represent them. Another utilizes a world-famous rock. Still another emphasizes the presence of caring hands. The point of these ads is to make you feel good about the company name so that the sales agent has an easier time breaking through buyer resistance. *None of this has anything to do with the quality of the product being sold.*

The other aspect of the sales pitch is made to the agents themselves. For example, a company will bring out prospective earnings charts to impress agents with the value of the policies being offered. Landau calls some of these agent sales pitches "optimistic." He's probably being kind. Thus, when an agent pitches a product as a big money-maker, take the assertion with a grain of salt. Ask the agent to trace the *actual earnings history of the company* as compared to the projections, to see how realistic the company has been in the past. (Yes, they can tell you. There are books that have the information available.) You should also look to the minimum earnings guarantee to see what your worst-case scenario is (barring the bankruptcy of the company).

Consumer Alert

Beware of smoke and mirrors when it comes to projected earnings. According to industry specialist Donald Reiser, president of Vest Insurance Marketing Corporation: "Obviously, no one can predict the future accurately 100 percent of the time. Projections are merely projections. But unless they are based on conservative, realistic assumptions and unless *all* the assumptions are disclosed, these proposals are not worth the paper they're printed on!"

Do Have the Earning Capacity of the Policy Evaluated

There are two principal ways to evaluate cash value insurance. One, the **surrender cost index**, is a tool that tells you how good a deal your cash value policy is. The index, which is computed by a complex formula too complicated to go into here, tells you what the projected cost of a proposed policy is. In order to be of benefit, the policies evaluated must be similar. *The lower the index number, the better the buy.*

In actuality, the index is of limited concrete value since it measures projected costs and values rather than what the actual measure of the policy will be. Of course, in order to determine the actual performance of the policy, you would need to see into the future.

Another method used to evaluate life insurance costs is called the **Linton yield method**. It measures the difference between what you could earn by buying term insurance instead of cash value policies and investing the money you save in premiums, compared with what you can expect to earn from a cash value policy.

Consumer Alert

NICO offers a service that will give you a *Linton rate-of-return comparison* for all of the cash policies you are comparing. The charge per policy is modest. The comparison will be performed by the president of NICO, J. Robert Hunter, a well-respected actuary. If you are interested, contact NICO at (703) 549-8050.

Do Buy Group Insurance

If you are eligible to purchase group insurance, think seriously about doing so. You will usually get better rates and will probably not have to take a physical to qualify. Many group policies are convertible to individual purchase should you lose your group member status.

For More Information . . .

If you would like more information on life insurance, there are some books that go into deeper detail than we can here since they deal exclusively with the topic of life insurance.

For the Consumers Union perspective, look for *Life Insurance: How to Buy the Right Policy from the Right Company at the Right Price*, by Trudy Lieberman and the editors of Consumer Reports Books (Consumer Reports Books, 1988). If the book is not in your local bookstore, write to Consumer Reports Books at 110 East 42 Street, New York, N.Y. 10017. A very valuable part of this publication is the comparison of most of the life insurance companies vis-à-vis each other.

For the view of an experienced life insurance agent, try *The Life Insurance Buyer's Guide*, by William D. Brownlie with Jeffrey

L. Seglin (McGraw-Hill Publishing Company, 1989). Unlike NICO and Consumers Union, Brownlie strongly supports the benefit of cash value plans over term insurance. The book is a little difficult to read but provides a different perspective from ours and thus can be a valuable tool in making the very individual decision of buying term or cash value life insurance. If you can't locate the book in your bookstore, call McGraw-Hill at (800) 2-MCGRAW.

You can also contact the following for sources of information on life insurance:

- **NICO. 121 Payne Street, Alexandria, Va 22314.** Ask to purchase their book, *Taking the Bite Out of Insurance: How to Save Money on Life Insurance*, by James H. Hunt. This book and NICO itself will recommend specific companies to do business with in purchasing your life insurance.

- **Your state insurance department.** They will have consumer information pertinent to life insurance issues.

- **The National Association of Life Underwriters.** 1922 F Street N.W., Washington, DC 20066. This trade association also helps consumers who have questions about life insurance coverage.

28

Term Life Insurance

Term life insurance can be defined as life insurance that is in effect for a specified period of time. This time period is called the term of the policy.

Seems pretty straightforward, doesn't it? Well, term insurance isn't quite as simple as it might at first appear.

The Characteristics of Term Insurance

There are some important things you should know about term policies before you buy.

What You See Is What You Get

With term insurance there is no accrual of cash value, no borrowing power, and no rights to any funds whatsoever once the term has expired without a claim. What you do get is a straight life insurance policy. Die within the life of the policy and your beneficiaries collect the dough.

Term Insurance Is Usually Renewable

Just as it is vital that your health insurance be noncancelable, it is essential that your term life insurance policy be renewable, and for the same reasons. If your policy is not renewable, the company can refuse to sell you more insurance at the end of the term if they consider you a poor risk (or for any reason at all, for that matter). Renewability allows you to maintain the policy in effect regardless of your health, as long as the policy is offered. (Note: Many term policies terminate the right to renew at a specific time, such as at age 65.)

The Company May Have the Right to Recheck Your Health

Renewability can be either with the company having the **right of reentry** or without that right, with some policies giving you a choice. Reentry is a term that describes the right of the insurance company to recheck your health at the end of the term to see whether you are a preferred, standard, or substandard risk (see page 54). In return for giving the company the right to reevaluate your insurability, the cost of your premium is reduced. If, upon reentry, the company deems you a poor risk, you can be hit with a major increase in your premiums. On the other hand, if the company likes what they see, you can save some big bucks.

The Price Goes Up Every Time You Renew

As you will recall from our discussion of mortality charges (see page 266), the price of life insurance rises for each year of your

Consumer Alert

If you choose a policy where the company has the right to reenter, *make sure you have the absolute right to renew* regardless of your health condition. Also, to avoid any unpleasant surprises, check to see that the policy provides a *maximum premium* you can be charged upon reentry if your risk factors are high.

life. This fact will be reflected in higher premiums each time you renew your term policy.

Many Term Policies Are Convertible

A **convertible** policy is one that can be exchanged for a cash value policy without reentry—that is, without your having to prove continued insurability. Thus, if you want a cash value type policy but can't afford the premiums just now, you can buy term and transfer policies later when you may have a little more padding in the old bank account.

Types of Term Policies

Term policies come in several varieties designed to fit the varying needs of a large populace.

Straight Term

Straight term insurance covers the beneficiaries for the time provided in the policy. *Straight term is not renewable*, which means that once the term has expired, you have no right to have the insurance continue in effect.

Yearly Renewable Term

As the name implies, **yearly renewable term** is taken out for *one year at a time*. As you would guess, the price of the policy rises every year you renew it. The life insurance company must keep the policy in effect regardless of your health status, as long as your premiums are paid.

Multiyear Renewable Term

Many companies offer terms that range from 5 years up to 25 years. During the term, the yearly premium will remain unchanged. At the end of the term, assuming you can renew, the price will be hiked considerably.

Term to a Specific Age

Some policies are sold to last until a specific age has been attained, typically 65 or 70. The premium will remain level during the term but will be priced so that the company receives a profitable return. Policies such as this are not generally renewable but are usually convertible.

Decreasing Term

Decreasing term insurance reverses the usual process of increasing premiums that pay for an unchanging face value. Instead, in this type of term insurance, the *premium remains unchanging but the face value decreases*. Thus, a policy with a face value of $100,000 when it is taken out may be worth only $90,000 a few years later. **Mortgage insurance**, which pays off the principal due on a mortgage or deed of trust upon the death of the insured, is a form of decreasing term insurance. In addition, some long term policies are specifically sold this way so as to have the maximum benefits available when the insured is younger and probably has a greater need to protect a growing family.

As a Job Benefit

Many employers and unions offer term life insurance as a benefit of employment. This is usually a group policy and protects the insured for a specific amount or for a multiple of the employee's annual salary.

Consumer Alert

If you have term insurance as a fringe benefit in excess of $50,000 face value, you may suffer an income tax consequence. Ask your accountant for details.

The Pros and Cons of Term Insurance

Advantages of Term

Many consumer organizations recommend term insurance as the life insurance of choice. In fact, both NICO and Consumers Union are very high on the term concept, believing that for most consumers it is the best buy for the money. They also point out the following "pros."

As you accrue value in a cash value policy, you are actually decreasing the exposure (potential out-of-pocket risk) of the insurance company. The reason for this is simple: *They only have to pay the face value* upon the death of the insured, not the face value plus the cash value. In other words, if you take out a $100,000 cash value life insurance policy and it accrues a $15,000 cash value before you die, the company is really only paying $85,000 of its own money when it pays your beneficiaries the face amount.

Most people can earn more money for themselves by purchasing term insurance and investing on their own the money they save in lower premiums (compared to cash value insurance). Cash value policies usually do not give you a terrific rate of return. You can do better yourself, *if* you invest the premium savings rather than spend it. (Unfortunately for some of us, that's a big *if*.)

According to NICO, annual renewable term insurance provides the most coverage for the least cost. Moreover, term insurance is often all a struggling young family can afford.

When you buy term insurance, more of your money is going to pay for the product rather than the commission. Agents make bigger percentages selling cash value policies than they do selling term insurance.

The primary purpose of life insurance is to protect loved ones against the consequences of premature death. Term insurance does this well without getting complicated or expensive.

Disadvantages of Term

As you might expect, the insurance industry sees things differently. Insurance professionals push term insurance as a temporary measure to be used only for *short-time protection* or *until a cash value policy can be afforded*. Because of the convertibility of most policies, insurance experts will also tell you that term policies are good to *guarantee you insurance at a later date*. Most insurance agents and executives will stress, however, that term insurance is not appropriate for long-term needs, for the following reasons.

If the insured doesn't die during the term of the policy, the premiums that have been paid all go down the drain. Cash value policies, in contrast, can accrue substantial sums that can be used at retirement or to help fund the kids' college education.

In later years, term insurance can become prohibitively expensive. This is not true with most cash value types of policies, which maintain a stable premium level throughout the life of the policy.

Mutual companies (see page 270) tend to pay very low dividends to term policyholders and higher dividends to cash value policyholders. Thus, by buying term insurance, you drastically reduce the benefit of buying a mutual policy.

Inflation eats up the real value of term insurance more readily than some cash value types of policies. The latter often allow cash value or paid dividends to be rolled over into a higher face value without increasing the premium.

Term insurance does not have many of the tax advantages of cash value life insurance.

Both sides have their points, but we give the contest to those who advocate term policies. Life in America is expensive as it is without paying the extra premiums for cash value insurance. But if you disagree, that's OK too. We don't care which type of policy you choose, as long as your choice is based on facts and on reason rather than on a salesperson's high-pressure pitch.

Understanding the Projection Charts

Life insurance is sold by asking the prospective buyer to compare projections as to premiums, earnings, and death benefits of different policies. You all know the scenario—the unnaturally bright and cheerful life insurance agent invites you to review his or her line of wares and immediately whips out a bunch of charts. Then, *whamo*—it's like being in a room filled with ether. Your eyes glaze over, you yawn, and the next thing you know, you're out in the sunshine with a new life insurance policy in your pocket—a policy you don't even remember buying.

Let's call these sleep-inducing charts **projection charts**. Projection charts can be of real assistance in helping you compare different policies before choosing the one you like best. In order to do your job as an informed and powerful consumer of life insurance, you must understand what these charts are telling you.

For our illustration we shall use excerpts from two actual projection charts given for term life insurance by two different companies. The first is an abridged version of an actual quote for life insurance in the amount of $150,000 for coauthor Wesley J. Smith, a 40-year-old nonsmoking male in good health. The policy is for a 10-year renewable term.

TERM INSURANCE PROJECTION CHART—EXAMPLE 1

Year	Death Benefit	Current Premium With Reentry	Current Premium Without Reentry	Maximum Premium Guarantee
1–10	$150,000	$372	$ 372	$ 372
11	$150,000	$631	$1,104	$2,347
12	$150,000	$631	$1,183	$2,509
[Years 13–19 Omitted]				
20	$150,000	$631	$2,102	$5,304

Renewal Privilege: Automatically renewable for successive one-year periods to age 95. *Conversion Privilege:* Convertible, without evidence of insurability for the full face amount of the policy during the first five policy years. Thereafter, convertible without evidence of insurability for 80% of the face amount. The conversion privilege may not be exercised on or after the policy nearest the insured's 70th birthday.

The following projection chart takes a different approach.

TERM INSURANCE PROJECTION CHART—EXAMPLE 2

Multiply death benefit below by number of thousands and then add $60 for policies over $100,000.

Age at Last Birthday	Male	Female
40	1.03	.95
41	1.09	1.00
42	1.17	1.05
43	1.25	1.10
	[Etc.]	

OK! *Wake up!* Here is the translation of the above charts.

Year

The year column in Example 1 refers to the number of years from the date of purchase of the policy. Some projection charts list the age of the applicant in numerical order rather than the above method. Example 2 is an illustration of this second type of listing.

Death Benefit

Example 1 lists the death benefit as requested by the applicant, $150,000. That's easy. The company in Example 2 makes it a little tougher but not much. They use a formula based on a unit price per $1,000 of face value. Thus, in the second chart, it takes 150 units to purchase a $150,000 policy.

Premiums

The annual premium in the first example (the current premium *with reentry*) for the first 10 years is $372. After the first 10 years, if the applicant had chosen to permit reentry, the annual premium for the next 10 years goes up to $631, assuming a continuation of standard rates.

It takes a little math to figure out the premium that would be charged in the second example. The formula to find the annual premium for a $150,000 death benefit would work like this:

> Multiply 1.03 × 150 (the number of $1,000 units desired) and then add $60. That price for this policy during a male applicant's 40th year would be $214.50 (1.03 × 150 plus 60). A female, who is statistically less likely to die, has a lower rate. Her premium would be $202.50 (.95 × 150, plus 60). The rate would have to be refigured for each year using the same formula but different multipliers.

You might wonder why the $372 premium in Example 1 is so much more than the $214.50 premium in Example 2. *If you were comparing these two policies, that would be a question you would want to ask the agent or representative.* The answers in this case are as follows:

- **The second example is an annual term policy quoted from a mail-order insurance company.** Its rates are lower because it doesn't have to charge for the agent's commission. This appears to be true even years into the policy. But then, those low rates are not guaranteed.

- **The 10-year term policy in Example 1 guarantees the rate for 10 years, while the annual term rate projection is only guaranteed for the first year.**

(Notice that there is no maximum premium guarantee in the second projection chart.) Thereafter, the rates may change and there would be nothing the annual term life insurance holder could do about it except pay or cancel the policy.

Consumer Alert

Always check to see whether future rates are guaranteed. This should be specified on the chart. If you don't have a guaranteed earnings and/or guaranteed maximum premium on your projections chart, then you don't have a maximum guarantee.

Compare the above to the premium quote in Example 1 when reentry is not allowed. The rates after the first 10 years are almost double the rates that will be paid if reentry is permitted and the policy reissued at the lower rate. Also note that in Example 1, if no reentry is permitted, *the policy becomes an annual term policy*, with the price rising every year beginning in year 11.

Maximum Premium Guarantee

After the expiration of the initial term, the projections set forth in the sales charts are just that, *projections*, no more and no less. Projections are rarely guaranteed. However, some companies will put a ceiling on the future premiums that can be charged, as the company in Term Insurance Example 1 does. Note that the ceiling is almost ridiculously high. This leaves the insurance company a lot of wiggle room. Insurance companies not only know how to wiggle, but give them half a chance and they'll shake, rattle, and roll!

Renewal Privilege

This term policy allows yearly renewal until age 95. Not shown in the example is the cost of the insurance at age 95—$53,997!

Conversion Rights

If a term policy is convertible, the terms of the right to convert should be listed in the projection chart. In this example, the policy could only be converted without new proof of insurability at $150,000 *for the first five years*. Also note that the right to convert terminates around the applicant's 70th birthday. *Conversion rights will differ from policy to policy, so be sure to compare this portion of the quote as well as the prices and benefits.*

Consumer Alert

Always keep the projection chart of the company you purchase your insurance from. In that way, if there is a future dispute, you will be able to enforce your rights as a policyholder.

Now that you have gotten your feet wet, let's tackle a somewhat more complicated aspect of life insurance: policies that accrue cash value.

29

Cash Value Life Insurance

When most people think about life insurance, they picture dollar signs in their mind's eye—the kind of policies that accrue money over the life of the policy. These are generically known as **cash value policies**.

Common Characteristics

Cash value policies come in several different varieties for your shopping perusal. These will be discussed in detail in the next chapter. For now, let's look at some of their common characteristics.

Accrued Value

Cash value policies accrue worth over time. That may be stating the obvious, but it is the most distinctive characteristic of these types of policies.

Higher Cost

Cash value policies cost more than term plans. The face values of the cash policies and term policies being equal, you will pay higher premiums for cash value life insurance than for term insurance. This is true for several reasons.

The insurance agent, if there is one, usually earns a higher commission with cash value life policies. Most cash value policies sold by agents earn a very high percentage of the first year's premium for the agent as a commission and lesser amounts per year as the insurance is continued in effect over time. Term policies usually pay far lower commissions. Thus, there is a "double whammy" effect: the commission percentage is higher for a cash value policy, and that increased percentage is based on a higher price.

The premium is working harder than a term premium. When you buy a term policy, the premium accomplishes the purchase of life insurance protection and that's it. On the other hand, when you buy cash value insurance, the premium buys the life insurance *and* provides the funds that are invested by the insurance company to earn you (and them) money. These earnings accrue as the policy ages.

Flexibility

Cash value policies are flexible. As we will discuss in greater detail, cash value policies may cost more but they can do more, too. They can be used as a *tax-deferred* way to accrue an estate; they can be used as *collateral* for a loan taken out against the cash value of the policy; and they can literally *pay for their own premiums*. In addition, the riders available for cash value policies usually give you greater latitude than those for term policies. For example, some cash policies allow you to collect a portion of your face value as a benefit *during your lifetime* (see Chapter 30).

Indefinite Periods

Cash value policies are sold for indefinite periods. Unlike term policies, most cash value type policies are sold for indefinite periods. In other words, the insurance doesn't lapse after a specific time but continues as long as premiums are paid. There are no issues of renewability or reentry to worry about as there are with term policies.

Borrowing Against the Policy

You can borrow against the worth of cash value insurance policies. When a policy has accrued cash value, it can be used as collateral to borrow against. Note, however, that if too much money is taken out, the policy can **fail**; that is, the amount in the account is not enough to pay for the death benefit. In that case no benefit will be paid upon the death of the insured. It is also important to remember that the insurance company will *charge you interest* on the money you borrow, and *the interest charged will be greater than the interest your money earns*. That difference is called the **net cost of borrowing**. One last point: Should you die while a loan is outstanding, the company will deduct what is owed and pay the balance to the beneficiaries.

Consumer Alert

Some companies pay higher dividends or interest as a reward to policyholders who do not borrow against their policies. This system is called *direct recognition*. If you don't expect to have to borrow against your policy, look for this feature that rewards you for your thrift.

Level Premiums

Cash value life insurance usually has a level premium. Unlike term insurance, which increases in cost at the end of each term, cash value life insurance premiums usually don't change as you grow older (although the increases in the mortality charge have already been factored into the cost). This can be a significant advantage in later years when renewed term policies might be too expensive to maintain.

There are exceptions to this rule, of course. Some cash policies are specifically designed to be more expensive at certain times than at others during the life of the policy. Some policies have a large one-time-only premium. These issues will be discussed in the next chapter.

Tax Benefits

There are tax benefits available with cash value policies. Life insurance is one of the few middle-class tax loopholes to survive the Reagan Revolution. Unlike most investment loopholes, life insurance escaped the knife of the 1986 Tax Reform Act. Among the tax benefits available in cash value policies are the following.

The worth that accrues as cash value is tax deferred. Assume you put money in the bank and also have a cash value life insurance policy. Over the years you earn $10,000 in interest from your bank savings and accrue $10,000 in cash value from your life insurance company. Is there a difference to Uncle Sam? You'd better believe it! You will have to pay income tax on every penny of interest you earn from the bank each and every year you earn it. Not so for the increased value of your life insurance policy. The government will leave you alone until you cash in part or all of your cash value, and even then you won't pay taxes on all $10,000 (see next benefit).

Premiums are deductible under certain circumstances. Premiums paid for life insurance are not deductible on individual income tax returns. However, they *can be deductible when with-drawing the cash value of the policy*. That's because the tax due on the money received (the cash value) is only taxable to the extent it exceeds the *amount of premiums that have been paid over the life of the policy*. If this amount is more than the cash value, the money can be received with *no taxes due whatsoever*. If not, the amount due in taxes will still be greatly reduced.

Let's see how this would work using our example of a $10,000 cash value. If you paid $8,000 in premiums to keep your life insured and to earn your $10,000, you will only have to pay taxes on $2,000. And if your total premiums exceed your cash value, you won't have to pay any taxes at all.

Money borrowed against cash value is usually not taxed. As was stated earlier, money borrowed against cash value is not taxed. This borrowing power gives you access to money without worrying about Uncle Sam's cut.

Consumer Alert

In order to avoid taxes on money borrowed, the IRS must recognize the policy as a bona fide life insurance instrument rather than an investment vehicle disguised as a life insurance policy. There are specific rules in that regard, so be sure to ask your accountant and life insurance agent whether the policy you have or are intending to buy qualifies under the IRS rules.

When the cash value portion is paid as part of the death benefit, it is not taxable at all. If you will recall the discussion on term insurance (see page 269), you will remember that the cash value of a life insurance policy merges with the death benefit when a claim is made. This effect is recognized by the tax code, which permits the cash value portion of the death benefit to be paid free of income tax when it is part of the death benefit. Thus, in our example, if you died leaving a death benefit of $50,000, the $10,000 that was the cash value portion of the death benefit would be paid to your beneficiaries free and clear of the IRS.

The monies paid to the beneficiaries are not usually subject to taxation. As discussed earlier (see page 265), when the beneficiary receives benefits, they are usually tax free. This includes the portion of the death benefit that constitutes insurance company proceeds (as opposed to cash value monies). Such life insurance benefits are free of income tax and usually *but not always* free from inheritance and estate taxes.

▶ **NOTE: This book does not purport to give tax advice. In order to be sure how your life insurance affects your taxes individually, consult your accountant or lawyer.**

Investment

The company invests your premiums to financially benefit you and itself. Buying cash value life insurance is sort of like staking a gold miner to a trip to the gold fields and sharing in the bounty he discovers. You give the company cash through higher premiums and, at least in theory, they use their considerable investment expertise to earn money from their "stake" through investments. There are advantages and disadvantages for you in this arrangement.

Disadvantage: The company exacts a charge for managing your money. Being capitalistic concerns, life insurance companies don't act for altruistic purposes. Thus, part of the money you invest with them accrues to their benefit and not yours.

Disadvantage: You usually have no control over the investments made. Once you have selected the kind of cash value life insurance you are going to buy, you usually have no control over how the company invests "your" money. Thus, if you do not want to invest in stocks but the company does, your premium dollars will be put into stocks. Similarly, if you want your premium dollars to be invested with a social conscience and your life insurance company has no such criterion (and it won't), your money might be put to work in places that would incur your disapproval.

Disadvantage: You have no flexibility. If you manage your own investments, you are free to move your money to wherever you think it will do the best for you. You can also hedge your bets by investing in a variety of ways. This usually isn't true when you invest in a cash value policy; you either sink or swim as the company does. There are a few exceptions to this rule. **Variable life insurance** (see chapter 30) allows some flexibility, as do many life insurance policies sold in Great Britain and Canada.

Advantage: You get two benefits for one price. Unlike other investments that only make you money, cash value life insurance provides a death benefit should you die. Plus, you have an investment that accrues value over the years.

Advantage: You receive tax benefits not available in other investments. As we've already detailed, the money earned in life insurance enjoys certain tax benefits not available in most other investments.

Advantage: You don't have to have a lot of money to become "an investor". Because you "invest" your money with the life insurance company a little bit at a time through your periodic premiums, you don't have to have a lot of money gathered together in one place to become an investor.

Advantage: Your money can work harder. There is an old adage that says, "It takes money to make money." One look at how the world really works will tell you that there is a great deal of truth to this statement. When you add your small premium to the total investment pool of the life insurance company, you become part of a very powerful investment force worth literally millions of dollars. Because the investment pool is so large, it can earn a higher rate of return than your premium could if it were put to work as an individual investment. (However, how much of that high rate gets into your pocket may be another question entirely.)

Advantage: Your money is invested by an expert. The people who manage life insurance company investments are experts in their fields. Thus, your small piece of the investment pie is managed in a way you might never be able to match, due to time, training, and the access that a large investment pool brings to the investment opportunity marketplace.

Advantage: There are often minimum earnings guarantees. Many companies guarantee a minimum level of earnings that you will receive for your premium investments. These minimums will not be high, but at least you know your money will earn something. That isn't always true of other investments.

Earnings Projections

Companies compete for your business using "projected earnings." When you are shopping for life insurance, the agent or sales representative will show you a chart that "projects" the future cash value of the policy as it accrues over time. These are called projection charts (here we go again with the charts). Often these charts are (to be charitable) overly optimistic. *In truth, no agent or company can tell you what your cash value will be*, since its future growth is directly dependent upon the success or failure of the insurance company's investment activities.

Cash Value Projection Charts

Among the most powerful baits that life insurance companies use to induce you to buy are the projected earnings charts that illustrate "how much money" you will earn by buying their life insurance. But beware, the charts are more smoke than fire.

Consumer Alert

Historically, the percentage of returns for cash value life insurance policies has been lower than what would have been earned had the same money been invested in bank passbook savings accounts. So always take the projected earnings estimate with a heavy dose of skepticism. It is only there to induce you to buy.

The following is a typical example of such a projection chart. It is an abridged portion of a quote given to Wesley J. Smith, the 40-year-old nonsmoker in good health you met earlier when discussing term insurance projection charts. The death benefit for the quote is $150,000.

CASH VALUE PROJECTION CHART

Age	End of Year	Annual Outlay	Projected Values Cash Value	Projected Values Surrender Value	Guaranteed Values Cash Value	Guaranteed Values Surrender Value
41	1	$1,791	$ 1,382	$ 0	$ 1,299	$ 0
42	2	1,791	2,881	1,005	2,598	878
43	3	1,791	4,488	2,604	3,933	2,286
44	4	1,791	6,236	4,336	5,290	3,714
[Ages 45–63 omitted]						
64	24	$1,791	$117,901	$117,901	$27,898	$27,898
65	25	1,791	131,725	131,725	27,550	27,550

Guaranteed values: Based on guaranteed interest rate of 4% and the guaranteed cost of insurance.
Projected values: Based on the current cost of insurance, which is subject to change, and the following interest assumptions > 9.54%.

Comparison with Term Insurance

Let's review the meaning of this chart and compare it to the term policies discussed in the last chapter. (The two term charts are repeated on page 312 for your convenience.)

- Note that **the annual premium is $1,382**, over $1,000 more than either of the term policies quoted at the same time for the same face value.

- **The value of the policy accrues quickly because it is expensive**. A lower monthly premium would accrue cash value at a lower rate.

- There is a vast difference between the projected value and the guaranteed value. **The guaranteed value is the only value that can be counted on**. The actual performance of the policy will probably come somewhere in the middle between the projected values and the guaranteed values.

- **The projected value is based, in part, on an interest rate of 9.54 percent**. This is probably an unrealistic expectation.

- **The "cash value" in this policy is the amount that can be borrowed against**. The "surrender value" is the amount to be received if the policy is canceled and its worth withdrawn.

- From ages 40 to 65, $44,775 will have been paid in premiums. The **guaranteed surrender** value at age 65, assuming that no money was borrowed against the cash value, is **$27,550**. This is **$17,225 less** than the premiums paid.

- In contrast, the 10-year renewable term policy quoted in the last chapter (Example 1) would have cost $32,805, using the current premium projections without reentry rights. This term policy would have cost $11,970 less than the cash value policy in premiums. However, **if the guaranteed surrender value**

TERM INSURANCE PROJECTION CHART—EXAMPLE 1

Year	Death Benefit	Current Premium With Reentry	Current Premium Without Reentry	Maximum Premium Guarantee
1–10	$150,000	$372	$ 372	$ 372
11	$150,000	$631	$1,104	$2,347
12	$150,000	$631	$1,183	$2,509
[Years 13–19 Omitted]				
20	$150,000	$631	$2,102	$5,304

Renewal Privilege: Automatically renewable for successive one-year periods to age 95.
Conversion Privilege: Convertible, without evidence of insurability for the full face amount of the policy during the first five policy years. Thereafter, convertible without evidence of insurability for 80% of the face amount. The conversion privilege may not be exercised on or after the policy nearest the insured's 70th birthday.

TERM INSURANCE PROJECTION CHART—EXAMPLE 2

Multiply death benefit below by number of thousands and then add $60 for policies over $100,000.

Age at Last Birthday	Male	Female
40	1.03	.95
41	1.09	1.00
42	1.17	1.05
43	1.25	1.10
[Etc.]		

is subtracted from the total cost of the premiums, the cash value policy will have actually cost less over the entire time period. On the other hand, if the $11,970 difference in premiums had been invested by the insurance consumer, a great deal of money could have been earned. (In further contrast, a typical mail-order annual renewable term policy (Example 2) would have cost a total of $19,778 in projected total premiums over the same 25-year time span. This is $24,997 less in premiums than the quoted cash value policy.)

As if all of this wasn't enough to think about, cash value policies come in several different types. The difference among them can be exciting to read about—if you are into minutiae and find the theories of accounting techniques to be the stuff dreams are made of. However, dull as it might be, the information can be important. The following chapter will identify the kinds of cash value policies, including annuities.

30

Vive la Difference: Cash Value Policies

Whole Life Insurance

A **whole life insurance policy**, as the name implies, remains in effect for the "whole life" of the insured; that is, until the insured's death or until the policy lapses due to cancellation, non-payment of premiums, or otherwise—whichever comes first.

There are three major types of whole life insurance: **traditional whole life**, **interest-sensitive whole life**, and **single-premium whole life**.

Traditional Whole Life

Traditional whole life insurance (TWL) is your basic garden variety type of cash value life insurance. In TWL, the insurance contract lasts until the insured is 100 years old or dies. If the insured makes it to 100, the benefits are paid as sort of a reward for a job well done.

Let's break this down a little further. Traditional whole life can be a **guaranteed cost policy** or a **nonguaranteed cost policy**.

Guaranteed cost policies. All of the guesswork is taken out of guaranteed cost policies. They provide a *guaranteed premium*, a *guaranteed cash value*, and *they pay no dividends or interest above that earned in accruing the guaranteed cash value*. This nonpayment feature makes these types **nonparticipating** policies—"nonpar" in insurance lingo.

Nonguaranteed cost policies. Some policies, while guaranteeing a fixed premium, fixed death benefit, and minimum fixed cash values, allow policyholders to benefit (or suffer, as the case may be) from the financial condition of the company. These TWL policies are called **participating policies** or "par" policies.

In a par policy, the company will pay dividends to the policyholder. A dividend is declared by the company based on its financial success (or lack thereof) over the previous year. Dividends are most often declared based on a unit price of $1,000. Thus, if a declared dividend is $1.25 and you have a $100,000 face value policy, you would multiply the total number of units in your death benefit (100) by the declared dividend. That total would be $125 ($1.25 × 100 = $125).

Depending on your particular insurance contract, dividends can be paid to you in one of several ways:

- In cash.

- Left in the policy to increase its cash value (also known as a cash reserve).

- Used to reduce the amount of your premium.

- Used to purchase minimal amounts of additional whole life coverage ($125 wouldn't buy much).

- Used to buy a one-year term policy.

Consumer Alert

If you are looking into purchasing a par whole life policy, be sure you understand your rights concerning paid dividends. The place to look is in the company's prospectus sheets. Or, ask your agent.

Interest-Sensitive Whole Life

Interest-sensitive whole life (ISWL) policies are something of a newcomer on the life insurance block. They were developed to allow stock companies to compete with mutuals during the days of high inflation when interest rates were very high.

Here is how interest-sensitive whole life compares to traditional whole life:

- **Both have level premiums.**

- **Both build up cash values, also known as cash reserves, over the life of the policy.**

- **Both have guaranteed minimum rates of return.**

- **The two differ in the method by which the policy gets beyond the minimum rate of earnings.** As you will recall, TWL uses the payment of dividends to create extra benefits to the policyholder. However, in ISWL *there is a fluctuating interest rate that is paid.* Sometimes this interest rate is tied to some economic indicator such as the interest rate on Treasury bills. At other times the interest rates are determined solely at the discretion of the insurance company.

Usually there are more options available to you in ISWL regarding the ways that the interest is used than with TWL. For example:

Some policies tie the price of the premium to the interest rates being earned. Thus, if the interest rate is high, the price of the premium will go down. If the interest rate is low, the premium will go up. In such policies there will be a maximum premium that can be charged.

Others tie the interest rate to the mortality tables and will actually reduce the death benefit if earnings are low. However, if the cash value gets high enough, the death benefit may go up since the death benefit must exceed the cash value by a defined percentage.

Still others use the interest rates to add to the cash value. This is done in greater or lesser amounts depending on the amount of interest being earned.

Thus, in summary, ISWL differs from TWL mainly in the way earnings are added to the value of the policy above the guaranteed minimums, with ISWL more tied in to the health of the economy as a whole and TWL more dependent on the performance of the insurance company itself. (The two often go hand in hand but not always.)

Single-Premium Whole Life

Single-premium life insurance, as the name implies, is sold with a one-time-only large sum premium paid by the policy owner when the policy is initially taken out. The amount of insurance obtained is dependent on the amount of the premium and the age of the insured.

Once the premium has been paid, the policy will accrue cash value by having interest added. The amount of interest will vary from year to year and will generally not be guaranteed beyond the first five years. There will be a guaranteed floor below which the interest rate cannot go. There will also be an interest rate projection, often called the **current rate**.

As with any cash value life insurance, you can withdraw the

reserve as you choose. However, there may be a penalty for any withdrawals that occur early in the policy.

The principal use of single-premium whole life has usually been as an investment tool, not for the purchase of life insurance protection. That's because the amount of life insurance you can buy, even with a $10,000 premium, is far less than you can obtain with other forms of life insurance. Lower premiums paid over an extended time, as occurs in other cash value policies, add up to a significantly higher amount of money actually paid and thus the purchase of higher face value protection.

Single-premium whole life policies have usually been used as a source of accruing tax-deferred earnings and as a source of collateral for borrowing money and thus having access to tax-free money. The companies that sell this product have tried to make it easy. For example, if you only borrow money you have earned in interest, the interest rate will be set in such a way that it matches the interest earned by your initial premium. Thus, in effect, you have an interest-free loan. If you borrow from principal, however, the company will take more than it gives.

Consumer Alert

Recent tax changes make loans against the accrued cash value of certain life insurance policies *taken out after June 21, 1988*, taxable. Single-premium policies do not escape this new tax law. Thus, be sure to consult your accountant or lawyer before purchasing this type of policy or using it as collateral to borrow money.

Universal Life Insurance

Technically, **universal life insurance** is a form of whole life insurance. In fact its official name is **adjustable-premium whole**

life. However, there are significant differences in the approach of traditional whole life and universal life, so for purposes of clarity, we will continue to use the universal life moniker.

Meeting the Need for Flexibility

Universal life was designed to cure some of the problems consumers have traditionally had with whole life insurance. Among these were the following:

- Consumers never knew what percentage of their premiums went to company costs.

- The rate of return was less than the consumer could make with other types of investments.

- There was little latitude in the plans to allow tailoring to match the consumer's needs.

Universal life has changed all that. The key word for universal life is *flexibility*. *You* tell the life insurance company how *you* want your policy to operate. *You* tell them how long you want the death benefit to be in effect. *You* tell them how long you wish to be obligated to pay premiums. *You* tell them how much you want to earn in cash value over the life of the policy. Once you have done that, they tell you how much the premiums will be to achieve the greatest likelihood of reaching your desired results.

Characteristics of Universal Life

Here are some of the aspects of universal life that you should know about.

Policyholders receive an annual statement. This tells you what percentage of your premiums went to company costs, mortality charges, and cash value. These entries are broken down on a monthly basis.

The cash value is more readily available to you. You can even make partial withdrawals. *However, if you withdraw cash value, you risk decreasing your death benefit.*

Early withdrawal of cash value (prior to 15 years or so) may trigger a tax consequence. Again, be sure to consult an accountant or attorney before withdrawing funds from your cash value life insurance to see what, if any, tax consequences will accrue.

Two cash accounts are kept. One is the accumulation account and the other is a cash value. The accumulation account reflects the total amount you've earned. The cash value account is the money you can actually get at. For a period of time, the cash account will be lower than the accumulation account. This is because universal life is usually **back-loaded**. This means that expenses (commissions, etc.), usually taken up front in whole life or term life (**front-loading**), are paid later in the policy. You can, of course, elect to have a front-loaded policy. However, until the expense "load" has been paid, the money you can withdraw is less than the total earned in the reserve account. Once the two merge, the load has been paid in full. (The cash value projection chart on page 310 is an example of a universal life policy prospectus.)

Universal life policies allow you to increase your coverage without paying costs and expenses all over again (loading). The company will, however, have the right to make sure you remain insurable. Think of this aspect as the right to increase benefits in return for the company's right of reentry (as to the increased benefit only).

Depending on your accrued cash value, you can sometimes skip payment of premiums. You can also overpay and have the extra money paid in credited to your account.

Consumer Alert

Universal life insurance salespeople often put great emphasis on the fact that you can "pay up" the policy like you can with certain whole life policies. In doing so, they may show you projections indicating when a policy will be paid up. There's no problem here *if you always remember that these are just projections and not guarantees*. The actual performance of the policy may differ. There will be a minimum interest rate guarantee, however.

You can elect to receive the death benefit in one of two ways:

- In the traditional way where the cash value is merged into the death benefit.

- Or you can receive *both* the death benefit and the cash value. Choosing this option will either cost you more in premiums or result in a slower increase in cash value.

If you decide to buy a universal life policy, be sure to keep a close eye on it and take advantage of its flexibility. Thus, if you add a child to your family, you may wish to think about increasing your policy's value. If you come into some extra money, you may wish to make a large payment to move your policy toward a paid-off status. Finally, be sure to review the statements you receive to make sure that the investment you thought you made remains the investment you desire.

Variable Life Insurance

Variable life insurance (VLI) allows the owner of the policy to invest in stocks and bonds as a means of accruing cash value while maintaining life insurance protection for the benefit of loved ones or other beneficiaries.

Investment Choice

When you purchase VLI, you will have the option of having your premium dollars invested in a common stock fund, a bond fund, a money market fund, or others—it's your choice. You can also change funds depending on the terms of the policy.

The cash investment fund is called the **separate investment account**. The funds of all of the policyholders are, in effect, a mutual fund operated by the insurance company. Thus, the company must have approval of the Securities & Exchange Commission to sell VLI. The amount of cash accrual for your account will depend on the success of the life insurance company's investment managers.

Other Features of VLI

- **Premiums are usually fixed and unchanging, similar to whole life**. However, some policies allow for a one-time-only premium or flexible premiums.

- **Most variable life policies are nonpar**. In other words, dividends will not be paid.

- **There is no minimum interest guarantee**. Therefore, the risk of loss for bad investments falls more directly on the policyholder than in other forms of cash value life insurance. However, the potential for high earnings may be better with VLI.

- **The amount of the death benefit may vary according to the success or failure of the investments**. If the investments do better than the anticipated return, the amount of the face value may go up. Conversely, if the investments do not do well, the face value may go down, *but not lower than the initial face value of the insurance.*

- **Tax benefits for VLI are similar to those available for other types of cash value insurance**. So are the rights to borrow against the cash value.

- **Charges made by the insurance company should be spelled out when you are reviewing the sales prospectus**. Note that most such policies provide for a substantial penalty for early cancellation of the policy (called **surrender charges**). Charges are also made for mortality risk, management of investments, and front-loading. The charges for VLI may be higher than for other forms of insurance.

Consumer Alert

Some policies guarantee that your death benefit cannot be lost due to poor investment performance. *If you buy variable life insurance, make sure that the policy contract has this guarantee.*

Is VLI a worthwhile form of life insurance? Consumers Union has its doubts. They advocate separating life insurance protection for loved ones from investment action. Also, if you are not an experienced investor, you may not want this type of policy since you won't have the business acumen to move your investment account among the investment options available to you.

Endowment Plans

Endowment insurance acts as both a life insurance plan and a way to guarantee funds to the owner of the policy if the insured lives beyond the term the insurance is in effect. In essence, endowment policies are savings plans guaranteed by life insurance.

Like term insurance, an endowment policy is taken out for a specific period of time, typically 20 or 25 years. This term is called the **endowment period**.

Like other life insurance policies, the insurance has a face value that will be paid to the beneficiary if the insured dies. However, unlike other policies, if the insured survives the term, the face value of the policy is paid to the *owner of the policy, not the beneficiaries*.

Premiums for endowment policies are *high*. This is because the money paid must do two things: pay for the cost of the life insurance, and build sufficient cash value to earn the face amount by the end of the policy term. For this reason, endowment policies are one of the least written types of life insurance.

Universities frequently use endowment plans to help raise money.

Annuities

Annuities provide periodic income payments over a specified term or for the life of the insured. The money to pay the income comes from the premiums paid into the annuity. These payments can be in a lump sum, periodic, or as the owner of the policy (the annuitant) determines. There can be more than one annuitant for the same policy.

Benefits for annuities are determined by the amount of the premium and the interest the annuity earns over time. Sometimes benefits can be arranged to begin immediately. If so, the lump-sum premium will have to be substantial. More often, benefits are deferred until a later time, typically as a preparation for retirement. If the annuity is deferred, tax benefits accrue similar to that of cash value life insurance.

Payments on the annuity can be for the lifetime(s) of the annuitant(s) (**life annuity**). They can also be for a specified time, whether or not the annuitant dies in the interim. If the payment is for life, the annuity will usually pay a higher income amount than if it is for a specified time. If a life annuitant dies, the company's only obligation is to refund the difference between the premium and the benefits paid, if any, with the company keeping any earnings that would have otherwise gone to the annuitant.

You can buy a combination of annuity and life insurance called a **split life insurance policy**. A split policy is a combination of an annual renewable term life insurance policy and an annuity paid on a yearly basis. The cost is somewhat akin to a cash value policy. Split policies are not available in every state.

Consumer Alert

The above described insurance plans are the generic names given by the industry to the different types of cash value plans. Most insurance companies give fancy names to their individual products. These names may or may not include the terms "whole life," "universal life," etc. Thus, when discussing these plans, ask the sales agent what kind of policy he or she is talking about. Remember, it is not the name that is important but the performance of the policy on your behalf.

This ends our discussion of the different types of cash value policies. The thing to remember is that each company will offer policy terms slightly different from the competition's. The main thing to do is compare and contrast these policies with one another, and don't buy until you find the one that seems just right for you.

31

Life Insurance Riders

Whether you purchase a term life insurance policy or cash value coverage, you may want to take a serious look at extras or options you can buy that can add to your protection. These are called **riders**.

Riders can be compared to the special equipment options you can obtain when you purchase a car. As a CD stereo adds to the price of a car, so too do riders add to your insurance premiums. Why buy them? Aren't the basic policies protection enough? The answer to that question is "not necessarily."

Generally, riders perform two very important functions:

- They add to or *extend the coverage* provided by the basic life insurance policy.

- They *protect the viability* of the life insurance policy itself.

Either function can spell the difference between full protection and exposure to the loss of benefits.

Extended Coverage Riders

Extended coverage riders provide a range of extra protections.

Accidental Death

Of all of the additions that can be purchased, the **accidental death rider** is probably the most famous. Popularly known as the **double indemnity** clause, the accidental death rider *increases the face amount of the policy should the insured die as a result of accident*. The increase is usually double the face amount (thus the term "double indemnity"), but it does not have to be. Some riders provide for even higher coverage if the accidental death occurs while on a common carrier such as a commercial jet.

Accidental death riders are normally available to augment just about any basic life coverage you can get. But before you buy, remember this: *Far more people die of natural causes than due to accidents*. The question also has to be asked whether an accidental death requires additional coverage compared to death from natural causes. Most consumer organizations discourage the purchase of this rider and suggest that the extra premium money is better applied to a higher amount of basic coverage.

If you are interested in an accidental death benefit rider, be sure to read the fine print before you buy. For example, many riders require that the death occur within 90 days of the accident. Moreover, look to see what happens if the cause of death is on the fine line between accident and natural cause, such as a person who is in an automobile accident and dies at the scene from a heart attack.

Cost of Living

Back in the bad old days of high inflation, the continuing increases in the cost of living would eat up the value of the face amount of life insurance faster than you could say the word "inflation." As a result, many insurance companies developed a rider that is, in effect, a one-year term policy that increases or decreases the basic coverage depending on what happens with the Consumer Price Index (CPI) and *without having to prove continuing insurability*. In essence, the **cost of living rider** indexes the face amount of the policy to protect its real value.

Here's how the rider works. Assume you have taken out a policy with a $100,000 face amount. Assume further that the CPI goes up 5 percent for the year. The next year, the rider will be worth $5,000 in increased benefits, with the owner of the policy charged for the increased coverage. This will continue year to year as long as the policy and rider remain in effect.

Guaranteed Insurability

When you decide to buy life insurance, the amount you buy may be fine for today, but who really knows how much will be enough tomorrow? For example, the amount of life insurance we need may go up as we increase the size of our family or incur greater living expenses by "moving up in the world" to a larger home or a more luxurious lifestyle.

You can protect yourself from this in several ways. One way is to buy term insurance where you get more insurance bang for your premium buck. But what if you want to purchase cash value insurance? Do you have to buy more than you need or can afford?

The answer is no. You can purchase a **guaranteed insurability rider** that allows you to *buy additional cash value at standard rates regardless of your insurability*. In essence, this rider is an option to purchase life insurance later at a price to be determined based on your age and the amount of insurance you elect to add to your coverage—not based on your health.

There are some things you need to know about guaranteed insurability riders before deciding to pay for the right to increase coverage:

- The rider is not available for term insurance.

- The rider is frequently only available to you in your younger years.

- There are time limits within which you must exercise your option to purchase increased coverage. After that you are out of luck. Be sure you understand this before you pay money for a rider that you may never get to use if you wait too long.

Term Insurance Rider

Many people have cash value policy tastes but a term policy pocketbook. Insurance companies recognize this but don't want to lose the profitability of selling you cash value insurance. Thus, they have created the **term insurance rider**, which gives you two, two, two policies almost for the price of one. One policy is a cash value type. The other is a term policy that allows you to keep the face value high for income protection. Then, when you are able, you can convert the term policy to a cash value plan.

Another term insurance rider allows term insurance to be bought for the spouse or children of a person who purchases cash value insurance. This term rider is called the **family rider**. Buying term insurance for other family members in this way allows you to avoid **double loading** (paying insurance company expenses, like commissions, twice), which would occur if the term policy was purchased separate and apart from the cash value policy.

Nondeath Benefit Payments

Some companies offer riders that will pay benefits *even if the insured does not die* but meets with some catastrophe.

Accidental dismemberment rider. This addition to the life insurance contract provides that all or a part of the death benefit will be paid if the insured loses body parts such as an eye or limb due to an accident. The amount paid under these riders depends on the body part lost. Look into the provisions of the rider to see the amount to be paid in the event of such accidental dismemberment.

Living insurance rider. This rider allows payment of benefits during the life of the insured should the insured suffer a catastrophic illness. For example, some of these riders will pay 2 percent a month of the face value if the insured needs long-term nursing home care. Others will pay percentages depending on the cause of the catastrophic illness (stroke, heart attack, renal failure, etc.).

Policy Protection Riders

Sometimes the most important rider you can buy *protects the very existence of your life insurance policy itself*. Here are some examples.

Waiver of Premium

This rider, many consumer and industry bigwigs agree, can be important to your complete life insurance protection. (However, support for this rider is not unanimous.)

With a **waiver of premium rider**, if you are disabled for a period defined in the rider, your obligation to pay the premium is waived. This can be of tremendous value if you become disabled for a long period of time. It will allow life insurance protection to continue in full force when you might otherwise have lost it because you couldn't afford the premiums. (Some waiver riders are less generous, allowing only that portion of the premium that pays for mortality charges to be waived during the disability.) There are several things to keep in mind about waiver of premium riders:

- Disability usually has a double definition. For the first two years or so, disability is usually defined as an inability to work at your usual or customary occupation. After that, the definition is broadened to include any gainful occupation.

- There is usually a substantial waiting period, most often six months, before the rider takes effect.

- Many riders have a cutoff date of age 65.

- These riders usually cost 4 to 10 percent of the premium amount.

Automatic Premium Loan

Are you a little disorganized? Sometimes forget to pay your bills for a month? Maybe you simply don't trust the mail and want to make sure you don't lose your benefits because of nonpayment of premiums? Well, good news—an **automatic premium loan rider** can protect you against lapse of coverage by permitting the company to automatically use dividends or issue you a loan from your cash value to pay for premiums if you otherwise fail to pay them.

Here's the best part: This rider should not cost you one red cent! That's right, it's gratis—one of the few real values left. All you have to do is check the appropriate box on the application and you're covered. (Be sure to keep a copy of your application.)

Spendthrift

When you accrue cash value in your policy, it might be subject to attachment by creditors should you fall into debt and lose court cases ordering you to pay your creditors. A **spendthrift rider** allows the cash value to be protected from creditors—unless you selected the provision for the purpose of defrauding creditors.

Part 6

Government Insurance Benefits

We, the people of the United States, in order to form a more perfect Union, establish justice, insure domestic tranquility, provide for the common defense, promote the general welfare, and secure the blessings of liberty to ourselves and our posterity do ordain and establish this Constitution for the United States of America.

—Preamble to the Constitution of the United States

What grand and glorious words our forefathers wrote when they created the United States of America. But it takes more than mere words to accomplish the grand and glorious purposes for which our government exists. It takes action and commitment. And yes, it takes money.

Happily, at least in the past, we have been able to muster all three. Since the Great Depression of the 1930s, the United States has increasingly been concerned with promoting the general welfare of its people. One way in which this has been accomplished has been in the creation of new and important social insurance programs that have gone a long way toward reducing the uncertainties and cruelties that life often has to offer the poor, powerless, or elderly.

Perhaps the most important of these government insurance programs is **Social Security**. Social Security is known mainly as an "old age pension" program established to ensure that those who have spent a lifetime working will have a source of income when their working days are over.

But Social Security accomplishes far more than that. It is a disability insurer, it provides a modest life insurance benefit to some families, and it helps defray burial costs. It is also an annuity program for those who have not personally worked but spent a lifetime as the homemaker and helpmate of a spouse who did.

Then there's **Medicare**, the national health insurance program enacted in the mid-'60s for senior citizens and the disabled. Thanks to this program, millions of our elderly are able to afford quality medical care that might not otherwise be available to them.

The United States also provides health insurance and other benefits for qualified veterans of the armed forces. The Veterans Administration, while severely beleaguered by budget cuts, can still offer certain **veterans benefits** that would not otherwise exist for these brave men and women who have sacrificed so much for their country.

State governments also have enacted insurance programs to help their citizens. **Unemployment insurance** softens the blow of a layoff from work. A few states also provide disability insurance to help those who, for health reasons, cannot work. And the **Medicaid** program, jointly funded by the federal government and the various states, helps bring at least some medical care to the poor.

In order for these programs to be more effective, they have to be understood by the people they are designed to benefit. That is the task before us. We will investigate the scope of the programs and get into the issues of who qualifies for assistance and who does not. Oh—not to worry. We will restrict ourselves to good old-fashioned American English—no bureaucratese allowed.

32

Social Security

It's hard to imagine a time in this country when we did not have Social Security. Yet, the truth of the matter is that the program is only a little more than 50 years old. Since its inception in the 1930s, it has become so deeply ingrained into the American way of life that we wouldn't know what to do without it.

Social Security is really three programs in one.

It is a retirement program. The most famous function of Social Security is as a retirement pension fund. As we shall see, the amount you get to collect depends on the money you have earned during your working years; the more you have earned, the higher your benefits. The amount you receive is also dependent upon when you decide to apply. If you apply at the earliest date possible, your 62nd birthday, you will receive lower payments than if you wait until age 70 before collecting. We'll discuss this and more, below.

It is a disability insurance program. A less famous function of Social Security is as a disability insurance system. If we become sick or injured to such an extent that we can no longer work for a living, Social Security can ride to the rescue by providing a monthly check. (Actually, "limp to the rescue" would be a better term, since the checks aren't all that high. But every little bit helps.)

It is an annuity program for dependents and survivors. Life can be cruel, especially when it takes a beloved breadwinner to the great beyond. Those who are left behind can face the very serious problems of simply putting a roof over their heads and food into hungry mouths. One important function of Social Security is to provide partial financial support for a deceased worker's family, when the kids are minors and/or during the surviving spouse's retirement years.

Retirement Benefits

Let's take a look at the most well known and highly utilized aspect of the Social Security system: retirement benefits. A common myth surrounding the retirement benefits paid by Social Security is that they are designed to fully support recipients in their retirement years. This is simply not true. Social Security has never been nor was it meant to be the sole source of support for recipients. Rather, it is designed to serve as a *supplement* to pension plans, savings accounts, and other forms of support for those who have primarily left their working years behind. The fact that some senior citizens must live solely on the sparse benefits paid by the program is one of the tragedies of modern American life.

As people prepare for retirement they begin to question how the program works. The following are some of the most common of these questions and their answers.

How Do I Qualify for Social Security?

Anyone who has ever received a paycheck knows that Social Security is not a gift from a benevolent government. To the contrary, workers obtain benefits the hard way; to quote a famous TV commercial, they "eeeeaaaarn them"—by paying taxes out of every paycheck. These payments are matched by their employers.

Qualifying for the program is relatively easy. It is done by earning what are called **work credits**. A work credit is measured in **quarters of coverage**, which translates into quarters of a year. You receive a credit by earning a minimum amount of money from *covered employment* per quarter. (Covered employment consists of any work for which you must pay Social Security taxes.) The amount of money differs depending on the years you worked. Self-employed workers must also pay into the system, only they pay double since they have to pay both their personal contribution as well as that of the "employer." (Most workers now come under Social Security, even federal workers, some of whom have been paying into the system since 1984.)

Once you have earned sufficient work credits (the amount will vary depending on the benefit requested), you qualify. For example, in 1990, if you earned 9¾ years' worth of credits at the age of 62, you are eligible for retirement benefits.

How Much Will My Check Be?

Unfortunately, Social Security does not pay enough to cover all of your retirement needs. But then, as we mentioned above, it wasn't designed to. The size of your check will depend upon the following.

The amount you have paid into the system. The amount you will ultimately receive is directly dependent upon the amount of taxes you have paid into the system. That's because the benefit is determined by taking an average of the covered employment income you have earned over the years.

The age at which you apply. Some people think that you can't qualify for benefits until reaching age 65. Not so. If you've met the work credits requirements that determine eligibility for retirement benefits, you can begin to receive them starting at age 62. There's a catch, though. Your benefits are reduced by 20

percent (less as you move closer to 65) and they remain reduced for the rest of your life. In order to receive full benefits, you do have to wait until age 65 (this will rise to age 67 by the year 2000). Some good news: If you wait to receive your benefits until *after* 65, you will receive a monthly premium (extra money) in addition to your standard benefits. The level of the premium rises until you celebrate your 70th birthday. Thereafter, there is no added payment for waiting, so there is no reason to hold off applying for your benefits beyond age 70.

Cost-of-living increases. Each January 1, your retirement benefits are increased in an amount equal to the rise in the cost of living based on the Consumer Price Index. Thus, if the CPI went up 6 percent in the previous year, so will your benefits.

Complicated formula. The exact amount of the payment you will qualify for is based on a formula that would make Einstein furrow his brow in mild confusion. In order to determine what your benefits are likely to be, you should:

1. Contact your local Social Security office. The phone number will be in the front of your phone book under U.S. Government listings.

2. Ask the good people at the Social Security office for a form called "REQUEST FOR SOCIAL SECURITY STATE-MENT OF EARNINGS." It will be mailed to you right away.

3. Fill out the form completely and return it by mail or in person to your local office.

4. Within a few weeks you will receive a written response setting forth your earnings history.

5. Using your earnings record, ask the office to figure out what your monthly benefits are likely to be. Their answer will give you a pretty accurate prediction of what your Social Security retirement benefits will be, so you can plan ahead.

Consumer Alert

Sometimes the government computations can be wrong. This can be a serious matter. If they have understated your earnings, they will also underpay your benefits. Thus, it is important that you check your records against the figures given to you in the earnings statement. If you think an error has occurred, you can correct it. There is a time limit, however. You have only three years, three months, and 15 days (39½ months) to find and correct any mistakes made in tallying your account. Thus, it is a good idea to have the Social Security Administration update your records for you every few years so that you can compare it with what you believe you have earned.

Consumer Alert

Because the United States is in such heavy debt, changes may be coming that could affect your Social Security check. One proposed change is for there to be some form of "means testing," wherein Social Security beneficiaries with high incomes might have their right to receive Social Security checks limited. Another potential change is the reduction or elimination or delay of annual cost of living adjustments in your Social Security check. Be sure to stay informed on this important issue and participate in the coming political debates on cutting the United States budget deficit.

Are My Benefits Subject to Income Tax?

The answer is yes and no. How's that for being unequivocal? Normally, Social Security benefits are not subject to taxation. However, if you are fortunate enough to have earned income and nontaxable interest in excess of about $25,000 for the year, your benefits could be taxed. Contact your Social Security office for more details.

Will My Benefits Be Reduced If I Work?

That depends on how much you earn. If your earned income exceeds approximately $8,200 at age 65 (less if you are close to 62), your benefits are subject to being reduced $1 for every $3 earned. Since these reductions vary depending on age and other factors, be sure to contact your local Social Security office to see exactly how the rules apply to you.

When Should I Apply for Benefits?

Considering the slow pace of bureaucracy, at age 40. All joking aside, you should give yourself about three months before you want benefits to commence.

Consumer Alert

If you apply before the age of 65, you will not be paid for any monthly checks you could have received had you applied earlier. However, after the age of 65, you can be repaid for up to six months' worth of checks you failed to receive because you did not apply in a timely manner.

What Should I Bring with Me When I Apply?

Besides a good book to read while you wait your turn in line, you should also be sure to bring the following:

- **Your Social Security Card or a record of the Social Security number you are making a claim under**. If you are making a claim based on another person's number (e.g., a deceased spouse), bring their card or number.

- **Proof of your age**. A birth certificate is best, but other records such as a baptismal record will do.

- **Your marriage certificate if you are applying as a widowed person on your deceased spouse's earning record**. See below.

- **Your W-2 form or a copy of your last federal income tax return**. You will need this in order to receive an accurate benefit, since the Social Security Administration will not have absolutely up-to-the-minute records of your earnings.

Dependents and Survivors' Benefits

An important function of Social Security is to provide benefits for dependents and other survivors of eligible workers. In essence, this is a form of life insurance that provides monthly support checks to eligible immediate family members of a deceased worker. These include minor children of a deceased working parent, and the widowed who are supporting minor children. Dependent retirement benefits are also payable to the widowed and qualified divorced spouses of eligible workers.

The following are some of the questions often asked by people interested in this aspect of Social Security.

Who Is a Dependent?

For purposes of Social Security, a dependent can be any of the following persons:

- **A spouse age 62 or older**. These persons can elect to receive benefits on the spouse's earnings or on their own, whichever would give a higher benefit. However, they cannot receive both.

- **A spouse under age 62 who cares for the deceased worker's child who is under the age of 16 or disabled**. If a spouse of a deceased worker takes care of the deceased worker's young or disabled children, that person will receive a monthly check to help with the children's support.

- **A disabled spouse under the age of 62**. See below.

- **A divorced spouse age 62 or older**. In order to qualify under an ex-spouse's earnings record, the marriage must have lasted for a minimum of 10 years.

- **Unmarried children of a deceased worker under the age of 18**. They also receive checks to help with their support.

- **Unmarried disabled children**. The disability must have occurred before the child was 22 years old.

Note that under the rules of Social Security, more than one of the above qualified dependents can claim Social Security benefits upon one worker's earnings. For example, assume a worker dies, leaving a wife and an eight-year-old daughter. The wife may be eligible for benefits since she's caring for a child under the age of 16, and the child will be eligible because she is under age 18.

How Much Will I Receive?

Benefits are based on the earnings of the deceased worker. The amount depends on the circumstances. Usually, a dependent or survivor receives a large percentage of what the worker would have been eligible for at age 65. Sometimes the amount is even 100 percent—for a surviving spouse who waits until age 65 to apply, for example.

Will My Benefits Be Reduced If I Receive a Pension?

If the pension is from a private employer or union, the answer is no. If it is from government service, the answer is maybe, depending on your individual circumstances. Ask your local Social Security office for more details.

What If I Go to Work?

Depending on how much you earn, you can lose benefits just as you would if you were receiving retirement benefits.

Disability Benefits

Social Security also pays benefits to workers who become disabled and thus cannot earn their own living. The following are the questions most frequently asked about this aspect of the program.

How Do I Become Eligible for Disability Benefits?

If you have earned enough work credits and you become disabled, you may be eligible for Social Security disability benefits. The amount of work credits you need will depend on your age and other circumstances. Check your local Social Security office if you have a question concerning your eligibility.

What Is a Disability?

The definition of disability for purposes of Social Security is somewhat different than it is in private disability policies (see Chapter 18).

The impairment can be physical or mental. Regardless of whether your disability is caused by a physical injury or is the result of a mental breakdown, you can qualify for disability if medical doctors will certify that you are indeed disabled.

The standard requires that you not be able to do any "substantially gainful work". This is a broader interpretation than the initial requirement for most private disability policies (not being able to perform your usual occupation). The Social Security

Administration has a list of impairments it considers disabling. If your condition is not on the list you must prove that the condition keeps you from earning a substantial living. What a substantial living is depends on your individual circumstances. Ask your Social Security office for details.

There is a time requirement. In addition to the above, the disability must be long term. Social Security requires that the disability will last or has lasted for at least 12 months or is expected to lead to death.

Can I Collect Other Disability Benefits Too?

As far as Social Security is concerned, the answer is yes. However, if the total benefits received are in excess of 80 percent of your usual earnings, your benefits may be cut. (Remember, however, that many private disability policies provide for a reduction of benefits based on other payments you receive, such as Social Security; see page 188.)

When Can I Collect Benefits?

As with any disability insurance program, there is a waiting period before benefits are collectible. Usually you must be disabled for at least five months before you are eligible to receive any benefits.

Does Social Security Review My Case?

Does Ronald Reagan believe in the free enterprise system? As with any disability insurance program, the benefit payer reserves the right to make sure the payee is entitled to continue to receive benefits.

Death Benefits

Social Security provides funds to help defray funeral expenses. The claim for the benefit must be made within two years of the death of the covered worker. The sum is admittedly very modest, in the mid-$200 range. This payment is limited to a spouse who was living with the worker at the time of death or to a spouse or a child who, in the month of death, is eligible for a Social Security benefit based on the worker's record.

Fighting Back

Many people are able to deal with the powers that be with little or no hassle beyond the usual bureaucratic delays. But what if you believe that the system has "done you wrong"? What do you do, punt? No, you get to work and appeal the wrong decision.

The Request for Reconsideration

As you would expect, there is an official form to fill out to get your request going. Your first step is to file a Request for Reconsideration. Don't procrastinate! You only have 60 days from the date you received the bad news to file your request.

Once you have filled out your request form, there's nothing to do but wait as caseworkers review the file. You will probably hear from Social Security with an answer within 30 days. If you don't, write a letter reminding them of their responsibilities to you.

The Administrative Hearing

If Social Security's decision doesn't go your way, you have the right to request a formal hearing. Again, turn to your local office to obtain the proper form. And *don't procrastinate*; you only have

60 days to request the hearing after the results of the Reconsideration are mailed to you.

The hearing itself is similar to a trial. You have the right to present testimony and have documents admitted into evidence. With so much at stake it is probably wise to hire a lawyer. If you do, be sure to hire one who has significant experience in Social Security matters; it is a very specialized field.

Filing an Appeal

If you still have not gotten your way and the money at stake or the principle of the thing is important enough for you to want to pursue your rights further, you can file an appeal with The National Appeals Council. Again, your local Social Security office will have the appropriate form. And again, *don't procrastinate*—you only have 60 days to file your appeal from the date you lost your hearing.

Bringing a Lawsuit

Finally, if you have exhausted all of the above avenues (known in the trade as administrative remedies), you can literally make a federal case out of the thing by filing a lawsuit. The expenses of your fight may really start to mount here, so be sure you are in the right before taking this step. You should also ask the lawyer to compute his or her fees and the costs of bringing the lawsuit to make sure the fight is worth the potential benefit. However, if you believe you are right and it's worth the time and money, go for it! Sometimes people do beat city hall.

33

Medicare

Medicare is a national health insurance plan designed primarily for the benefit of older citizens. However, older adults are not the only beneficiaries of this important program. Certain disabled people, such as those with kidney failure, also qualify for Medicare.

A popular misconception about Medicare is that it will pay most or all of a senior's health care costs. Unfortunately, that was never the case. Medicare was designed only to *assist* with these expenses. In fact, statistics show that *the costs that Medicare doesn't pay are nearly as substantial as those it does.*

There are three principal topics that need to be covered when it comes to Medicare: what it covers; what it does not cover; and how seniors can find private insurance coverage to pay for the difference. We will discuss the first two topics in this chapter. The third issue, the purchase of private policies to supplement Medicare benefits, will be handled in Chapter 36.

Medicare benefits are continually changing. We have included accurate figures and coverages for 1992. For updated information, contact your nearest Social Security office.

Qualifying for Medicare

In order to qualify for Medicare you have to be one of the following:

- **Age 65 and eligible for Social Security retirement benefits**, either directly or as a survivor or dependent.

- **Age 65 and ineligible for Social Security retirement benefits** (and you pay a fee to join Medicare).

- **Under age 65 and eligible for Social Security disability benefits for the previous 24 months** (whether you actually received them or not).

- **Under age 65 and suffering from kidney failure**, if you qualify based on sufficient Social Security work credits.

Since relatively few people have problems qualifying for Medicare, we will not concentrate on this issue. If you have any questions regarding eligibility, contact your local Social Security office.

Medicare Part A (Hospitalization)

Medicare comes in two parts, entitled **Part A** and **Part B** (oh, those clever bureaucrats). Part A is a form of hospitalization insurance. Here are some of the important features as it exists today.

Coverage is free. The benefits of Part A are free if you are eligible for Social Security. Once you qualify for Medicare and properly apply at your Social Security office, you are automatically covered under Part A.

You can join even if you are ineligible for Social Security. If you are one of those few unfortunate people over 65 who don't qualify for Social Security, you may be able to join Medicare by paying a fee. The cost is quite high, in excess of $200 per month. Because Medicare coverage is not cheap, review your other health insurance options before signing up. However, if you have had severe health care difficulties in the past, Medicare may be the only health insurance plan you will be able to obtain. (If you can't afford to buy into the program, consider applying for Medicaid. See Chapter 34.)

How Much Will It Pay?

Medicare will pick up a large portion of your hospitalization expenses. Here's how this aspect of Medicare operates. The numbers we give you here are valid for 1992. They are, of course, subject to change and will be going up in the years to come.

- **There is a $652 deductible per hospitalization.** This means the first $652 comes out of your pocket.

- **Days 1–60 are paid by Medicare.** This covers the vast majority of hospitalizations.

- **Days 61–90, you pay $163 per day.** This can add up fast.

- **Reserve days.** Medicare helps pay for your care in a hospital for up to 90 days in each benefit period. Medicare Part A includes an extra 60 hospital days you can use if you have a long illness and have to stay in the hospital for more than 90 days. These are called reserve days. *Caution:* Reserve days are not renewable. Once they are used, they are gone forever. During 1992, if you used a reserve day, your share of the hospital bill was $326 per day.

The moral of the story: Don't get so sick that you have to be hospitalized more than 60 days.

The DRG System

After you pay your deductible, all of your hospital bill is picked up by Medicare through day 60. Sounds good, huh? Well, there's a small catch. Payments to the hospital are based on the **diagnostic related group (DRG) system**, which could end up forcing you to leave the hospital before your health really permits. Here's how the DRG system operates.

The diagnosis. When you become ill, your doctor makes a diagnosis of what is wrong. This diagnosis becomes the basis for determining whether you are entitled to benefits; hospitalization will only be paid for if it is medically necessary. As we shall discuss immediately below, the diagnosis also affects the level of compensation received by the hospital.

Preadmission review. In some nonemergency cases, your doctor must submit a request to Medicare to get permission to admit you to the hospital before surgery or other medical procedures are performed. This requirement is waived if the delay in treatment would harm you.

The payment. Let's assume you are diagnosed as having a medical problem—we'll call it disease X—which requires hospitalization. The DRG system will have determined how long sufferers of disease X remain in the hospital on average. Let's assume that the average hospitalization for the condition is five days. In that case, the good people at Medicare will pay the hospital for five days' worth of care.

The result. The purpose of the DRG system is cost containment. But cutting monetary expenses can come with a very high human price tag. Many doctors claim that the system is causing their patients to be released sooner and sicker than ever before.

This is because, *under DRGs, the financial incentive for the hospital is to get you out the door as fast as possible.* Going back to our hypothetical example of disease X, the hospital receives a five-day payment from Medicare *regardless of the actual time you spend in the hospital.* If you are released in three or four days, the hospital makes a profit. On the other hand, if you are hospitalized for nine days, the facility will lose money on your care.

If they want you out. You'll know that your doctor or hospital wants you out if you receive a written Notice of Noncoverage. Defenders of the DRG system claim that it is against the law to release a patient under the system before it is safe to do so. And that is true. However, in the real world the potential for abuse is high. In fact, several medical professionals we've interviewed on the subject insist that at least some hospitals count the days a patient can stay *in advance* and begin planning the discharge almost as soon as the hospital admission procedure has been completed.

A Notice of Noncoverage doesn't mean that the hospital will send some burly orderlies to your room to pick you up and leave you on the curb wrapped in a blanket. But it does mean that the cost of your continued hospitalization will be on you. With the cost of average hospital care running in excess of high-priced hotel suites, and with older people generally being very reluctant to take a financial risk, few people elect to stay in the hospital beyond their allotted time, even if they would be physically better off doing so.

The DRG system is anti-patient in its effect if not its purpose. But the potential adverse effects can be combated and reduced if you or a family member act as an informed and assertive consumer. Be prepared to fight back if the need arises.

Fighting Back

If you believe you or a loved one is getting the bum's rush to be discharged from the hospital, you are not helpless. Here are some of the measures you can take to protect yourself or family members from the downside of the DRG system.

Ask your doctor to go to bat for you. Hospitals depend on their doctors on staff (those eligible to hospitalize patients at the facility) to literally stay in business. Thus, doctors have real power, power that can be the difference between an early discharge and those few extra days that can mean so much to a full and complete recovery.

If your doctor believes you should not be released, ask him or·her to go to the hospital administration and ask that you be allowed to stay. Remember, *it is against the law for the hospital to try to get you released before you are medically ready*. Your doctor should remind them of that.

Get copies of your medical records. You have the absolute right in most states to see your own medical records and receive a copy of them. You also have the right to receive decisions regarding your Medicare coverage in writing. Getting these records in writing is important if you plan to take the next step: the right of appeal.

Appeal the decision. If you or your doctors don't agree with the Notice of Noncoverage, you can appeal. If you do, you will be dealing with an entity entitled the Peer Review Organization (PRO). Once you receive your Notice of Noncoverage, you will have *two days* of Medicare paid hospitalization left. Thus, *don't procrastinate!* Pick up the phone and call the PRO and tell them you want to appeal.

The consequences. If you appeal, you may wish to remain in the hospital if you or your doctor believe that is the best medical course for you to take. If you win your battle at the PRO, part or all of the extra hospitalization will be paid by Medicare (or eaten by the hospital). If you lose, the charges for the amount of time you remained in the hospital after your two-day notice will come out of your pocket.

Services Besides Hospitalization

Part A covers some types of care outside the hospital as well.

Skilled nursing home. Another benefit you have under Part A is skilled nursing care. If you need inpatient nursing care at a skilled nursing facility after a hospitalization, Part A may help pay for your care. The first 20 days are picked up by Medicare. In 1992, days 21–

Consumer Alert

Officially, your covered care cannot be terminated without written notice from the hospital. Thus, if your doctor or hospital tells you that your benefits are terminating, demand the written notice so that you can appeal.

100 would have cost you $81.50 a day. After that, you're on your own.

Medicare has six conditions, *all* of which must be met if you are to receive benefits for skilled nursing care. These conditions are as follows:

1. Your condition requires daily skilled nursing or skilled rehabilitation services that, as a practical matter, can only be provided in a skilled nursing facility.

2. You have been in the hospital at least three days in a row (not counting the day of discharge) before you are admitted to a participating skilled nursing facility. (*Note:* If you were not hospitalized, you will receive no benefits.)

3. You are admitted to the facility within a short time (generally 30 days) after you leave the hospital.

4. Your care in the skilled nursing facility is for a condition that was treated at the hospital.

5. A medical professional certifies that you need, and you receive, skilled nursing or skilled rehabilitation services on a *daily* basis.

6. Your Medicare intermediary does not disapprove your stay. (The intermediary is the private insurance organization that processes Medicare claims.)

Home health care. With the DRG system bringing about earlier hospital releases, the existence of home health care has become quite important. Happily, Medicare will pay limited benefits for part-time skilled home health care as long as all of the following conditions are met:

1. Your care should include intermittent skilled nursing care, physical therapy, or speech therapy.
2. You are confined to your home.
3. You are under the care of a physician who determines you need home health care and sets up a home health plan for you.
4. The home health agency providing services is participating in Medicare.

There is no time limit for these benefits. Medicare pays (as of 1992) for all approved and covered home health care visits, with the exception of durable medical equipment, which is 80 percent covered.

Covered home health care services include:

Part-time nursing
Physical or speech therapy

If you are receiving any of the above, you may also be entitled to:

Occupational therapy
Part-time home health aids
Medical social services
Durable medical equipment

You are **not** entitled to homemaker services or 24-hour private duty nursing care. If you are leaving the hospital, ask your doctor if he or she will prescribe home health care. Don't be shy or bashful; unfortunately, many doctors forget that you may be entitled to this benefit.

Hospice care. Medicare will pay benefits for hospice care for those who have been diagnosed as having a terminal illness. Hospice care is designed to maintain a quality life for the patient without taking efforts to prolong life. Hospice benefits are available for both the patient as well as the family, if the patient is being cared for at home. Medicare covers two 90-day periods of hospice treatment and one additional

30-day period if the care remains necessary. In 1992, the patient was responsible for 5 percent of the cost of outpatient drugs or $5 toward each prescription, whichever was less. If the patient is placed in a facility so the family may have respite time, the patient pays a modest fee for the inpatient care.

As you can see, the scope of Part A is relatively limited. For the rest of the Medicare story, let's take a look at Part B.

Medicare Part B (Major Medical)

Part B is the medical insurance portion of Medicare. Unlike Part A, Part B is not free. However, the premiums are modest, costing $31.80 per month in 1992, a figure that will be increasing as time marches on. For most people, the premium is deducted from their Social Security checks.

In order to become covered under Part B, you must actively enroll in the program. Moreover, it is very important to your financial health that you enroll in a timely manner. Your initial enrollment period is a seven-month time span that begins three months before the month you first meet the eligibility requirements for Medicare. If you fail to enroll during your time of eligibility, you can sign up only during "general enrollment periods," which occur every January 1 through March 31, with benefits beginning in July of that year. You may also be charged a premium penalty for late enrollment.

Part B is similar to a medical/surgical private health insurance policy. It covers the following services.

Medical Bills

If medical services are medically necessary, Medicare will help pay for them. Services such as surgery, outpatient hospital care, other forms of medical treatment, diagnostic tests, and diagnostic physical exams are covered. Unfortunately, Medicare will not pay for many preventive procedures such as routine physicals and inoculations, although benefits are available for flu shots.

Reasonable charge. Benefits are paid on the basis of what is called a **reasonable charge**. What is a reasonable charge? Whatever Medicare says it is. A reasonable charge is not necessarily the actual charge made by the doctor. In fact, it is usually *less* than the actual charge. After a modest deductible, $100 in 1992, *Medicare pays 80 percent of the reasonable charge*. You pay the balance.

Accepting the assignment. The amount you will ultimately be responsible for depends on whether your doctor is willing to **accept assignment**.

If your doctor accepts assignment, he or she agrees to receive payment directly from Medicare. In return, he or she agrees to accept the charge Medicare deems as reasonable as the *entire charge* for the doctor's services. Having a doctor who accepts assignment can save you some significant dollars, as the chart below will demonstrate.

If your doctor refuses to accept assignment, he or she will demand payment in full from you and you will receive partial reimbursement from Medicare. In such cases, you still only receive 80 percent of what Medicare states is the reasonable price for the service, regardless of what the doctor actually charges you.

The following chart illustrates the difference. Assume you have already paid your yearly deductible. Your doctor charges you $1,000 for covered services rendered. Medicare rules that the reasonable charge allowable is only $750. Here's how that would work out under both payment methods:

SAVINGS WITH ACCEPTANCE OF ASSIGNMENT

	M.D. Accepts Assignment	M.D. Does Not Accept Assignment
M.D. actual charge	$1,000	$1,000
Reasonable charge allowed by Medicare	$750	$750
Medicare Pays M.D.	$600 (80% of $750)	Nothing. Patient pays M.D.
Medicare Pays Patient	Nothing. M.D. Paid directly by Medicare	$600 (80% of $750)
$ out of patient's pocket	$150 ($750 reasonable charge − $600 payment from Medicare)	$400 ($1,000 actual charge − $600 payment from Medicare)

Consumer Alert

Medicare publishes a list of most of the doctors in your area who will accept assignment. These doctors are known as Medicare participating physicians and the list is called the *Medicare Participating Physician/Supplier Directory*. It is available through most local senior citizen organizations or your local Social Security Office.

Medically necessary charges. In addition to setting the reasonable price of a rendered medical service, Medicare reserves the right to judge whether the performed service was actually "medically necessary." If it is determined by Medicare that the charges were not medically necessary, you have two choices: pay the entire bill yourself, or appeal—whereupon you will probably have to pay the entire bill yourself, since many appeals are lost. Appeals work similarly to Social Security appeals. For more details, consult with your local Social Security office.

What Else is Covered

- **Outpatient hospital care**. Increasingly, many minor surgeries are done on an outpatient basis. This means that you don't stay overnight in the hospital. Medicare pays for 80 percent of the approved charges made by the hospital.

- **Ambulance services**. The cost of an ambulance to or from a hospital or skilled nursing facility is covered if the trip is medically necessary.

- **Durable medical equipment**. Durable medical equipment, such as a hospital bed or wheelchair, will be covered under Part B if it is deemed medically necessary. So will items such as pacemakers or prosthetic devices.

- **Administered drugs**. Shots administered to you in or outside of a hospital are covered. Other prescribed medication is not covered.

- **Outpatient therapy**. Outpatient physical and speech therapy are covered if they are deemed medically necessary.

- **Chiropractors**. Under limited circumstances, chiropractic manipulations are acceptable for Medicare benefits.

- **Second opinions.** If your doctor advises you to undergo surgery, Medicare will pay for a second opinion. If the original opinion and the second opinion differ, Medicare will pay for a third opinion.

As you can see, even if all of your medical care is covered under either Part A or Part B, you can have some significant expenses to pay out of your own pocket. Thus, many Medicare recipients take out private insurance, so-called **medi-gap policies**, to pay some of the difference. Medi-gap policies will be discussed in Chapter 36.

Medicare and HMOs

As you will recall from our discussion of health insurance (see Chapter 16), an HMO receives monthly payments and in return takes care of most of the member's medical needs at little or no extra cost. What does that have to do with Medicare? If you choose, you can *exchange your benefits under Medicare for HMO membership* by joining one that will accept Medicare monthly payments in return for your coverage. You are allowed to drop an HMO and get back on Medicare if you're not happy with the exchange. For more on HMOs, refer back to Chapter 16.

If you are interested in transferring your coverage to an HMO, remember the following:

- **You lose your rights under Medicare.** Once you are a member of an HMO, the rights set forth earlier in this chapter do not apply to you. Your rights are limited to those you receive as an HMO member. If you receive services not approved by the HMO, you will have to pay the bill.

- **HMOs vary greatly.** The services and extra charges vary greatly from HMO to HMO. So does their emphasis on geriatric medical services. So do yourself a favor: shop around before you sign up.

- **Choose an HMO that offers service superior to that provided by Medicare.** When you join an HMO, you are giving up freedom of choice with regard to the doctors and hospitals that serve you. Thus, make sure that the HMO offers services such as preventive care or prescription benefits that are not currently available through Medicare.

- **Make sure the HMO is financially sound.** There has been a rash of HMO bankruptcies in recent years. Thus, you must take steps to make sure the HMO you choose is financially sound.

Consumer Alert

Ask the HMO to send you a financial statement. Also, check with the Department of Corporations in your state to see if the HMO has had complaints. Be sure to ask your insurance agent specifically about the financial status of the HMO and have him or her confirm it in writing.

34

Other Government Insurance Benefits

Social Security and Medicare are by far the most famous government insurance benefits available to Americans today. However, they are by no means the only ones. Both federal and state governments offer a wide range of programs to assist the deserving and to help provide for the general welfare.

Veterans Benefits

There was a time when it seemed that the government couldn't do enough for veterans of the military service, especially after World War II. **Veterans benefits**, especially in the areas of education and housing, helped build postwar America into the greatest economic machine the world had ever seen.

But all of that changed. Eventually, the deeply felt gratitude that the American people and government felt toward veterans faded as World War II slipped into the mists of history. The controversy that was the war in Vietnam broke the nearly unanimous support the American people had accorded veterans of the armed services. That, and the terrible expenses of assisting the wounded and broken soldiers of the Vietnam experience, as well as budget deficits and the resulting cost cutting, acted in concert to reduce the benefits that veterans are entitled to receive from their "grateful" government.

Still, the Veterans Administration provides some very worthwhile benefits for certain veterans of the military. The following is an overview of the breadth and scope of those benefits.

Who Qualifies

If you are interested in veterans benefits, the threshold question you must answer is whether you are qualified to receive any benefit at all. The specific answer will depend on the program you are interested in, but some general standards apply.

You must have been in the armed forces of the United States. The question of whether you are a veteran is sort of like whether you are pregnant: either you are or you are not. There is no middle ground.

You must have served for over 24 continual months. If you joined the military after September 7, 1981, there is a time-of-service requirement. You cannot have served less than 24 months of *continual active duty*. This provision does not apply to veterans who have a compensable service-connected disability or who were discharged close to the end of an enlistment period due to hardship or for a disability incurred in the line of duty.

There are often time limits within which you must apply for benefits. For some veterans benefits, the "use it or lose it" rule applies. For example, you must apply for the Veterans Educational Assistance Program within 10 years after your discharge. Other benefits, such as medical services, have no such time limits.

You cannot have been dishonorably discharged. There are several categories of military discharge, ranging from "honorable" through "general discharge" to "dishonorable" or a "bad-conduct discharge." Many people think that only honorably discharged veterans are entitled to benefits, and for some programs that's true. More often, however, an other-than-honorable discharge will not serve as a bar to benefits. However, if you are dishonorably discharged or received a bad-conduct discharge, you are barred from the services of the Veterans Administration.

You may have to have suffered a service-connected disability or injury. Many but certainly not all of the programs administered by the Veterans Administration require that the beneficiary have suffered a service-connected disability or injury, or at least give preference to injured veterans.

Veterans Health Care Benefits

Many veterans health benefits come as close to pure socialized medicine as the government will allow. The most famous of these health care benefits are those associated with medical care, specifically the Veterans Administration hospitals and clinics that serve a wide range of health needs for qualified veterans.

It is important to note that there are eligibility requirements you must pass if you wish to receive care at a VA hospital. In fact, there is a priority system that can leave some qualified veterans waiting out in the cold for service if their local VA hospital is full.

VA hospital priority cases. You receive priority of care at VA hospitals if you are:

- rated service connected.

- retired from active duty for a disability incurred or aggravated while in the service.

- in receipt of a VA pension.

- eligible for Medicaid.

- a former POW.

- in need of care for exposure to a toxic substance such as Agent Orange.

- an "atomic veteran" such as those who participated in the atomic bomb tests of the early 1950s.

- have a yearly income less than $15,833 with no dependents or $18,999 if you are married (as of 1990).

Other eligible veterans. Veterans who earn too much to receive priority but who still have low incomes are also eligible for care on a space-available basis. Veterans who are not low-income can also receive treatment if there is room for them, but they must pay for the privilege.

Other health care services are available to some veterans depending on eligibility. These include *nursing home care, in-home care, outpatient medical treatment, travel reimbursement for medical appointments, treatment for substance abuse,* and *readjustment counseling,* just to name a few. To learn the exact nature of these and other services, and their differing eligibility requirements, contact your local VA office and ask for the booklet *Federal Benefits for Veterans and Dependents.*

Education Programs

One of the most successful programs of the Veterans Administration was the **GI Bill**, under which millions of World War II and other veterans received substantial financial assistance while obtaining an education. The veterans of that era did not have to make financial contributions to the program while in active service. Unfortunately, that program expired and is no longer available. It has been replaced by the following programs.

Veterans Educational Assistance Program. This program is available to veterans and current military personnel if they signed up after December 31, 1976, and before March 31, 1987, and meet other eligibility requirements.

The program requires active service personnel to contribute between $25 and $100 out of each military paycheck to pay for future educational expenses. In return, the government will match $2 for every $1 contributed by the participant. Thus, if a veteran deposits $3,000 into the program, he or she will be entitled to receive $6,000 in monthly checks while pursuing an education. The participant will receive monthly benefits equal to the number of months he or she contributed into the plan. The amount received will be determined by the amount in the individual veteran's fund and the number of monthly payments he or she is entitled to receive.

The Montgomery GI Bill. This program provides educational benefits for individuals entering the military after June 30, 1985. Servicepersons entering active duty after that date will have their basic pay reduced by $100 a month for the first 12 months of their service unless they specifically elect not to participate in the program.

Under the Montgomery plan, if the serviceperson has been active for the required time periods, which can be a combination of active and reserve status, he or she is entitled to receive a payment of $300 a month for 36 months while obtaining an education. More can be received if the VA administrators decide additional payments are appropriate. There is also a plan for certain reservists who can receive $140 a month for 36 months if they meet the eligibility requirements.

Vocational rehabilitation. Eligible veterans can receive up to four years' worth of full-time training or its equivalent in part-time training. Participants in the program also receive modest monthly payments, generally in the $300 range, as well as assistance in finding work after the rehabilitation is complete. In order to qualify for this broad program, the veteran must meet the following three conditions:

1. He or she suffered a service-connected disability in active service that entitles the veteran to compensation.

2. He or she was discharged or released under other than dishonorable circumstances.

3. The VA determines that the veteran needs vocational rehabilitation to overcome an impairment to his or her ability to prepare for, obtain, or retain employment consistent with the person's abilities, aptitudes, and interests.

Other programs. There are other educational programs available to qualified veterans—for example, a special program for those deemed unemployable and veterans receiving a pension. For more details, contact your nearest Veterans Administration office or veterans assistance organization.

GI Loans

Many veterans are eligible for loans to help them purchase a home, whether it is a house, condominium, mobile home, or other manufactured residence. The program is also open to veterans who wish to improve their homes, including the installation of solar heating and/or cooling and weatherization improvements. The benefits of obtaining a GI home loan are very broad and can make the difference in attaining the dream of home ownership. These loan benefits include:

- An interest rate that is usually lower than conventional rates.

- Usually, no down payment.

- A long amortization repayment period.

The VA also offers group life insurance, death and burial benefits, and pensions. For more information contact your local Veterans Administration office or write:

Veterans Administration
Washington, DC 20420

Medicaid

Medicaid is a federally aided, state-operated program of health care assistance for the poor who are aged, blind, disabled, or families with dependent children. The program is funded by the federal government in partnership with the respective states. Currently, over 25 million people receive some form of assistance from Medicaid.

Each state is allowed to make its own rules concerning what is and is not covered by Medicaid, subject to some very loose federal guidelines. Because each state has different rules, you will have to contact your local human services office to check the eligibility requirements in your area.

Medicaid must, at minimum, cover the following for eligible recipients:

- Inpatient hospital or skilled nursing facility care

- Outpatient hospital services

- Laboratory and X-ray services

- Doctor's services

- Home health care

- Transportation costs to and from medical care

Many states provide more than this basic care. Some will pay for eyeglasses, dental care, prescription drugs, and other services such as inpatient psychiatric treatment. The level of care available depends, in large measure, on the commitment of your state to the health care of its neediest citizens.

A large portion of Medicaid payments goes to nursing homes to pay for the skilled nursing care of the elderly who cannot afford it themselves. Because nursing home care can run in excess of $2,000 a month and because Medicare only has limited nursing home benefits, many families turn to Medicaid to enable their elderly relatives to be cared for at a nursing home.

There's only one catch: In order to qualify for Medicaid, the patient must literally spend down his or her assets almost to the point of bankruptcy. Thus, a lifetime of work and accumulation can be wiped out in months. Many consider this state of affairs to be a national scandal, and it can be expected to be one of the political hot spots as the baby boomers continue on their march toward retirement.

For more information on Medicaid, contact your local department of social services or welfare office.

Supplemental Security Income

Supplemental Security Income, or SSI as it is known in the vernacular, is a joint federal and state program that guarantees a minimum level of income to the poor elderly, disabled, and blind. Although the program is administered through the Social Security system, the standards for qualifying for Social Security have no relevance to eligibility for SSI.

You have to be poor to qualify for SSI, and we mean *really poor*. Not only must your income be below the poverty level (the amount will vary from state to state), but you cannot own much property. You can own your home and a modestly valued car. Beyond that your assets cannot exceed $2,850 for a couple, $1,900 for a single person.

The point of the program is to put a few bucks into your pocket that can make the difference between eating macaroni and cheese versus eating cat food. The level of money you will receive if you are eligible for the program will vary from state to state but usually runs between $350 and $800 a month, depending on where you live. Of course, if you work and earn money above the level allowed under your state's program, your benefits will be reduced.

For details on the benefits and eligibility standards in your state, contact your local Social Security office.

State Programs

So far we've dealt with federally operated programs and those that are the joint responsibility of the individual states and the feds. There are also state-administered programs that can bring great benefit to their recipients.

The individual nature of these numerous programs from state to state precludes their detailed descriptions in this book. However, the following are some of the typical state programs.

Unemployment Insurance

In a capitalistic nation, there is no guarantee that the job we have today will be there tomorrow. At one time in our history, this economic fact of life brought untold hardship to many who through no fault of their own found themselves out of work.

There is no question that it is tough to lose a job. But there is some padding available, at least for the financial consequences of being laid off. The unemployment compensation programs of the various states are designed to reduce the financial problems associated with losing a job without robbing the recipient of the incentive to go out and find new work. The programs available around the country share some important common facts.

The cost of unemployment insurance is usually paid by the employers of each state. Only a few states require that employees contribute to the unemployment fund. Most of the financial burden for the program falls on state employers.

In order to qualify for benefits, a worker must pass eligibility requirements. While the requirements vary from state to state, they will usually feature the following.

There must have been previous employment. There is always a minimum number of weeks that an employee must have worked before he or she earns the right to receive benefits.

The unemployed worker must be looking for a new job. You can't just sit on your duff and expect to receive benefits. You must prove to the unemployment people that you are actively looking for work. However, you are not required to accept a job at substantially lower wages for similar work, nor can you be forced to become a strikebreaker.

You must file a claim for benefits. As you would expect, the state isn't going to come looking for you, but you must apply. (After all, they wouldn't want to cheat you out of all of that time you will get to spend waiting in line.) You should file for benefits just as soon as you qualify, since there will be a waiting period before you can receive assistance.

You must be able to work. If you are not healthy enough to work, you cannot receive unemployment compensation. In such cases, look to see if your state has a disability insurance program to assist you.

Grounds for denying benefits. Benefits may be denied for reasons including:

> Receiving severance pay
>
> Receiving workers compensation benefits
>
> Being dismissed from a job for cause
>
> Quitting a job without a valid reason
>
> Refusing suitable work

The benefits you will receive will be a percentage of your total income. The caps on benefits, unfortunately, are usually quite low. The maximum number of weeks you can receive benefits will vary from state to state, but 26 weeks is probably the most common. During times of economic trouble these time limits are often extended. The point of all of this, of course, is to help you while you are between jobs—but not so much that you get used to the idea of receiving state benefits.

State Disability Insurance

Five states (California, Hawaii, New Jersey, New York, and Rhode Island) and Puerto Rico have temporary disability benefit programs designed to partially reimburse you for wages lost due to sickness or injury. The disability cannot be caused by con-

Consumer Alert

If you are a veteran of the U.S. armed forces, you are entitled to apply for unemployment benefits if you can't find work upon leaving military service. However, you must wait four weeks before applying for benefits and can only receive benefits for *13 weeks* (other unemployed workers can receive benefits for 26 weeks).

ditions under which workers compensation (see Chapter 37) would foot the bill.

In order to qualify for state disability, you must meet three different requirements:

- **You must have been employed.** The time requirements differ from state to state.

- **You must be disabled.** The usual definition is that of the private disability policy: being unable to perform your usual occupation or employment (see page 185). New Jersey has the stricter requirement that the recipient be unable to earn a living at all.

- **You must get through a waiting period.** As is common with private plans, a waiting period must be met before benefits begin. The amount of time varies from state to state.

The state programs will usually provide a defined percentage of your wage as a benefit. Typically, this is 55 percent of your usual wage. There is also a cap that keeps the maximum payment you can receive relatively low.

State disability is usually funded by withholding taxes taken out of employees' paychecks, usually with some participation by employers. The amount of withholding varies from state to state.

Most states do not have disability insurance programs. If yours does not, think extra seriously about purchasing a private disability insurance policy (see Chapter 18). After all, most families do not have the liquidity to finance a prolonged period of unemployment, and who wants to lose all they've worked a lifetime to acquire because of a severe illness or injury? Even if your state has a disability program, be sure to investigate the private policies sold in your area since the state benefits can be pretty low.

There are many other state and federal insurance programs. Time and space do not permit them to be listed here. For example, the federal government sells flood insurance, and some states are considering state health insurance programs. All states have some form of welfare available to the neediest of their citizens, including food stamps. Operation Head Start gives disadvantaged youngsters a boost to prepare for their education. For specific information on these and other programs available in your state, contact your senator or representative or your local human services or welfare office.

35

Consumers' Agenda

The government is not taking care of your business. Both Medicare and Social Security have become political footballs, to your detriment.

The federal government is threatening the future viability of the Social Security system. Starting in 1990, there began a series of Social Security tax hikes designed to assure current taxpayers that money will be there when it comes time to pay their benefits. Instead of saving money like it is supposed to, the government is robbing Peter to pay Paul.

In this case "Peter" is the Social Security trust funds designed to accumulate money to pay for the bulge in claims that will be made by the baby boomers when they reach retirement age. "Paul" is the ravenous federal budget deficit, which our esteemed politicians cannot seem to tame. In order to hide the true size of the deficit, funds raised by tax payments for Social Security are being "borrowed" by the general fund and placed on the books as assets of the government. The purpose of this hat trick is to make it appear to you, the American taxpayer, that the size of the federal deficit is smaller than it really is. This is not only dishonest—it may threaten the very viability of the Social Security system.

This irresponsible behavior must stop. Write your senators, your representatives in Congress, and the president. Demand that they stop cooking the books of the United States. The addresses to write are:

(Name of Representative or Senator)
Senate (or House) Office Building
Washington, DC 20510 (Senate) or 20515 (House)

President George Bush
The White House
Washington, DC 20500

With regard to Medicare, the government started to go in the right direction but chickened out. For a brief and shining moment in 1989, Congress enacted new and expanded catastrophic care coverage for Medicare beneficiaries. The following expanded benefits were among those briefly put on the books:

Unlimited hospitalization. After an initial deductible, patients in the hospital would have had unlimited care for covered hospital services.

Prescription benefits. For the first time, Medicare would have paid for prescription medicines after a deductible. With the price of even the simplest antibiotics ranging from the ridiculous to the outrageous, this would have been a very important benefit.

Skilled nursing home care. Under the expanded law, no prior hospitalization would have been required before skilled nursing could be covered. In addition, the limit of covered days would have been increased to 150.

Cap on Part B expenses. Under the new law, there would have been a cap placed on out-of-pocket expenses of the patient under Part B.

All of this was lost because Congress and the president insisted that the additional coverage be paid for by surcharging wealthier senior citizens rather than paying for the changes out of the general treasury fund, as the rest of Medicare is paid for. As you might expect, the affected seniors took severe umbrage to being singled out for a tax surcharge, and they used their political muscle to have the program rescinded (although limited benefits were retained for the poor).

As things now stand, Medicare continues to have some significant coverage gaps, gaps that deprive older people of quality health care and of reimbursement dollars they could use for a more productive retirement.

Let's make the decade of the '90s the time when human concerns again become a priority of the U.S. government. Write your representative demanding that the Social Security Trust Fund be protected. Demand that catastrophic care be reenacted and this time funded in an equitable fashion. It's your government and it will respond, but only if *you* get involved.

For More Information

You may wish more details about Social Security than a book of this type can offer. You should first contact your nearest office of the Social Security Administration. You may also consult the following books:

Social Security, Medicare and Pensions
by Joseph L. Matthews and Dorothy Matthews Berman (fourth edition)
(Berkeley: Nolo Press, 1988)

Life Begins at 50: A Handbook for Creative Retirement Planning
by Leonard J. Hansen
(Hauppauge, NY: Barron's Educational Series Inc., 1989)

Part 7

Insurance to Fill That Special Need

There are several types of insurance policies that don't quite fall into the previous chapters. That doesn't mean they are not important. Some, in fact, are vital if the consumer is to have a complete insurance umbrella in place to protect against the trials and tribulations of modern life.

One of the fastest growing specialty markets is the field of **senior citizens insurance**. It's not that seniors don't have the same insurance needs as the rest of us, such as auto insurance and property coverage. But when it comes to health insurance, older people do have some unique concerns: "How do I cover myself for the medical expenses not paid by Medicare?" "What can I do to prepare myself and my family in case I need nursing home care?" "Should I buy one of those life insurance policies aimed at older Americans?" These are very important and relevant questions, and the insurance industry has attempted to supply answers.

Medicare supplement insurance, known as **medi-gap coverage**, is designed to cover many health bills left unpaid by Medicare. **Convalescent home insurance** pays benefits for nursing home care. There is also an experimental project under way in four communities in the United States that seeks to keep seniors out of nursing homes altogether. Called **social health maintenance organizations**, these programs may be pointing a way to a future where seniors can receive long-term care without having to spend all of their money to get it.

There are also **life insurance policies** marketed specifically to the middle-aged and to seniors. Very real questions can be raised about the value of these policies—and we will raise them here.

We will also take a look at the all-important area of workers compensation. **Workers compensation** provides for medical care, disability, and other benefits for employees injured on the job. Understanding this extensive no-fault system of personal injury insurance is vital for all workers.

Finally, we will look at a slowly growing field of insurance known as **prepaid legal** or **group legal coverage**. Lawyers are expensive, and many people are unable to pursue their legal rights because they can't afford to hire a lawyer. Prepaid legal insurance is designed to take some of the bite out of the high cost of justice.

Let's start by taking a look at the insurance issues of vital interest to senior citizens and those who love them.

36

Senior Citizens Insurance

In this chapter we will look at four types of insurance policies that are of unique interest to older citizens. The first three of them have to do with health insurance. These are medi-gap policies, which fill in the blanks left by the partial coverage accorded by Medicare; convalescent home insurance, another policy designed to cover what Medicare does not; and social health maintenance organizations (SHMOs), an experimental program that deals with issues such as home health care. The fourth type is life insurance policies marketed specifically to the middle-aged and seniors. We'll see that these policies may offer less than meets the eye.

Medi-Gap Policies

As you will recall from our discussion on Medicare in Chapter 33, almost as many health care expenses are *not* paid for by Medicare as *are* paid for. This fact of Medicare life has led to a boom industry in the sale of supplemental health insurance policies, popularly known as medi-gap insurance.

There is a great deal of misunderstanding about medi-gap insurance and a lot you need to know. Many people think that medi-gap policies are a panacea, that they provide all that is needed to fill in the payment blanks left by the Medicare laws as they now exist. Not so. *No policy on the market pays for every expense not covered by Medicare.* And, according to Consumers Union, many provide lower benefits than the consumer thinks.

As with most areas of life, knowledge is power. The more you know about a subject, the better you will be able to deal effectively with it. This truth goes double for medi-gap insurance, since the more you know, the better able you will be to buy the policy that's just right for you.

Benefit Gaps Versus Coverage Gaps

It is important for those looking into medi-gap policies to understand that there are two different areas where Medicare fails to pay all health care expenses. Let's call these **benefit gaps** and **coverage gaps**.

Benefit gaps.   There are many benefit gaps under Medicare, where money is payable for covered medical services, *but not enough to pay the entire expense*. For example, under Part B, Major Medical, you owe a deductible before any benefit is payable to your doctor. You must also pay 20 percent of the "reasonable cost" of your care, or more if your doctor does not "accept assignment." Those funds that must come out of your pocket constitute the Medicare benefit gaps.

Coverage gaps.   Medicare also has significant coverage gaps—areas of health care *where no benefits are payable at all*. For example, if you go in for a routine annual checkup, Medicare will pay nothing toward the cost. Nor will Medicare usually pay for any prescription medicines. These coverage gaps also cost seniors a pretty penny.

The distinction between these two gaps can be very important. *Medi-gap policies are usually designed to cover benefit gaps only. Coverage gaps remain.* It is the rare insurance policy that will pay for a significant service that is not at least partially paid for by Medicare.

Consumer Alert

A major form of deceptive salesmanship occurs when medi-gap sales personnel state or imply that their insurance will pay for everything Medicare does not. *The simple fact is that no policy pays for everything that Medicare does not pay.* If any salesperson tries to tell you otherwise, make the rascal prove it by going through the policy step by step and showing you in black and white how all of the benefit and coverage gaps are filled.

Medi-Gap Policies Are Not Sold by the Government

Another area of confusion exists as to who actually sells these policies. There are many unscrupulous operators out there in insurance land who imply that they are affiliated with the government in some way. According to Consumers Union, this is usually done by playing word games with consumers.

Here's how the "con" works: A company is formed whose sole purpose is to generate leads for private insurance agents who sell medi-gap policies. These leads are obtained by mailing senior citizens a card, which appears to be official government business, warning of "dangerous gaps" that might exist in their health care coverage. The card asks older adults to respond by mail inquiring as to how to protect themselves.

What these "official notices" don't tell you is that they are really fronts for private insurance carriers or agents who are using the official-looking form as a lead-in to try to soften you up for the "sell." Once you have responded to the scare tactics of the lead company, your name, address, and phone number are then sold to the insurance agent, who calls and hustles a sale.

Many consumers buy insurance in this way, believing they are purchasing government-affiliated insurance protection. *They are not. No such government insurance exists.* Medi-gap insurance is sold only on the private market. As with all other forms of coverage, medi-gap policies should only be purchased if the benefits are worth the premiums and if the company is financially sound and ethical in the way it does business with its customers.

The Government Does Regulate Medi-Gap Insurance

Open enrollment requirements. As of November 5, 1991, people age 65 or older cannot be denied medi-gap insurance for six months immediately following enrollment in Medicare Part B, nor can they be charged higher premiums because of health problems. However, despite this guarantee, your medi-gap policy may not provide services for a preexisting condition until a six-month waiting period has passed.

New standardized policies. The federal government, reacting to the high level of shoddy business practices that have existed in the medi-gap insurance industry, requires that states regulate medi-gap insurance to limit insurance companies from offering more than 10 standard policies. One of the 10 must be a basic policy offering a "core package" of benefits, and all policies must contain at least those benefits found in the core package. The basic policy must be available in all states. The basic policies should be on the market in 1993.

To find out when the new standardized policies will be available in your state, and which of the 10 policies will be approved for sale, check with your state insurance department.

Medicare SELECT policies. A new, reduced-cost type of medi-gap policy is due on the market. It is called Medicare SELECT. Medicare SELECT is similar to a PPO (see Part 3), where, for a reduced premium, you agree to use the services of designated health care professionals called preferred providers. The states in which SELECT policies should become available are Alabama, Arizona, California, Florida, Indiana, Kentucky, Michigan, Minnesota, Missouri, North Dakota, Ohio, Oregon, Texas, Washingon, and Wisconsin.

Comparing Benefits

The medi-gap policy you ultimately select should be long on coverage and short on coverage gaps if you are to get a policy that is worth the premiums you will be paying. In order to find such a company you *must do your homework*. That means taking the time to compare at least five different policies and preferably more.

When comparing policies, ask the sales agent these questions or look at the sales literature to find the answers.

Is the Part A deductible covered? As you will recall, there is a substantial deductible per occurrence under the hospitalization portion (Part A) of Medicare. This deductible is most likely the only charge you will have to pay if you are hospitalized, since the vast majority of hospitalizations under Medicare last for far less than 60 days. Thus, if a medi-gap policy does not pay for most or all of this initial out-of-pocket expense, it may be offering you less than you think you are paying for.

What is covered if there is a long hospitalization? It is statistically doubtful that you will suffer a prolonged hospitalization. But if you do, it is important that you be covered by medi-gap insurance for the copayments that are your responsibility under Medicare, beginning on the 61st day of hospitalization. Unfortunately, when your rights to receive Medicare coverage for a hospital stay terminate, so do your benefits under most medi-gap insurance policies.

Does the policy cover skilled nursing home copayments? As you will recall from our discussion of Medicare, benefits for skilled nursing home care do exist, but only under limited circumstances. Even when Medicare covers the care, the patient must pay $81.50 a day after the first 20 days and the entire bill after 100 days. Unless your private supplemental coverage will pay for a large portion of the copayments, you could be stuck with a substantial bill. Once again, don't expect your supplemental policy to protect you from the coverage gap that begins after 100 days.

Is the Part B deductible covered? Of somewhat less importance is coverage of the major medical (Part B) deductible. The entire deductible is only $100 in 1992, and that applies per year rather than per occurrence. So, while medi-gap assistance here is nice, it is not as important to your financial health and well-being as are other aspects of coverage.

Is the Part B 20 percent copayment covered? Medicare patients are personally responsible for 20 percent of the "reasonable" charge allowed by Medicare for procedures covered under Part B. Most, if not all, medi-gap policies do cover this expense. But be sure to ask, just in case.

Is there coverage for excess charges made under Part B? This can be very important. As you will recall, some doctors do not accept assignment when treating Medicare recipients. This can have profound financial consequences. Not only will you have to personally pay for 20 percent of the "reasonable charge" allowed by Medicare but you will also have to pay the difference between what the doctor actually charges and what Medicare says is "reasonable." This can turn your pocketbook into a black hole. Unfortunately, most medi-gap policies will not pay for excess charges. However, a few do. Thus, *you should make a point of looking for a policy that covers part or all of any excess charges*, since you may not always be able to use doctors who agree to accept assignment.

What other coverages does the policy offer? There are other coverages you should look for when purchasing medi-gap insurance. These include:

Consumer Alert

Sometimes benefits in policies have no real value. For instance, Consumers Union tells the story of one medi-gap policy it ran across that provided medi-gap benefits for *midwife* care. Now, unless a miracle of biblical proportions has occurred, we doubt whether the company has had to process any claims from senior citizens requesting reimbursement for the expenses of delivering a baby. So make sure you don't pay for benefits you will *never* have to use.

Foreign country coverage. Medicare does not cover you if you need medical care while traveling in a foreign land. Thus, if you plan to travel, you may want to find a policy that will protect you abroad.

Prescription benefits. This is one of the few coverage gaps that is sometimes filled by medi-gap insurance. If a prescription benefit is important to you, find out the details and add the information to your comparison list.

Private-duty nursing. There is a limited benefit for private nursing under Medicare. Some medi-gap policies supplement this with increased benefits for medically necessary private nursing services.

Hospice services. Under Medicare, a maximum of 7 months hospice care is paid for. However, nature doesn't always run its course within the time limits established by bureaucracy. Thus, you may wish to find a policy that supplements hospice care after Medicare payments are exhausted.

Other coverages. Some medi-gap policies also provide modest accidental death benefits or other incidental coverages. These should be thought of as of marginal importance and should not be the basis for making the purchasing decision.

Look for the Downside

It is important to remember that medi-gap policies are a form of health insurance. Thus, you need to look at the downsides of the policies as well as the coverages you can expect. (We suggest you review the chapters on health insurance in Part 3.) In particular, look out for the following.

Are there preexisting conditions clauses? Many policies will have such clauses that could restrict your rights to benefits. Usually, these entail a waiting period before the preexisting condition will be covered. If you have such a problem, you may want to look for a policy that does not require a waiting period.

Is the policy guaranteed renewable? No health insurance policy is worth very much if the company can cancel or refuse to renew it because of the health of the policyholder.

Do premiums increase as you get older? Some policies increase in price as the policyholder ages.

Are there elimination periods? Some policies promise an indemnity payment for each day the policyholder spends in the hospital. Of these, however, many require an elimination period, usually a wait of several days, before any benefits are paid. Since most hospitalizations are relatively brief, elimination periods may serve only to eliminate the company's obligation to pay benefits.

Consumer Alert

Both state and federal laws govern the sale of medi-gap insurance. If you believe you have been the victim of illegal or unethical sales practices, contact your state insurance department and/or federal officials. The Medicare Hotline can be reached toll-free at (800) 638-6833.

MEDI-GAP POLICY COMPARISON CHART

Policy	A	B	C	D	E
Part A deductible covered?	no	no	yes	yes	yes
Part B deductible covered?	no	no	no	no	yes
Part B additional deductible covered?	yes	no	yes	yes	yes
Part B expenses in excess of $5000 covered?	yes	no	yes	yes	yes
Coverage for difference in reasonable charge and charge of doctor?	no	no	no	30%	after 1st $200
Skilled nursing facility covered?	no	no	medicare copayment from 100th through 365th day	copayment through 100th day	through 100th day
Other benefits	none	none	limited private duty nurse	none	none
Premium at age 70 (yearly)	$215.40	$207	$450–$567	$789 (male) $684 (female)	$711 male $606 female
Comments			group plan only		

Compare Premiums

The prices of medi-gap policies vary widely based on several factors, including benefits paid, exclusions and preexisting conditions clauses, and the skill of the insurance company managers in running a productive and efficient business. Your job as a consumer is to *take your time* and compare the policies available. Only by pursuing your purchase in a careful, methodical, and businesslike manner will you be able to find the highest level of benefits for the premium your checkbook can afford. Of course, you should also make sure that the company that offers the best coverage is also fiscally secure so that it will still be in business when a claim is made.

Use the chart on page 391 when comparing medi-gap policies. It is taken from the California Department of Insurance and compares actual policies available in that state. As you will see, prices and services vary widely. Also, remember that these policies may not be the same as those available to you.

Some "Don'ts" When Shopping for Medi-Gap Policies

Last but not least, remember the following "don'ts" when shopping for medi-gap insurance.

Don't buy multiple policies. You will only be duplicating basic benefits while giving yourself little additional protection. Unfortunately, a lot of people make this mistake.

Don't pay cash for your policy. Always write a check and make it out to the insurance company, not the agent.

Don't cancel an old policy until the new policy is fully effective. If you decide to change policies, be sure to keep your old one in full force and effect until all waiting periods or other impediments to full coverage have expired.

Don't buy a policy if you are eligible for Medicaid. If you are one of the unfortunate group of older Americans who live below the poverty line, you may qualify for Medicaid. If you do, it should provide adequate additional insurance protection for you beyond what Medicare pays. Save your meager resources for other necessities of life, like rent and food.

Don't purchase policies that have restricted disease clauses. Some policies pay benefits only for specific diseases, such as cancer. These restricted policies are rarely worth the money.

Don't be pressured into your purchase. Some seniors have a difficult time resisting the old hard sell (you're not alone). If an agent tries to fast-talk you into signing on the dotted line, be sure to resist. The agent's come-on may be a smoke screen to mask inadequate benefits offered by the company represented. In such cases, just say, "Thank you for your help. May I keep your sales brochures? I want to compare your policy with others offered on the market."

Consumer Alert

Once you purchase a medi-gap policy, you will have time under state law to review the policy to make sure it lives up to its claims (usually 30 days, but ask to make sure). Take advantage of this consumer protection. *Read your policy carefully.* If it seems inadequate, cancel it and find another within the allotted time.

Convalescent Home Insurance

A major worry of seniors and their families is the ruinous cost of nursing home care. Unfortunately, should you or a loved one be placed in a nursing home for long-term care (as opposed to treatment for a specific malady), Medicare usually will not pay any of the price, nor will medi-gap insurance policies.

A type of insurance has recently been developed, however, that may help pay for the terribly burdensome costs of long-term convalescent hospital care. This is the convalescent care insurance policy, also known as **nursing home insurance** or **long-term care insurance**.

One of the first questions that may come to mind is, "What are my chances of having to go to a nursing home?" As with most such questions, it depends on whom you ask.

The American Association of Retired Persons (AARP) suggests that 60 percent of all families have faced the need for long-term care in a nursing home. The California Department of Insurance is a little more optimistic. They claim that 40 percent of all persons age 65 or older will have to be placed in a nursing home at some time in their lives. Of these, approximately half will stay for less than three months and thus may be entitled to receive benefits from Medicare; the rest will stay long enough to incur significant out-of-pocket expenses.

The Health Insurance Association of America tells us that starting in the year 1990, approximately 7.7 million people will require long-term care at any given time. This figure will probably rise as the "graying of America" continues.

Why consider a convalescent home insurance policy? For most people, there are at least four reasons:

- Nursing homes are expensive, generally averaging approximately $2,000 a month, a price that can only go up in the future.
- Medicare pays no benefits for long-term custodial care.
- Medi-gap policies probably won't pay either.
- In order to qualify for Medicaid, the patient must deplete his or her estate to the point of poverty. Many seniors worry themselves sick over this because they deeply want to leave their estates to their children.

These are important reasons for *considering* the purchase of a long-term-care policy. That doesn't mean you should necessarily buy one. After all, you have more to do with your money than buy insurance. Besides, you may decide that the benefits and exclusions simply aren't worth the costs.

Let's get to the heart of the matter. What does long-term-care insurance pay for?

Nursing Home Care

Most of the benefits paid by long-term-care policies go to defray the fees charged by nursing homes. Generally, these are indemnity-types policies that will pay you a specified sum, say $50 or so, for each covered day you spend in a nursing home.

Most policies divide nursing home care into three kinds:

- **Skilled nursing care:** When the patient must be cared for by medical personnel such as doctors and nurses 24 hours a day.
- **Intermediate care:** When the patient doesn't need 24-hour medical supervision but can't live alone.
- **Custodial care:** The lowest level of assistance, which focuses not on medical treatment but on matters of daily living such as bathing, meals, and toilet requirements.

Consumer Alert

Some convalescent home insurance policies wiggle out of paying benefits by excluding coverage for custodial care. *Such policies virtually defeat the purpose of buying long-term-care insurance* since many nursing home placements are made just because of the need for custodial care. So, make sure that all three are covered in any policy you select, and make sure you understand the definitions set forth in the policy concerning levels of care.

In-Home Care

Some policies provide limited benefits for in-home health care. In-home care can be very expensive, too, so this benefit can be of real service. Unfortunately, according to the AARP, many policies require a prior hospitalization or a stay in a skilled nursing facility before you have the right to receive in-home benefits. Avoid such policy language if you can.

Questions to Ask

As with all other forms of insurance, knowing the restrictions and exclusions of coverage are vital to a complete understanding of these policies and to making an informed and intelligent purchasing decision. They are usually nonnegotiable. When comparing the convalescent care policies that are available in your community, find out the following.

Are preexisting conditions excluded?   There is usually a preexisting conditions exclusion that requires a long waiting period before benefits will be payable for any long-term care required by any preexisting condition. *Be sure you understand the terms of the preexisting conditions clause before you buy.*

Is there an Alzheimer's disease exclusion?   Alzheimer's disease is a form of dementia that strikes many elderly people. In fact, it is the fourth leading cause of death among adults in the country. Before the disease kills its victims, it progressively destroys their minds, beginning with forgetfulness and ultimately leading to inability to care for themselves at all. Virtually every Alzheimer's victim will eventually have to be confined to a long-term-care facility. Thus, with Alzheimer's on the rise, it pays to be safe and find a policy that *includes* benefits for Alzheimer's or other forms of dementia as part of its protective umbrella. Those that don't just may not be worth the money.

Must there be a prior hospitalization before benefits kick in?   If so, you may be buying a pig in a poke. According to Consumers Union, *60 percent of all nursing home placements occur without a prior hospitalization.* Thus, if policy language excludes benefits for nursing home placements made with no prior hospitalization, it creates a crater-sized loophole!

What are the time limits of coverage?   Few policies pay lifetime benefits. Most place some form of time limitation on coverage. According to Arizona insurance agent Helen L. Abbott, most policies provide for two, four, or six years of coverage. She states that the four-year time is the most popular. Obviously, the longer the coverage, the better-protected you are against the bankruptcy

Consumer Alert

When it comes to long-term-care insurance, you may elect an individual policy rather than a group policy. This is one area where an individual policy may actually provide better protection. That's because few group policies prohibit nonrenewal by the insurance company, while most individual policies do. On the downside, you will probably pay more for individual coverage.

potential of long-term care. Of course, the longer the coverage, the higher the premium.

Is there an elimination period?   To decide whether the premium is worth the benefit, you need to know if you must wait for a period of time before benefits commence. Long waiting periods somewhat defeat the purpose for which the insurance is purchased.

Is the policy renewable?   As we have stated previously (see pages 145, 390), a health insurance policy that the company can refuse to renew due to your health isn't worth much more than the paper and ink used to print it. Long-term-care policies are no exception. *You should only purchase policies that are guaranteed renewable for life or until all policy benefits have been paid.*

Is a "waiver of premium" rider available?   Some policies allow you to cease paying premiums if you have been placed in a nursing home for more than 90 consecutive days. If you can afford this coverage, it makes sense.

Can you purchase riders to fight inflation?   Most long-term-care policies pay specific indemnity payments to the insured rather than a percentage of the total bill. Thus, insurance agent Helen L. Abbott recommends that you seriously look into riders that will increase the benefit level as the price of care goes up. Otherwise, your indemnity payment will not rise while the cost of care probably will. This means that more will have to come out of your pocket without the rider as the cost of care rises like a one-way elevator.

Is a long-term-care policy really worth the price? Consumers Union doesn't think so. They issued a press release in 1988 criticizing the cost of the policies, which generally run *in excess of $200 a month*, and the restrictions many policies place on benefits. The insurance industry has responded by stating that the kinks are being worked out and greater benefits are being provided all the time. Who is right? Well, in a free country, the answer is up to you.

SHMOs

Clearly, we have a problem in dealing with the long-term-care needs of senior citizens, and it's a big one. According to the AARP, more than 8 million people, most of them senior citizens, require assistance with personal living. Fifty-one percent of the costs for caring for these people comes out of private pockets.

The AARP believes that an expansion of Medicare benefits is the answer to this social dilemma. We agree. However, the political realities don't bode well for such an expansion, what with the massive federal deficit casting a nationwide shadow. Congress couldn't even save catastrophic care coverage (see page 376).

All may not be lost. Four pilot programs currently being marketed are designed to provide a private alternative. These are called social health maintenance organizations (SHMOs). SHMOs were started in 1984 when Congress authorized these pilot programs. They combine the services of an acute-care HMO with long-term-care benefits to help keep people out of nursing homes.

Seniors who live in communities serviced by an SHMO can join in the same way they would sign up for an HMO: they trade their Medicare benefits for the right to receive services under the program. Once this is done, they receive medical services as they would in any HMO. But SHMO members also benefit from a case management system. Case managers are hands-on professionals who work to arrange for home care and other services the plan members may need. Among the expanded services offered by SHMOs are the following:

Home nursing care

Physical and occupational therapy

Meal delivery

Homemaker services

Medical transportation

Adult day care

Emergency response systems

Respite care (to allow full-time caregivers a break).

The SHMOs have yet to prove that they are the answer to the long-term-care dilemma. However, if you or a loved one happens to live in an area serviced by the pilot programs, they may be worth looking into. The four communities where SHMOs are offered are: Brooklyn, New York; Minneapolis, Minnesota; Long Beach, California; and Portland, Oregon. If you are interested in the concept or would like more information, contact:

Brooklyn
Elderplan Inc.
1276 50th Street
Brooklyn, N.Y. 11219
(718) 438-2600

Minneapolis
Seniors Plus
2829 University Avenue S.E.
Minneapolis, Minn. 55414
(612) 623-8697

Long Beach
Senior Care Action Network
521 E. 4th Street
Long Beach, Calif. 90802
(800) 247-5091

Portland
Medical Plus II
Kaiser/Permanente
4610 S.E. Belmont
Portland, Ore. 97215
(503) 233-5631

SHMOs are the brainchild of the good people at Brandeis University, who keep tabs on how the programs are working. If you would like their input, contact:

Dr. Walter Lutz
Brandeis University
Heller School
Waltham, Mass. 02254
(617) 623-8697

Senior Life Insurance

In recent years a growing number of insurance companies have focused much of their marketing emphasis on selling life insurance to senior citizens and the middle-aged. You know the ones—where the famous actor, his hair now turned gray, trumpets, "You can't be turned down for any reason. No medical exam required! Think about it, life insurance for only $4.95 a month!"

Too Good to Be True

If these ads sound too good to be true, it's because they probably are. After all, why would insurance companies try to sell life insurance to folks who have arrived at an age where most life insurance companies either don't want them or price the policies so high that few can afford to buy? Are they crazy? Yeah, like a fox.

A close look at these policies generally reveals the following:

The life insurance is sold in units of coverage. One unit of coverage for these policies is usually worth between $600 and $1,000 in death benefits. Thus, in order to have insurance that pays any sizable death benefit at all, you will have to purchase a lot more than one unit. If you do, your monthly premium can quickly add up to $25 or $30 per month.

The policies don't pay real benefits for the first year or two. The reason these policies don't demand medical exams is that there are no real benefits payable for an extended period of time. Should a death occur during the waiting period, the only benefit is likely to be a refund of premiums (although some will pay if the death is accidental).

The bulk of the death benefits are for accidental deaths. Many of these policies have different death benefit schedules. If the death is accidental, the benefits are much higher than if the insured dies of natural causes. Since fewer deaths occur in our later years because of accident rather than natural causes, there is less likelihood that the maximum death benefit will be payable.

The benefits go down as your age goes up. These "senior life insurance" policies are a form of term insurance (see Chapter 28). But they take a slight twist on the usual formula. Rather than raise the premiums, they lower the benefits as the insured grows older. For example, one policy we've reviewed promised $44,400 in total benefits depending on age. Well, the only person who could ever qualify for that high level of return was a woman, age 40–44, who spent $19.95 a month in premiums and died an accidental death more than a year after taking out the policy. A woman who died accidentally at age 68 would receive $21,800, but if she died of natural causes, *the policy would only pay $3,000.* Beyond that, the fine print contains an interesting exclusion allowing the company to wiggle out of paying benefits if the accident that results in the insured's death is caused by age or infirmity.

Now, if your hair is turning gray and the term "middle-aged spread" is taking on a whole new meaning to you, these "mature adult" life insurance policies may be the only life insurance you can find that won't cost you an arm and a leg. But before you do buy, do yourself a big favor and check to see whether the benefits are worth the premium. We expect that you will decide they are not.

37

Workers Compensation

Every day, millions upon millions of Americans wake up and cheerfully sing, "Hi-ho, hi-ho. It's off to work I go." Well, maybe they don't sing exactly. Grumble might be a better word. And the words they mutter are probably more along the lines of the popular bumper sticker, "I owe, I owe, so off to work I go."

Whether we like it or not, we are a nation of workers who earn our bread, either literally or figuratively, by the sweat of our collective brows. For some, work is simply a place to earn a paycheck. For others, it provides an opportunity for self-expression and a way to contribute to society. Many use their place of employment for developing friendships and gaining a sense of belonging. Unfortunately, the work site is also where millions of workers meet injury or employment-related disease, which may leave them broken in body and sometimes in spirit.

If you ever become one of the unfortunates who suffer injury and disease at work, there is a form of no-fault insurance available to you to help alleviate the costs. This system of law is called **workers compensation**.

It wasn't always so. At one time in our history, workers who were injured on the job had to like it or lump it, unless they were able to file a lawsuit and prove that their employer caused their injuries by reason of negligence or other civil misconduct. This legal form of class warfare led to a crisis for both workers and employers in the early years of the 20th century. Workers suffered because it wasn't easy to win a lawsuit, especially with a conservative judiciary and with the defense of contributory negligence (see page 69) effectively barring financial recovery for many workers who may have partially caused their own injuries. (Please see discussion of the tort system in Chapter 42.) The defense of "assumption of the risk," which held that the employee assumed the risk of injury when he or she took the job, also made it difficult to successfully sue an employer.

Out of that horrible system came agitation for change. The reforms that followed virtually eliminated the right of injured workers to sue their employers. In return for giving this shield against liability to employers, workers were guaranteed medical care for their injuries and compensation for the time they had to miss work, regardless of the cause of the work-related accident. And, of course, this reform led to a brand new kind of insurance to pay for the whole thing, called workers compensation insurance.

Today, workers compensation laws are in place throughout the United States and Canada. The system has expanded beyond that originally contemplated, to include work-caused illness as well as injury. There is a downside, however. For many, the benefits received are terribly low, creating not so much a safety net but a few slender threads that may cushion the fall but not prevent permanent financial injury.

Rules of the Game

Here's a general overview of how the workers compensation system operates.

State Variations

Each jurisdiction has different laws. While there have been congressional efforts to mandate minimum benefits under workers compensation laws, these bills have not moved out of committee and are effectively stalled. As a result, each state remains free to establish its own standards of coverage, which vary widely depending on the commitment of each jurisdiction to workers' rights. The procedures for resolving differences between worker and employer vary by state as well.

Who Is Covered

With the exception of agricultural and domestic workers, most employees come under the provisions of workers compensation. However, the worker must be an "employee" as opposed to an "independent contractor." While each state has its own law defining the difference, an *employee* is generally someone who is paid to perform a task for pay under the immediate direction of his or her employer, while an *independent contractor* is paid to perform a task but is not supervised directly concerning how the work gets done.

Employers Pay the Costs

Although employees primarily receive the benefits of workers compensation, they don't have to pay for the insurance that provides those benefits. Employers do. In fact, civil and sometimes even criminal penalties can be brought against an employer who fails to provide for employee coverage, whether through a private insurance company, adequate self-insurance, or a nonprofit state compensation insurance fund (where available).

Settling Disputed Cases

Most states have special administrative systems to handle disputed cases. These states have established administrative hearing boards outside of their court systems to handle workers compensation cases that cannot be resolved by the parties themselves. Because courts of law do not generally handle workers comp cases, there are no juries and the rules of evidence are more lenient than would otherwise be true. This allows cases to be decided with far less fuss and bother than would be required in a full-blown trial.

The Injury or Illness Must Be Work Related

In order to qualify for benefits under the workers compensation statute, the injury or illness must be work related. Sound simple? Well, it usually is but not always. For example, what if Peter Bluecollar is in an auto accident while driving to his job as an assembly-line worker? Is that compensable? Probably not, since he didn't have to drive as part of his job. But what if the person in the accident is a traveling salesman? In that circumstance, the injury might be covered, since traveling to and from appointments could be considered one of the requirements of the job.

In addition to compensating for injuries sustained in industrial accidents, workers compensation will also pay benefits for sufferers of some occupational diseases. An occupational disease is one that arises out of and in the course of employment and is peculiar to that occupation. For example, coal miners suffer from a horrible lung disease called black lung. (Sufferers of black lung are covered under both federal and state compensation laws.) There is also a growing controversial trend in some states to award benefits for illness caused by stress or for heart attacks, if the malady can be shown to have been partially caused by the work environment.

Workers compensation is a pure no-fault system, so it doesn't matter whether the injury was caused by the worker, a fellow employee, or the employer. The worker who drops a heavy box on his own foot will receive the same rights under workers comp as the coworker who hurts his back trying to lift the box off his injured coworker.

The Role of Attorneys

You don't have to hire a lawyer if you wish to pursue your rights under workers compensation. You can represent yourself, and many states allow nonlawyers such as union representatives to assist in workers' cases. However, despite the fact that workers comp systems are designed to remove fault from the process and seek to simplify the resolution of disputes, attorneys remain integral to the successful operation of the system.

Why? Few insurance companies pay benefits gladly, even when they can't dispute that certain benefits are due. If there is any way to eliminate or reduce benefits, the company will often make a grab for the brass ring by disputing all or part of the worker's claim. For example, the company may contest the extent of the injury that is work related. Or they may claim that the worker is fit and doesn't need to continue receiving medical care. When disputes arise, workers often hire lawyers to fight for their rights.

Workers compensation lawyers are usually paid on a contingency fee based upon a percentage of the award or as ordered by the workers compensation judge or hearing officer.

Benefits Payable Under Workers Compensation

There are several significant benefits available to workers (and/or their families) who qualify for workers compensation. Usually, they include the following.

Consumer Alert

Workers compensation is a unique field of law, with its own set of rules and procedures. Thus, if you have to hire a lawyer to assist you with a claim, make sure he or she has substantial experience in the field. A lawyer who only "dabbles" in workers compensation may not know all of the buttons to push on your behalf or how to push the buttons most effectively. Also note that some states allow lawyers to become certified specialists in the field in much the same way that doctors can specialize in narrowly defined areas of medical expertise.

Medical Payments

A major benefit payable under workers compensation is the payment of the medical bills incurred because of the work-related injury or illness. Most workers have the following questions about their work-related injuries and treatment.

Are all of my medical bills covered? With very few exceptions, all of your medical bills are covered by workers compensation as long as they arise out of a work-related injury. This includes doctor's bills, prescription medication, the costs of durable medical equipment, and most other conventional forms of medical treatment. However, disputes often arise between the employee and the employer's insurance company as to the necessity of certain medical procedures or the length of treatment.

Can I choose my own doctor? In many states, the answer is yes. In others, you must choose from an approved list of physicians who work in the field of industrial injury. Some states give the employer the right to choose, while you may choose a second doctor to review the diagnosis and recommendations of the employer-selected doctor.

Is there a waiting period before benefits begin? As to medical bills, no.

Rehabilitation

In addition to medical payments, workers compensation will pay for rehabilitation. This may come in the form of physical rehabilitation, designed to get the worker on his or her feet and back into the "old salt mine."

A very important part of the right to rehabilitation involves vocational rehabilitation, which teaches new job skills to the injured worker. The purpose of the training is to help the worker find a new field of endeavor when an industrial injury prevents the worker from continuing in his or her former occupation. If you find yourself in the workers compensation system and believe that you can no longer work at your former job, *you must apply* for vocational rehabilitation; the benefit is not automatically given.

If you are receiving rehabilitation and you cannot go to work, you will be entitled to receive temporary disability payments and other reimbursement. If you must travel to receive your training, you will be reimbursed for the extra expenses you incur.

Temporary Disability Payments

If your injury is so serious that you must miss work, you will be entitled to receive payments from workers compensation to partially reimburse you for lost wages. The following are usually the issues of concern to those suffering from a temporary disability.

How long will I receive temporary disability? You will be entitled to receive payments as long as you cannot work, or until you are determined to have "healed" as much as you are going to. At this point, you may be entitled to permanent disability or other payments.

How much will I receive? Unfortunately, probably not enough. One of the downsides of no-fault insurance systems is that they usually don't pay adequate benefits. Workers compensation is typical in this regard.

Payments will usually range between 60 and 80 percent of the worker's wage. Since the benefits are not taxed, this reduction in income is not usually a problem. However, real difficulty often arises for workers in higher income brackets because maximum amounts, or caps, are placed on benefits. No matter what the worker earns, he or she will not receive any money beyond the maximum allowed by state law. Some states, such as Connecticut, have reasonable caps ($671 per week). Most, however, do not. For example, according to the United States Chamber of Commerce, in Florida the maximum payment is $362 per week; in New York, $300; in Georgia, only $175. If you are used to living on $4,000 per month and face a cap in benefits, you could be headed for the financial equivalent of Custer's Last Stand.

Is there a waiting period? As with any disability insurance, the answer is yes. The length of the waiting period will vary from jurisdiction to jurisdiction but will usually range from three to seven days. If the injury is enough to keep you off the job for more than a few weeks, retroactive benefits to the date of injury will usually be paid.

Total Disability

If your injury is so serious that you are found to be totally disabled, you will receive lifetime payments. The size of these payments will be approximately the same as temporary disability benefits. Sometimes, however, the insurance company makes a lump-sum cash payoff instead. In such cases, the size of the lump sum will depend on an actuarial determination of what the disabled worker can expect to receive over his or her lifetime.

Permanent Partial Disability

More often than becoming totally disabled, workers find themselves permanently disabled but not so badly injured that they can never work again. In these circumstances, workers compensation will usually have a preset *schedule of benefits* that specifies what the worker is to receive based on the injury. For example, in Alabama, a worker who loses an eye will be entitled to $27,280. In Arkansas, the same injury is worth $16,465, while Wisconsin pays $34,375.

If your injury is one not listed on the schedule, a hearing officer will usually decide on the amount you will receive based on factors such as your reduced earning capacity or your "percentage of disability." If you are partially but permanently disabled, be sure to look into your rights to receive vocational rehabilitation.

Survivors Benefits

If a worker is killed in an industrial accident, his or her immediate dependents are also entitled to receive workers compensation. According to the United States Chamber of Commerce, such payments to survivors total 14 percent of all benefits paid under the workers compensation systems.

Payments made to spouses and children (during their minority) are based on a percentage of the deceased worker's wages. Usually the amount is based on how many mouths there are to feed. Thus, if only a spouse remains behind, the percentage will range anywhere from 35 to 60 percent. If the worker also leaves children, the percentage rises, usually to the 66⅔ percent range.

However, in Alberta, Canada, the share of a worker's salary payable to survivors is 90 percent!

There are also caps on the size of the payments. Thus, the families of upper-income workers are likely to face a significant decline in living standards unless the surviving spouse is gainfully employed, otherwise protected by life insurance, or has a significant estate to fall back on. Social Security survivors benefits also can make life a little easier for those who are left behind.

Consumer Alert

A big worry some workers have is whether their bosses can punish them for availing themselves of workers compensation benefits. The answer to that concern should be no. Labor laws prohibit sanctions against workers who apply for benefits and provide for monetary compensation for such misconduct. However, an employer cannot be forced to keep the injured worker's job open indefinitely while awaiting his or her return. If you have any worries in this regard, check with your union representative, your office of workers compensation, or a lawyer who practices in the field of labor law for the particular laws of your state.

Obtaining Workers Compensation Benefits

Receiving workers compensation benefits can be as easy as pie or as difficult as pulling teeth without an anesthetic. If you are ever injured on the job, here's a general overview of how your case is likely to progress.

Notification of Employer

If you are hurt at work, the first thing you should do is report the incident to your supervisor. There is usually a time period within which you must notify your employer or risk losing the right to receive benefits. Typically you have 30 days to make your report. *Don't procrastinate.*

Filing the Claim

If the injury is one that necessitates significant medical treatment or requires you to lose time from work, you should file a formal claim with your employer. When you do, ask your employer for literature that will tell you about the specific remedies and procedures available to you in your state. Each jurisdiction has different procedures and forms for filing claims. These forms should be available from your employer, union, or the local office that administers workers compensation. (See the front of your phone book under state phone numbers.) You may also want to hire a lawyer to file your claim on your behalf.

The following information is generally required when you make a claim:

Your complete name and address

Employer's name and address

Your Social Security number and birthdate

Your occupation

A description of the accident

A list of your injuries

Names and addresses of doctors and/or hospital that treated you

It is important to be as clear and concise as you can be when filling out the claim form since it will provide the basis for everything that is to follow.

Employer's Response

There will often be some sort of response required of the employer. Sometimes the employer will agree that the injury is compensable and will certify the accuracy of your claim. At other times, the employer may deny liability—stating, for example, that the injury was not work related. In any event, the employer's insurance company will be handling the matter both as to legal representation and the payment of benefits.

The Investigation

Once the claim has been filed, some benefits (such as temporary disability or medical bills) may be paid immediately. If not, a hearing may have to be held in front of a workers compensation hearing officer or judge to determine what, if anything, the worker is entitled to receive.

Treatment

If the injury is serious or ongoing, the worker will be treated as long as it takes to get well or to achieve as much of a recovery as can reasonably be expected under the circumstances. During this time, many workers feel as if they are in limbo because they don't know how things are going to turn out. But you can't rush Mother Nature, and until the treatment is complete, many workers remain out of work, forced to survive on the meager benefits of temporary disability.

Final Determination

When the case is ready, there will be a final determination of benefits due the injured worker. If the insurance company and the worker agree, a stipulation is entered into setting forth the terms of the agreement. This stipulation becomes the basis for the ruling of the workers compensation hearing board regarding the worker's case. If the parties cannot agree, a hearing is held and a workers compensation judge or hearing officer makes the final decision regarding permanent disability or other claims the worker (or, in the case of a work-related death, the worker's family) may make.

Appeals

If the worker or insurance company is unhappy with the results of the hearing, there is always the right to appeal. Appeals often are heard by workers compensation appellate boards, but courts of law can also be brought into the act. As a result, the appeals process can literally take years.

Reopening the Case

If the injured worker suffers a relapse, the case can be reopened and reevaluated. For the specifics of how this is done, contact your state industrial or workers compensation commission or board, an employees' representative such as a shop steward, or a workers compensation attorney.

Other Things You Should Know

There are a few other things you need to know about workers compensation:

- **You may be entitled to transportation costs** if you travel to receive medical or rehabilitational care. Thus, keep track of the mileage and/or get receipts for bus fare, etc.

- **There is a statute of limitations** for bringing workers compensation cases. **Don't procrastinate.**

- **Workers compensation is a no-fault system** and thus you are not entitled to damages for pain and suffering, even if you will spend the rest of your life in a wheelchair or in pain.

- **The insurance company has the right to have you examined** by a doctor of its choice and at its expense. Many cases of workers compensation litigation concern disputes between insurance company doctors who claim that a worker can return to his or her job and the worker's doctor who says otherwise.

- **In some circumstances you can file a lawsuit** as a result of your injury. In such cases, you will not be limited to workers compensation benefits but can collect all that the law and a jury say you are entitled to. These cases usually involve third-party-caused injuries. For example, let's say you work for a tree-trimming service. You are busy clipping a curbside tree when you are hit by a car. Under such circumstances you would be entitled to workers compensation because you were injured on the job. However, you would also be entitled to sue the driver who hit you because he or she is not protected by the workers compensation shield against lawsuits.

Consumer Alert

If your employer or the insurance company does not pay benefits in a timely manner, you may be able to file a motion with the workers compensation hearing board to have your employer penalized by way of additional surcharge payments made to you.

- **Your employer must usually keep your fringe benefits in full force and effect** as long as you are on workers compensation temporary disability. This is very important since the loss of a benefit such as health insurance could be very costly indeed.

- **There is usually a state fund** from which benefits can be paid to you if your employer does not have insurance or is under-self-insured.

For more information, contact your local union representative, your employer, your state's workers compensation board, or a workers compensation attorney.

Finally, we feel we must criticize the system as it currently exists:

- It generally takes too long for workers to receive the complete benefits they're entitled to.

- You can go broke trying to live off of workers compensation benefits because of the monetary caps placed on payments, which keep the maximum benefits payable very low.

- The system as it exists degrades workers by forcing them to undergo repeated medical examinations.

- Workers compensation benefits currently do not cover enough occupational diseases. If a disease is covered, the burden of proof is too difficult on the worker, frequently resulting in denial of benefits. One such disease is byssinosis, a lung disease caused by inhaling cotton dust.

38

Prepaid Legal Insurance

Lawyers—everyone seems to hate them. The legal profession is probably the only one about which joke writers never seem to run out of material. There are even whole books filled with anti-lawyer jokes.

Jokes and put-downs aside, lawyers are as American as apple pie and are essential to the peaceful functioning of society. They are hired to write wills. They help people with real estate transactions. They help facilitate adoptions. They defend those accused of crimes. They promote civil liberties and protect civil rights. They are solicited whenever there's a divorce (which means they work a lot). A lawyer is often the second person an injured accident victim calls, right after the doctor—sometimes even before. In short, for better or worse, lawyers are part and parcel of the American experience, and sooner or later most people need to retain one.

The Expense of Legal Services

However, lawyers are expensive—and expensive with a capital E. Clients frequently have to pay in excess of *$150 or $200 an* *hour* for legal services. That amounts to more than $2 a minute! If your lawyer sneezes and blows his nose, you could be out 10 bucks!

This may be a bit of an exaggeration, but the simple fact of the matter is that lawyers are too pricey for most consumers to afford. Thus, many would-be clients tend to walk away from a legal dispute, not because they think they are in the wrong but because it will cost too much money to prove they are in the right. For a society that prides itself on the rule of law, this is a disturbing and sorry state of affairs.

Of course, the rich and powerful and the large corporate interests have no problem. They have enough money to hire enough lawyers to choke a whale. And they usually do, which is one reason why the justice playing field is tilted in their favor. Poor people receive assistance from public defenders, bar associations whose members do some free work, and legal aid (or what's left of it after the Reagan budget cuts). But what help is there for the middle and lower classes? Unfortunately, not much.

The Insurance Solution

Increasingly, private insurance is being marketed around the country to assist middle-class folks with the cost of legal service. These programs are marketed in several ways: credit card companies offer group rates, unions and employee groups obtain legal insurance as a fringe benefit, and people purchase individual policies, just to name a few. According to the American Prepaid Legal Services Institute, 13 million Americans were covered by some form of prepaid legal insurance in 1987 and the number has increased in the years since.

The various policies that are being marketed today differ in the specific services they offer. However, some general principles apply to most coverages. Here is an overview of what you can expect to find in a typical prepaid legal insurance policy.

Greater Access to Lawyers

One of the major points of emphasis made by providers of prepaid legal insurance is that it gives the insured general, everyday access to lawyers. Most people have legal questions they need answered from time to time: "What can I do if my neighbor's tree is endangering my gazebo?" "Can I sue the dry cleaner for ruining my new red sweater?" "How can I avoid probate expenses when I die?" "Do I have to reveal that a mudslide damaged my house three years ago, if I decide to sell it?" Most people simply don't have a lawyer on retainer they can call to answer these kinds of questions.

Most prepaid plans solve this problem by allowing access to lawyers for the purpose of answering legal questions. Sometimes the access is by toll-free telephone number. In other plans, the insured is given a list of lawyers in the community who have promised to "be there" should a question arise. This access to accurate legal information is one of the most valuable benefits of prepaid legal insurance plans.

Money Savings

Another important benefit of these policies is that they can save you money if you retain a lawyer to handle a legal problem. For example, wills may be offered at reduced price or even no cost at all. Name changes, bankruptcies, and simple divorces may be available at fixed discount prices. The lawyer's usual hourly fee may be cut for insured clients, or the percentage in a contingency case may be lowered.

Restrictions on Freedom of Choice

Just as with an HMO in the field of medicine, clients who use legal insurance frequently have to choose from lawyers on a list given to them by the insurance carrier. These lawyers, known as a panel, have contracted with the insurance company to provide services at reduced cost. If you go outside the panel, you have to pay the full price.

Other prepaid legal systems allow you to use any attorney of your choice and receive reimbursement from the insurance company for covered services that were rendered. Often this is done on an indemnity basis. For example, if you have a legal document prepared, the insurance might pay $50 and you would be responsible for the balance.

Premiums

The premiums are usually reasonable. The prices charged by the various prepaid legal plans vary, depending on the level of services offered and the percentage of the total fee that is covered by insurance. Plans come for as little as $12 a year. These provide basic question answering and not much else. Other policies cost as much as $300 per year and are much more comprehensive.

Questions to Ask

If you are interested in prepaid legal insurance, make sure you investigate the following issues.

Are the lawyers screened? The services you receive under a prepaid legal services plan are only as good as the lawyer who performs the work for you. Thus, if your plan requires you to choose from a panel of attorneys, you should ask the plan administrators what, if anything, they have done to screen these lawyers to make sure they have the ability to do the job. You should also take the time and effort to screen the lawyer yourself, checking for experience, the ability to communicate with you respectfully and clearly, and whether you feel confident in the lawyer.

Exactly what services are covered? You need to know what services you can expect to have provided at little or reduced cost. The following list is typical.

Free legal services:

> Unlimited phone calls to an attorney
>
> One hour of free in-office consultation
>
> Free letter writing

Reduced fees:

> Personal injury cases
>
> Landlord-tenant disputes
>
> Divorce
>
> Drunk driving defense
>
> Traffic court
>
> Representation in civil lawsuits
>
> Motions to expunge juvenile records
>
> Adoption proceedings
>
> Tax planning
>
> Drafting wills and trusts

What services are not covered? Every insurance contract has exclusions, and prepaid legal insurance is no exception. Typically these plans exclude highly specialized services, such as patent law or Securities & Exchange Commission representation. Legal disputes between two members of the same group or prepaid legal plan may also be excluded. Tax audits aren't usually covered, nor are business lawsuits (although businesses can purchase their own prepaid legal insurance).

Costs are not covered by insurance. *Costs* are the out-of-pocket expenses incurred during litigation for other than lawyers' fees. Cost items include filing fees, investigators' expenses, the price of a deposition, and payment to experts to testify. Costs in a $5,000 case will be in the hundreds of dollars. In a larger case, the costs can run into the thousands. In huge cases, costs can run into five and even six figures! So look before you leap into a lawsuit, even if your legal fees are reduced by insurance.

Are the policies worth the price? Of course, this is the big question. If you have extra money sitting around or find yourself having to consult with lawyers on a regular basis, or if the premium is low (or even free, when supplied as an employment fringe benefit), the answer may be yes. However, make sure that more important policies, such as auto, health, and life insurance, are firmly in place before purchasing a prepaid legal protection plan. After all, first things first. Most of us would have little occasion to benefit from a prepaid legal plan.

Part 8

Standing Tall

In all fairness, it must be said that many people who file claims with insurance companies run into relatively little trouble. However, far too many are not so lucky. Every day, on radio talk shows, in letters to the editor, and in personal conversations, consumers gripe about the poor service they receive from insurance companies.

For some, the complaints center around being "nickled and dimed" to distraction concerning a claim. You know the scenario: You file a claim and the company doesn't reject it but offers to pay less than you think you are entitled to—maybe the amount in dispute is a few bucks, maybe more. Not that the smaller fights aren't important—they are. After all, if the insurance companies are able to save themselves a few bucks per claim, the total dollars that are taken out of consumers' pockets each year will amount into the tens of millions.

For others, the troubles can go far deeper. As irritating as a "cat fight" with an insurance adjuster can be over minor items such as the value of a stolen stereo, these problems pale in comparison to the plight of the unfortunate consumers who find themselves in danger of being aced out of insurance benefits altogether. These fights often turn into battles royal, taking years of litigation and costing thousands of dollars in legal fees.

So we now come to the place where the rubber meets the road. In this section, we will be dealing with several important topics: how insurance is regulated and how you can use the regulatory agencies to your advantage; how to prepare in advance for the day you must file an insurance claim; the process of filing claims; and how to successfully struggle with your insurance company if you disagree about the extent of benefits you are owed.

We will also discuss some changes in the law that we think are necessary if consumers are to get a fair deal in their relationships with their insurance companies. Unfortunately, as things now stand, the insurance industry holds most of the cards. But there is a potent tool that can bring down insurance companies that deal maliciously with their insureds: the bad faith case. Its potential to even up the playing field must be unleashed if consumers are ever going to be able to consistently insist on a fair shake from the insurance industry.

So let's get to it as we paraphrase a famous rallying call of the 1960s: Power to the consumer, right on!

39

Regulation:
Fact or Fiction?

It is safe to say that the insurance industry is *supposed* to be one of the most regulated industries in the United States. After all, each state has a department of insurance charged with regulating all aspects of the insurance business within its respective jurisdiction. Unfortunately, when it comes to the topic of state regulation, that is about the only thing that *is* safe to say. The issue of state oversight has become one of the hot spots of political debate in the country today.

It wasn't always so. Early efforts at state regulation were primarily designed to keep the insurance industry honest by taking steps to ensure the solvency of companies selling insurance. This became an acute problem in the latter part of the 19th century, when far too many companies became overzealous in cutting their premiums in order to attract business, only to go belly-up when too many policyholders made claims. Thus, originally, much of the regulatory emphasis was on preventing premium pricing that was too *low*.

The current battle lines concerning regulation had their genesis in 1944 when the U.S. Supreme Court issued a ruling on a case entitled *Paul v. Virginia*. In this case, the court ruled that the practice of price fixing in certain insurance companies violated the antitrust laws. More important, and for the first time, the court stated that insurance sold across state lines was interstate commerce and thus was subject to regulation by Congress.

Well, the insurance industry bellowed like a stuck pig. For one thing, the decision would have allowed federal antitrust standards to apply to insurance. (You must remember, this was in the days when the government took antitrust laws seriously.) No more sharing of statistics, no more common use of pricing information. Here was a chance for the industry to be forced to engage in pure competition! Plus, the industry was also concerned that companies would have to serve two masters, state regulators as well as federal. Clearly, a crisis was at hand.

After intense lobbying by the industry, Congress came riding to the rescue with the McCarran-Ferguson Act, which, to put it graphically, gutted the *Paul* case. Under the McCarran-Ferguson Act, the federal government was forced to keep its hands off insurance regulation in most instances. Otherwise, the individual states were given the power to rule the insurance roost. This was just fine with the insurance industry, which could use its immense power and fortune to persuade state legislatures and regulatory boards to see things its way.

Thus was the current mess—er, system—born. Today, 50 different states have created 50 different sets of rules regarding the same kinds of insurance, which are sold in 50 different state markets. These rules and regulations are created by state legislatures and administered by the governors' offices through insurance commissions or boards.

Under current law, the following are among the areas generally regulated by the respective insurance commissions.

Rate Regulation

This area of state power probably receives more public attention than any other since it has a direct and significant impact on each insurance consumer's pocketbook. In theory, rates are supposed to be regulated rather like baby bear's porridge in "Gold-ilocks and the Three Bears"—not too high, not too low, but just right.

Of course, this is easier said than done, especially regarding rates that may be too high. How do you determine what rate is too high, especially in an industry whose books make hiero-glyphics look like the text of the old Dick and Jane reading books? ("Look, Dick, see Jane pay. Pay, pay, pay.") The issue of what constitutes fair pricing is a controversy that is raging all over the country.

Many insurance commissions are criticized for being too lax regarding rates. Many consumer advocates point to current law allowing different insurance companies to utilize the same ratings bureaus as a prime cause of the problem. A ratings bureau com-piles the statistics we talked about in Chapter 6 and publishes recommended rates to its subscribers. Critics allege that this permits a form of price fixing that hinders competition. On the other hand, supporters argue that this practice promotes fair regulation since the ratings bureaus are themselves state-regulated.

Consumer Alert

There is a growing trend in the area of property/cas-ualty insurance to do away with direct regulation of rates in favor of a pure market system that would the-oretically allow competition to determine the best and fairest prices. But this won't work if rating bureau sta-tistics and recommendations continue to be the pri-mary basis for pricing decisions. If you're going to have competition, do it the old-fashioned way and prevent the insurance companies from exchanging informa-tion with one another, which tends to blunt the com-petitive forces of the marketplace.

Reserve Levels

Insurance companies are required to set aside money to ensure against their insolvency. This money is called a **reserve**. Reserves come in several types; the two of primary interest to this discussion are the **loss reserve** and the **policy reserve**.

Loss Reserves

The loss reserve is found in the area of property/casualty insurers (such as auto and homeowner's insurance). It is the amount of money that the insurer estimates it will have to pay out on all claims it has received or expects to receive based on past performance, but has yet to pay. To guard against insolvency, regulators do not allow the loss reserves of companies to be set too low.

Policy Reserves

Life insurance companies are required to maintain policy reserves sufficient to pay future claims. A policy reserve is the amount of money that is anticipated to be needed to pay policy obligations in the future based on one of several formulas that compute mortality tables (see page 266), anticipated interest earnings, and the like.

Surplus and Dividends Requirements

As you will recall from our earlier discussion on the different types of insurance companies (see page 12), mutual companies keep surpluses and pay dividends to policyholders. Many states limit the size of surpluses so that policyholders can be better assured of receiving fair dividends.

Licensing

State laws govern the method by which insurance companies are permitted to do business within each state. The company must be licensed by the state (except for companies that do business through the mail), which permits state authorities broad leeway in determining the licensing standards the companies must meet and gives them a powerful (if rarely used) tool to control insurance company malfeasance.

States also license insurance brokers and agents. Usually, an applicant must pass a written test in order to receive a license (see pages 18–19). The states also have the power to revoke licenses for cause (i.e., if an agent commits fraud upon his or her customers). It is generally agreed that state regulation of agents and brokers is inadequate, as is state regulation of most of the professions.

Regulation of Policy Language

Because insurance policies are complicated contracts, state insurance commissioners have the power to allow or disallow policy language, especially if it is ambiguous, deceptive, or easily subject to misunderstanding or misrepresentation. Some require uniform language so that all policies of the same type written in the state read the same.

Consumer Assistance

Insurance commissions also provide valuable consumer assistance, such as providing price comparisons about companies licensed within the state, and protecting consumers from company abuse. It is important to note that the adequacy of consumer protection provided by state commissions varies widely from state to state, ranging from total absence to mediocre at best.

The worst mistake consumers make in dealing with insurance companies is that they expect regulators to take care of their problems and don't act as powerful and informed consumers on their own behalf. The old saying, "God helps those who help themselves," is true, especially regarding your own insurance. We'll teach you how to help yourself in the following chapters.

40

Creating a "Paper Trail"

In many ways, the relationship you establish with your insurance company is like the interactions between nations when they enter into treaties: a mutually beneficial business relationship. As with most treaties, you each have your own rights and responsibilities, which, if followed, should lead to peaceful and harmonious transactions between you.

Unfortunately, insurance consumers often discover, just as nations do in the international sphere, that we don't live in a perfect world. Sometimes they find that being in the right isn't enough—that far too often "might makes right." Thus, it falls upon us to do with our insurance companies what Ronald Reagan advised the United States to do with the Soviet Union: "Trust, but verify."

How is that done? Sure, the United States and the Soviet Union have the ability to monitor each other's performance of treaty obligations. They enjoy a parity of power. If the Russians explode a bomb in the atmosphere, we will know it immediately. If the United States invades Kamchatka, the Russian response will be quick in coming.

But consumers don't have the power or money that an insurance company does. Consumers can't inspect the books of an insurance company. They can't grill the CEO as to how the company treats its customers. They can't force insurance companies to "do the right thing." Can they?

As a matter of fact they can, *if*—and it's a big if—*they prepare ahead of time for a dispute*. Just as nations who are not at war prepare for war, just in case, so too should you prepare for the "battle of the insurance claim," just in case. You can do this by creating your own **paper trail**.

The Importance of the Paper Trail

What is a paper trail? *It is the evidence of the history of your business affairs with your insurance company* as set forth in documents, letters, brochures, and claims for benefits. Remember, despite all of the advertising aimed at you by insurance companies designed to make you feel all gooey inside at how much they care about you, the insurance business is in reality cold and impersonal. Decisions concerning you, your policy, and any claims you make are not going to be based on personalities, sob stories, or feelings of friendship, but rather on words—words contained in a contract called an insurance policy.

Insurance companies put great store in words. They use words and their interpretation of them as the basis for all they do in their business affairs with their customers. In fact, it is their mastery of policy language and of the words contained in relevant statutes (and the fact that they helped write many of these laws) that allows the insurance industry to exercise such tremendous power.

The facts of life being what they are, the best way for you to exercise a little consumer power of your own is to likewise master the words that control your insurance relationship. So words must become your primary weapon, too—words printed in sales brochures, words told to you by your insurance agent, the words you ultimately put into your claim for benefits, not to mention the words contained in your insurance policy itself. If you reach the point of having to go to battle with your insurance company, you must have the proper words at your disposal and understand their proper usage.

Get Organized

The first step you must take as a strong and powerful consumer is to marshal your "word troops." The only way you will be effective at this is if you get organized. Here's how.

Set Up an Insurance File

Most of us are pretty casual about the way we keep our business records. We toss them in drawers, stick them between the covers of books, and sometimes even throw them away. This is a big mistake. How can we hope to "engage the adversary" if we don't know where our troops are?

So, the first thing we should do is organize an insurance file. How you do it is, of course, up to you, but we suggest the following.

Establish a place to keep your records. You should keep all of your business records in one place. That way, in time of need you won't have to organize a search party just to find the name of your agent or a copy of your insurance policy.

The best thing to do is to buy a small filing cabinet, fireproof if you can afford the cost. If you can't afford a filing cabinet, then spend a few bucks on a sturdy cardboard filing box available at most stationery stores or a sturdy moving box available through moving companies or stores that sell boxes. In any event, the filing container should be large enough to hold all of your insurance files as well as other business papers such as tax returns and receipts from the purchase of merchandise.

What you will need. Setting up your file will be easy. Everything you need can be found at your local stationery store. Here's what to buy:

> An "accordion style" file holder
>
> Manila file folders
>
> Identification tabs

Place an identification tab labeled "Insurance" on the accordion file. Then label one manila folder for each kind of insurance policy you have (auto, health, homeowner's, life, etc.).

File your records in the appropriate file. You should then take all of your insurance records and file them: your auto insurance papers in the auto insurance file, your homeowner's documents in the homeowner's file, and so on.

Keep Your File Up to Date

The point of all this, of course, is to allow you to have the information you will need concerning your insurance at your fingertips. For the system to work, you must continue to update your files as new policies come in, as you correspond, make claims, and pay premiums. Whatever you do, don't put off today's filing for tomorrow. Otherwise, you might end up having to turn your house upside down looking for the information you need to make a claim or make it stick.

Always Get Everything in Writing

You should make it a habit to conduct all of your business interactions in writing. Thus, always get the following down on paper in good old-fashioned black and white.

All sales promises. You will be making purchasing decisions based on the information you are given by your insurance agent or other sales representative. Remember, insurance companies will be bound by what their agents promise you. Of course, there are many agents and sales representatives who are honest and conduct their professional duties with fidelity to ethical guidelines. Many, however, sell company products that have serious shortcomings, and there are those who are downright dishonest. And there is always the possibility of a mistake or a good-faith miscommunication between you. Thus, you should get all sales promises in writing and keep the documents in the event the policy you receive is not the same as the policy you have been promised. In that regard, *take written notes about what the agent told you* and keep them for future reference.

Consumer Alert

Agents will usually use sales brochures or other written documents to help sell their product. Always *keep these* in your insurance file if you buy a policy. If the oral representations are not supported by company documents, ask the agent to put the promises made to you in writing and ask the agent to date and sign it. Then file the document in your insurance file so that it will be there in the event of a dispute. In that way, if any funny business should occur, you will have written proof that your version of the facts is true.

Binders. If the agent is empowered to bind the company (see page 39), you should obtain the binder in writing. If you have been promised coverage over the phone, ask the agent to send you a binder in the mail. You should also send your own *confirming letter* concerning the coverage you have purchased, making sure you keep a copy for your own records. For example:

October 3, 1991

Alfred Millionseller
Big Bucks Insurance Company
8888 Big Bucks Drive
Profit City, Arkansas 88989
    Re: The Coverage I Have Purchased

Dear Mr. Millionseller:

The purpose of this letter is to confirm our conversation of Oct. 3, 1991, wherein the following occurred:

1) You told me that you were authorized by the Big Bucks Insurance Company to bind them to issuing an insurance policy to me.

2) You have issued an oral binder to me, as set forth below. The binder took immediate effect, which means I am currently covered by auto insurance.

3) My coverage is as follows:
   A. Liability coverage is $50,000 per person, $100,000 per accident.
   B. Property damage coverage is $50,000.
   C. Uninsured motorist coverage is $30,000 per person, $60,000 per accident.
   D. Med pay is $5,000.
   E. Collision and comprehensive coverage was purchased with a $500 deductible.

4) I understand the premium will be $540, which shall be payable in three equal installments plus a $10 service charge. The premium is for one year's worth of coverage.

5) I shall receive my formal policy within 30 days.

Thank you for your courtesy and cooperation. I look forward to doing business with you.

Very truly yours,

John P. Smartconsumer

Declarations pages. As you will recall from Chapter 5, the declarations page will tell you the exact levels of coverage you have purchased, as well as any riders or endorsements you have added to your insurance protection. It will also tell you your policy number, which you should use in all of your correspondence with the insurance company about your coverage. *Always review the declarations page to make sure it corresponds with the coverage you believe you have purchased.*

Insurance policies. The company will also mail you the insurance policy itself. *Be sure to read it*, paying special attention to benefits, exclusions, your duties under the policy, and how to file a claim.

If you have any questions about your policy, be sure to call the agent or company to have your concerns clarified. Again, *take notes* so that you have a written record of what was discussed. For example, if you wonder whether your personal computer is covered under your homeowner's policy, call and get the answer from your agent. Then, *write a confirming letter* setting forth your understanding of what you were told and keep a copy for your records.

Bills. You will be sent bills or invoices for payment of your premiums. When you mail in the payment, note on your copy of the invoice the date you made the payment and the check number. *Also, be sure to write your policy number on the check*, in case your check gets separated from the portion of the invoice you send in with your payment. Keep your portion of the invoice, as well as the canceled check of your payment. *Always pay by check or money order so that you will have a receipt* to prove you made the payment. *Never pay by cash.*

Company correspondence. During your relationship with the insurance company, you will receive correspondence about various matters from time to time. Keep copies of these letters (other than advertising that you don't respond to) as well as any replies you make.

Records concerning the subject of the insurance policy. Each policy you buy covers something or someone. Thus, it is a good idea to keep the "vital statistics" of the insured person or property in your insurance file. For example, in your automobile insurance file you would want to keep a copy of your automobile purchase contract, the license number, the engine identification number, and a list of extras that might raise the value of the car. With homeowner's or renter's insurance you should make an inventory of your personal possessions (your agent will have an inventory form you can use).

Claim forms. It is a good idea to keep blank claim forms in your insurance file before you need to use one. In that way, you will know the kinds of information the company will want should you apply for benefits. (We will discuss claims in the next chapter.)

Claims made. If you ever need to apply for benefits, be sure to keep a copy of the claim forms you have filled out. In fact, unless the claim is a minor one, you should set up a new manila folder, identify it, and keep all of the records of the claims transaction in the new file.

Benefits paid. If you receive benefits, make a copy of the draft you receive and any other documents that may come with it, such as a **release**. (A release acknowledges payment in full and releases the insurance company from any further obligation arising out of your claim.)

The Paper Trail Is a Money-Saver

We know this is a lot of work and most of us don't have secretaries to do our filing for us. But by keeping organized and creating a paper trail, you can give yourself a very important boost in your dealings with your insurance company.

You will give yourself a better understanding of your coverage. Knowledge is power, and the more you know about your insurance protection, the better you will be able to use your insurance intelligently and to best effect.

You are more likely to catch mistakes. Insurance people are human, and humans make mistakes. These mistakes can come back to haunt you if you are not careful or can complicate the processing of a claim.

It will be easier to file claims. If you get organized at the start, it will be much easier for you to file claims later on since most of the information you will need will be right at your fingertips. No frantic hunts through old shoe boxes, no begging the insurance agent for copies of records, no panic attacks because you have lost vital information.

It will help you get better service. The key to getting good service from an insurance company is to win the war of words. If the words of the sales pitch, the policy itself, or other documents support you, you will probably win. If not, you will probably lose. But there is also a kind of no-man's-land that occurs if the word record is incomplete or nonexistent. *In such cases, the adjuster or other insurance executive, knowing which side his or her toast is buttered on, will probably give the benefit of the doubt to the company.* Out of such gray areas are lawsuits made—expensive, aggravating, ulcer-creating lawsuits. So do yourself a favor: keep meticulous records. The conniption fit you avoid could be your own.

It will provide ammunition if you and your company get in a fight. If you and your company come to legal blows over your coverage, you will need all of the ammunition you can get to press your claim or to give to your lawyer. Having all necessary documents in hand will greatly simplify your life and could save you money. Remember, if an attorney has to pursue the insurance company to secure records you should have in your own file, he or she will charge you for the work. Better and cheaper to have everything on hand for your attorney ahead of time. Not only will the contents of your file help your attorney in giving legal advice but it will also save you money.

And if all this is not enough to motivate you, remember: Your insurance company is keeping records of its own and will use them to its advantage. When trouble comes, any advantage to the company becomes a corresponding disadvantage to you.

41

Filing Your Claim

The most important thing you will ever do as a consumer of insurance is to file a claim. After all, the whole point of buying insurance in the first place is to be able to say to your insurance company after suffering a loss, "Here, take care of this problem for me." That's why you work so hard to find the right coverage. That's why you pay all of those premiums. That's mainly why the insurance industry exists at all.

So, now that you're finally at the place where money flows your way instead of the other way around, you will want to do things right. There may be a lot at stake. Maybe your house burned down. Perhaps you crashed your car into a bridge. It could be that your appendix had to be removed. Whatever the claim might be, now is definitely not the time to fumble the ball as you race toward the insurance benefits goal line.

How the Claims Process Works

The process of having your claim filed may go as smooth as silk, or it may make you feel like you've gone over Niagara Falls in a barrel. Much of the smoothness or turbulence of the process will depend on the extent to which you understand the claims process and how to get the most out of it.

The following is a typical blow-by-blow description of what happens when you file a claim.

Notification to the Insurance Company

In every policy, your duties regarding company notification of a pending claim will be spelled out. For example, you may be required to notify the company within 30 days. In order to avoid unnecessary trouble in obtaining your benefits, *make sure you understand your responsibilities under the contract and that you comply with them.*

Notification can occur in several ways, which will be specified in the policy. Perhaps you will make notification by telephoning your agent. Or there may be an adjuster's number to call. Whatever the case, upon notification, you will be asked to file a formal claim.

Consumer Alert

Failure to meet all of the technicalities and formalities of company notification will not necessarily mean you will lose your benefits. But it could, so why take a chance?

Filing the Claim

In order to reap the benefits of the premiums you have sowed, you will have to file a formal document with the insurance company requesting that benefits be paid. This document is called a **claim**. The claim should be delivered or mailed to the location designated in the policy or as instructed by your agent or insurance company representative. And remember, always keep a copy for your records.

The Investigation

Once the claim has been properly filled out and sent in, red lights go off in the company office, the call to general quarters is sounded, and the company goes into its "We're from Missouri" mode. In other words, you will have to prove your right to receive benefits.

The first thing the company will do is to assign an **adjuster** to handle the claim. The adjuster is the person who is charged with making sure that your claim is properly investigated and then paid or refused. The adjuster may be an employee of the company or may be an independent contractor with whom the company has a deal to handle their claims.

The first thing the adjuster will do is to check your coverage to see if it is in full force and effect. Insurance is a hard-ball business. If there is a legal way for the adjuster to deny that you are protected by the coverage, he or she will take advantage of it. For example, if you have not paid your premiums or there are exclusions that apply, the company will take full advantage of the circumstances and put up a wall of resistance to paying benefits. Once the wall is up, you may have to hire a lawyer to break it down, if it can be broken down at all.

The next step the adjuster takes is to thoroughly examine the assertions made in your claim. At this stage, you will be asked to document your request for benefits. For instance, if you lost a couch in a burglary, you may have to prove when you bought it and how much you paid. If your spouse dies and you file a claim for life insurance benefits, you will be asked to produce a certified copy of the death certificate.

The adjuster may also attempt to verify the facts set forth in your claim by contacting independent witnesses or by looking at official documents, such as a police report made at the scene of an automobile accident. Other things will be looked at as well. For example, has the insured acted in such a way as to worsen the damages payable by the insurance company? If so, the adjuster may recommend that the company refuse some or all of the benefits requested. The adjuster will also try to determine the "true value" of the loss. Except in the most basic cases, the company probably won't take your word for how much it is obligated to pay.

Ultimately, the adjuster issues a recommendation to the insurance company regarding your claim. That recommendation may be to pay the claim. If so, a proof-of-loss form will be prepared by the adjuster for your signature along with his or her report. If the adjuster decides it is appropriate for the company to resist the claim, he or she will recommend that strategy to the company. Or the adjuster may suggest that the claim be partially paid and partially resisted.

Based on the adjuster's recommendations and the contents of the insurance company file, the company will then make its decision regarding your claim, and you will be notified of that decision by mail.

Performance Is Given

If you and the insurance company are of one accord regarding your claim, the company will perform its obligation to you under the terms of the insurance contract. For example, if you are being sued and you are protected by liability coverage, the company will agree that it is its responsibility to defend you in court and to pay damages up to the policy limits. Under these circumstances, you will be directed to the attorney who will be handling your case. Later, payments may be made to the person bringing suit.

More often, you will be paid directly. If you are so paid, you will be issued a written draft, a document akin to a cashier's check. You may be asked to sign a release in order to obtain your draft. In any event, unless there is a specific agreement to the contrary, your signature on the draft constitutes acceptance of the payment as payment in full. At this point, the file is closed forever unless you can show that the company somehow induced you to accept an inadequate payment using fraud, coercion, or some other form of unfair business practice.

If You Agree to Disagree

If you and the company cannot come to terms concerning the loss, you will have two options: take what they will pay and go on with your life; or, to paraphrase the famous football cheer, "lean to the left, lean to the right, refuse to take it, and, fight, fight!" Fighting insurance companies will be discussed in the next chapter.

Tips on Filing Claims

Since the insurance company will be reviewing your claim with a somewhat jaundiced eye, it is vital that you conduct yourself in a proper and businesslike manner. Here are some tips that should help you avoid unnecessary problems when your claim is being adjusted.

Be Thorough and Meticulous

The quality of the work you put into the claim form will be the first impression that the adjuster will have of you and your loss. It is only natural that a claim that is clear and concise will make a far better impression on the adjuster than one that is filled out in unintelligible handwriting, is smeared, or is written in an unclear and imprecise manner.

For example, if the claim form asks you to describe your version of an auto accident, there is a right way and a wrong way to give the requested information.

The right way: I was driving Eastbound on Main Street at approximately 35 miles per hour. Approximately 100 yards east of the intersection with

Second Avenue, my right front tire blew out and I lost control of the car. The car crashed into a tree. I have pictures taken at the scene of the accident, which will be made available upon request.

The wrong way:

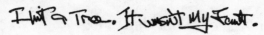

In the first example, the adjuster is given the specifics of the accident that gave rise to the claim. The fact that photographs back up the story can only give the adjuster confidence that you are speaking with a straight tongue. The specificity and clarity of the claim will also make it easier for the adjuster to investigate the case efficiently and quickly. The quicker the investigation, the sooner your benefits stop earning interest for the insurance company and start going to work for you.

On the other hand, the claim made in the second example is of little use to the adjuster, who will have to take the time and effort to determine your version of what happened before proceeding with the independent investigation. Such poorly filled-out claim requests can only delay your rightful benefits.

When you fill out a claim form, be sure to fill out every portion of the document. Otherwise, the adjuster will have to send it back to you for completion or try to reach you by phone to get the additional information. Incomplete forms do nothing but delay your benefits.

Don't hesitate to attach additional pages to your claim if necessary. Most claim forms do not allow sufficient space to fully describe the facts and circumstances that give rise to the claim for benefits. If you find there is not enough space to do a thorough job, attach additional pages in support of your claim. These are called "attachment pages" and should be identified as such.

Tell the Truth

Tell the truth, the whole truth, and nothing but the truth. Sometimes people tend to embellish (to put it politely) their claim. Others withhold vital information that might be damaging to their chances of recovery. These can be very serious mistakes. Not only is it dishonest to lie or mislead by silence, it might be a crime—the crime of **insurance fraud**. And what good are benefits paid to you if you are in jail?

Beyond the threat of criminal penalties, lying on a claim form, even a "little white lie," can lead to some very unpleasant results. For one thing, the adjuster will distrust you and may recommend that the company dig in its heels and conduct a protracted investigation. Moreover, if push comes to shove and you wind up in a lawsuit over the claim, your lying could become a big issue in the case and cause a jury, judge, or arbitrator to disbelieve even those portions of your story that are true.

So, be like George Washington. Never tell a lie to your insurance company. Otherwise you are likely to reap delay, discord, and the loss of otherwise rightful benefits.

Remember: It's a Business Relationship

Don't be "fooled" by a nice adjuster. Most adjusters are pleasant and courteous in their dealings with claimants. Of course, this is as it should be. However, *the polite and friendly attitude of an adjuster does not make him or her your friend*. Your relationship with the adjuster is a *business relationship*, and he or she will be trying to get the best obtainable deal for the company. Never forget that. So be nice and courteous too, but don't allow yourself to be led down a garden path into agreeing to accept less than you are entitled to.

Be Courteously Assertive

The flip side of the coin to the last point is for you to be courteously assertive with the adjuster. If you have taken the time to organize your file, to read your contract and the declarations page, you should have a pretty good general idea about how much you are entitled to receive in benefits. When dealing with the adjuster, be polite but don't be afraid to stand up for what you think is right. Don't allow yourself to be pushed into a settlement. It never hurts to tell the adjuster you want to sleep on the proposal.

Consult Your Agent

Don't be afraid to discuss the matter with your insurance agent. Your agent represents the insurance company, but his or her bread and butter is earned by servicing clients like you. The agent's business depends on goodwill, and word of mouth is the principal way goodwill is achieved. Thus, your agent will want you to tell your friends how much he or she helped you in your time of need. So, don't be afraid to consult your agent to ask for assistance when filing a claim.

Get Legal Advice If Necessary

Don't hesitate to seek legal advice if it is warranted. Lawyers may be a pain in the wallet, but failing to consult one when you have a serious question concerning your rights under the policy can cost you even more.

Read Before You Sign

Read everything before you sign it. Once you have signed a document, it will be presumed that you read and understood it. So be sure you do exactly that before you sign anything. Otherwise, all the whining in the world may not be able to undo a mistake.

Document Your Claim

Be prepared to support your claim with documentation. The better you document your claim with receipts, pictures, and/or other evidence, the higher the chances that your claim will be processed smoothly and efficiently and that you will be believed. This is a very important purpose of the paper trail discussed in the last chapter, and it's why you should keep your receipts, letters, and other documents in one place.

Do Your Homework

Don't be afraid to do a little legwork. When disputes arise over a claim, they usually have less to do with the issue of *whether* benefits are owed than with the *amount* of benefits owed. If you feel you are being shortchanged, don't be afraid of digging in and doing a little homework to prove you are right. For example, if the company says your stolen car is worth $8,000 and you know it's worth at least $10,000, hit the pavement. Talk to car dealers, look up the classified ads, and if it looks like you are right, document your proof and send it to the adjuster.

Ask Questions

If you have any questions about the process, don't hesitate to ask. Always write down the answers and place them in your insurance file. In that way, if things don't go according to what you were told, you will have notes to look back on to support your position. Notes will also help keep you from making mistakes of your own in case you later remember the conversation incorrectly. And, if you will pardon our nagging, never forget the power or importance of the confirming letter.

Don't Be Afraid to Go to the Top

If you are unsatisfied with the manner in which your adjuster is handling your claim, don't be afraid to contact his or her supervisor. You can call and complain, and then *always* write a confirming letter detailing your objections. Write the letter carefully and think it through. You may even want to hire a lawyer to write the letter for you, since it could become evidence should you get into litigation with the company.

The following is a sample letter of complaint:

October 30, 1991

We-Won't-Pay Insurance Company
Attn: Marilyn Bosslady, Supervisor
8282 Recalcitrance Lane
Boise, Idaho 88448

Re: Claim #423453—Policy #HO 324567

Dear Ms. Bosslady:

I have been a policyholder with We-Won't-Pay Insurance Company for over five years. During that time, I have never been late paying my premiums and have always fulfilled my obligations under our contract of insurance.

On September 1 of this year, I was in an auto accident. On September 3, I filed a claim, a copy of which I have enclosed.

The adjuster assigned to my claim is Clarence Dolittle. I regret to inform you that Mr. Dolittle has not performed his duties in a satisfactory manner. Specifically, I have the following complaints:

1) He has been discourteous. Specifically, he waits days before returning phone calls. He also has been sarcastic and demeaning in his attitude toward me.

2) He has procrastinated in his investigation. When Mr. Dolittle was assigned our file, I asked him how long the process would take. He told me three weeks. It has now been more than seven weeks and yet the claim has not been processed.

3) He has refused to acknowledge the information we have sent him regarding the value of our car. Mr. Dolittle has orally advised us that our car was worth $8,000. But we have proof that cars of the same model and year are selling in the classified section for $10,000. (Copies enclosed.)

Under the terms of our policy, we are entitled to receive the fair market value of our car. We believe that our documentation proves our point.

I would like to discuss these matters with you so that the misunderstanding can be cleared up and my claim can be processed. I can be reached during the day at 555-4434. My home phone is 555-0678.

Thank you for your courtesy,

Mary P. Indignant
8383 Victim Lane
Boise, Idaho

CC: Clarence Dolittle

Remember, when writing a letter of complaint:

- Always use your claim number and your policy number when communicating with the company about your claim.

- Support your contentions with documents whenever possible.

- Outline all complaints in a clear, concise, and unemotional manner. This is a business letter, and the credibility of what you contend will be judged by how you write it.

- Always let the person you are writing to know where you can be reached during business hours.

- Always send a copy of your complaint to the person you are complaining about. It will show you have class. Also send copies to legislators who may be active on behalf of consumers in your state and to your state department of insurance.

If the supervisor doesn't give you satisfaction, don't be afraid to go right on up the line to the chairman of the board. (You should be able to get the names and addresses of company officers by calling their home office. Your agent or local company rep will be able to give you the address and phone number of the home office.) The worst thing that can happen is that you receive no satisfaction, which will leave you in the same place you were before you wrote the letters. Besides, the old saying about the squeaky wheel getting the grease is often true, so if you are unhappy, "squeak" away!

Sometimes, however, even the best-intentioned and most capable consumer runs into a wall of insurance company resistance. When this happens, you have to be prepared to fight for your rights, which is the subject of the next chapter.

42

We Have Not Yet Begun to Fight

We've all heard insurance horror stories. Stories, for example, about an insurance company canceling an auto policy just because the policyholder dares to file a claim. Stories like the one about the health insurance company that became insolvent, but kept collecting premiums even though it couldn't pay benefits. Stories about an insurance company that refused to defend its customer when he was sued for millions of dollars.

The problem faced by consumers is not that disputes will arise with insurance companies. In any industry that engages in millions of arms-length business transactions each year, there are going to be disputes. Most of these disputes, in fact, are good-faith differences of opinion. However, some are the result of malice and greed.

The problem is, whether the insurance company is in good faith or bad, the deck seems overwhelmingly stacked in its favor. This leaves consumers feeling helpless, angry, and at the mercy of their adversary, like the lonely knight in shining armor who has been sent out without a sword to fight the powerful dragon.

Insurance company executives will tell you that this is so

much paranoia; that it is the insurance companies that are at risk; that the companies are at the mercy of greedy lawyers who file frivolous lawsuits that cause insurance companies to pay benefits they don't really owe. Not so, cry consumer advocates; just because you are paranoid, they say, it doesn't mean someone is not really after you.

Whether you believe insurance companies are "dollar monsters" out to devour every greenback they can get their greedy little hands on; or whether you think the insurance industry is the victim of consumer misunderstanding and the attacks of antibusiness political forces, it is vital that you know how to assert yourself if you find yourself in a dispute with your own insurance company. After all, you won't likely be able to win the game if you don't understand the rules.

Internal Remedies

Most consumers believe that a disagreement with an insurance company can have one of two outcomes: either the consumer gives up and is walked upon, or lawyers get into the act and the proclamation goes out to "let the lawsuits begin." Happily, there is a middle ground between those two extremes.

Informal Complaints

Before you go to the time and expense of hiring a lawyer and bringing out the big guns, you may be able to prevail by complaining to your insurance company itself.

Letters of complaint, which we discussed in the last chapter, often work. Mel Budnick, owner of the Trident Insurance Agency in Los Angeles, tells the story of a friend of his whose house burned down. The man was a deputy sheriff. He and his wife had three children and five pets. Happily the family escaped harm in the fire, but all of the pets were killed.

For some reason, the adjuster got it into his head that the fire was the result of the policyholder's arson. Not that there was any evidence pointing to the case as "an insurance fire"—the adjuster just had a hunch (or maybe he had indigestion that day). In any event, he refused to approve the claim, which left the family between a thick rock and a very hard place.

The impasse was broken by a simple letter of complaint to the adjuster's supervisor. The letter worked because the policyholder had his facts lined up in a row, and he set them forth precisely and specifically. The man also provided ample documentation to back up his claim. Finally, he made a point of quoting the language of the policy itself. His exercise in consumer power led to a just reward: the unreasonable adjuster was overruled and the family's home was rebuilt . . . where they presumably now live "happily ever after."

Meet the Decision Makers

As we have repeatedly warned you, insurance is a very impersonal business. The people who set the rates or decide the benefits rarely interact with the policyholders themselves. However, humanity can be brought into the equation if you ask to meet personally with the decision makers to discuss your dispute.

If you decide to "take a meeting" to discuss the controversy, *prepare* before you enter the lion's den. Remember, the executives you will be meeting are businesspeople who are prepared to stand up for their company but who also have been trained to spot the times when the company may be in the wrong. Here are some things to remember.

Do your homework. Your dispute will be won by the facts or lost by the facts as they appear to the decision makers. So, make sure you do the following:

Bring a copy of your policy. Your policy will usually set forth all of the rights and obligations of each side. Highlight the policy language you believe supports your position so that it can be discussed in the meeting. You should also be prepared to show the executive where the company has gone wrong according to its own policy language.

Bring documents that support your claim. You must be prepared to back up as much of your side of the story as you can by objective documentation. If a picture is worth a thousand words, so are documents that support your story.

Know the history of your file. You should be prepared to answer any question the executive might have. Thus, be sure you have thoroughly reviewed your own insurance file (see Chapter 40) before you attend the meeting.

Know your legal rights. If the dispute has the potential to turn nasty or if it involves a lot of money, you may wish to bring an attorney with you to the meeting. At the very least, you should have consulted a lawyer so that you can learn your legal rights before you meet with the insurance representative.

Avoid unnecessary emotionalism. When you go into the meeting, don't rant and rave and act like a maniac (even though your insurance company has made you feel like one). Such irrational and rude behavior is only likely to set the insurance company position in concrete. On the other hand, you can't be afraid to show the human side of your problem, since that is a primary purpose of a face-to-face meeting. Tell the executives of the pain and suffering their mistake is causing you. Explain how justice delayed in your case is justice denied. Show them pictures of your kids if you think it will help them see you and your problem in a sympathetic light.

Take notes. It is important that you continue to blaze your paper trail by taking notes about what you and the insurance company executive said at the meeting. If push ultimately does come to shove, court testimony may be taken about the meeting and you will want to be able to keep your facts straight.

Be willing to compromise. Don't be too rigid in your search for a solution. Instead, look for an acceptable compromise that will satisfy both you and your insurance company. Remember, half a loaf is better than none, especially when the whole loaf may be unobtainable.

Follow up. Whether the meeting results in a settlement, a compromise, or an agreement to meet at 40 paces, always follow it up with a courteous confirming letter. Also, if you are asked to take any action at all, such as finding a receipt or providing the name of a witness, *don't procrastinate*—get right to it. Remember, the insurance company won't take your claim any more seriously than you do.

Pursue Policy Remedies

At this point, if you can't reach a satisfactory conclusion to your dispute, you can either raise the white flag or declare that you have just begun to fight. If you choose the latter course, your next step is to pursue the remedies available to you that are provided within the insurance contract itself.

The usual policy remedy the insured must pursue if he or she disputes an insurance company decision is **arbitration**. An arbitration is similar to a trial but it is not held in a court of law in front of a judge or jury. Rather, it is held in front of a private individual or individuals whom the parties have agreed by contract to accept as the person(s) who will decide the dispute.

Arbitrations come in two types for your litigating pleasure:

- **Nonbinding.** A nonbinding arbitration allows the case to be heard but permits either side to bring a formal lawsuit if they are not satisfied with the result.

- **Binding.** A binding arbitration resolves the matter once and for all. In a binding arbitration, there is no right to a subsequent trial, appeal, or other remedies available to the loser of a case in court.

Whether the arbitration will be binding or not will depend on the contract language of your policy and the laws of your state and/or whether you and the company have agreed to make it binding.

Arbitrations can be very handy. For one thing, they permit each side to present its case before an impartial third party. Often, this outside opinion is sufficient for the case to be resolved. For another, arbitrations usually are much speedier than waiting for a trial at law, which can often take years to reach a conclusion. Finally, arbitrations are more informal than trials and thereby allow some insureds to pursue a remedy without going to the expense of hiring a lawyer.

On the other hand, arbitrations can be very unfair to consumers. For example, *the consumer has to pay for the right to seek justice.* Here's why. In insurance arbitrations, the consumer usually retains and pays for one arbitrator, as does the insurance company. Then these two arbitrators agree on a third arbitrator whose services are paid for equally by both sides. The problem here is that *the consumer may have to pay hundreds or even thousands of dollars seeking justice*—and that doesn't include the price of an attorney should the policyholder decide to retain one. This "price of justice" is only a drop in the bucket for the insurance company but it may be an ocean to you. Many disputes go unpursued by wronged consumers simply because the price of justice is too high.

Before you go into an arbitration, seriously consider hiring an attorney. Remember, your insurance company will probably be represented by one, and the arbitrators may be lawyers too. Beyond that, if you represent yourself, you will have to file papers according to arbitration rules established in your state and you will have to speak for yourself, a task that can be daunting to those not used to speaking in public or in pressure situations. At the very least, consult a lawyer before you represent yourself so you can make sure your analysis of your case is not lacking in an important way.

Once the arbitration is complete, you will be notified of the decision by mail. If you win, pat yourself on the back and see whether the insurance company accepts the decision (in a nonbinding arbitration). If you lose, decide whether you want to regroup and fight again in court. If the arbitration was binding, pray that you win. If you lose, consult an attorney to see whether you can appeal to the courts to vacate the decision.

File a Lawsuit

If you cannot settle your dispute with your insurance company by informal means or by way of arbitration, you may have to sue. For many, that's like going from the frying pan into the fire, since you will now be dealing with lawyers in addition to the insurance company. But unfortunately, sometimes a lawsuit is the only way to go.

Lawsuits involving insurance disputes come in several forms.

Breach of Contract

The most usual action taken against an insurance company will be suit for breach of contract. As we all know by now, an insurance policy is a contract. A contract is a formal agreement where the contracting parties each make promises to each other that will be enforced by law. If your insurance company doesn't keep a promise made to you in the policy, it is called a **breach of contract**.

There are several remedies for damages suffered from breach of contract. One involves a court order compelling the breaching party to keep its promise. This is called "specific performance." More often, the remedy is an order compelling the losing party to pay the damages the breach of contract caused to the winning party. Thus, if the insurance company promised in a homeowner's policy to pay to rebuild your house in the event it is destroyed by fire, your damages will be the cost of rebuilding your house.

There is a large problem for consumers in having their remedies against the insurance company limited to breach-of-contract damages. For one thing, there is no repayment for the emotional turmoil the battle has caused. For another, the incidental expenses of pursuing the case, such as time taken off from work to go to court, usually are uncompensated. Even attorneys' fees usually aren't paid. Attorneys' fees are not part of your damages when you sue for breach of contract unless the contract being litigated specifically calls for such fees to be paid to the winning party. And guess what? Most insurance policies do not allow for the recovery of attorneys' fees as a remedy available in the event of breach of contract. That's why bad-faith cases (see below) need to be expanded.

Bad-Faith Cases

We are sure it comes as no surprise when we say that insurance companies are more powerful than you are. They have more money, more lawyers, more of everything it takes to get their way in their relationship with you as a policyholder.

But what do *you* have? A contract (your policy) that can be enforced in a court of law. True enough. But too often, that's simply not enough to get the insurance company to do the right thing since your remedy for breach of contract is merely to make the insurance company do what it was obliged to do all along. In other words, there is no real punishment for breaching a contract, and this makes it far too easy for the company to say to you, "See you in court," rather than to comply with its duties under the policy.

All of this has inspired lawyers who represent policyholders to look for a way to punish insurance companies by "suing in tort" in addition to breach of contract. The most effective tort thrown against insurance company bastions is known generically as **bad-faith litigation**.

Without turning this into a law school dissertation, bad faith exists when an insurance company violates its legal duty to treat you fairly. This legal duty arises as soon as you enter into the contract, because the law implies that each contracting party has a duty to treat the other fairly with regard to the subject matter of the contract. Under this theory, then, breaching a contract can also be a tort, if the breach is done in such a way as to violate the "covenant of good faith and fair dealing."

Suing in tort can bring more in damages to the consumer than merely suing for breach of contract. That's because the remedies available go far beyond those for breach of contract. They include emotional damages, other economic losses (such as time lost from work pursuing the case), and perhaps attorneys' fees. Beyond that, under circumstances where the insurance company acts with "malice, oppression, or fraud," the person wronged by the tortious conduct may be able to get an award of punitive damages against the insurance company. You are more likely to get a lawyer to take the case on a contingency basis in a bad-faith case than you will be in a breach of contract case.

Punitive damages are payments ordered by a court to the wronged party *above and beyond the monetary amount actually lost*. They are intended to punish wrongdoing. More important, they are intended as a deterrent to future bad conduct, both by the party ordered to pay the punitive damages and by those who hear about the judgment.

There are two types of bad-faith cases.

First-party cases. An example of a first-party case is when your insurance company deals directly with you in bad faith by arbitrarily and unreasonably withholding benefits. A classic example is the health insurance company that arbitrarily decides it will not pay for a medical service covered under the policy. In such circumstances, if the excuse given by the company for withholding benefits doesn't wash, the insured may have a right to recover for bad faith, depending on the law of the state and whether the health insurance was a fringe benefit from work or an individual policy (see Consumer Alert on page 464).

Third-party cases. Sometimes, as in an auto accident situation, your insurance company has a duty to defend you and to pay damages for your misconduct up to and including the limits of the policy. But what if the damages are more than the policy limits? Well, unless you have an umbrella policy (see Chapter 24), you will have to pay the extra out of your own pocket.

Out of this backdrop come bad-faith cases arising out of third-party cases. If you get sued, for example, and your insurance company fails to settle the case reasonably, they may be exposing your pocketbook. Under such circumstances, you may be able to sue on the grounds of bad faith. Likewise, if they fail to defend you, a bad-faith case might arise.

Consumer Alert

The law of bad faith is extremely complicated and is continually evolving. Thus, we can only touch the tip of the iceberg in our discussion here. If you believe you have suffered from the bad faith of your insurance company, be sure to consult a lawyer who is an expert in the field of insurance litigation.

One of the primary benefits of suing in tort, as opposed to limiting your case against your insurance company to breach of contract, is the greater likelihood of finding an attorney who will take your case on a contingency basis. Contingency fees allow you to fight large and powerful institutions like insurance companies without having to bankrupt yourself in the process. This is why insurance companies hate contingency fees and are always lobbying legislatures to limit their availability to you. On the other hand, if you have to pay a lawyer $150 or more per hour, the company will try to force you to spend a lot of money in attorneys' fees as a way of getting you to give up the case.

Consumer Alert

Bad-faith cases are under continual attack by insurance companies and business interests because they force them to play fairly. Unfortunately, with conservatives in power in many places in the country, bad-faith cases have been sharply curtailed in recent years. For example, the U.S. Supreme Court has ruled out bad faith in health insurance cases if the health insurance was obtained by the insured as a fringe benefit of work or union membership.

Other tort remedies may be available to you in addition to bad faith. Fraud, intentional infliction of emotional distress, and breach of fiduciary relationship have all been used to bring miscreant insurance companies to their knees. To see whether any of these or other remedies apply in your case, consult an attorney who is an expert in insurance litigation.

If you are interested in how down and dirty a fight with an insurance company can become, we strongly suggest you read *Payment Refused: A Crusading Lawyer's Dramatic Cases Against Insurance Companies*, by William M. Shernoff and Thelma O'Brien (Richardson and Steirman, 1986).

Report Your Company

Insurance companies are regulated in all 50 states and in all the provinces of Canada. This regulatory power gives consumers another avenue in their quest for truth, justice, and the American (or Canadian) way.

One of the important functions of state insurance departments is to assist consumers in getting an even break from their insurance companies. Thus, if you feel like Don Knotts in the wrestling ring with Hulk Hogan, you may wish to put your state insurance department in the ring for you.

State insurance departments are supposed to handle many pressing problems for consumers, including:

Improper denial of claims

Unreasonable delays in settling claims

Illegal cancellation or termination of policies

Misrepresentation by a broker or agent

Misappropriation of funds paid in trust to an agent or broker

Premium disputes

Be sure to hold your state's insurance department to these standards.

Insurance departments don't handle every insurance dispute. For example, HMOs may not come under the jurisdiction of the department of insurance, and workers compensation is generally administered by its own state agency.

If you decide to file a complaint against your insurance company, you should do the following:

- **Call the department and ask for complaint forms.** They will be mailed to you.

- **Fill out the form carefully.** Be as specific as possible. Be sure to keep a copy for your records.

- **Send *copies* of supporting documents to support your claim**, such as your policy, canceled checks, letters, and other relevant matter.

You should receive notification of receipt of your complaint within a few weeks. At that time you will be given a file number. Be sure to use the file number in all future correspondence concerning your claim.

Unfortunately, many insurance departments are toothless tigers with neither the money nor the legal authority to energetically "advocate" for the consumer. And far too often, the leaders of the departments come out of the insurance industry, where they intend to return when their time of state service is over. Many complain that these "revolving door regulators" kowtow to insurance companies rather than vigorously pursue their regulatory functions. Still, it may be your only hope of achieving justice without the hassle and expense of going to court, so give your insurance department the old college try.

The Consumer Can Win

There are, however, instances of consumers winning their battles with insurance companies with the help of insurance departments. Two such cases involved Geico Insurance Company, which issues policies to more than a million people nationwide. Geico

Consumer Alert

Another area your state insurance department can help you with is getting a straight answer as to why a claim has been denied. In such cases, ask your department to assist you in getting the *specifics* of your case. With that information in hand, you will be able to decide what your next step should be.

prides itself on its low auto insurance rates for good drivers, but policyholders have often ended up paying more than they bargained for. Geico has been quick to raise its rates and even cancel the policies of people who have been involved in accidents or violations of the law—no matter how minor the accident or violation, no matter who was at fault.

In the first instance, a woman named Doris Lichter, who had held a policy with Geico for 15 years, learned that her policy had been terminated. In the two years prior to the cancellation notice, she'd been involved in two accidents, for which Geico had paid $1,600 in damages. Although she wasn't charged by the police in either case, Geico determined that her driving record was "unacceptable" for continued coverage. To back up their decision, Geico pointed to studies that placed Doris in a group of drivers three times as likely to have another accident in the following year. In fact, Geico insisted that it was almost statistically certain Doris would have this accident.

These claims of "certainty" didn't make sense to Doris's husband, a trained statistician. He investigated the source of the statistics cited by Geico, which turned out to be studies published by the California Department of Motor Vehicles. While the studies did show that Doris's two accidents placed her in a group of drivers more likely to have another accident, there was no way—according to the statistics—to predict *who* in that group would have those accidents.

Raymond Peck, the author of the California DMV studies,

said that he'd never heard of an instance where the statistics had been so misused. He wrote a letter of support for Doris Lichter, who then appealed the case before the Maryland Insurance Commission, and won. Geico was forced to renew her policy.

The Lichters' victory didn't stop Geico from canceling policies for questionable reasons. In a second case, Steve Pequeeny had his auto insurance canceled after the company had paid a $90 claim and Pequeeny had received a speeding ticket for going 63 in a 55-MPH zone. Pequeeny also appealed his case before the Maryland Insurance Commission, and won. This time, the Commission found Geico's own internal driver studies invalid.

The guidelines regulating insurance companies vary widely from state to state, but if you believe your policy has been unfairly canceled, call the consumer action group in your area and find out whether it's worth challenging.

Guarantee Funds

Imagine the frustration of paying premiums over the years and then when it comes time to file a claim, calling your insurance company only to hear those fateful words, "We're sorry, the number you have called has been disconnected."

Unfortunately, from time to time insurance companies do go out of business or become bankrupt. This can leave many policyholders in the lurch, which could be disastrous to their economic health.

Luckily, most states have guarantee funds whose function it is to pay most, if not all, of the benefits that are owed by a company that has gone belly-up. Money for the funds comes from insurance companies themselves. These funds have alleviated a great deal of suffering over the years.

However, six states have failed to pass laws compelling guarantee funds in the field of health and life insurance. This is an inexcusable state of affairs, leaving the policyholders at risk—perhaps, in the case of health insurance, of their very lives. The "gang of six" are Alaska, California, Louisiana, New Jersey, Colorado, and Wyoming. If you are a citizen of one of these jurisdictions, contact your state legislators and demand that a guarantee fund be put into full force and effect. You are never truly secure without one.

If you have any questions about guarantee funds, contact your state insurance department (see Appendix C) for the address and telephone number of the fund administrator in your state.

Now that you know some of the things you can do to stand tall against your insurance company, let's look at some of the obligations insurance companies should owe you, your community, and society as a whole.

43

Consumers' Agenda

Despite the efforts of consumers, lawyers, sympathetic regulators, and legislators, the balance of power in insurance matters is weighted overwhelmingly against you. This unfortunate circumstance won't change unless the laws do, and the laws won't be changed unless you get active and make it happen.

Here are some thoughts about how the disparity of power can be equalized.

Increase the applicability of bad-faith laws. Bad-faith laws are under constant attack by the insurance industry in those jurisdictions where they have been put into effect. In order to strengthen this remedy, it should be specifically provided for by statute (as opposed to court interpretation) as a remedy that consumers can take against insurance companies that treat them unfairly. Consumers need to organize and barrage their elected officials with letters and phone calls demanding that bad-faith laws or similar statutes be made a part of state codes. If necessary, the ballot initiative process should be used (where available) so that the control the insurance industry exerts in most legislatures can be diminished.

Allow attorneys' fees to be recovered if an insurance company is found to have breached a contract. Money talks—especially to the insurance industry. Thus, in addition to implementing bad-faith cases, laws need to be passed permitting litigants to collect their attorneys' fees as part of the court judgment when they successfully take their insurance companies to court, as occurs already in many federal and state consumer, environmental, and civil rights litigations. In that way, recalcitrant insurance company executives will know there will be a price to pay for refusing to pay due benefits.

Make the office of insurance commissioner an elected post. As it stands now, most insurance commissioners around the country are political appointees. This allows them to be insulated from the citizens they are serving. However, if the post becomes an elected one, the commissioner will sooner or later have to answer to the people, thereby giving you, the voter, more power. And if you have more power, chances are the insurance departments will be more likely to *truly regulate* the insurance industry rather than merely giving lip service to the concept of state oversight. They will also be more responsive to consumer complaints, making it *less likely that you will have to sue* to get satisfaction for a bona fide complaint.

Establish voluntary mediation boards. Most consumer disputes with insurance companies do not involve big bucks. This makes it harder to fight if they "do you wrong," because of the high cost of seeking justice. This imbalance can be rectified by each state establishing voluntary mediation boards or other dispute resolution mechanisms where consumers and insurance companies can resolve problems without having to pay high court filing fees or hiring high-priced lawyers.

Fight insurance industry attempts to further stack the deck. The insurance industry is engaged in a full-court press seeking to further tilt the litigation playing field in their favor. In state after state, they are trying to put caps on the money they can be forced to pay for damages owed. In state after state, they are trying to restrict the availability of contingency fees to you the consumer, because contingency fees give you a fighting chance against their might and power. And in state after state, they are trying to limit your power to sue all of those who may have had a hand in causing you damages if you are injured. These efforts must be fought. Otherwise, there will be a biased system where consumers pay full premiums but receive only limited benefits in return. And if contingency fees are lost to the average litigant, only the wealthiest consumers will be able to afford a lawyer to fight their own insurance companies.

There should be nationwide standards for insurance regulation. The effectiveness of state regulation varies depending on the comparative strength of consumers and the special-interest forces of the insurance industry. Minimum federal standards should be established concerning the level of insurance regulation each state must follow.

Epilogue: Toward Greater Expectations

Expectations influence the present and directly shape the future. Unfortunately, in the area of insurance, consumer expectations have been low and unfocused for far too long. As a result, the insurance industry has become delinquent in its role as sentinel for the health and safety of all Americans.

Had we expected the automobile insurance companies of the fifties to promote safety, we would have avoided deaths and injuries due to poor door latches, faulty seat belts, sharp edges on dashboards, and impaling steering columns. If currently we expect casualty insurance companies to act effectively against the promotion of alcoholic beverages and to invest their considerable resources into methods of rehabilitation, we can help prevent numerous deaths and injuries due to drunk driving. And if we expect life insurance companies to lead the struggle in the war against tobacco addiction, or fire insurance companies to push for a reduction in the number of fires due to cigarette smoking, we can help save countless lives, prevent injuries, and minimize property damage. All of which will reduce the incidence of expensive claims due to death, injury, disease, and property damage; substantially lower our premiums; and put the insurance industry back on track as advocates of health and safety.

At one time, loss prevention and safety advancement were important objectives of insurance companies. Nearly three centuries ago, Lloyds of London underwriters would only write insurance for vessels traveling to the Orient if ship owners took important safety precautions such as installing lifeboats. In 1894, the industry established Underwriters Laboratories for issuing seals of approval for fire-prone electrical devices and connectors. During the nascent development of elevators and boilers, insurers led the way in insisting on safety standards and equipment improvements, such as those for elevator cables and industrial boiler monitoring.

Now, however, the insurance industry is on a "cost-plus" kick; that is, in order to receive more investment income on your premium dollars, insurance companies would rather charge you $1,000, say, and pay out $500 in claims than charge $500 and pay $250 in claims. And as long as they can keep raising their prices in tandem with rising claims payments, there will be no incentive for change. It is only when consumers revolt and slow down this rising spiral that the insurance industry will invest significant amounts of time, effort, and money into reducing claims.

We have the technology to produce safer and more effective products. Yet statistics show that the yearly casualty count in the workplace and the marketplace continues to run into the millions. In fact, according to researchers at the National Academy of Sciences, nonintentional injuries are the *number one cause of death* for Americans under forty-four years of age. The insurance industry has the ability to significantly alter these statistics by creating and investing in loss-prevention programs. Domestic casualty companies alone hold assets of about *$400 billion*, while life insurance companies hold *nearly a trillion*. Still, the insurance companies of today, with few exceptions, are notorious underachievers in loss prevention.

One exception is the Hartford Steam Boiler Inspection and Insurance Company. The leading insurer of boilers and machinery, this firm believes in working with its customers to prevent costly accidents, to the customers' benefit as well as to its own.

In fact, according to the October 2, 1989 edition of *The Hartford Courant*, the company has compiled some impressive statistics that prove the benefit of loss prevention. Thanks to its safety programs, Hartford has paid out in claims about half of what most other insurers have. This has contributed to an increase in dividends seven times since 1984 and a return on equity over the past decade in the 25 to 30 percent range, or more than double the average for the property/casualty industry. Would that the rest of the industry follow Hartford's lead!

There are many ways that insurance companies can control and minimize hazards that cause injury and death:

Disclosure of information.   Insurance companies are in a unique position to disclose information about hazards to those responsible for ensuring safety, as well as to the public. Unfortunately, information sharing outside the insurance industry is virulently resisted. For example, in a letter published in the *New York Times*, Stanley Bulback, Director of Communities United for Research and Education for AIDS, noted the resistance by insurers to scale down escalating insurance claims by promoting AIDS education (a significant method of controlling the spread of the disease and maximizing its treatment) through newsletters sent with customer billing statements.

David V. MacCollum, former president of the American Society of Safety Engineers, suggests that insurance companies collect data on injuries caused by particular hazards and maintain a central data bank on hazard information. These companies should publish annual summaries of all hazard-related injuries and deaths and share information about ultrahazardous products (such as defective car models) and conditions (such as asbestos contamination) to both law enforcement officials and the public. Thus advised about hazards that are dangerous to life and limb, officials and individuals could take action to root out safety offenders and to avoid injury, leading to a safer environment for all.

Rating and coverage. Insurance companies can use their own ratings systems to penalize insureds who do not improve safety. They can also require implementation of hazard prevention measures as part of the insurance contract, particularly after a claim is submitted and the specific measures are identified. After a legitimate claim is paid, the insurer can routinely conduct a hazard analysis of the product or condition, refusing to continue coverage until all the hazards cited are removed and the risk of injury reduced.

Petitioning regulatory agencies. Insurance companies and their hundreds of thousands of agents across the country can also use their very significant political leverage before regulatory and legislative bodies to effect safety improvements. Virtually all regulatory agencies that set health and safety standards provide opportunities for outside input. So do legislative bodies through committee hearings. Many consumer organizations and individual citizen activists participate in these opportunities. Yet insurance companies, which fight so hard to maintain their own regulatory and legislative prerogatives, have largely steered clear of advancing public health and safety before these same agencies and legislatures. Even in the important area of auto safety, only the Insurance Institute for Highway Safety has petitioned occasionally for auto safety recalls, but has almost never requested new or stronger vehicle safety standards. Imagine the impact if the insurance industry became a major player in the field of improving safety regulation by advocating such products as more durable bumpers or reduced polluters.

Litigation. We all know that insurance companies are not strangers to lawsuits. Unfortunately, they usually take the role of resisting claims and essentially defending hazards. A luminous exception occurred when State Farm Mutual Automobile Insurance Company, the nation's largest insurance company, petitioned the United States Court of Appeals to review the National Highway Safety Administration's 1981 recision of the automatic restraint standard. In 1983, the United States Supreme Court gave the victory to State Farm and rule the recision illegal. Countless lives have been saved by this decision. We need more such insurance company advocacy in the future.

A promising development that has yet to prove itself was the establishment in 1989 of the Advocates for Highway and Auto Safety, the industry's own response to the victory of Proposition 103 in 1988. Funded by the insurance companies and cochaired by insurance and consumer group leaders, Advocates has identified a number of critical issues and is developing strategies to address federal and state policy priorities, including the National Highway Traffic Safety Administration (NHTSA) Reauthorization Bill; safety belt and motorcycle helmet use legislation; auto crash parts legislation; five MPH bumper standards; passive restraint for vans and light trucks; rollover crash protection standards; roadside sobriety checkpoints; youth driving; and open container legislation.

Research and development. Insurance companies devote insufficient effort toward research and development in the areas of hazard and disease prevention. David M. Pharis, president of the Philadelphia-based S. T. Hudson International, which specializes in loss control, complained in the May 21, 1986 issue of *Journal of Commerce* that risk managers do not deal sufficiently with the engineering aspects of safety promotion and that insurance companies do not allocate adequate funds for this important area of risk control. In fact, as James Tye, director of British Safety Council, has frequently pointed out, the phrase "risk management" is used in most American insurance circles to mean *financial* risk management and not loss prevention through greater safety.

Setting standards in their own shops. Insurance companies can lead by example—by setting standards for their own loss prevention and hazard control. For example, the Travelers Insurance Company was the first insurance company to convert its entire auto fleet in 1989 to driver-side air-bag cars. Allstate and U.S.A.A. have purchased several hundred air-bag–equipped cars. Unfortunately, other companies, such as Prudential and Metropolitan, have lagged behind.

The insurance industry's overall indifference to loss prevention and its failure to apply loss prevention programs to major environmental, product, and professional hazards obviously contributes to higher commercial, professional, and personal insurance prices. Thus consumers suffer because the industry does not help to reduce claims by engaging in loss prevention.

We have a right to expect more from the insurance industry. For it is here, in the area of loss prevention, that the interests of consumers and the companies that serve them coincide. There is no reason—moral, financial, or political—for the insurance industry not to meet our greater expectations, if, as individuals and through the collective political will, we make it known that we want the industry to get busy making the workplace, automobiles, highways, emergency rooms, schools, homes, offices, and every other environment safer and more secure places in which to exist. Such increased emphasis on loss prevention would not only expand insurance companies' profits but would also contribute significantly to the betterment of the health and safety of everyone. This is how we will truly win the insurance game.

Appendices

Appendix A

Glossary

Actual cash value: The cost of repairing or replacing damaged property with property of the same kind and quality and in the same physical condition. Also known as the replacement cost.

Adjuster: The person assigned by an insurance company to determine its obligations under a policy when a claim is made.

Agent: A licensed insurance professional who represents insurance companies. Agents are paid by commission from the company they represent when they sell you a policy.

Annual renewable term: A term life insurance policy that is renewed on a yearly basis.

Annuity: An investment whereby you pay premiums now in order to receive an income later.

Arbitration: A nonjudicial adversarial hearing to determine the rights and obligations of the parties to an insurance contract.

Auto insurance shared market: A program that allows otherwise uninsurable drivers to obtain auto insurance. The profits and losses under the program are usually shared by all of the auto insurance companies that sell insurance in the state.

Bad faith: A form of tort whereby an insurance company breaches its contractual obligation to treat its insureds in good faith.

Basic policy: Traditional fee-for-service health insurance that covers both hospitalization and surgical/medical.

Beneficiary: The person who is entitled to receive the proceeds from a life insurance policy.

Benefits: Proceeds paid pursuant to an insurance company's obligation under a policy.

Binder: An agreement entered into between the consumer and the insurance agent obligating the insurance company to provide immediate coverage until the actual policy is issued. Binders are usually issued only in property and casualty insurance.

Breach of contract: The wrongful failure to perform the obligations set forth in a contract. In an insurance contract, failure to pay benefits due under the policy is a breach of contract.

Broker: A licensed insurance agent not affiliated with an insurance company, who works for the consumer and helps him or her find the best policy at the best price. The commissions are paid by the insurance company.

Cancellation: The termination of an insurance policy.

Cap: Maximum payments that will be made under a policy of insurance.

Cash value life insurance: Life insurance that accrues financial worth during its existence.

Claim: A formal request made by an insured for benefits pursuant to the terms of an insurance policy.

Commercial insurance: Insurance sold to businesses, organizations, and institutions, as opposed to insurance sold to individuals.

Commission: A percentage of a premium paid to an agent as compensation for the sale of an insurance policy.

Comparative negligence: An aspect of personal injury law whereby an injured person can collect damages only in the percentage he or she was not at fault in causing an accident.

Contingency fee: A fee arrangement with a lawyer whereby he or she receives a percentage of the money actually collected on the client's behalf.

Contributory negligence: An aspect of personal injury law that prohibits an injured party from collecting any damages if he or she was even partially at fault in causing an accident.

Conversion rights: The right contained in an insurance policy or established by law, which permits an insured to convert one form of coverage into another. Typically occurs in term life insurance policies allowing conversion of the policy into cash value life insurance.

Coordination of benefits: Provision in a group health insurance policy that permits companies to decide who pays benefits if more than one group plan is in effect. Also used to avoid paying benefits—i.e., the "birthday rule" (see page 147).

Copayment: The insured's obligation to make payments concurrent with payments paid under a policy of insurance. Typically found in fee-for-service health insurance policies.

Coverage: The scope of protection provided under an insurance policy.

Damages: The injury and/or financial loss suffered by someone, giving rise to the right to receive compensation from the person causing the injury or loss.

Declarations page: A page that summarizes insurance policy benefits.

Decreasing term: A term life insurance policy whereby benefits are reduced each year rather than having the premiums go up.

Deductible: Monies that must be paid by the insured before his or her insurance company is obliged to pay benefits under the policy.

Defendant: The person who is sued in a lawsuit.

Depreciation: The decrease in value of property due to physical wear and tear and the passage of time.

Dividend: Payment made by a mutual insurance policy to policyholders or to their policies as a distribution of company earnings.

Endorsement: Extra coverage that can be purchased at an increased premium to provide protection above and beyond that provided in a property/casualty policy.

Exclusion: A provision in an insurance policy that explicitly denies coverage for specified losses.

Exclusive agent: An insurance agent who works for only one company.

Face amount: The amount to be paid under a life insurance policy in the event of the death of the insured.

FAIR Plan: A federal government insurance industry cooperative plan (Fair Access to Insurance Requirements) allowing property insurance to be sold to those who would otherwise have difficulty obtaining coverage.

Fault system: The traditional method of determining who must pay damages in an auto accident case based on who was in the wrong.

General damages: Noneconomic losses in a personal injury case. Pain and suffering are a form of general damages.

Group: A collection of people who share a common interest and who join together for the purposes of purchasing insurance at reduced rates.

Guarantee fund: A fund designed to pay partial benefits to those entitled to receive benefits from a defunct insurance company.

Indemnity payments: Insurance payments made on the basis of a specific dollar amount. Typically occurs in hospitalization policies where a specific amount is payable for each covered day of hospitalization.

Insurable interest: An exposure to loss that gives rise to the right to purchase insurance to protect against such potential loss.

Insurance fraud: The crime of obtaining or attempting to obtain benefits from an insurance company by intentionally providing misinformation or withholding relevant information.

Insured: The person who is protected under a policy of insurance.

Loading: The part of an insurance premium that goes to pay the insurance company's expenses, such as the sales agent's commission and clerical costs.

Loss: Damages caused to someone due to injury to person, destruction of property, or the incurring of liability to others.

Mortality charges: Base rates for determining the pricing of life insurance premiums, based on statistical tables showing death rates for various classes of people.

Mutual company: An insurance company in which ownership is held by the insurance policyholders themselves.

Negligence: A civil wrong where one person breaches the duty of care to another person, causing damages.

No-fault insurance: A system of auto insurance where limited benefits are paid to the insured without regard to whether he or she was at fault in an accident.

Peril: A possible cause of loss, such as fire or earthquake in a homeowner's policy, or theft in an automobile policy.

Personal articles floater: An endorsement to a homeowner's policy, which provides all risk coverage for scheduled valuable personal property, subject to a minimum number of exclusions.

Personal insurance: Insurance sold to individuals to protect them in their personal lives, as opposed to commercial insurance.

Plaintiff: The person who brings a lawsuit.

Policy: A contract of insurance.

Policy owner: The owner of rights in an insurance policy, who has the power to exercise control over the policy.

Preferred risk: A person with a lower risk of loss than the average. A preferred risk will usually pay lower rates.

Premium: The money paid for insurance coverage.

Proof of loss: A written statement made by the policyholder for the insurer regarding a claim, so that the insurer may determine its liability under the policy.

Punitive damages: A cash payment awarded to a plaintiff in excess of monetary damages to punish a civil wrongdoer who has engaged in intentional misconduct.

Rate: The cost of a unit of insurance, on which the premium is based.

Rating bureau: An organization, supported by insurance companies, that provides advisory, rating, statistical, and other services to the insurance industry. The antitrust exemption for insurance companies enables them to use rating bureaus.

Renewable term insurance: Term life insurance whereby the insured has the right to renew coverage at the end of the term without regard to his or her health.

Reserve: An amount representing actual or potential liabilities of an insurance company, set aside to cover these obligations.

Rider: Extra coverage purchased in a life or health insurance policy.

Risk: The chance that a loss will occur.

Settlement options: Alternative modes of paying the proceeds of a life insurance policy.

Special damages: Out-of-pocket damages suffered by the injured party in a personal injury lawsuit.

Standard risk: A person or insurable piece of property that presents an average risk of loss.

Stock company: A life insurance company owned by stockholders and operated for profit.

Substandard risk: A higher-than-average risk of loss.

Term insurance: A life insurance policy that remains in effect for a specific period of time. Term policies do not accrue cash values.

Third-party coverage: Insurance to pay damages caused by the negligence of the insured to third parties.

Tort: A civil wrong, other than breach of contract, that gives rise to liability.

Underwriter: The person who is responsible for determining the insurability of an applicant and the rates that person will pay for insurance if accepted as a policyholder.

Uninsured motorist coverage: Coverage in an auto insurance policy that pays benefits to the insured for personal injury caused by a driver who did not have auto insurance.

Universal life insurance: A type of whole life policy (also called adjustable-premium whole life) that allows the customer flexibility in choosing and changing terms of the policy.

Variable life insurance: A type of cash value life insurance policy giving the policy owner the choice of investing in stocks, bonds, and money market funds.

Waiting period: A form of deductible expressed in time rather than dollars. No benefits under a policy will be paid if there is a waiting period until the period has expired.

Whole life insurance: A type of cash value life insurance policy that remains in effect for the lifetime of the insured or until the policy lapses; in contrast to *term insurance*.

Workers compensation: A system, operating under varying laws in each state and Canadian province, of paying workers for medical care and disability payments with regard to work-related accident and illness. Workers compensation is funded by insurance paid for by employers.

Insurance Coverages Not to Buy

The following is a reprint of an article written by J. Robert Hunter, the founder of the National Insurance Consumer Organization. It is reprinted with the permission of J. Robert Hunter.

Don't Buy These Insurance Policies

- Air travel insurance
- Life insurance if you're single
- Life insurance if you're married with no children and your spouse has a good job
- Life insurance on your children
- Insurance that only pays if you're hurt or killed in a mugging
- Contact lens insurance

- Rental car insurance

- Mortgage insurance

- Life or health insurance sold to cover a car loan or other loan (credit insurance)

- Health insurance on your pet

- Health insurance that pays $100 a day if you are in the hospital (indemnity health plan)

- Rain insurance (pays if it rains during your vacation)

Why Shouldn't You Buy These Policies?

You should buy insurance to protect yourself from *all kinds* of *severe* financial distress. Thus, you should buy insurance that comprehensively covers you against *catastrophic* dollar losses.

It is unwise to use insurance to protect yourself against sure things, such as the first doctor's visit of the year. It is also unwise (and expensive) to protect yourself only against part of the risk when a catastrophic loss could occur. For instance, what good is a cancer insurance policy when you have a heart attack? You need to be protected for the economic consequences of all illnesses. To buy only specific illness coverage is like buying toothpaste a squeeze at a time—and that's expensive.

You probably do need the following coverages:

- Life insurance if you have dependents

- Health insurance

- Auto insurance

- Homeowner's insurance

- Disability insurance

You probably need nothing else if you buy these coverages properly.

Let's see why each item on the "don't buy" list is a "no-no."

Air Travel Insurance

If you have dependents, you need to be covered for the economic consequences of your premature death from *any* cause, be it heart attack, auto accident, or air crash. You are not worth more dead from an air crash, *and*, if an air crash happens, your family has someone to sue (a luxury you don't have if the much more likely heart attack occurs).

Air insurance costs too much and pays back only about 10 cents for each dollar of premiums. It is *not comprehensive* and should be avoided.

Life Insurance If You're Single

If you have no dependents, there is no economic reason to buy life insurance since there is no economic catastrophe associated with your death.

Life Insurance If You're Married with No Children and Your Spouse Has a Good Job

Talk this one over with your spouse. If he or she can get along on the income he or she makes, there would be no economic catastrophe if you died.*

Life Insurance on Your Children

All of these life insurance examples carry emotionally catastrophic implications: none more so than the death of a child. However, *in the purely economic sense*, the loss of a child is *non-catastrophic*.

---

*Author's note: If you are planning a family, you may want to buy life insurance since the younger you buy it the less expensive the initial premiums are likely to be and the more likely you will be able to qualify for an economically superior policy.

Mugging Insurance

Here is a classic example of "junk" insurance. It pays if you die or are hurt in a mugging. It pays very limited benefits as well. Avoid it in that it is *not comprehensive* and is covered by good life and health policies which do cover comprehensively.

Contact Lens Insurance

These policies pay if you lose a contact lens. The cost of the premium is about equal to the cost of a lens at a discount eyeglass store. *Not catastrophic.*

Cancer Insurance

As discussed above, *not comprehensive*.

Rental Car Insurance

These policies cover $500 to $1,000 of damage *you cause* (your fault) to a rental car. Since NICO recommends deductibles of this size on your own car, why cover it on someone else's? Also, the cost of it is too expensive. The $500 deductible coverage is typically $5 a day, $1,825 a year. You would have to average 3½ accidents a year to break even. *Non-catastrophic.*

Mortgage Insurance—Credit Insurance

These two protect you if you die and still have payments due on your house or your car or other large purchase. You should use good annual renewable term (ART) life insurance to protect yourself and your family against all of the economic consequences of your death if you have dependents, including these loan things. It is much more expensive to buy life insurance under mortgage or credit policies than under ART.

Pet Insurance

Pets are dear to us, but the cost of health care is low and is limited by the fact that the absence of third-party players has, mercifully, hindered the development of CAT scans for dogs. It is almost impossible today to spend $200 on a pet's health problem. *Non-catastrophic* and likely to increase the cost of pet health care.

$100 a Day Health Insurance

The costs of a hospital stay are several times this non-catastrophic coverage which pays $100 a day while you are in a hospital. Get good health insurance and don't waste your money on these policies.

Rain Insurance

This pays if it rains over a specified amount during your vacation. This is wholly non-catastrophic. Use the premium to go to the theater if it rains while you are away.

For more information on NICO write to: 121 Payne Street, Alexandria, Virginia 22314, *or call* **(703) 549-8050.**

Appendix C

Insurance Departments: United States and Canada

United States

STATE	ADDRESS	TELEPHONE
Alabama	135 Union St. #160 Montgomery, AL 36130-3401	205/269-3550 FAX 205/240-3194
Alaska	333 Willoughby Ave. 9th Floor P.O. Box "D" Juneau, AK 99811-0800	907/465-2515 FAX 907/463-3841
American Samoa	Office of the Governor Pago Pago American Samoa 96797	011-684/633-4116
Arizona	3030 N. 3rd St. Suite 1100 Phoenix, AZ 85012	602/255-5400 FAX 602/255-4722
Arkansas	400 University Tower Bldg. 12th and University Streets Little Rock, AR 72204	501/371-1325 FAX 501/371-5723

United States

STATE	ADDRESS	TELEPHONE
California	100 Van Ness Ave. San Francisco, CA 94102	800/233-9045 FAX 415/557-3076
Colorado	303 W. Colfax Ave. 5th Floor Denver, CO 80204	303/620-4300
Connecticut	165 Capitol Ave. State Office Bldg. Room 425 Hartford, CT 06106	203/297-3801 FAX 203/566-7410
Delaware	Rodney Bldg. 841 Silver Lake Blvd. Dover, DE 19901	800/282-8611 FAX 302/736-5280
District of Columbia	613 G St., N.W. 6th Floor Washington, DC 20001	202/727-7421
Florida	Attn: Steve Liner State Capitol Plaza Level 11 Tallahassee, FL 32399-0300	800/342-2762 FAX 904/488-6581
Georgia	2 Martin L. King, Jr. Dr. Floyd Memorial Bldg. 704 West Tower Atlanta, GA 30334	404/656-2056
Guam	855 W. Marine Dr. Agana, Guam 96910	011-671/477-1040 FAX 011-671/472-2643
Hawaii	1010 Richards St. Honolulu, HI 96813	808/548-5450 FAX 808/543-2721
Idaho	500 S. 10th St. Boise, ID 83720	208/334-2250 FAX 208/334-2298
Illinois	320 W. Washington St. 4th Floor Springfield, IL 62767	217/782-4515 FAX 217/782-5020

United States

STATE	ADDRESS	TELEPHONE
Indiana	311 W. Washington St. Suite 300 Indianapolis, IN 46204-2787	800/622-4461 FAX 317/232-3548
Iowa	Lucas State Office Bldg. 6th Floor Des Moines, IA 50319	515/281-5705 FAX 515/281-3059
Kansas	420 S.W. 9th St. Topeka, KS 66612	800/432-2484 FAX 913/296-2283
Kentucky	229 W. Main St. Frankfurt, KY 40602	502/564-3630 FAX 502/223-4011
Louisiana	950 N. 5th St. Baton Rouge, LA 70801-9214	504/342-5328 FAX 504/342-3078
Maine	State Office Bldg. State House Station 34 Augusta, ME 04333	207/582-8707 FAX 207/582-8716
Maryland	501 St. Paul Place Stanbalt Bldg. 7th Floor South Baltimore, MD 21202	800/492-6116 FAX 301/333-1229
Massachusetts	280 Friend St. Boston, MA 02114	617/727-3357 FAX 617/727-7189/x.299
Michigan	611 W. Ottawa St. 2nd Floor North Lansing, MI 48933	517/373-9273 FAX 517/335-4978
Minnesota	500 Metro Square Bldg. 5th Floor St. Paul, MN 55101	612/296-4976 FAX 612/296-4328
Mississippi	1804 Walter Sillers Bldg. Jackson, MS 39205	601/359-3569 FAX 601/359-2474
Missouri	301 W. High St. 6 North Jefferson City, MO 65102-0690	314/751-2640 FAX 314/751-1165

United States

STATE	ADDRESS	TELEPHONE
Montana	126 N. Sanders Mitchell Bldg., Room 270 Helena, MT 59601	800/332-6148 FAX 406/444-3497
Nebraska	Terminal Bldg. 941 "O" St., Suite 400 Lincoln, NE 68508	402/471-2201 FAX 402/471-4610
Nevada	Nye Bldg. 201 S. Fall St. Carson City, NV 89710	800/992-0900 FAX 702/885-3937
New Hampshire	169 Manchester St. Concord, NH 03301	800/852-3416 FAX 603/224-1427
New Jersey	20 W. State St. CN325 Trenton, NJ 08625	609/292-5363 FAX 609/633-3601
New Mexico	PERA Bldg. 500 Old Santa Fe Trail 4th Floor Santa Fe, NM 87501	505/827-4500 FAX 505/827-4734
New York	160 W. Broadway New York, NY 10013	800/522-4370 FAX 212/602-0437
	Agency Bldg. #1 Albany, NY 12257	518/474-6600 FAX 518/473-4600
North Carolina	Dobbs Bldg. 430 Salisbury St. Raleigh, NC 27611	800/662-7777 FAX 919/733-6495
North Dakota	Capitol Bldg. Fifth Floor Bismarck, ND 58505	800/247-0560 FAX 701/224-4880
Ohio	2100 Stella Court Columbus, OH 43266-0566	800/282-4658
Oklahoma	1901 N. Walnut Oklahoma City, OK 73105	405/521-2828
Oregon	21 Labor and Industries Bldg. Salem, OR 97310	503/378-4271 FAX 503/378-4351

United States

STATE	ADDRESS	TELEPHONE
Pennsylvania	Strawberry Square 13th Floor Harrisburg, PA 17120	717/787-5173 FAX 717/783-1059
Puerto Rico	Fernandez Juncos Station 1607 Ponce de Leon Ave. Santurce, Puerto Rico 00910	809/722-8686 FAX 809/724-5197
Rhode Island	233 Richmond St., Suite 237 Providence, RI 02903-4237	401/277-2246
South Carolina	1612 Marion St. Columbia, SC 29201	803/737-6117
South Dakota	Insurance Bldg. 910 E. Sioux Ave. Pierre, SD 57501	605/773-3563 FAX 605/773-4840
Tennessee	Volunteer Plaza 500 James Robertson Pkwy. Nashville, TN 37219	800/342-4029 FAX 615/741-4000
Texas	1110 San Jacinto Blvd. Austin, TX 78701-1998	512/463-6464 FAX 512/463-0866
Utah	160 E. Third St. Heber M. Wells Bldg. Salt Lake City, UT 84145	801/530-6400
Vermont	State Office Bldg. Montpelier, VT 05602	802/828-3301 FAX 802/828-3306
Virginia	700 Jefferson Bldg. 1220 Bank St. Richmond, VA 23219	800/552-7945 FAX 804/786-3396
Virgin Islands	Kongens Gade #18 St. Thomas, VI 00802	809/774-2991 FAX 809/774-6953
Washington	Insurance Bldg. AQ21 Olympia, WA 98504	800/562-6900 FAX 206/586-3535
West Virginia	2019 Washington St. East Charleston, WV 25305	800/642-9004 FAX 304/348-0412

United States

STATE	ADDRESS	TELEPHONE
Wisconsin	123 W. Washington Ave. P.O. Box 7873 Madison, WI 53702-7873	800/236-8517 FAX 608/266-9935
Wyoming	Herschler Bldg. 122 W. 25th St. Cheyenne, WY 82002	307/777-7401 FAX 307/777-5895

Canada

PROVINCE	ADDRESS	TELEPHONE
Alberta	Ministry of Consumer and Corporate Affairs 22nd Floor 10025 Jasper Ave. Edmonton, Alta. T5J 3Z5	403/422-1592
British Columbia	Ministry of Finance and Corporate Relations Ste. 1100-865 Hornby St. Vancouver, B.C. V6Z 2H4	604/660-2947
Manitoba	Department of Consumer and Corporate Affairs 1142-405 Broadway Ave. Winnipeg, Man. R3C 3L6	204/945-2542
New Brunswick	Department of Justice 364 York St. P.O. Box 6000 Fredericton, N.B. E3B 5H1	506/453-2541
Newfoundland	Department of Consumer Affairs and Communications 2nd Floor, Elizabeth Towers 100 Elizabeth Avenue St. John's, Nfld. A1C 5T7	709/729-2594
Northwest Territories	Department of Justice Government of the Northwest Territories Yellowknife, N.W.T. X1A 2L9	403/920-8055

Canada

STATE	ADDRESS	TELEPHONE
Nova Scotia	Department of Consumer Affairs Insurance Division 5151 Terminal Road P.O. Box 2284 Halifax, N.S. B3J 3C8	902/424-4690
Ontario	Ministry of Financial Institutions 5160 Yonge Street 15th Floor N. York, Ont. M2N 6L9	416/250-7250
Prince Edward Island	Department of Justice P.O. Box 2000 Charlottetown, P.E.I. C1A 7N8	902/368-4564
Quebec	Inspector General of Financial Institutions 800 Place d'Youville 8th Floor Quebec, (Que.) G1R 4Y5	418/643-5783
Saskatchewan	Department of Consumer and Commercial Affairs 1871 Smith Street Regina, Sask. S4P 3V7	306/787-8999
Yukon Territory	Department of Consumer and Corporate Affairs P.O. Box 2703 Whitehorse, Yukon Y1A 2C6	403/667-5257

Appendix D

Bibliography

In this book we have attempted to give you all of the information you need to be effective and powerful consumers of insurance products. But no book, however comprehensive, should be relied upon as the exclusive authority. If you are interested in digging deeper into the subject, the following books may be of interest.

General Interest

Alford, Ron. *The Crime of the Century—Insurance*. Owners Action Plan, 1988.

Doroshow, Joanne and Adrian J. Wilkes. *Goliath: Lloyd's of London in the United States*. Washington DC: Center for the Study of Responsive Law, 1988.

Hansen, Leonard J. *Life Begins at 50: A Handbook for Creative Retirement Planning*. Hauppauge, NY: Barron's Educational Series, Inc., 1989.

Mehr, Robert I. *The Fundamentals of Insurance*. 2d ed. Homewood, IL: Richard D. Irwin Inc., 1986.

Property/Casualty Fact Book. New York: Insurance Information Institute, published yearly.

Sharing the Risk: How the Nation's Businesses, Homes, and Autos Are Insured. 3d ed. New York: Insurance Information Institute, 1989.

Shernoff, William M. and Thelma O'Brien. *Payment Refused: A Crusading Lawyer's Dramatic Cases Against Insurance Companies*. New York: Richardson and Steirman, 1986.

Tobias, Andrew. *The Invisible Bankers*. New York: Linden Press, 1982.

Health Insurance

Hogue, Kathleen, Cheryl Jensen, and Kathleen McClurg Urban. *The Complete Guide to Health Insurance: How to Beat the High Cost of Being Sick*. New York: Walker and Company, 1988.

Matthews, Joseph L. and Dorothy Matthews Berman. *Social Security, Medicare and Pensions: The Source Book for Older Americans*. 4th ed. Berkeley: Nolo Press, 1988.

Stark, Sharon L. *Health Insurance Made Easy . . . Finally*. Shawnee Mission, KS: Stark Publishing, 1989.

Life Insurance

Brownlie, William D. and Jefferey L. Seglin. *The Life Insurance Buyer's Guide*. New York: McGraw-Hill Publishing Co., 1989.

The editors of *Consumer Reports*, and Trudy Lieberman. *Life Insurance: How to Buy the Right Policy at the Right Price*. Mount Vernon, NY: Consumers Union Books, 1988.

Hunt, James H. *Taking the Bite out of Life Insurance*. Alexandria, VA: National Insurance Consumers Organization, 1988.

Appendix E

Consumer Insurance Resources

A. M. Best Company, Inc.
Ambest Road
Oldwick, NJ 08858-9988
201/439-2200

Center for the Study of Responsive Law
P.O. Box 19367
Washington, DC 20036
202/387-8034

Champaign County Health Care Consumers Organization
(CCHCC)
44 Main St., Suite 208
Champaign, IL 61820
217/352-6533

Committee for National Health Insurance
1757 N St. N.W.
Washington, DC 20036
202/223-9685

Consumer Insurance Interest Group
9321 Millbranch Place
Fairfax, VA 22031
703/836-9340

Consumer Reports
256 Washington St.
Mount Vernon, NY 10553
914/667-9400

Federal Emergency Management Agency
Federal Insurance Administration
500 C St. S.W.
Washington, DC 20472
800/638-6620

Insurance Information Institute
110 William St.
New York, NY 10038
212/669-9200
Hotline 800/221-4954

Insurance Services Office, Inc.
175 Water St.
New York, NY 10038
212/487-5000

National Association of Insurance Commissioners
12 Wyandotte Plaza
120 W. 12th St., Suite 1100
Kansas City, MO 64105
816/842-3600

National Association of Life Underwriters
1922 F St. N.W.
Washington, DC 20066
202/331-6000

National Association of Professional Insurance Agents
400 N. Washington St.
Alexandria, VA 22314
703/836-9340

National Insurance Consumer Organization (NICO)
121 N. Payne St.
Alexandria, VA 22314
703/549-8050
Hotline 800/942-4242

Appendix F

Excerpts, Sample HO 3 (Homeowner's) Insurance Policy*

Section I—Property Coverages

Coverage A—Dwelling

We cover:

1. the dwelling on the **residence premises** shown in the Declarations, including structures attached to the dwelling; and

2. materials and supplies located on or next to the **residence premises** used to construct, alter or repair the dwelling or other structures on the **residence premises**.

This coverage does not apply to land, including land on which the dwelling is located.

*Includes copyrighted material of Insurance Services Office, Inc. with its permission. Copyright, Insurance Services Office, Inc. 1990.

Coverage B—Other Structures

We cover other structures on the **residence premises** set apart from the dwelling by clear space. This includes structures connected to the dwelling by only a fence, utility line, or similar connection.

This coverage does not apply to land, including land on which the other structures are located.

We do not cover other structures:

1. used in whole or in part for **business**; or

2. rented or held for rental to any person not a tenant of the dwelling, unless used solely as a private garage.

The limit of liability for this coverage will not be more than 10% of the limit of liability that applies to Coverage A. Use of this coverage does not reduce the Coverage A limit of liability.

Coverage C—Personal Property

We cover personal property owned or used by an **insured** while it is anywhere in the world. At your request, we will cover personal property owned by:

1. others while the property is on the part of the **residence premises** occupied by an **insured**;

2. a guest or a **residence employee**, while the property is in any residence occupied by an **insured**.

Our limit of liability for personal property usually located at an **insured's** residence, other than the **residence premises**, is 10% of the limit of liability for Coverage C, or $1000, whichever is greater. Personal property in a newly acquired principal residence is not subject to this limitation for the 30 days from the time you begin to move the property there.

Special Limits of Liability. These limits do not increase the Coverage C limit of liability. The special limit for each numbered category below is the total limit for each loss for all property in that category.

1. $200 on money, bank notes, bullion, gold other than goldware, silver other than silverware, platinum, coins and medals.

2. $1000 on securities, accounts, deeds, evidences of debt, letters of credit, notes other than bank notes, manuscripts, passports, tickets and stamps.

3. $1000 on watercraft, including their trailers, furnishings, equipment and outboard motors.

4. $1000 on trailers not used with watercraft.

5. $1000 on grave markers.

6. $1000 for loss by theft of jewelry, watches, furs, precious and semi-precious stones.

7. $2000 for loss by theft of firearms.

8. $2500 for loss by theft of silverware, silver-plated ware, goldware, gold-plated ware and pewterware. This includes flatware, hollowware, tea sets, trays and trophies made of or including silver, gold or pewter.

9. $2500 on property, on the **residence premises**, used at any time or in any manner for any **business** purpose.

10. $250 on property, away from the **residence premises**, used at any time or in any manner for any **business** purpose.

Property Not Covered. We do not cover:

1. articles separately described and specifically insured in this or other insurance;

2. animals, birds or fish;

3. motor vehicles or all other motorized land conveyances. This includes:

   a. equipment and accessories; or
   b. any device or instrument for the transmitting, recording, receiving or reproduction of sound or pictures which is operated by power from the electrical system of motor vehicles or all other motorized land conveyances, including:
      (1) accessories or antennas; or
      (2) tapes, wires, records, discs or other media for use with any such device or instrument;

   while in or upon the vehicle or conveyance.

   We do cover vehicles or conveyances not subject to motor vehicle registration which are:

   a. used to service an **insured's** residence; or
   b. designed for assisting the handicapped;

4. aircraft and parts. Aircraft means any contrivance used or designed for flight, except model or hobby aircraft not used or designed to carry people or cargo;

5. property of roomers, boarders and other tenants, except property of roomers and boarders related to an **insured**;

6. property in an apartment regularly rented or held for rental to others by an **insured**;

7. property rented or held for rental to others off the **residence premises**;

8. a. books of account, drawings or other paper records; or
   b. electronic data processing tapes, wires, records, discs or other software media;

   containing **business** data. But, we do cover the cost of blank or unexposed records and media;

9. credit cards or fund transfer cards except as provided in Additional Coverages 6.

Coverage D—Loss of Use

The limit of liability for Coverage D is the total limit for all the coverages that follow.

1. If a loss covered under this Section makes that part of the **residence premises** where you reside not fit to live in, we cover, at your choice, either of the following. However, if the **residence premises** is not your principal place of residence, we will not provide the option under paragraph b. below.

   a. **Additional Living Expense**, meaning any necessary increase in living expenses incurred by you so that your household can maintain its normal standard of living; or
   b. **Fair Rental Value**, meaning the fair rental value of that part of the **residence premises** where you reside less any expenses that do not continue while the premises is not fit to live in.

   Payment under a. or b. will be for the shortest time required to repair or replace the damage or, if you permanently relocate, the shortest time required for your household to settle elsewhere.

2. If a loss covered under this Section makes that part of the **residence premises** rented to others or held for rental by you not fit to live in, we cover the:

   Fair Rental Value, meaning the fair rental value of that part of the **residence premises** rented to others or held for rental by you less any expenses that do not continue while the premises is not fit to live in.

   Payment will be for the shortest time required to repair or replace that part of the premises rented or held for rental.

3. If a civil authority prohibits you from use of the **residence premises** as a result of direct damage to neighboring premises by a Peril Insured Against in this policy, we cover the Additional Living Expense or Fair Rental Value loss as provided under 1 and 2 above for no more than two weeks.

The periods of time under 1, 2 and 3 above are not limited by expiration of this policy.

We do not cover loss or expense due to cancellation of a lease or agreement.

Additional Coverages

1. **Debris Removal.** We will pay your reasonable expense for the removal of:

   a. debris of covered property if a Peril Insured Against causes the loss; or

   b. ash, dust or particles from a volcanic eruption that has caused direct loss to a building or property contained in a building.

   This expense is included in the limit of liability that applies to the damaged property. If the amount to be paid for the actual damage to the property plus the debris removal expense is more than the limit of liability for the damaged property, an additional 5% of that limit of liability is available for debris removal expense.

   We will also pay your reasonable expense for the removal of fallen trees from the **residence premises** if:

   a. coverage is not afforded under Additional Coverages 3 Trees, Shrubs and Other Plants for the peril causing the loss; or

   b. the tree is not covered by this policy; provided

the tree damages covered property and a Peril Insured Against under Coverage C causes the tree to fall. Our limit of liability for this coverage will not be more than $500 in the aggregate for any one loss.

2. **Reasonable Repairs.** We will pay the reasonable cost incurred by you for necessary repairs made solely to protect covered property from further damage if a Peril Insured Against causes the loss. This coverage does not increase the limit of liability that applies to the property being repaired.

3. **Trees, Shrubs and Other Plants.** We cover trees, shrubs, plants or lawns, on the **residence premises**, for loss caused by the following Perils Insured Against: Fire or lightning, Explosion, Riot or civil commotion, Aircraft, Vehicles not owned or operated by a resident of the **residence premises**, Vandalism or malicious mischief or Theft.

The limit of liability for this coverage will not be more than 5% of the limit of liability that applies to the dwelling, or more than $500 for any one tree, shrub or plant. We do not cover property grown for **business** purposes.

This coverage is additional insurance.

4. **Fire Department Service Charge.** We will pay up to $500 for your liability assumed by contract or agreement for fire department charges incurred when the fire department is called to save or protect covered property from a Peril Insured Against. We do not cover fire department service charges if the property is located within the limits of the city, municipality or protection district furnishing the fire department response.

This coverage is additional insurance. No deductible applies to this coverage.

5. Property Removed. We insure covered property against direct loss from any cause while being removed from a premises endangered by a Peril Insured Against and for no more than 30 days while removed. This coverage does not change the limit of liability that applies to the property being removed.

6. Credit Card, Fund Transfer Card, Forgery and Counterfeit Money.

We will pay up to $500 for:

a. the legal obligation of an **insured** to pay because of the theft or unauthorized use of credit cards issued to or registered in an **insured's** name:

b. loss resulting from theft or unauthorized use of a fund transfer card used for deposit, withdrawal or transfer of funds, issued to or registered in an **insured's** name;

c. loss to an **insured** caused by forgery or alteration of any check or negotiable instrument; and

d. loss to an **insured** through acceptance in good faith of counterfeit United States or Canadian paper currency.

We do not cover use of a credit card or fund transfer card:

a. by a resident of your household;

b. by a person who has been entrusted with either type of card; or

c. if an **insured** has not complied with all terms and conditions under which the cards are issued.

All loss resulting from a series of acts committed by any one person or in which any one person is concerned or implicated is considered to be one loss.

We do not cover loss arising out of **business** use or dishonesty of an **insured**.

This coverage is additional insurance. No deductible applies to this coverage.

Defense:

a. We may investigate and settle any claim or suit that we decide is appropriate. Our duty to defend a claim or suit ends when the amount we pay for the loss equals our limit of liability.

b. If a suit is brought against an **insured** for liability under the Credit Card or Fund Transfer Card coverage, we will provide a defense at our expense by counsel of our choice.

c. We have the option to defend at our expense an **insured** or an **insured's** bank against any suit for the enforcement of payment under the Forgery coverage.

7. **Loss Assessment.** We will pay up to $1000 for your share of any loss assessment charged during the policy period against you by a corporation or association of property owners. This only applies when the assessment is made as a result of each direct loss to the property, owned by all members collectively, caused by a Peril Insured Against under Coverage A—Dwelling, other than earthquake or land shock waves or tremors before, during or after a volcanic eruption.

This coverage applies only to loss assessments charged against you as owner or tenant of the **residence premises**.

We do not cover loss assessments charged against you or a corporation or association of property owners by any governmental body.

8. **Collapse.** We insure for direct physical loss to covered property involving collapse of a building or any part of a building caused only by one or more of the following:

a. Perils Insured Against in Coverage C—Personal Property. These perils apply to covered building and personal property for loss insured by this additional coverage;

b. hidden decay;

c. hidden insect or vermin damage;

d. weight of contents, equipment, animals or people;

e. weight of rain which collects on a roof; or

f. use of defective material or methods in construction, remodeling or renovation if the collapse occurs during the course of the construction, remodeling or renovation.

Loss to an awning, fence, patio, pavement, swimming pool, underground pipe, flue, drain, cesspool, septic tank, foundation, retaining wall, bulkhead, pier, wharf or dock is not included under items b, c, d, e, and f unless the loss is a direct result of the collapse of a building.

Collapse does not include settling, cracking, shrinking, bulging or expansion.

This coverage does not increase the limit of liability applying to the damaged covered property.

Section II—Liability Coverages

Coverage E—Personal Liability

If a claim is made or a suit is brought against an **insured** for damages because of **bodily injury** or **property damage** caused by an **occurrence** to which this coverage applies, we will:

1. pay up to our limit of liability for the damages for which the **insured** is legally liable; and

2. provide a defense at our expense by counsel of our choice, even if the suit is groundless, false or fraudulent. We may investigate and settle any claim or suit that we decide is appropriate. Our duty to settle or defend ends when the amount we pay for damages

resulting from the **occurrence** equals our limit of liability.

Coverage F—Medical Payments to Others

We will pay the necessary medical expenses that are incurred or medically ascertained within three years from the date of an accident causing **bodily injury**. Medical expenses means reasonable charges for medical, surgical, x-ray, dental, ambulance, hospital, professional nursing, prosthetic devices and funeral services. This coverage does not apply to you or regular residents of your household except **residence employees**. As to others, this coverage applies only:

1. to a person on the **insured location** with the permission of an **insured**; or

2. to a person off the **insured location**, if the **bodily injury**:

   a. arises out of a condition on the **insured location** or the ways immediately adjoining;
   b. is caused by the activities of an **insured**;
   c. is caused by a **residence employee** in the course of the **residence employee's** employment by an **insured**; or
   d. is caused by an animal owned by or in the care of an **insured**.

Index